Communicating in the Anthropocene

Environmental Communication and Nature: Conflict and Ecoculture in the Anthropocene

Series Editor: C. Vail Fletcher, University of Portland

This interdisciplinary book series seeks original proposals that examine environmental communication scholarship. In the Anthropocene era, the period during which human activity has become the dominant influence on climate and the environment, the need for highlighting and re-centering nature in our worldviews and policies is urgent, as collapsing ecosystems across the globe struggle to survive. Topics might include climate change, land use conflict, water rights, natural disasters, nonhuman animals, the culture of nature, ecotourism, wildlife management, human/nature relationships, food studies, sustainability, eco-pedagogy, mediated nature, eco-terrorism, environmental education, ecofeminism, international development, and environmental conflict. Ultimately, scholarship that addresses the general overarching question "how do individuals and societies make sense of and act against/within/out of nature?" is welcomed. This series is open to contributions from authors in environmental communication, environmental studies, media studies, rhetoric, political science, critical geography, critical/cultural studies, and other related fields. We also seek diverse and creative epistemological and methodological framings that might include ethnography, content analysis, narrative and/or rhetorical analysis, participant observation, and community-based participatory research, among others. Successful proposals will be accessible to a multidisciplinary audience.

Recent Titles in This Series

Water, Rhetoric, and Social Justice: A Critical Confluence, Edited by Casey R. Schmitt, Theresa R. Castor, and Christopher S. Thomas

Environmental Activism, Social Media, and Protest in China: Becoming Activists over Wild Public Networks, By Elizabeth Brunner

Natural Disasters and Risk Communication: Implications of the Cascadia Subduction Zone Megaquake, Edited by C. Vail Fletcher and Jennette Lovejoy

Critical Environmental Communication: How Does Critique Respond to the Urgency of Environmental Crisis?, By Murdoch Stephens

Natural Disasters and Risk Communication: Implications of the Cascadia Subduction Zone Megaquake, Edited by C. Vail Fletcher and Jennette Lovejoy

Communicating in the Anthropocene: Intimate Relations, Edited by C. Vail Fletcher and Alexa Dare

Communicating in the Anthropocene

Intimate Relations

Edited by
Alexa M. Dare and C. Vail Fletcher

LEXINGTON BOOKS
Lanham • *Boulder* • *New York* • *London*

Published by Lexington Books
An imprint of The Rowman & Littlefield Publishing Group, Inc.
4501 Forbes Boulevard, Suite 200, Lanham, Maryland 20706
www.rowman.com

6 Tinworth Street, London SE11 5AL, United Kingdom

Chapter 3: Henderson Poem: Henderson, Donna. 2019. "Much Raining." *Writing Our Watershed: Luckiamute River and Ash Creek* (Second Edition), edited by Gail Oberst, 44–45. Independence: Luckiamute Watershed Council.

British Library Cataloguing in Publication Information Available

Library of Congress Control Number: 2020949683

∞™ The paper used in this publication meets the minimum requirements of American National Standard for Information Sciences—Permanence of Paper for Printed Library Materials, ANSI/NISO Z39.48-1992.

Contents

Foreword: Undisciplined Stories   ix
Carol J. Adams

Acknowledgments   xiii

1   Introduction: Intimate Relations for Earthly Survival   1
    Alexa M. Dare and C. Vail Fletcher

PART I: GRIEF, RESILIENCE, AND STORYTELLING   **11**

2   Vigilant Mourning and the Future of Earthly Coexistence   13
    Joshua Trey Barnett

3   Presence and Absence in the Watershed: Storytelling for the
    Symbiocene   35
    Emily Plec

4   The Trouble with Resilience   53
    Jessica Holmes

5   Solastalgia and Art Therapy in Climate Change   69
    Chelsea Call

6   Living (in) Spider Webs: More-than-Human Intimacy in
    Installation Art by Tómas Saraceno   73
    Katharina Alsen

PART II: NONHUMAN COLLABORATORS: OYSTERS, BIRDS, AND ELEPHANTS 79

7 The Permeable Heart: Mindfulness in Animal-Human Communication 81
Peggy J. Bowers

8 Intimacy on the Half-Shell: Place, Oysters, and the Emerging Narrative of Virginia Aquaculture 85
Anne K. Armstrong, Richard C. Stedman, and Marianne E. Krasny

9 i am naiad: Becoming Benthic 105
laura c carlson

10 Ada Clapham Govan and "Birds I Know": Ecological Intimacy in a Mass-Mediated Sisterhood 111
Peter W. Oehlkers and Anna Ijiri Oehlkers

11 Dialogic Elephant and Human Relations in Sri Lanka as Social Practices of Cohabitation 127
Elizabeth Oriel, Deepani Jayantha, and Amal Dissanayaka

12 ocean medicine, mother medicine, sky medicine 147
Michaela Keeble

PART III: PLANTS AND OTHER FAMILY MEMBERS 153

13 Weirding Wellness: Mushrooms, Medicine, and the Uncanny Renaissance of Psilocybin in the Chthulucene 155
Josh Potter

14 Multispecies Motherhood: Connecting with Plants through Processes of Procreation 173
Mariko Oyama Thomas

15 Plant Persons, More-than-Human Power, and Institutional Practices in Indigenous Higher Education 197
Keith Williams and Suzanne Brant

16 OAK 215
Marybeth Holleman

17 Objects/Ecologies: *Jardin d'Incertitude le système écologique et l'objet technologique* 217
Christianna Bennett

PART IV: NONHUMAN AGENCY, ACTIVISM, AND LEGAL PERSONHOOD — 223

18 If the Ocean Were a Person — 225
Jenny Rock and Ellen Sima

19 Personal Affairs: Litigating Nonhuman Animal Personhood in the Anthropocene — 231
S. Marek Muller

20 Tahlequah's Internatural Activism: Situating the Body and the Intimacy of Grief as Evidence of Human-Caused Climate Change — 253
Madrone Kalil Schutten

21 Never the Same River Twice: How Legal Personhood of Rivers Affects Perceived Stability of Policy Solutions — 275
Carie Steele

22 The Titans at the Heart of the Anthropocene: Diving into the Nonhuman Imagery of Leviathan — 299
Patrícia Castello Branco

23 Listen to the Lake: Nature as Stakeholder — 321
Kathy Isaacson

24 The Geo-Doc: A Proposed New Communications Tool for Planetary Health — 325
Mark Terry

PART V: GENDER, EARTHLY INTIMACIES, AND OTHER TROUBLE — 331

25 Intimate Dwelling and Mourning Loss in the (m)Anthropocene: Ecological Masculinities and the Felt Self — 333
Todd LeVasseur and Paul M. Pulé

26 The Climate Gaze and Koalas in Extremis — 353
Lyn McGaurr and Libby Lester

27 From Fatbergs to Microplastics: New Intimacies of an Extruded World — 371
Paul Alberts

28 Doğa İçin Çal (Play for Nature) — 387
Çağrı Yılmaz

29 Subversive Art: Communicating the Climate Crisis on a
   Planetary Scale   393
   Catherine Sarah Young

Index   397

About the Editors, Contributing Authors, and Artists   405

Foreword

Undisciplined Stories

Carol J. Adams

In the beginning was a story, and we settled into the story, comforted, knowing that even though there would be tension, probably trauma, and even terror as we moved through the story, a reconciliation was guaranteed before the ending. Traditional endings are optimistic, providing closure. Beginnings can be pessimistic, because they assume the trajectory of the story will resolve the pessimism, set things right. Does assuming there can be a happy ending to a story function like resilience approaches to climate change, that assume the climate emergency of our era can be transcended, be overcome?

Thinking forward, now, in the Anthropocene, which I see as a shorthand term for conveying the challenges of our climate emergency, means living with despair and grief—vigilant mourning, as Joshua Trey Barnett calls it; vulnerable mourning we might say.

Once upon a time in the Anthropocene, there was a need for new stories, new approaches, new methodologies, for the end of the story seemed to be written and the reassurances had dropped away like passenger pigeons shot from the sky.

In these pages, we learn of

polar bear fatigue
glaciers calving
ice loss
algal blooms
more than human grieving
fox and elephant funerals
species decimated and disappeared
animals butchered

serial killing machines called "trawlers"
orcas grieving
poisoned watersheds
rivers of sludge
climate grief
koalas with bandaged paws

We are reminded about how much has been lost.

Perhaps, now, the book and its finiteness signal to us the many endings that have already transpired. The endings of ice caps and great auks. The losses described herein are earth shattering and water quaking. Grief becomes a part of our lives, this ecological mourning. Here you are, grief, my friend, reminding me of what and who I cherish:

the Labrador duck
the Carolina parakeet
the Heath hen
the elephants under threat
the people whose names are on the AIDS quilt
the dead in the pandemic of 2020

A pandemic that we know has been mishandled in the United States by a racist, xenophobic, misogynist president put in place by an electoral system created to protect slavery and favor the slave states. A pandemic resulting from anthropocentric priorities that maintain animal agriculture, one of the major sources of viruses that jump to the human from animals.

This anthology opens a space of engagement, a process of interrogating the local and keeping the eye on the global. The chapters affirm our ability to be thinking, caring, relational, engaged beings. They call for our attention, not just the attention of reading, but the attention of, well, *attention,* as Simone Weil defined it: all our neighbor asks is that we ask, "What are you going through?" and listen to the answer. Making associations, finding relationships, cherishing relationships, perceiving

coral reefs
grouse in tall grass
oysters
purple finch
chickadees
rose-breasted grosbeak
hawks
shrikes
blue jays

Asking

ants
pigeons
wolves
octopuses
mushrooms
cranes
oaks
salmon
mussels
the western pond turtle

"What are you going through?"

In the pages that follow, the authors name the ruptures caused by an anthropocentric worldview and they rupture that normativity. Our language is one of hubris and mastery, and stories of intimate relations have to resist the inertia of dominant narratives. They require the discipline of attention but must be free of any one discipline. We find new forms of communication in

owl gratitude
the dialects of trees
fungal fables
an imaginary garden
incomplete mourning
interactive art

seeking to undo

the tourist gaze
the white gaze
the male gaze
the anthropocentric gaze
the colonial gaze
the climate gaze

The chapters in these pages help to unsettle categories, giving us undisciplined stories. They speak of animals, vegetables, mushrooms and oysters, psychedelic boom and fungal bloom, of cripping animal law and notions of personhood for rivers. And they suggest art as equally important as activism and scholarship; art *as* activism and scholarship but also as a way to respond to pessimism, depression, anomie, and alienation. Art is a form of intimate relations.

I found myself in relationship to artists who shared their work with me after reading *The Sexual Politics of Meat*. Even when they are addressing painful subjects, I sense the optimism of art itself, that it can intervene, that it can meditate on disaster in a way different from other forms. This is liberating. The sections devoted to art offer such perspectives, providing antiphonal voices within the book.

While we sleep, snails are in the world, leaving a trail. Moving at their own pace—one we usually only see by its trace—they traverse over soil and concrete. When the sun shines in a certain way, we can see their trails. We can see where they have been. In these chapters, I like to think that ecofeminism is the snail trail, illuminating what came before, for I am heartened by how ecofeminist themes move in and out of different chapters. Over the past fifty years, ecofeminist writings have emphasized relationality over autonomy, identified problematic value hierarchies and the accompanying function of false dualisms, and expanded the feminist ethics of care to a more-than-human world. Ecofeminism contributes immensely to the dismantling of the siloed nature of scholarship, as it articulated the overlap and intersections of oppressions of race, gender, sex, species, earth, and sea. And ecofeminism helped to lift up the writings of Simone Weil, whose notion of attention grounds intimate relations. Ecofeminism helped catalyze animal studies, posthumanist studies, animality studies, and ecostudies.

From ecofeminism we learned how first we anthropomorphized humans, then we anthropomorphized the other animals, as it suited us. Ecofeminism also maintains a commitment to understanding how representations work to reinforce dominance or facilitate liberation. I like to think about the ways that ecofeminism has helped with the unmaking of dominant narratives, inspiring the new approaches we find here, the resistance to locating resistance in any one discipline.

A book offers evidence of connections threading through it, like that snail's trail across concrete. In these pages, we find the traces of relationships among writers, influences, inspirations. So many disruptions needed; so many boundaries crossed.

A snail trail suggests movement and messaging in a nonanthropocentric way. We are vigilant about the need to resist, resist even our own formulations.

The work of unmaking is a challenging one. Unmaking distinctions reinforced through hierarchies, undoing silos of learning that restrict approaches, unsettling categories.

Enjoy the undisciplining in *Intimate Relations*.

Acknowledgments

ALEXA

I acknowledge the stolen land upon which this book was composed, and the generations of indigenous caretakers whose history and intimacies with all living beings have been systematically forgotten by many who now call Portland home. We started this book with a tiny seed of an idea, and we are so grateful to all of the authors in this volume whose visions of intimacy exceeded and expanded on our own initial ideas well beyond our wildest hopes for the project. Sophie Downing was an outstanding research assistant and is a beautiful person. Her care for the project and her careful, cheerful work was more than we deserved. I am so grateful to Vail Fletcher, the best co-conspirator and a brilliant visionary. She has an amazing ability to see the world as it could be and to convince others that such a world is possible. And, finally and most importantly, gratitude beyond words to Pat and Franny who remind me, always, that to be human is to exist in webs of mutual beneficial interdependence. My life would be so impoverished without their love and labor and laughter.

VAIL

I acknowledge and dedicate this work to the young squirrel, lucky to be born in the Spring of COVID-19 as humans retreated inside their walls, who stood distracted by a nut in the middle of the road near my farmhouse this week. I saw you, dear squirrel, in those very last moments trying to decide which way you should go to escape, so you might have one more day on this magical sphere floating in space, but it was too late. I also dedicate this work to the human driving that car who most certainly must have seen this young earthling standing there with some time to spare, and yet did not care? I watched for your brake lights, though they never came. Maybe you were on your phone? Maybe you, too, like the squirrel were distracted until it was too late? And to the driver directly behind me, when I pulsed my own brakes in some sort of theatrical attempt to demonstrate or mimic the actions needed to maybe save this dear life, proceeded to speed up alongside me just after the squirrel spun out from under the car, its blood already staining the ground— after I had already started my guttural screaming, tears instantly soaking my face—to throw his upper body into his passenger seat and almost out the open window, to angrily wave his middle finger at me while also telling me to fuck off. This book is for you, too. And when I returned home just a couple of hours later, I saw you again, squirrel, already disappeared into the pavement, now indistinguishable. But I'll see you forever. This is our current life in the Anthropocene. And so, this book is for all of the ways and times *you,* dear stranger, and I have missed an opportunity to care more deeply, to pay more attention to each other, to love *all* of our neighbors more intimately. I also want to acknowledge Alexa, my most intellectual and kind friend and colleague. Of course you are everything good and beautiful in this world. To Greg, Huckleberry, Poppy, and all the nonhuman animals and more-than-human beings that I share my life with, I love you more than you know. May you always find joy.

Chapter 1

Introduction

Intimate Relations for Earthly Survival

Alexa M. Dare and C. Vail Fletcher

STORIES OF CONNECTION

The purpose of this book is to tell a different story about the world. Humans, especially those raised in Western traditions, have long told stories about themselves as individual protagonists who act with varying degrees of free will against a background of mute supporting characters and inert landscapes. Humans can be either saviors or destroyers, but our actions are explained and judged again and again as emanating from the individual. And yet, as the coronavirus pandemic has made clear, humans are unavoidably interconnected not only with other humans but with nonhuman and more-than-human others with whom we share space and time. Why do so many of us humans avoid, deny, or resist a view of the world where our lives are made possible, maybe even made richer, through connection? The title of this Introduction is inspired by Donna Haraway who has consistently and creatively argued that storytelling is an especially powerful tool for, well, saving the world and ensuring multispecies survival. In *Staying with the Trouble* (2016), Haraway muses poetically that

> It matters what matters we use to think other matters with; it matters what stories we tell to tell other stories with; it matters what knots knot knots, what thoughts think thoughts, what descriptions describe descriptions, what ties tie ties. It matters what stories make worlds, what worlds make stories. (12)

We are inspired by a new crop of genre-bending (often feminist) writing that draws from art, philosophy, history, science fiction, ecology, biology, and even quantum physics to offer different stories about the urgency of our contemporary epoch (variously characterized as the Anthropocene or

1

the Chthulucene or the Capitalocene) and to lay the groundwork for the mass changes needed to counteract violent, degrading, and world-destroying "business as usual" practices: industrial agriculture, fossil fuel extraction and consumption, and ecosystem degradation, among others. Books like *Arts of Living on a Damaged Planet: Ghosts and Monsters of the Anthropocene* (Tsing, Swanson, Gan, Bubant 2017), *Staying with the Trouble: Making Kin in the Chthulucene* (Haraway 2016), and *The Mushroom at the End of the World: On the Possibility of Life in Capitalist Ruins* (Tsing 2015) attempt to tell stories about the world that recognize how humans are deeply interconnected with nonhuman animals and ecosystems. The purpose of this storytelling is not just symbolic. The writers see these more expansive views of biological interconnection as having the potential to resist capitalist/neoliberal practices in ways that more traditional political or scientific arguments have been unsuccessful.

COMMUNICATING ABOUT COLLAPSE

The Anthropocene, the human-shaped geologic era we now occupy, presents challenges too huge to comprehend, damage too tragic to contemplate, and a reality that mocks the wholly insufficient language of "solutions" many humans yearn to imagine. We have spent too long fretting about the impossibility of "fixing" the damage that humans have done to the environment, whether climate change, mass extinction, or ecosystem destruction. And the vast majority of the writing about both environmental destruction and possible (or impossible) solutions is from a human-centered perspective with limited acknowledgment of the web of entangled relations that make up our human-nonhuman world. Again and again, researchers and activists alike bemoan the way in which scientific findings (even those that confirm worst-case predictions from earlier research) do not lead to action or change. There is no shortage of approaches to environmental communication that suggest best practices for how to communicate in this crisis era of climate change, mass extinction, worsening pollution, and environmental degradation, yet here we are, more than thirty years after James Hansen broke with scientific norms for how to communicate about scientific findings in public and urged policymakers and the public to take global warming seriously with few significant changes—public, private, or governmental—to address these issues. The carbon-based economy is alive and well, and in a July 2020 research paper, the researchers note that "it now appears extremely unlikely that the climate sensitivity could be low enough to avoid substantial climate change (well in excess of 2°C warming) under a high-emissions future scenario" (Sherwood et al. 2020, 5). The purpose of this edited volume is to offer a view of life in the Anthropocene where communication is at the heart of our ability to reckon with both the now-ness of environmental crisis and the future of other ways of being-in-relation with our earthly companions. To say that communication is a central feature of the Anthropocene is to argue that communication can be understood as an interface between humans, nonhumans, and the land. Communication, for our purposes, is not simply the transfer of information, but is a connector, an articulator, a mechanism for building connections and networks. Importantly, humans are always communicating with each other, with nonhuman beings, and the land, although in Western cultures we tend to think of communication as something unique to humans and to reduce communication to language. As Emily Plec (2012) suggests in one of the first communication books devoted to human-nonhuman communication, researchers must expand "our understanding of communication beyond that very human obsession with the structure and substance of verbal utterances. Animals, including humans, speak not only via vocalization but also in scent, posture, eye gaze, even vibration" (3). The chapters in *Intimate Relations* reach far beyond the "structure and substance of verbal utterances" and offer insight into a wealth of possibilities for recognizing and honoring modes of connection with living beings.

INTIMACY

In this volume, we suggest a view of communication as intimacy. We use this concept as a provocation for thinking about how we humans are in an always-already state of being-in-relation with other humans, nonhumans, and the land. Inspired by Kath Weston, whose (2017) *Animate Planet* offers several cases that describe "new intimacies" between humans, animals, and their surroundings, we argue that "intimate relations" offer an explanation of both environmental degradation and of alternative worlding. The concept of intimacy offers a way of thinking about the entanglement and interconnectedness of human-nonhuman relations and the ways in which such entanglement is often overlooked by humans. But this is only part of the story. Intimacy, as a concept, includes resonances of love, care, commitment, and sensuousness. To think with intimacy is to think about being-in-relation in a particular way that *centers* care: for each other and the earth. Care is a way of characterizing the filaments of interconnectivity that bind us together. Especially in this moment of aerosolized transmission of a deadly pathogen, our cultural ideas about connectivity are a jumbled mix of contradictory values: On the one hand, many of us are longing for a pre-pandemic version of human connection that includes touch and physical presence. And yet we also feel anxiety at the proximity of seen and unseen strangers, human and nonhuman, whose

closeness can literally sicken or kill us. Pity the humans who, having been
fed a steady diet of anthropocentric individualism their entire lives, must now
navigate the material contradictions that entanglement presents to their narratives of individuality. The writers and artists in this volume tell stories of how
to live in connection with other beings in the face of crisis.

ENTANGLEMENT

The notion of "entanglement" that we use here is inspired by Karen Barad,
who draws from her expertise in both quantum physics and feminist theory.
In an influential 2003 article, she proposes what she calls relational ontology
as a corrective to overly discursive approaches to social worlds. Drawing
insights from quantum physics about the inseparability of the observer and
the observed (i.e., that there is no "thing" to be studied that exists prior to the
entanglement of researcher-object), Barad names this kind of entanglement
an intra-action (as opposed to interaction) in which all elements, human, and
nonhuman become together. She explains that "'human bodies' and 'human
subjects' do not preexist as such; nor are they mere end products. 'Humans'
are neither pure cause nor pure effect but part of the world in its open-ended
becoming" (Barad 2003, 821). To think about ecosystems as entangled means
that we have to see human actions as always-already tied to, influenced by,
and complicit in the actions of other parts of the world, human and nonhuman. Typical ideas about "saving the environment," for example are challenged by this perspective. There is no "environment" separate from the
human savior that can be acted on. Glenn Albrecht (2016) offers another way
of thinking about entanglement in his plea for "Exiting the Anthropocene and
Entering the Symbiocene." He proposes that the way out of the Anthropocene
is to "affirm the interconnectedness of life and all things" (13) and to see such
symbiosis as a model for a new politics and way of living.

BEING-IN-RELATION

Intimacy offers a framework for developing alternative ways of thinking
about agency-in-relation. Donna Haraway, who builds lovely speculative
worlds filled with what she calls "oddkin," suggests how new forms of relationality might offer insights into more sustainable ways of living. In her
2016 book *Staying with the Trouble*, she explains the title by suggesting that
staying with the trouble "requires making oddkin; that is, we require each
other in unexpected collaborations and combinations, in hot compost piles.
We become-with each other or not at all. That kind of material semiotics is

always situated, someplace and not noplace, entangled and worldly" (Haraway 2016, 4). Agency here is radically relational and intertwined. Kath Weston, in her engagement with human-nonhuman relationality describes how intimacy with nonhuman others can be "animated" in various sites. So while we might always-already be entangled with other humans and nonhumans, Weston suggests a way to "activate" or "animate" (2017, 4) such relations such that we might recognize or reframe how we see complex social-material issues. To consider human interactions with the world as entangled intimacy is to work within the tradition of posthumanists (and other eco-philosophers) who strive to "decenter the human" in the humanities. Rosi Braidotti (2016), for example, notes that "a posthuman ethics for a non-unitary subject proposes an enlarged sense of interconnection between self and other, including the nonhuman or "earth" others, by removing the obstacle of self-centered individualism" (Interview with Veronese 99). Such a shift from self-centered individualism to an intimate, entangled subject requires new stories, new lexicons, new values.

To use intimacy as a frame for this book, we center two components of relationality: interconnectedness and affect. We propose that individualism and human exceptionalism—two guiding truths in Western philosophy—obscure the many ways in which humans, nonhumans, more-than-humans, and the land are co-dependent, symbiotic, entangled, and otherwise wrapped up in each other's stories. There is power in telling stories that background individualism and instead strive to notice some of the complex ways that humans are a part of (not apart from) the world. Our focus on intimacy also has an affective component. Affect is the often-overlooked force that binds us together—that, if we look more closely at it, offers clues for how to be (and how we are) entangled with nonhuman others. In this book, we ask how engaging affective questions in unlikely ways, forms, and places opens up new possibilities for how we understand environmental crisis and how the seeds for how to live differently are already planted.

COMMUNICATING (IN) THE ANTHROPOCENE/CAPITALOCENE

We "locate" the chapters in this volume within the context of the Anthropocene, or perhaps more accurately the Capitalocene. While both the Anthropocene and the Capitalocene can seem bleak in their terrible destructive enormity, we approach our current era with a steely hope and a desire to, as Anna Tsing proposes, find "life in capitalist ruins." Timothy Morton (2013) has argued that the Anthropocene should be understood as a "hyperobject," a concept that, in its hugeness, is almost impossible to comprehend. It is both urgent and on a different scale altogether from the day-to-day life of most people. Traditional (social) scientific methods and typical forms of science communication have been ineffective in fully engaging the magnitude and complexity of climate change, mass extinction, and other large-scale environmental changes. Rather than re-hashing suggestions for how to better tailor messages to audiences or how to (re)frame environmental communication, our volume engages the hyperobject through the lens of intimacy. Using evocative and engaging examples that cut across traditional disciplines, the chapters in this volume take seriously the idea that worlds are made (and remade) through mundane, everyday practices. The communication discipline has a rich tradition of research and theory that examines how mundane everyday practices "construct" social worlds (influenced by sociological theories that privilege the way in which social structures are constructed rather than fixed or natural). Our volume seeks to expand this sense of construction by paying attention to how interspecies intimacy, entanglement, and relations form the building blocks of the Anthropocene. To use intimacy as a guiding framework for thinking about relations and relationality in the Anthropocene, our goal is to offer a new and accessible way to consider both environmental harm and possibilities for seeing and living otherwise. We see how the thread of mass extinction is unavoidably connected to the thread of systematic forms of racist disenfranchisement and the creation of sacrifice zones. The world-changing effects of human (masculine) violence are on full display in 2020. (Climate) refugees detained in inhuman conditions, unrelenting state-sponsored (police) violence against Black, Indigenous and People of Color, and widespread environmental degradation, especially in communities of color, are impossible to look away from. The chapters below offer rich and impassioned examples of what it might look like to truly accept that we are all entangled in relations of intimacy.

AN INVITATION AND BEGINNING

We have arranged the below story into five sections according to what we perceive as naturally forming pairings of ideas and/or perspectives, but we acknowledge that these works could easily be arranged again and again in varying ways to reveal and tell different contrasting stories. Some of these chapters are in tension, offering opposing viewpoints that could lead our audience to feel disjointed. Yet all of this work disrupts commonly held narratives in Western culture by centering intimacy and intimate relations as paramount for our survival.

Part I of the book, Grief, Resilience and Storytelling, immediately acknowledges the deepness of what we are currently grappling with (or not!) in the

Anthropocene. It is a recognition that we are experiencing collective despair and that our usual ways of coping are no longer viable. Instead the reader is invited to walk-into our grief and stay there until we can see ourselves anew in our entanglement: To see compassion, love, and care as centerpieces to our relationship with our planet. And then this section offers trouble. Resilience is not enough. Many of our tools are not going to be enough. We are going to need to reimagine ourselves and our capabilities.

Part II, Nonhuman Collaborators: Oysters, Birds, and Elephants, demands more intent listening and attention to specific species and urges the reader to consider how nonhuman animals communicate with us and indeed are collaborators, resistors, and disruptors within our human-animal worlds. They are not passive actors, instead they are autonomous creatures with imagination, resolution skills, and do communicate with each other and us. Authors from across the globe recognize how oysters, birds, and elephants use their agency, and as a method of disrupting anthropocentric thinking, *strategically anthropomorphize* (Bennett 2010) these nonhuman animal persons, inviting them to speak for themselves. These contributions are often charming, always tender, and pointedly asking for recognition of the problems we humans create for our earthly co-inhabitants.

Part III, Plants and Other Family Members, is a fun adventure into the rhizomatic understory of plants. Here, the authors crack open the tightly held belief that plants are cognitively inanimate, unknowable, and not human co-conspirators. In its place, the reader is offered the most fantastic peek into how mushrooms, plant reproduction and motherhood, and plant personhood are critical and unique intellectual, metaphorical, and literal collaborators in our human adventure and life cycle. This section makes you weep as you recall all the times and ways you refused to "see" plants as friends and family members, and yet what you are left with is not shame or remorse (although you could easily feel these things, too) but a call to ground yourself in roots, deep empathy, and psilocybin.

Part IV, Nonhuman Agency, Activism, and Legal Personhood, is pragmatic and sensible. It helps us further consider and untangle legal framings and policy obligations that feel outdated and immoral but still real barriers to our environmental intimacy revolution. Legal Personhood, the role of imagery and technology, and mediated understandings of nature all unfold here. These authors know that the master's tools will never dismantle the master's house (Audre Lorde 1984), and yet they delightfully encourage and demand that we don't throw the baby out with the bathwater in our desperation to create our new world. We need to find pathways *through*.

Part V, Gender, Earthly Intimacies, and Other Trouble, turns the reader upside down with its blinding reminder of all that we have forgotten about our problematic behavior as humans. Our convenience culture, our addiction to plastics, our *imperialist, white-supremacist, capitalist, patriarchal* (bell hooks 2013) culture that erodes our opportunities for peace, healthy soil, and interspecies connection is put forth and interrogated with a painful obviousness of where we have gone astray. The outcomes of these human ways are crushing: enormous wildfires that kill a billion animals, seething toxic masculinities that undermine any attempts at gentleness as a way of being in the world, and the congealed floating masses of slime and junk and grease in our oceans and sewers. It's painful and necessary to have this mirror held up, and still our authors lessen the blow by reminding us of how we can still proceed in deepening our relationships and perhaps even enjoying our time here on earth more.

The chapters in this book vary in their appearance, tone, and style. In our attempt to disrupt what Plec calls "that very human obsession with the structure and substance of verbal utterances" (2015, 3), in addition to the full-length chapters, we wanted to include a collection of chapters that represent *Arts-Based Knowing*. These are twelve contributions from individuals on the frontlines of poetically reimagining our futures, using art, poetry, speculative prose, and other creative forms. These contributions are powerful invitations to world-making: art functions to plant us in the ground that birthed us, bringing us down into the depths of our emotions and exploding our hearts as we recognize how much longing we have for intimacy with our surroundings. Because, you see, we have not been fully born until we can commune with all of the flora and fauna and more-than-human charisma of our universe and planet.

We hope reading this book changes you—that it plucks you up and throws you into a river of reflection, remembrance, and reverence. It is a prayer, really, absent religion and human-centered thinking—a prayer for your beingness, becomingness, and for your consideration of our earthly intimacies as part of you.

BIBLIOGRAPHY

Albrecht, Glenn A. 2016. "Exiting the Anthropocene and entering the Symbiocene." *Minding Nature*, 9, no. 2: 12–16.

Barad, Karen. 2003. "Posthumanist Performativity: Toward an Understanding of How Matter Comes to Matter." *Signs: Journal of Women in Culture and Society* 28, no. 3: 801–31. https://doi.org/10.1086/345321.

Bennett, Jane. 2010. *Vibrant Matter: A Political Ecology of Things.* Durham: Duke University Press.

Haraway, Donna J. 2016. *Staying with the trouble: Making kin in the Chthulucene.* Duke University Press.

hooks, bell. 2013. Writing Beyond Race: Living Theory and Practice by bell hooks. New York: Routledge.

Lorde, Audre. 1984. "The Master's Tools Will Never Dismantle the Master's House." *Sister Outsider: Essays and Speeches*. Ed. Berkeley, CA: Crossing Press. 110–114.

Morton, Timothy. 2013. *Hyperobjects: Philosophy and ecology after the end of the world*. University of Minnesota Press.

Plec, Emily, ed. 2012. *Perspectives on Human-Animal Communication : Internatural Communication*. London: Taylor & Francis Group. Accessed August 21, 2020. ProQuest Ebook Central.

Puig de la Bellacasa, M. 2017. *Matters of care: Speculative ethics in more than human worlds*. University of Minnesota Press.

Sherwood, Steven, Mark Webb, Kyle Armour, Piers Forster, Gabriele Hegerl, Stephen A. Klein, J. Rohling Eelco, et al. 2020. An assessment of Earth's climate sensitivity using multiple lines of evidence. *Reviews of Geophysics*, 58: https://doi.org/10.1029/2019RG000678.

Tsing, Anna L. 2015. *The mushroom at the end of the world : On the possibility of life in capitalist ruins*. Princeton University Press.

Tsing, Anna L., Heather A. Swanson, Elaine Gan, and Nils Bubandt 2017. *Arts of living on a damaged planet: ghosts and monsters of the Anthropocene*. University of Minnesota Press.

Veronese, Cosetta. 2016. "Can the Humanities Become Post-human? Interview with Rosi Braidotti." *Relations* 4, no. 4.1: 97–101. https://doi.org/10.7358/rela-2016-001-vero.

Part I

GRIEF, RESILIENCE, AND STORYTELLING

Chapter 2

Vigilant Mourning and the Future of Earthly Coexistence

Joshua Trey Barnett

Mourning is all too often described as a kind of untethering, a severing of the ties that bind one to another. Consider Sigmund Freud's account in "Mourning and Melancholia." "The fact is," Freud explains matter-of-factly, "that when the work of mourning is completed the ego becomes free and uninhibited again" (1953, 154). Having finished this "work," Freud's mourner emerges emancipated. Mourning would, therefore, seem to consist of unweaving intimacies and relinquishing the emotional bonds that bind us to who and what exceed the self. This is perhaps what we mean when, in ordinary language, we speak of "getting over" the death of another or "moving on" in the wake of a loss.

Yet, mourning is not simply—nor, I would add, usually or even ideally—a kind of abandonment. Impoverished is the idea that we must "let go" of what has been lost in order to free ourselves up to establish new bonds, new connections, new intimacies. And, indeed, there may be something deeply unethical in the demand to grieve privately and efficiently, to carry out the work of mourning as quickly and completely as possible. There are other ways. "Mourning," Jacques Derrida once wrote, "*must* be impossible. Successful mourning is failed mourning" (2004, 159). In this stunning inversion of Freud's explanation, Derrida not only thrusts mourning's very possibility into question. More importantly, Derrida also destabilizes the notion of *successful* mourning. Whereas Freud believed that "successful" mourning meant liberating oneself from the other, Derrida claims that the only mourning we could rightly call "successful" is that which *fails* to emancipate the survivor from the lost. This Derrida describes as "the law of mourning," namely, "that it would have to fail in order to succeed" (2001, 144). As opposed to "getting over" the lost object, then, we find ourselves called to "hang on."

It is precisely to this call to hang on—to refuse to abandon who or what has been lost—that I wish to attend in this chapter. Indeed, I will consider the ways in which a refusal to "get over" what has been lost might contribute to the work of earthly coexistence—to the work, that is, of striving to dwell more peacefully upon the earth and of collaborating with our more-than-human cohabitants in ways that are mutually beneficial. As Timothy Morton reminds us, "Existence is always coexistence" (2010, 4). Though we may hope or believe that we are essentially autonomous individuals, the fact is that we *are* only insofar as we are connected to others. Thus, how we comport ourselves entails consequences that ramify beyond our own lives, influencing human and more-than-human ways of being on earth. All things are (more or less directly) interconnected. The work of earthly coexistence involves us in conscious efforts to dwell within those connections in ways that do less harm and that preserve opportunities for others to flourish.

In both the wake and the face of mass extinction, rampant habitat degradation, ecological devastation, and earth systems disruption, perhaps we ought to stay with our grief and, thus, confront the diminishment of our shared worlds without seeking to simply escape our sorrow. Born of bereavement, our sorrow is a sign of our deprivation, a sign that we have lost something significant, something that mattered, something irreplaceable. Our grief for what exceeds the human is a symptom of connection, familiarity, and love, of what Douglas Burton-Christie calls "our sense of participation in and responsibility for the whole fabric of life of which we are a part" (2011, 30). Our mourning is also an act of fidelity, a pledge of loyalty, a work of remembrance; through mourning, we preserve our connection to what has died, been destroyed, or otherwise disappeared. More to the point, our mourning is a way of caring and enacting our concern. Or, as Terry Tempest Williams has eloquently put it, "Our grief is our love" (2019, 214).

Since we express and enact our love for the earthly by and through our mourning, it makes sense to consider sustained grief and persistent mourning. Along these lines, I will attend in this chapter to what I call "vigilant mourning," a practice of tarrying with our grief, of remaining awake to those beings and ways of being on earth which have already been lost and of staying alert to those which today find themselves under threat of erasure. From the Latin *vigilia*, "watch, watchfulness, wakefulness," and *vigilāre*, "to keep awake," enacting vigilance entails persisting in a state of wakefulness and alertness, attending and attuning, observing and protecting, guarding and keeping. Etymologically, the English verb *mourn* derives from the Indo-European base of the word *memory*, the Gothic *maurnan*, "to worry, concern oneself," the Old High German *mornēn*, "to sorrow," and the Old Saxon *mornon*, "to be sorrowful or troubled." In mourning vigilantly, we remain with our sorrow and we watch for losses to come. Vigilant mourning is unresolved and active;

unfinished and resistant. When we grieve for what exceeds the human, and especially when we refuse to bring our grief to a "successful" end, R. Clifton Spargo suggests that our "unresolved mourning becomes a dissenting act, a sign of an irremissible ethical meaning" (2004, 6). This "dissenting act" is one of the conditions of earthly coexistence; maintaining our sense of connection with what has been lost, on the one hand, and remaining awake to what might yet be lost, on the other, we establish an enduring bond between the living and the dead, a bond which renders us responsible to one another. Mourning vigilantly is one of the ways we might enact our earthly responsibility.

Attending to past losses and anticipating future ones, the work of vigilant mourning orients us within what Aldo Leopold once described as "a world of wounds" (1970, 197). In practice, vigilant mourning may take any number of forms but either *persistence* or *repetition* is key to its rhetorical, ethical, and political force. In the pages that follow, I sketch some contours of vigilant mourning by thinking with two examples: a Monument to the Passenger Pigeon (*Ectopistes migratorius*) located in southern Wisconsin's Wyalusing State Park and the annual international Remembrance Day for Lost Species (RDLS). Whereas the immovable monument reveals the significance of endurance, the perennial RDLS sheds light on the force of recurrence. Both examples provide models of "hanging on" to what has been lost, models which complement and enrich one another. Before turning to these specific instances of vigilant mourning, though, it will be useful to return to our starting point and outline the beginnings of a theory of vigilant mourning.

TOWARD A THEORY OF VIGILANT MOURNING

For better and for worse, Freud's "Mourning and Melancholia" remains with us today as a specter of sorts, both informing and haunting how we understand loss and grief. As Ashlee Cunsolo and Karen Landman remark in their introduction to *Mourning Nature*, "Freud laid the foundations for a belief that healthy mourning would eventually come to completion, and this theory still characterizes much discourse on mourning" (2017, 9). In "Mourning and Melancholia," Freud sought to distinguish the defining characteristics of his titular concepts. Essentially, Freud maintained, the work of mourning moves us to accept our loss, acknowledge our new reality, relinquish our attachments to the lost object, and, thus, free ourselves up to forge new bonds with new objects. This view of mourning is sometimes described as "compensatory," as the loss of one object is made up for by gaining another. Through mourning, we divest and detach from what we have lost. "The testing of reality," he remarked, "having shown that the loved object no longer exists, requires forthwith that all the libido shall be withdrawn from its attachment to this object" (1953, 154). This so called "requirement" to detach frequently incites a psychic struggle. As the mourner tries to preserve the lost other in their mind, they also attempt to abandon the libidinal position that binds them to what they have lost. "Each single one of the memories and hopes which bound the libido to the object," Freud explained, "is brought up and hyper-cathected, and the detachment of the libido from it accomplished" (1953, 154). Liberated from their attachments to one object, Freud's mourner was free to "move on" to another.

If Freud's mourner moves on, his melancholic gets stuck. "Instead of transferring attachment outward to a new object-cathexis," writes Catriona Mortimer-Sandilands, "the melancholic internalizes the lost object as a way of preserving it" (2010, 334). Both Freud's mourner and melancholic bring the other inside themselves. "The ego wishes to incorporate this object into itself," Freud explained, "and the method by which it would do so, in this oral or cannibalistic way, is by devouring it" (1953, 160). Whereas the mourner is able to fully "digest" the internalized other, the melancholic suffers a pro-found case of indigestion. The melancholic's inability to move on from their grief Freud regarded as a kind of "failed" mourning. And because a failure to mourn could lead to self-beratement and, in the most severe cases, self-harm or suicide, Freud understood melancholia as aberrant, pathological, and potentially morbid. Melancholia sometimes leads to "an overthrow, psycho-logically very remarkable, of that instinct which constrains every living thing to cling to life" (Freud 1953, 156). The melancholic turns against himself and against the very desire to live on in the wake of loss. No wonder, then, that Freud understood abandoning the loved and lost object as crucial to the mental health of his patients.

A few years later, Freud significantly revised his earlier position on melan-cholia. Reflecting on his claim that the melancholic's identification with the lost object prevented him from successfully mourning, in *The Ego and the Id* Freud observed: "At that time, we did not appreciate the full significance of this process and did not know how common and how typical it is" (1960, 23). Whereas Freud once believed that melancholic identification threatened the subject's very being, he now claimed that the subject becomes who and what it is through devouring and *partially* digesting lost loved objects. Indeed, he concluded that "it is possible to suppose that the character of the ego is a pre-cipitate of abandoned object-cathexes and that it contains the history of those object-choices" (1960, 24). If the "character of the ego" is formed through the sedimentation within the psyche of lost loved ones, objects, fantasies, and ideals, it no longer makes sense to distinguish between a "healthy" mourning and an "unhealthy" melancholia. As Judith Butler notes, Freud "changes what it means to 'let an object go,' for there is no final breaking of the attachment." Rather, she continues, "we see that letting the object go means, paradoxically, not full abandonment of the object but transferring the status of the object from external to internal" (1997, 134). In bringing what has been lost within ourselves, we maintain—rather than relinquish—a connection to the dead, destroyed, or otherwise disappeared.

Although Freud eventually and reluctantly embraced incorporation as an aspect of mourning, Derrida regarded it as essential to ethical relationality. Indeed, Derrida saw in mourning an opportunity to enact our fidelity to the lost other. In what, though, might such fidelity consist? Derrida wrote of "an interminable mourning," a mourning with neither beginning nor end (2001, 158). Rather than relinquishing our relations after a predictable period of mourning, Derrida claimed that we should seek to maintain our connections with who or what we have lost. "For Derrida," as I have written elsewhere, "the ethical task of mourning consists in letting the other, the wholly other, live on in our thoughts and our deeds" (Barnett 2019b, 291). These relationships play out at the psychic as well as the social level, which are, of course, always already entwined. We mourn individually and privately, to be sure, but the work of mourning is also undertaken by communities. We have a collective responsibility to keep lost (ecological and earthly) others "alive" through our thoughts, our speech, and our acts of creation and commemoration. By doing so, we safeguard the other from total or absolute loss.

Resistance and protection merge in mourning. Predicated on a refusal to relinquish the ties that bind the survivor to their lost object, ethical mourning preserves who or what has been lost, enabling the lost other to survive, to live on. Following Derrida, in *The Ethics of Mourning* Spargo considers what he describes as "a resistant and incomplete mourning" (2004, 13). Against cultural demands to mourn and move on, Spargo conceives of grief as an occasion for a belated, impossible—but nevertheless significant—gesture of protection. "Though it may proceed under the aspect of fantasy," Spargo contends, "this imagined protection recalls or introduces a willingness to risk oneself imaginatively for another" (24). Mourning reveals not only how we are entangled with others, but it also unconceals a desire to defend them against absolute loss—the loss, that is, of both matter and memory. Although we did not, or could not, intervene on their behalf before they were lost, through mourning we hold the other close, refusing to abandon them a second time. And while no act of mourning can resuscitate who or what has been lost, nonetheless mourning exposes "an ethic exceeding self-concern," an ethic that connects the living and the dead, an ethic that binds us, without end, to the memory of the other (24). This belated act of protection might serve, too, as a model for relating to what remains with us, with those beings and ways of being on earth that have not yet been lost. Striving to preserve the memory of what has already been lost, in other words, may inspire us to anticipate and ward off other losses to come.

Vigilant mourning may comprise mostly private rituals of remembrance. Consider, for example, Roland Barthes's *Mourning Diary*, a collection of fragmentary texts that the French philosopher and cultural critic began assembling in the wake of his mother's death on October 25, 1977. In the years after her death Barthes added, sometimes several times a day, to a slowly amassing pile of brief, often obscure written remarks about his mother, her death, and especially his ongoing sorrow. A bit more than a month after her death, he wonders: "Does being able to live without someone you loved mean you loved her less than you thought?" (2010, 68). A certain anxiety underwrites Barthes's question: is his grief enough? "I ask for nothing," he wrote on July 1, 1978, "but to live in my suffering" (174). "Anything that keeps me from my suffering," he had written the day before, "is unbearable to me" (173). For Barthes, grief was a sign of continuing connection. Therefore, not to grieve—not to suffer—would have signaled the severing of that connection. It was the possibility of this severing, not his own suffering, that Barthes felt was "unbearable." In both content and form, Barthes's *Mourning Diary* performs a kind of vigilant mourning: just as the author of these fragments explicitly avows his grief, so too does he return to it again and again for years before his own untimely death in 1980. Barthes refuses to "let go," chooses to abandon neither his mother nor his grief. His words and deeds tether him, interminably, to his *maman*.

If Barthes's *Mourning Diary* illustrates an initially private act of vigilant mourning that later became public, the AIDS Memorial Quilt provides a powerful example of how vigilant mourning has been enacted in public. From humble beginnings in 1987, the Quilt has grown to encompass nearly 50,000 three-foot-by-six-foot memorial panels, each one designed and sown to commemorate the life of someone—and, in many cases, more than one person—who has died of AIDS ("The AIDS Memorial Quilt" 2020). The Quilt is a poignant reminder of how persistent, public mourning works not only to keep us awake to past losses but to invite us to remain alert to the possibility of losses to come. Particularly when who or what has been—or might be—lost has been relegated to what Butler calls the status of the "ungrievable" (2002; 2004; 2010), publicly mourning becomes an act of resistance. In "Mourning and Militancy," Douglas Crimp tends to the often-fraught relation between grief and activism. In the early years of the AIDS pandemic, Crimp notes, "Public mourning rituals [could] often seem, from an activist perspective, indulgent, sentimental, defeatist" (1989, 5). To mourn in the midst of pandemic can feel like capitulation, like giving up on life, like giving in to loss. And yet, as the title of Crimp's essay makes clear, we need not see "Mourning and Militancy" as opposed. The "and" here is significant, for it links the anger and the sorrow at the heart of the AIDS Memorial Quilt. We must fight the injustice of every death, but we must also mourn those losses publicly and persistently. When the work of mourning moves from the private to the public sphere, it becomes one of the conditions of possibility for new ways of relating to and caring for others, of attending to loss while also celebrating and supporting life.

With these two examples in mind, I want to return briefly to the question of how vigilant mourning might support the work of dwelling peacefully on earth with our more-than-human cohabitants. We live in a time of devastating ecological transformations and profound planetary disruptions. We are losing biodiversity. Long-standing relationships are breaking down. Habitats and ecosystems are transforming beyond recognition. Systems that humans once imagined beyond our control are now clearly under our influence. Given the scope and scale of the damage, it is unsurprising that individuals and communities alike are experiencing grief. Ecological grief, as Ashlee Cunsolo and Neville Ellis characterize it in one of the first empirical studies on the topic, is "the grief felt in relation to experienced or anticipated ecological losses, including the loss of species, ecosystems, and meaningful landscapes due to acute or chronic environmental change" (2018, 275). Ecological grief is both backward-looking and forward-looking, retrospective, and anticipatory. It is possible both to mourn the extinction of the passenger pigeon, gone now for more than one hundred years, and to grieve for what we are likely to lose in our own lifetime—the polar ice caps, for example, which are melting six times faster now than they were just three decades ago (Carrington 2020). Every day we learn of new ecological crises, of recent and imminent losses. For better and for worse, we are burdened with both an awareness of previous losses and with forms of knowledge that enable us to anticipate those losses which are as yet on the horizon.

Situated between past and future losses, we find ourselves dwelling, as Leopold put it, "in a world of wounds" (1970, 197). Amid these losses, the environmental philosopher Thom van Dooren claims, we are called "to face up to the dead and to our role in the coming into being of a world of escalating suffering, loss, and extinction" (2014, 143). Differently put, we are called not only to confront ecological and earthly losses but also to acknowledge the responsibility that we individually and collectively bear for creating and/or reproducing worlds in which such losses are not only possible but increasingly—lamentably—common. We live, van Dooren explains, in "shared worlds," which means that we need to come to terms with the fact that we are vitally bound up with and responsible to others. "Grief," as Donna Haraway writes, "is a path to understanding entangled shared living and dying" because it exposes the fact that "we are in and of this fabric of undoing" together (2016, 39). And so, in some significant sense, to mourn what exceeds the human is to recognize our intricate and inextricable imbrication with this imperiled earth. This recognition is the beating heart of earthly coexistence.

PERSISTENCE: THE MONUMENT TO
THE PASSENGER PIGEON

Let's consider *Ectopistes migratorius*, a species of avifauna once prevalent across much of central and eastern North America. As the Smithsonian Institution notes, its scientific name suggests "a bird that not only migrates in the spring and fall, but one that also moves about from season to season to select the most favorable environment for nesting and feeding." Etymologically, "*Ectopistes* means 'moving about or wandering,' while *migratorius* means 'migrating'" ("The Passenger Pigeon" n.d.). This doubly itinerant bird was and is known to most as the passenger pigeon. For more than a century, though, humans have dwelt on earth without passenger pigeons. On the first day of September in the year 1914, the last surviving passenger pigeon—dubbed "Martha" in honor of the United States' original First Lady, Martha Washington—died in captivity at the Cincinnati Zoo.

Martha's death was, in many ways, unremarkable: billions of passenger pigeons on the continent had already died, after all, and most well before 1914. Martha's death was simply the final nail in the proverbial coffin. Indeed, as Thom van Dooren reminds us, "the immensity and significance of extinctions cannot be captured within these singular events, as though a species might be deemed to be extinct or not solely on the basis of the presence in the world of at least one individual of that kind/lineage" (2014, 11). In the end, a single specimen does not a species make. By the time the last individual perishes, an entire way of being in the world has already disappeared from the face of the earth. Yet, in another sense, Martha's death was extraordinary precisely because it punctuated such a tremendous loss. "At the time that Europeans first arrived in North America," the natural historian Joel Greenberg notes, "passenger pigeons likely numbered anywhere from three to five billion," making it "the most abundant bird on the continent, if not the planet" (2014, 1). Less than 100 years before Martha died, yet another naturalist, the famed John James Audubon, published an account of his encounters with the species. In his *Ornithological Biography*, Audubon remarks that, "The multitudes of Wild Pigeons in our woods are astonishing. Indeed, after having viewed them so often, and under so many circumstances, I even now feel inclined to pause, and assure myself that what I am going to relate is fact." Audubon then describes a time in 1813 when a flock of passenger pigeons took several days to pass over the Ohio River Valley, blocking out the sun as they migrated to a new food source. Thus, slightly more than a century before the last passenger pigeon died, Audubon was "struck with amazement" at the species' abundance (1831, 320). Ninety-nine years later, the old abundance had withered away altogether.

Or, rather, the once-prolific passenger pigeon population had been withered away. The species' demise was not inevitable. It was, rather, an achievement—the result of a two-pronged assault on both the birds themselves and their habitat. While people indigenous to North America had dwelt alongside passenger pigeons for centuries without significantly diminishing either their populations or their habitats, Greenberg notes, the "newly arrived Europeans looked at the masses of pigeons both with wonder and hunger" (2014, 69). The new arrivals killed the passenger pigeons with their bare hands, with poisons, with arrows; they clubbed them to death, trapped them with nets, shot them from the skies. Their flesh was consumed, and their feathers were used to make pillows and other soft goods. To the European immigrants the passenger pigeons must have seemed an inexhaustible resource, another sign of the New World's riches. So prolific was *Ectopistes migratorius* that even Audubon struggled to fathom their extinction: "They are killed in immense numbers," he wrote, "although no apparent diminution occurs" (1831, 323). Even as Audubon witnessed the large-scale destruction of passenger pigeons, he nevertheless believed that "nothing but the gradual diminution of our forests [could] accomplish their decrease" (1831, 325). Of course, many of the old-growth forests that once provided habitat and sustenance for the species were diminished through deforestation. Oak, beech, and chestnut trees yielded the mast upon which passenger pigeons relied for their survival. So, when large populations of these trees were sent down the river to provide materials for a growing nation or when they succumbed to fatal diseases, passenger pigeons surely suffered.

Although humans struggled to anticipate the extinction of *Ectopistes migratorius* even as they witnessed—and, in some cases, participated in—the destruction of "immense numbers" of these birds, the profundity of their loss has, nonetheless, not been entirely lost on humans. In more ways than one, the demise of the passenger pigeon has summoned forth a kind of vigilant mourning engendered by public expressions of grief, expressions which continue to awaken us to the profound absence the loss created. The Cincinnati Zoo, for instance, maintains a permanent memorial to the species ("Passenger Pigeon Memorial" n.d.). And in Washington, D.C., outside the Smithsonian Institution's Museum of Natural History, stands a large-scale bronze sculpture of a single passenger pigeon. The sculpture is part of artist Todd McGrain's "Lost Bird" (O'Brien 2016) series, which also includes memorials to other extinct birds like the great auk, Labrador duck, Carolina parakeet, and heath hen. But these are not the only memorials to *Ectopistes migratorius*. More enduring still is the Monument to the Passenger Pigeon in southwestern Wisconsin.

Perched atop the summit of Sentinel Ridge, the Monument to the Passenger Pigeon overlooks the confluence of the Wisconsin and Mississippi rivers near

the still-small town of Prairie du Chien, Wisconsin. Thirty-three years after
the last passenger pigeon died, on May 11, 1947, members of the Wisconsin
Society for Ornithology dedicated the memorial. In the Society's newslet-
ter, aptly (and still) titled *The Passenger Pigeon*, one Gertrude M. Scott
recounted that, after a celebratory luncheon,

> members of the Society and many park visitors who were attracted by the
> unusual idea of erecting a monument to an extinct species of fauna, began gath-
> ering on Sentinel ridge, overlooking the broad Mississippi with its extensive
> wooded bottomlands, which is here swelled by the waters of the Wisconsin. The
> neat and imposing stone monument was the focal point, its face covered by a
> square of black cloth. (1947, 58–59)

Following several speeches, Scott explained, the Society's president, J.
Harwood Evans, "presented the plaque and monument to the State of
Wisconsin" (Scott 1947, 61). W. J. P. Aberg received the Society's gift on the
state's behalf and drew the ceremony to a close by promising that the monument would be "carefully guarded and watched daily." And, Aberg added, "if
vandals try to molest it, their efforts will be prevented, for the joy it will give
to the future and [the] sorrow that is necessary to dedicate monuments of this
kind" (quoted in Scott 1947, 61).

Whether any vandals ever tried to "molest" the Monument to the Passenger
Pigeon, I do not know. When, quite by accident, I visited the monument
exactly seventy-two years to the day after it was dedicated, however, it was
still perched on the edge of Sentinel Ridge and looked much as it did in the
pictures from 1947. The handsome, sturdy monument sits beneath the cano-
pies of mature oak trees, which on sunny spring days cast dappled light upon
the memorial. A stout stone column draws visitors' attention toward a bronze
plaque featuring an impression of a solitary passenger pigeon alighting on a
single oak branch. The inscription reads: "Dedicated to the last Wisconsin
passenger pigeon shot at Babcock, Sept. 1899. This species became extinct
through the avarice and thoughtlessness of man." I ran my fingers across
these raised words, touched the stone that surrounds them, sat upon the
benches that flank the plaque, looked out over the Mississippi River valley,
and felt the absence of the very birds to which the monument invites visitors
to attend. The monument awakens visitors to what is not present—to one of
the "flight ways," to use van Dooren's (2014, 27) evocative term—that no
longer inhabits or animates the landscape within which they now find themselves. The very presence and persistence of these bits of stone and bronze
hold open a space for vigilance, a space in which we are summoned to witness the overwhelming loss to which the monument attests.

Those who erected the monument hoped it would endure for decades and centuries to come and, thus, serve as a reminder of what has been squandered and a warning against hubris and greed. Leopold was among the crowd of bird lovers assembled under the oak trees in May 1947 to witness the dedication. Prior to the event, Leopold prepared an essay to mark the occasion. Attendees of the ceremony received a pamphlet titled *Silent Wings: A Memorial to the Passenger Pigeon* (W. E. Scott 1947), within which "On a Monument to the Pigeon" was first printed (Leopold 1947). A slightly revised version was included in Leopold's classic book, *A Sand County Almanac and Sketches Here and There*. As he put it there,

> This monument, perched like a duckhawk on this cliff, will scan this wide valley, watching through the days and years. For many a March it will watch the geese go by, telling the river about clearer, colder, lonelier waters on the tundra. For many an April it will see the redbuds come and go, and for many a May the flush of oak-blooms on a thousand hills. Questing wood ducks will search these basswoods for hollow limbs; golden prothonotaries will shake golden pollen from the river willows. Egrets will pose on these sloughs in August; plovers will whistle from September skies. Hickory nuts will plop into October leaves, and hail will rattle in November woods. But no pigeons will pass, for there are no pigeons, save only this flightless one, graven in bronze on this rock. Tourists will read this inscription, but their thoughts will not take wing. (1949b, 110–11)

In this brief passage, Leopold condenses long periods of times into 148 words: "days and years" are here represented by phenological events—seasonal rhythms that recur each year (see Barnett 2019a). March after March, geese will fly by. November after November, hail will fall from the sky. The monument, Leopold notes, will persist throughout the "days and years" to come; it will preside over, and watch over, "this wide valley." The monument, in other words, will persist. It is itself vigilant. In remaining on Sentinel Ridge, the monument marks time's passage by pointing to a past that most of us cannot remember and gesturing toward a future for which we are all, collectively, responsible.

Persistence is one of vigilant mourning's modes, one of the ways in which we enact and share our resistant, unresolved grief for what has been lost. Against the command to "move on" in the wake of a loss, and against the demand to detach from that which has disappeared, persistence performs a refusal to abandon the ties that bind us to the lost other. Etymologically, the English verb *to persist* derives from the Latin *persistere*, meaning "to continue steadfastly." In ordinary language, to persist is to "continue firmly or obstinately in a state, opinion, purpose, or course of action, [especially] despite opposition, setback, or failure." Persistence embodies an unwavering commitment or resolve. But persistence, of course, is not only a characteristic of persons. A material thing—say, a monument—may also persist, which is to say "remain or continue in existence." As a material manifestation of our grief for *Ectopistes migratorius*, the Monument to the Passenger Pigeon steadfastly remains in place. Its physical endurance corresponds to and animates the persistence of our shared grief for the passenger pigeon. Matter and memory merge. Despite the passage of time and the corrosive force of the elements, the memorial holds its ground. It continues; it carries on. And in doing so, the Monument also holds open—or, better yet, generates—a scene within which visitors might be moved to perceive the loss of that to which it was designed to draw our attention. Precisely because modern visitors have never encountered passenger pigeons, and thus have no memories of the species, the Monument's enduring existence makes possible the persistence of a collective yet discontinuous mourning, an expression of grief born not of individual experiences but, rather, of material reminders of what once was.

Standing atop Sentinel Ridge alongside the Monument to the Passenger Pigeon, a sense of vigilance comes naturally. Like the memorial itself, visitors stand on the precipice of a steep bluff scanning the wide-open Mississippi River valley. The perspective one gains from this position is itself wide and encompassing. Visitors look out over the edge toward the horizon, over the forests and valleys below. Wakefulness and watchfulness come easy here. The physical presence of the monument makes the absence of *Ectopistes migratorius* all the more conspicuous. That is to say, the persistence of the memorial transforms how I understand and interpret the otherwise abundant, lively scene that unfolds before me when I survey the verdant valley below. The monument unconceals a context within which we can make sense of the many beings and ways of being that continue to populate this place. Prolific though life may appear here, that is, the memorial reveals the prior diminishment which has imperceptibly given shape to this scene. It contests our sense of the inevitability or naturalness of the scene within which we find ourselves embedded: it demands that we question the very taken-for-grantedness of the ecosystems we cohabit. The Monument asks us to acknowledge that this once was—and could have, under other conditions, remained—a place where passenger pigeons flocked to eat, to roost, to breed. And so, by extension, it also invites visitors to recognize that those beings and ways of being we witness at the edge of Sentinel Ridge are themselves vulnerable to destruction and loss.

Persistence invites the wakefulness and watchfulness crucial to vigilant mourning in yet another way. The material endurance of the Monument sets the stage for occasional gatherings, gatherings which mark the passage of time and enable newcomers to feel grief for a species long since eradicated from earth. Precisely because it persists in place, the monument becomes the scene for such assemblies. In 2014, to mark the one-hundredth anniversary of the extinction of the passenger pigeon, dozens of people gathered at Sentinel Ridge to remember the birds and rededicate the monument. Stanley Temple, an ecologist at the University of Wisconsin who both coordinated and spoke at the ceremony, remarked that

> today, a century after the bird's extinction, the tragic story of the passenger pigeon needs to be retold—not only because most people have forgotten it, but also because it provides important lessons for the present and the future as we confront and unprecedented mass extinction of species as a result of our actions. [. . .] The Passenger Pigeon Monument stands as a permanent reminder of what we have lost. (2014)

The rededication ceremony was one part of a wider set of international goings-on in 2014 created to "retell" the story of the passenger pigeon. Because the memorial is a "permanent reminder" of the loss of *Ectopistes migratorius*, it stands to reason that people will gather on that ridge in the year 3014 to again acknowledge the ecological costs of human actions and to publicly mourn the death of billions of birds. Perhaps we will assemble there in 2047 to mark the hundredth anniversary of the memorial itself. As long as Sentinel Ridge is open to the public, some people will make pilgrimages to the Monument, as my partner and I did in 2019. Still others will stumble upon it while hiking. So long as the memorial endures, it will host gatherings, orchestrated and serendipitous alike, of people who, because of its presence, will be able to feel the absence of the passenger pigeon in the hills and valleys of Wisconsin. The Monument's persistence underwrites our collective and continued capacity to mourn not only for *Ectopistes migratorius* but also to anticipate ecological and earthly losses that are as yet still on the horizon.

REPETITION: REMEMBRANCE DAY FOR LOST SPECIES

In thinking with the persistence of the Monument to the Passenger Pigeon, we have begun to unearth another of vigilant mourning's modes: *repetition*. Whereas the memorial creates both a place and an occasion for routine gatherings, vigilant mourning is also sustained by more ephemeral yet perennial performances of grief. Consider the RDLS, an international constellation of events held annually on November 30 since 2011. The Remembrance Day is, according to its organizers, "a chance each year to explore the stories of extinct and critically endangered species, cultures, lifeways, and ecological communities" ("Remembrance Day for Lost Species" n.d.). In practice, the RDLS is decentralized, fragmented, open to interpretation: organizers across the globe stage and orchestrate various events and happenings in their own regions, often connected by a central theme. "Original Names" was the theme in 2019; participants were invited to "celebrate the ways that humans have named, loved, and lived with their human and non-human kin" ("2019: Original Names" 2019). Local organizers were called upon to explore and share local stories about extinct and endangered species, to create artworks, hold ceremonies, investigate indigenous ways of knowing, and to engage in restorative acts, such as picking up refuse on the beach, planting trees, and gardening. In 2019 alone, several dozen events were held in Australia (where RDLS began), many European countries, and throughout the United States. Though the details of these gatherings shift from year to year, the pattern repeats, thereby occasioning recurrent, even "interminable" (Derrida 2001, 158) mourning.

Structurally, RDLS embodies resistance to the Freudian idea of "moving on" in the wake of a loss by demonstrating that, although grief is not necessarily continuous or even all-encompassing, it does recur. Though the intensity of one's sorrow may wax and wane, grief is ultimately unresolvable. The pain associated with loss comes and goes; the despair we feel in the face of future losses ebbs and flows. But neither the pain nor the despair goes away entirely. In his *Mourning Diary*, Barthes writes, "What I find utterly terrifying is mourning's *discontinuous* character" (2010, 67). Grief often surfaces unexpectedly—a sound, word, image, smell, taste, or some other totally ineffable quality can reinvigorate, out of the blue, and beyond our control, the sorrow and the suffering that we had, for a while, evaded. We are assailed by grief. Because it is perennial, the RDLS suggests that the work of mourning is unending, that we never mourn "once and for all." We never rid ourselves, thankfully, of those we have loved and lost. Each year, as fall gives way to winter, RDLS events take shape in dozens of cities and rural sites across the globe, thus reopening or agitating extant wounds and bringing us to mourn once again. And so, in some sense, the regularity and repetition of these events over the years mimics the unpredictable upsurges of grief and models an ethical relation to both the dead and to those who find themselves under threat of erasure. While RDLS is not itself unpredictable, its repetition creates the structural conditions under which our mourning for what exceeds the human might arise anew.

In particular, repetition merges with ritualization in the activities of the RDLS. Year to year, participants mourn different species and ecosystems. In 2014, for instance, many of the events focused on the loss of the passenger pigeon since it was the one-hundredth anniversary of its extinction. While these specifics matter, perhaps the repetition of the symbolic act of mourning itself matters most. By transforming ecological mourning into a cultural ritual, the RDLS establishes a *history* of mourning. This history lends legitimacy to future acts: we have mourned before, and we shall mourn again. By creating a legacy of mourning, the RDLS works to "enfranchise" ecological grief and, thus, to demonstrate that it is acceptable to mourn for what exceeds the human. Legitimizing the pain and sorrow associated with past environmental catastrophes shifts our orientation to future losses, too. Indeed, because the RDLS ritualizes ecological grief, it produces an anticipatory structure for mourning the more-than-human. As November 30th approaches every year, so too does RDLS and the works of mourning it occasions. Just as we can anticipate the coming of Earth Day, the arrival of Hanukkah, or any other sacred or secular ritual, so too can we await the coming of RDLS. Because it takes the form of a ritual, we find ourselves poised between the past and future of ecological mourning—aware that the ecological grief we are feeling now is by no means novel, and secure in knowing that an opportunity to publicly express that grief will once again emerge.

We should not overlook the significance of rituals for coping with loss. Generally speaking, all cultures possess diverse yet well-established rituals for mourning the loss of human lives. Of course, wakes, eulogies, funerals, and graveside ceremonies are common within the dominant U.S. culture. When someone dies, these and other rituals often follow. And yet, this dominant culture does not possess a sophisticated or well-established set of rituals or expectations for mourning what exceeds the human. It is for this reason that some scholars describe ecological grief as "disenfranchised" since it "isn't publicly or openly acknowledged" (Cunsolo and Ellis 2018, 275). Mortimer-Sandilands argues that "there is something of an emotional void [. . .] when it comes to the mass destruction of the natural world" (2010, 338). This "emotional void" emerged, Mortimer-Sandilands argues, in part because there are so few opportunities to collectively confront and grieve the ecological losses we often hear about: "There are few if any public rituals of environmental mourning (which are different from public announcements of environmental catastrophe, of which there are plenty), little keening and wailing for extinct species or decimated places (which are different from lists or maps of them, of which there are also plenty)" (338). Without a ritual, we may find ourselves at a loss for mourning what exceeds the human. That is, even though we might experience a sense of bereavement when we endure or learn about an ecological loss, without identifiable rituals we may not know what to "do" with our grief. Rituals, precisely because they are repeated over time, provide a framework within and through which we can express and share grief, as well as bond over our shared vulnerability to ecological loss. Each year, by orchestrating an array of mourning rituals, the RDLS adds to our collective capacity for grappling with ecological catastrophe.

A wide range of mourning rituals are practiced each year on the RDLS. As I noted earlier, in 2014, many participants publicly mourned the loss of the passenger pigeon, even in places where *Ectopistes migratorius* never dwelt. Take, for instance, Emily Laurens's "sand art installation" at Llangrannog beach in Wales. Laurens's artistic "work explores themes of loss, transformation, memory, and letting go" in relation to "the current ecological crisis" (Laurens n.d.). In a blog post on her website, Laurens reflects on the creation of the work: "November the 22nd. The tides are right. And that matters when it comes to sand drawing. Starting at or just before low tide gives you time to complete your drawing and then watch as it disappears. Watch and wait for the tide to take away what has been created" (2014). Working with the tides, according to tidal logics, Laurens set about inscribing ephemerality itself: the end of the work, anticipated at the beginning of the work, was disappearance. With rakes and other implements, Laurens and friends traced passenger pigeon silhouettes into the sand. At ground level, the drawings dwarf the human bodies that made them. From above, the silhouettes in relief resembled the shadows of birds flying overhead, a temporary reminder of the vast flocks of wild pigeons which once traversed the skies above North America.

Unlike the Passenger Pigeon Monument in Wisconsin, Laurens's sand drawings are meant *not* to endure but to deteriorate—not to last, but to wither away with the tide. Etched into stony, mobile sediment, depressed into the shifting earth, each of the avian icons awaits its own undoing, its own demise. The work itself is anticipatory. It awaits its withdrawal, dramatizing the disappearance of the species it seeks to commemorate. As Laurens put it, "In the blond brown sands I draw a small flock of pigeons, like shadows passing overhead. And then I watch them disappear" (2014). What is a work of commemoration, a work of mourning, that disappears? Commemoration means a call to remember, an awakening to what has passed, an observance of what has been lost. The word also suggests preservation and safeguarding, but we must ask whether to preserve or to safeguard means only to let endure. Grappling with disappearance can be a way of safeguarding against future losses; restaging past losses so that we can witness them anew invites us to reflect on the time of extinction. And thinking about the time of loss may perhaps enable us to imagine, and to seize upon, opportunities for intervention. Laurens's sand drawings invite us to remember not just the extinct but the process of extinction, to not only *not* forget the species but to bring the extinction, the collective loss, to light as well, to let disappearance be seen. "We need," Laurens contends, "to find new ways to express [our] love and [of] commemorating the passing of places, ecosystems, and species" (2014).

And so it is with the tides, which rush in and retreat, scouring the impressions made in the sand by Laurens and others. The tides wash away what has already passed away, and in doing so they bring the withering away to light. Yet, there is something about the tidal logic that does not jive with the extinction of the passenger pigeon. *Ectopistes migratorius*, after all, did not succumb to the earth's recurrent processes. It was not a natural cycle that wiped these birds from the face of the earth: it was humans who systematically ruined their habitat and who shot them from the skies. It was humans who reduced them from billions to zero in only a few generations. So, even as the tidal cycle poignantly lets disappearance be seen, it perhaps also masks the more nefarious forces at work in making another way of life impossible. The inevitability of the tides, analogous perhaps to the certainty of death, is not quite analogous to *anthropogenic* extinction. The tides come no matter, but to banish another species from the earth is a decision enacted in everyday practices. And, like all decisions, it might have been otherwise.

My aim in this chapter, though, is neither to praise nor to critique specific instances of ecological mourning. And besides, we should tread cautiously when writing about grief. I am not interested in prescribing some modes of mourning and admonishing others. What matters most is that we understand how different modes of mourning capacitate us for the difficult yet necessary work of earthly coexistence. Repetition, like endurance, is crucial to what I have called "vigilant mourning." Recall that to be vigilant means to remain awake and to become alert. Through the RDLS, participants perennially attend to those losses that have already occurred. But they are also attuned to those species, landscapes, ecosystems, and relationships that now find themselves under threat of erasure. As they hold wakes for the dead, they raise awareness about what remains. Each November, the RDLS mingles grief with protection. This ritualization of mourning represents a refusal to abandon neither what has been lost nor our extant attachments to what remains. Returning again and again to dwell on the loss of the more-than-human, the RDLS compels us not only to remember what has come and gone but also to hang on to those beings and ways of being with whom and with which we continue to cohabit the earth.

CONCLUSION

We live in a time characterized by enormous ecological devastation and profound planetary transformation. Amid the Anthropocene, the death, destruction, and disappearance of the more-than-human world have become undeniable—though not inevitable—dimensions of earthly coexistence. Lamentably, we confront losses of many kinds on many scales: mass extinction, habitat degradation, ecosystem collapse, and earth systems disruption. The toll is tremendous. To dwell in the Anthropocene is to live with an awareness of these losses. But it is also to be haunted by humanity's—and, thus, one's own—complicity in practices both spectacular and mundane that are responsible for the accumulation of ecological and earthly losses.

Grief and mourning are appropriate, legitimate responses to these losses. They are, I would wager, necessary if we wish to dwell more peacefully, and less violently, upon the earth. And yet, as I have argued elsewhere, we should not take ecological grief for granted (Barnett 2019b; 2020). That we *should* mourn is clear enough. That we *will* mourn is more tenuous a declaration. It is certainly true that, most of the time, most of us pass our days, and perhaps our lives, without genuinely acknowledging, much less tarrying with, either the specificity or the immensity of losing what exceeds the human. Besides a few exceptional examples, few of us can even name species of flora and fauna that have been extirpated in decades and centuries past. As a whole, we know even less about those animals and plants who find themselves under threat of erasure today.

And so, we need to treat ecological grief less as a natural, inevitable response and more as an achievement. If and when we register more-than-human losses *as* meaningful losses, if and when we publicly express our grief, we should not regard these acts as givens. Such acts of mourning are, rather, remarkable accomplishments. What, though, makes our ecological grief possible? Aldo Leopold suggested that knowledge and intimacy are crucial antecedents for mourning the more-than-human (e.g., see Leopold 1949a, 44–50). I suspect Leopold is right, but I also believe that several rhetorical conditions often set our mourning into motion—names, archives, and images, to name just a few. Being able to name another species, for example, is vital to recognizing not only its presence but also its absence. Thus, although naming often enacts a certain violence, it is nevertheless one of the preconditions for registering—and, by extension, for mourning—the disappearance of another species, habitat, ecosystem, or geological epoch (Barnett 2019b). Names enable us to identify, in several senses, precisely what and who are at stake. Similarly, some images also capacitate us for the work of ecological mourning (Barnett 2020). Consider, for instance, time-lapse and satellite photography of melting glaciers, which enable us to see and to imagine the intensity and immensity of sea ice loss. Much more could be said about these and other rhetorical conditions. My point here is simply that ecological mourning is underwritten not only by personal connections with what has been or might be lost; it is made possible, too, by our encounters with particular rhetorical conditions.

In the preceding pages, I have begun to describe some rhetorical conditions that do more than set our ecological grief into motion. Indeed, my aim here has been to consider what capacitates us for sustained mourning—mourning that is characterized by a certain vigilance, a refusal to relinquish the ties that bind us to the beings and ways of being with whom we coexist. It is important that we recognize and mourn ecological losses, but it is crucial that we conceive of that work outside the bounds of Freud's early formulations in "Mourning and Melancholia." Our ambition, individually and culturally, should not be to "move on" in the wake of so much loss. Arguably, doing just that—*refusing* to mourn the more-than-human—has delivered us to our current planetary crisis. Generations of humans have witnessed, and participated in, the diminishment of the natural world. That we still do so suggests that many, perhaps most, of us remain all too ready to quickly and efficiently abandon the beings and ways of being scattered in our species' violent wake. Owning up to those losses, and our complicity, requires something of us that can be difficult to muster. In *Mourning Nature,* Cunsolo and Landman (2017, 5) speculate on why humans so often resist grappling with ecological grief: "Perhaps it is because grief work is deeply painful and, at times, debilitating?" It is for this reason that I turned in the preceding pages to some instances when people turned toward, and not away from, their feelings of grief.

The examples I discussed in this chapter offer models of what sustained, vigilant mourning might look like in practice. In the memorial's material endurance, we discover a physical and persistent reminder of what has been lost, as well as a gathering place where, for as long as the monument remains, people can be moved to apprehend the absence of the passenger pigeon. The monument's presence cannot, of course, guarantee that visitors will mourn, but it does contribute to our collective capacity to grieve one of the "flight ways" humans have banished from the earth. And in the ritualized repetition of the RDLS, we discover an array of practices which further add to our shared ability to tarry with our ecological grief. The RDLS transforms ecological mourning into a perennial performance, one among many activities undertaken each autumn to recognize and respect the ties that bind the living to the dead—and, importantly, to the living. When we publicly, collectively mourn what exceeds the human, we normalize and legitimize those feelings of pain and sorrow that follow from ecological losses. The more we grieve for what has already been lost, the better prepared we will be to notice, and to mourn, those losses which are yet to come. Poised between the past and the future, our task is to become vigilant, to become awake and alert to the joys and sorrows of earthly coexistence.

BIBLIOGRAPHY

"2019: Original Names." 2019. Remembrance Day for Lost Species. 2019. https://www.lostspeciesday.org/?page_id=14.

Audubon, John James. 1831. *Ornithological Biography, or An Account of the Habits of the Birds of the United States of America.* Philadelphia, PA: Judah Dobson.

Barnett, Joshua Trey. 2019a. "Irrational Hope, Phenological Writing, and the Work of Earthly Coexistence." *Communication and Critical/Cultural Studies* 16 (4): 382–91.

Barnett, Joshua Trey. 2019b. "Naming, Mourning, and the Work of Earthly Coexistence." *Environmental Communication* 13 (3): 287–99.

Barnett, Joshua Trey. 2020. "Grievable Water: Mourning the Animas River." In *Water, Rhetoric, and Social Justice: A Critical Confluence*, edited by Casey Schmitt, Christopher S. Thomas, and Theresa Castor, 273–91. Lanham, MD: Lexington Books.

Barthes, Roland. 2010. *Mourning Diary*. Translated by Richard Howard. New York: Hill and Wang.

Burton-Christie, Douglas. 2011. "The Gift of Tears: Mourning and the Work of Ecological Restoration." *Worldviews* 15 (1): 29–46.

Butler, Judith. 1997. *The Psychic Life of Power: Theories in Subjection*. Stanford, CA: Stanford University Press.

Butler, Judith. 2002. *Antigone's Claim: Kinship between Life and Death*. New York: Columbia University Press.

Butler, Judith. 2004. *Precarious Life: The Powers of Mourning and Violence*. London: Verso.

Butler, Judith. 2010. *Frames of War: When Is Life Grievable?* London: Verso.

Carrington, Damian. 2020. "Polar Ice Caps Melting Six Times Faster than in 1990s." *The Guardian*, March 11, 2020. https://www.theguardian.com/environment/2020/mar/11/polar-ice-caps-melting-six-times-faster-than-in-1990s.

Clewell, Tammy. 2004. "Mourning Beyond Melancholia: Freud's Psychoanalysis of Loss." *Journal of the American Psychoanalytic Association* 52 (1): 43–67.

Crimp, Douglas. 1989. "Mourning and Militancy." *October* 51: 3–18.

Cunsolo, Ashlee, and Neville R. Ellis. 2018. "Ecological Grief as a Mental Health Response to Climate Change-Related Loss." *Nature Climate Change* 8: 275–81.

Cunsolo, Ashlee, and Karen Landman. 2017. "Introduction: To Mourn beyond the Human." In *Mourning Nature: Hope at the Heart of Ecological Loss and Grief*, edited by Ashlee Cunsolo and Karen Landman, 3–26. Montreal: McGill-Queen's University Press.

Derrida, Jacques. 2001. "By Force of Mourning." In *The Work of Mourning*, edited by Pascale-Anne Brault and Michael Naas, 142–64. Chicago: University of Chicago Press.

Derrida, Jacques, and Elisabeth Roudinesco. 2004. *For What Tomorrow . . . A Dialogue*. Translated by Jeff Fort. Stanford, CA: Stanford University Press.

Dooren, Thom van. 2014. *Flight Ways: Life and Loss at the Edge of Extinction*. New York, NY: Columbia University Press.

Freud, Sigmund. 1953. "Mourning and Melancholia." In *Collected Papers*, edited by Joan Riviere, IV:152–70. London: Hogarth Press.

Freud, Sigmund. 1960. *The Ego and the Id*. Edited by James Strachey. Translated by Joan Riviere. Standard Edition. New York, NY: W.W. Norton & Company.

Greenberg, Joel. 2014. *A Feathered River Across the Sky: The Passenger Pigeon's Flight to Extinction*. New York: Bloomsbury.

Haraway, Donna. 2016. *Staying with the Trouble: Making Kin in the Chthulucene*. Durham, NC: Duke University Press.

Laurens, Emily. n.d. "About." *Emilylaurens* (blog). n.d. https://emilylaurens.wordpress.com/about/.

Laurens, Emily. 2014. "Remembrance Day for Lost Species." *Emilylaurens* (blog). November 28, 2014. https://emilylaurens.wordpress.com/2014/11/28/remembrance-day-for-lost-species/.

Leopold, Aldo. 1947. "On a Monument to the Pigeon." In *Silent Wings: A Memorial to the Passenger Pigeon*, edited by Walter Edwin Scott, 3–5. Madison, WI: Wisconsin Society for Ornithology.

Leopold, Aldo. 1949a. *A Sand County Almanac and Sketches Here and There.* New York, NY: Oxford University Press.

Leopold, Aldo. 1949b. "On a Monument to the Pigeon." In *A Sand County Almanac and Sketches Here and There*, 108–12. London: Oxford University Press.

Leopold, Aldo. 1970. "The Round River." In *A Sand County Almanac with Essays on Conservation from Round River*, 188–202. New York, NY: Ballantine Books.

Mortimer-Sandilands, Catriona. 2010. "Melancholy Natures, Queer Ecologies." In *Queer Ecologies: Sex, Nature, Politics, Desire*, edited by Catriona Mortimer-Sandilands and Bruce Erickson. Bloomington, IN: Indiana University Press.

Morton, Timothy. 2010. *The Ecological Thought.* Cambridge, MA: Harvard University Press.

O'Brien, Liz. 2016. "Passenger Pigeon Lands a Permanent Perch." Unbound: Smithsonian Libraries. October 10, 2016. https://blog.library.si.edu/blog/2016/10/10/passenger-pigeon-lands-permanent-perch/#.XpyVF6tKjdc.

"Passenger Pigeon Memorial." n.d. Cincinnati Zoo & Botanical Garden. Accessed April 19, 2020. http://cincinnatizoo.org/plan-your-visit/exhibits/passenger-pigeon-memorial/.

"Remembrance Day for Lost Species." n.d. Remembrance Day for Lost Species. Accessed April 22, 2020. https://www.lostspeciesday.org/.

Scott, Gertrude M. 1947. "Society Meets in May at Madison." *The Passenger Pigeon* 9 (2): 54–62.

Scott, Walter Edwin, ed. 1947. *Silent Wings: A Memorial to the Passenger Pigeon.* Madison, WI: Wisconsin Society for Ornithology.

Spargo, R. Clifton. 2004. *The Ethics of Mourning: Grief and Responsibility in Elegiac Literature.* Baltimore, MD: Johns Hopkins University Press.

Temple, Stanley. 2014. "A Bird We Have Lost and a Doubt We Have Gained." Wisconsin Academy of Sciences, Arts & Letters. 2014. https://www.wisconsinacademy.org/magazine/bird-we-have-lost-and-doubt-we-have-gained.

"The AIDS Memorial Quilt." 2020. The NAMES Project Foundation. 2020. https://www.aidsquilt.org/about/the-aids-memorial-quilt.

"The Passenger Pigeon." n.d. Smithsonian. n.d. https://www.si.edu/spotlight/passenger-pigeon.

Williams, Terry Tempest. 2019. *Erosion: Essays of Undoing.* New York: Sarah Crichton Books.

Chapter 3

Presence and Absence in the Watershed

Storytelling for the Symbiocene

Emily Plec

> Our most dependable insurance against calamity resides in the fellow feeling and generosity of those who live near us . . . Our truest security lies where it always has, in community solidarity and neighborliness. . . . Telling the tale of the cranes as they wing their way north over our upturned faces, enacting in rituals the wondrous return of each species from the brink of extinction—while marking in story, and ceremony, the demise of those species we let slip from the real, so that we'll remember, collectively, the awesome cost of our hubris (Abram 2010, 290).

This chapter is about choices—the ones we have, the ones we make, and those choices that appear to be dictated by forces beyond our control. Like any intimate human relationship, our relationships with the more-than-human world are complex, multifaceted and, ideally, rooted in compassion and care. I began to choose the more-than-human world as a focus of study because I had learned so much about other humans from studying communication. Theorizing about what I term "internatural communication" (Plec 2013) is widespread and crosses many disciplines, as are popular cultural texts about animals, trees, and bees that appear on best seller lists or inspire films.[1] Critical theorists from Gilles Deleuze and Jacques Derrida to Donna Haraway and others have laid rich ground from which these explorations grow.

In *Becoming Animal*, David Abram describes what is needed for restoration of an ecological balance, for connection with our animal selves. Advocating for the regeneration of oral culture, including the story telling and ritual enactments described in the epigraph, Abram highlights the role that festivals and ceremonies play in marking presence and absence, as well as shaping memory: "These are ancient and elemental ways to awaken our own animal senses, binding the imagination of our bodies back into the wider life of the animate earth" (Abram 2010, 290). Abram's writings probe and permeate the philosophical membrane separating humans from those with whom we share an earthly coexistence. I long to translate his eloquent and spiritually esoteric insights into pragmatic terms that can help me make sense of the Anthropocene in terms of the everyday, lived experiences of three groups of people: community members (in this case, mostly rural landowners), conservation biologists, and environmental advocates. I'm interested in what they can show us about living in the Anthropocene in a way that enables the experience of another era, one defined, for humans, by intimate earth relational values—care, compassion, responsibility, and love.

Why these three sometimes overlapping groups? For almost three decades I have been either directly or peripherally engaged in work with watershed councils, which tend to be composed of local landowners, environmentalists, and conservation experts. As a teenager, I learned about the concept of watersheds from my high school biology teacher, who also prompted me to get involved with our local watershed council where I conducted youth outreach programs with local elementary schools to teach kids (and hopefully their caregivers) about hazardous products and practices and the importance of groundwater health and protection. The idea and work of the council immediately made sense to me. Watersheds provide clear hydrological and geological boundaries that can create localized identities for communities on the basis of their shared bio-region.

As watershed council members (and students in Mary Fowler's Biology class) learn early on, a watershed is an area of land (a drainage basin) that includes all of the rain, snowmelt, rivers, and streams that feed a common body of water. Watersheds are intimately connected to all of their inhabitants, who depend upon safe and available water supplies for survival, as well as spiritual sustenance. Fr. Terry Ehrman describes "watershed theology" as an extension of St. Francis of Assisi's emphasis upon the interconnectedness of all things: "Humans belong to and live and work within larger ecological systems, and watersheds are natural units of those systems. Thinking with watersheds connects humans to the rest of the biological community of species that also live there and to the abiotic aspects—air, water, and rock" (Ehrman 2019).

It is my contention that "thinking with watersheds" can produce the kinds of insights and intimate relationships that can bring an end to the agony caused by careless anthropocentric contamination in the forms of dams, pollution, habitat destruction, deforestation, and intensive agriculture (an agony that philosopher Glenn Albrecht (2005) calls "solastalgia"). As Cunsolo and Landman point out in *Mourning Nature*, "Given the immense challenges our planet currently faces, we need a mechanism for moving into new terrains of thought that may provide avenues for thinking with and through environmental challenges, for encouraging action, and for potentially cultivating new emotions in fruitful ways" (Cunsolo and Landman 2017, 6). Watersheds are an old mechanism that can move us into new terrains of thought, engaging us directly and concretely in action for the benefit of the environment.

Since the early 2000s, my primary habitat has been the Luckiamute River watershed, located in western Oregon's Willamette Valley. The main stem of the river is approximately eighty-two miles long with abundant streams and creeks throughout the basin, including the thirty-six-mile sub-watershed of Ash Creek. According to the Luckiamute Watershed Council (LWC), 87 percent of the land in the watershed is privately owned, with the main uses being forestry and agriculture. I joined the watershed council and served a couple of terms as a member, often helping to coordinate educational and community engagement projects involving university students, in addition to assisting with grant-writing and strategic planning activities. I found that my work on the council deepened my appreciation and awareness of my home place and its natural resources. I was inspired by their collective commitment to conservation.

The main thread woven through this essay is a theoretical one, stitched to what Amy Propen and others have termed "compassionate conservation" (2018, 6) or a slightly modified and perhaps more intimate version of it. Because watersheds are material and symbolic assemblages, they are constituted by inhabitants, events, and meanings that are beyond the control of any single species. Invasive species alter the ecology of a watershed but natural spaces are never pure; breezes, animals, and waterways carry new community members, contaminating and complicating all our relations. "We are contaminated by our encounters," writes Anna Lowenhaupt Tsing in *The Mushroom at the End of the World*; "they change who we are as we make way for others" (2015, 27). She then argues, "Contamination makes diversity. Contamination creates forests, transforming them in the process. Because of this, noticing as well as counting is required to know the landscape" (Tsing 2015, 29–30). This is watershed council work—noticing (opportunities, destruction, changes); counting (species, plantings); knowing the landscape and finding out what you can do to improve the counts, restore a balance, preserve a place; and engaging in what Mark Bekoff (2014) terms "rewilding."

What I am advocating is "compassionate contamination," premised on Tsing's understanding of contamination as collaboration: "Collaboration means working across difference, which leads to contamination" (Tsing 2015, 28). Human beings, particularly those embroiled in industrial and postindustrial capitalist economies, are constantly contaminating watersheds by leaching lead and other heavy metals, hydraulic fracturing of precious shale formations, ignorant disposal of household hazardous chemicals, to name just a few of our species' special means of destruction. But these are all (to varying degrees)

malicious, violent, or harmful examples of contamination that construct a subject position for the natural world as either unwilling collaborator or victim.

Thinking with watersheds enables us to consider "compassionate contamination," a kind of intimate, relational collaboration manifest in relationships
between people and the landscapes they love. Compassion is understood and
defined in a wide variety of ways and literally evokes the idea of suffering
with another. Associated with acts such as forgiveness and benevolence,
compassion also enables us to tolerate our own shortcomings as humans
implicated in harmful contamination as we seek to offer genuine care and
engage the more-than-human world with kindness. This working and communicating across species lines, too, is contamination but, as Tsing highlights, it is contamination as collaboration.

Taken together, Tsing's orientation toward contamination, entangled with
Barnett's discussion of naming/mourning, philosopher Glenn Albrecht's
neologistic concepts of "solastalgia" (Albrecht 2005) and the "Symbiocene"
(Albrecht 2020), and Robert Cox's "locus of the irreparable" (Cox 1982),
point toward a transformative rhetorical and ecological inhabitation, one
that approaches what Albrecht calls "Sumbiotude" (2019). This quaternary
articulation enables us to think about "compassionate contamination" in intimate, relational terms—as intentional engagement in acts of loving care with
unique (named) and precarious (potentially mourned) others in particular
moments of assemblage.

THINKING WITH WATERSHEDS:
INSCRIBING THE SYMBIOCENE

Near Fanno Ridge in the Coast Range of Western Oregon, a woman closes
her eyes and imagines a drop of water and its journey should it "fall into the
tributaries of the Luckiamute River" rather than down the western slope of
the range right to the ocean (Oberst 2019a, 6):

> It must negotiate the creeks that feed the Little Luckiamute, and then, the rain-
> drop must navigate its way east into the larger Luckiamute River past Helmick
> Park and into the Willamette River past Independence, past Salem, north to
> Portland, where it turns west as it joins the Columbia River. Hundreds of miles
> and miles and miles later, finally, this ponderous drop is now part of billions of
> others as it splashes into the Pacific, where it joins the Siletz and thousands of
> other rivers. And one day, maybe millions of years from now, or maybe tomor-
> row, a drop will lift into the air again on a hot day, or on a stormy wave, or in a
> typhoon, and the cycle of water will begin again as another drop falls near Fanno
> Ridge, where I am standing. (Oberst 2019a, 6)

Her observations provide an analogy for the "difficult and cyclical work of a watershed council" (Oberst 2019a, 6) and, at the same time, illustrate the insignificance of the human species when placed in an epochal context. As Andrew McMurry puts it, "On the cosmic timeline, humankind constitutes considerably less than a blip. If a dog year is seven human years, a human year is 180,000,000 universe years" (2018, 1). As an era, the period referred to as the "Anthropocene" shrinks geologic time in a manner reflective of humans' greatest ecological harms. Epochally speaking, it covers the emergence of large-scale, organized human societies right through to our unknown future as a species. Barnett describes it as "the moment when natural and human history blurred into one another, when humankind began to express itself as a planetary force" (Barnett 2019, 295).

Returning to the story of the raindrop, the analogy falters "because, unlike the raindrop, we have choices, if we make our choices to improve the watershed, then the good work of our volunteers eventually cycles back to us in the form of healthier lands, better water, falling on our heads, running down our mountains, filling up our streams, returning to us" (Oberst 2019a, 6). Whether or not raindrops exercise some sort of aquatic agency, our attitudes toward land and water (and all who inhabit it) require a new vocabulary. The "Symbiocene" is "the next era in human and Earth history where reintegration of the Anthropos (humans) with the Sumbios (symbiotic life)" is complete (Albrecht 2020). "Sumbiotude," the state of being or way of life that will sustain humanity in the Symbiocene, "involves contemplation and completion of a lifespan with the loving companionship of humans and nonhumans" (Albrecht 2020). It is an intimate relationship grounded in compassionate contamination.

In the LWC's *Writing Our Watershed*, and other texts like it, paths into the Symbiocene are worn by words. These are stories of connection to the land, of the intimacy of presence and grief due to absence, of new life introduced and indigenous lives lost. In short, they are stories of compassionate contamination as collaboration. They create spaces of mourning for rivers straightened and forests clear cut. They offer resources for noticing, naming, and acknowledging entanglements. For, as Tsing points out, "Sometimes common entanglements emerge not from human plans but despite them. It is not even the undoing of plans, but rather the unaccounted for in their doing that offers possibilities for elusive moments of living in common" (Tsing 2015, 267). Watershed work, like the writers who relate to it in this collection of essays, exposes these elusive moments of living in common.

First, the noticing and naming: "At a fork in the road, we stop a minute and look up into the canopy closed tight over our heads with Douglas fir, maple, alder. We both call out the names of plants: He chants in Latin: oxalis, rubus, vaccinium, gaultheria, polystichum, prunus. I sing in common language:

Sweet grass, salmonberry, huckleberry, salal, sword fern, mountain cherry" (Oberst 2019b, 32). The passage reminds us that some acquire their naming practices from formal education while others from the common language of communities, and sometimes we know our neighbors by different monikers at different times. Reflecting on divergent naming practices, Barnett says, "We must ask . . . what kinds of relations, a particular name brings into view, into being. We must also remain open to the possibility that acts of naming might draw us into closer connections with the more-than-human world" (Barnett 2019, 289). If, indeed, naming is deeply related to grievability, then naming the other "is to honor their singularity, so also their mortality, their radical lose-ability" (292); in other words, their uniqueness and precarity.

As mentioned previously, this description of the forest illustrates two nomenclatures for our cohabitants, scientific and "common" names. Barnett points out, "Scientific names gather together what we call species and, in doing so, enable us to gather around and to take care of species" (Barnett 2019, 294). They "lessen the distance . . . between those who have been lost and those who survive" (294). But anthropomorphic "proper names" also perform important relational work. "The proper name prefigures death by calling attention to the singularity of just this being" (293), further emphasizing uniqueness as part of the appeal of connection, whether the celebration of presence or the solastalgic mourning of absence.

An ecologist and former project manager marks both presence and absence in the watershed through both noticing and naming—trees, fish, birds, rocks, flows, roads, plants, barriers, and even garbage:

> Dappled sun illuminates water striders, bigleaf and vine maples, alders, and a few Douglas fir trees. Caddis flies appear on fresh water boulders at the old town site of Black Rock, where Weyerhaeuser now reigns supreme. This is cutthroat trout water overflown by dippers and belted kingfishers. Skipping stones and spawning gravel are found where three river forks converge at a locked gate. I am fly fishing amidst trash.
>
> I think of what I see, hear, feel, taste, and smell at the creek today. Then I think of what those senses would have led me to experience 200 years ago at this same location. Large cutthroat now replaced by many small fish. Well-sorted gravel under mammoth conifer logs replaced by bedrock "cleaned" of all "debris," except for the beer cans and Pampers. Cathedral forest of 500-year-old western red cedar, hemlock and Doug fir are now replaced by small bigleaf maple and red alder. Native American and elk trails now are replaced by Polk County and Weyerhaeuser logging roads. Rippling, bubbling waters have been replaced by the sounds of log trucks and 747s from PDX. Once salal, rhododendron and giant ferns ruled, now Himalayan blackberries and Japanese knotweed dominate. (Cairns 2019, 22–23)

The juxtaposition of past and present, of nature's artful diversity against human culture's rapacious consumption (the sights and sounds of the watershed supplanted by beer cans, diapers, logging roads, trucks, and airplanes) and commitment to privatizing property (the locked gate), reveals a dominant dialectical tension in environmental discourse. The passage also frames the contrast in terms of relations of power-over rather than power-with: the new "trash" ecology is reigning, ruling, and dominating what was once grand, pristine, native, and peaceful.

In her writings about zoos, Tema Milstein discusses several dialectics, including "mastery-harmony" which contrasts the ideology of human control over nature with a perspective that "values holistic cooperation and positions so-called progress . . . as damaging ecological balance and any possibility of harmony" (Milstein 2013, 164). That nonnative, *invasive* species should come to dominate the landscape described above is a fact that can be held like a mirror to reflect the entanglement of inheritors of the settler colonial imagination grounded in that same destructive ideology of mastery. Mastery can also enable a pathology alluded to in the epigraph by David Abram and known as "hubris syndrome" (Owen 2008, cited in MacSuibhne 2009, 212). Hubris syndrome can be briefly described as a reckless belief in one's own rightness—whether that be the rightness of human rule over nature or the rightness of our choices when it comes to environmental conservation efforts.

The dialectic of mastery-harmony is doubly reinforced in the conclusion of the essay, where the ecologist-turned-author describes a trout as "a fellow creature" and ends with a confidence often found in the discourse of mastery, overwriting a fear grounded in the disharmony of human decision-makings:

> I worry that the natural disturbances, such as flood, fire and drought, that once determined the form and function of our ecosystems have been replaced by today's human-driven stressors, like road building, fire suppression, and pollution. The outcomes are far different. I'll cope with this feeling by continuing to apply a lifetime of knowledge to fixing the damage we have done. (Cairns 2019, 23)

The "worry" described here is symptomatic of solastalgia, the sickness or suffering that accompanies "a feeling of dislocation; of being undermined by forces that destroy the potential for solace to be derived from the present" (Albrecht 2005, 48). Linking the concept to Aldo Leopold's notion of "land health" and contemporary research on "place pathology," Albrecht distinguishes solastalgia from other disruptions of identity linked to a sense of "home" (2005, 45–47). Acknowledging "the damage we have done" (the "awesome cost of our hubris," in Abram's terms) becomes a means of acknowledging complicity and committing to caring for our ever-contaminated, ever-collaborating, and adapting environment.

Solastalgia can occur wherever place identity is challenged, but unlike nostalgia which would prompt a desire to return to a past state, it manifests in the will "to sustain those things that provide solace" (Albrecht 2005, 49). A favorite fishing hole, a beloved hiking trail, the meadow in which young deer always appear in springtime, a mountain spring, our backyard birds, or ancient petroglyphs; we seek to protect and sustain those whom we know intimately. And when they appear to be on the brink of destruction or extinction, forever altered beyond familiarity, we mourn them, often by name. Abram believes that, as humans, we close ourselves off from our creaturely sensations "lest we succumb to an overwhelming grief—a heartache born of our organism's instinctive empathy with the living land and its cascading losses. Lest we be bowled over and broken by our dismay at the relentless devastation of the biosphere" (Abram 2010, 7). This may be so, but our apathy is self-inflicting. The contamination that occurs when we suffer *with* the warming and changing natural world, when we tolerate the discomfort of our creaturely sensations to the point of *feeling deeply* the pain of that relentless devastation, is the metaphorical yeast needed to ferment corrective human action. It is no wonder that the ancient notion of ethos (or the character of the rhetor) is related to habitat (*ethea*).

Albrecht recognizes this potential and need. He points out, "New and powerful technologies have enabled transitions to occur to social and natural environments at a speed that makes adaptation difficult if not impossible . . . those who suffer from [solastalgia] might actively seek to create new things or engage in collective action that provides solace and communion in any given environment" (2005, 49). The work of watershed councils (and their project managers) is often to make decisions founded upon an understanding of contamination as collaboration. We know that we will not eliminate the knotweed or ever fully abate the invasive scotch broom and blackberries and we may long for control. But only as a mechanism for enforcing mutual collaboration, allowing the native plants to flourish, the indigenous earthworms to return, without eradication. As if anyone without a herd of hungry goats and a hundred years can eradicate Himalayan blackberries. Now that's hubris!

Albrecht goes on to point out that the "most poignant moments of solastalgia" occur when an environment with which we have an intimate relationship is transformed. "Watching land clearing (tree removal) or building demolition, for example, can be the cause of a profound distress that can be manifest as intense visceral pain and mental anguish" (49). In Oregon, from old growth ancestors to fast-growing cedars and firs no older than the majority of my university students, trees are cut and killed by the millions annually.[2]

Such agonies abound in watershed work. The anguish can be found in the announcement of unusually low fry counts in stream surveys of once abundant salmon rivers, in the toxic runoff from fertilized fields and pesticide-drenched orchards, in the dangerous algal blooms increasingly common in our ever-warming rivers and lakes, or the dwindling numbers of animals and plants unique to the region. This, too, is the work of naming and counting, of noticing alterations and adaptations. Consider, for example, local landowner and non-native Oregonian Ron Nestlerode's essay about the creek and forests where he lives and creates conditions of solace and communion by gardening and nurturing the land. He depends upon the water for all manners of sustenance. Nestlerode's essay opens with a poem that ends with a complex, unmarked question, hinting at their intimate relation: *Could my creek be Fuller* (2019, 11).

> I can see the ridges of the mountains that form this watershed. I have hiked through most of it many times. To the southeast I can see the scar on the mountainside where OSU did another "experimental" clear cut. . . . To the northwest is where Weyerhaeuser brought in two tree dragons and mowed the hillside in four days. They started the machines at 3:30 in the morning and quit after dark. But, I am still surrounded by plants. To the northeast, an absentee land owner has been logging his section of the watershed for longer than I have lived here. You have to hike through the forest to notice that it has been cut. He takes out a few truckloads of logs every year. (Nestlerode 2019, 12)

Here, the massive mowing operation of the multinational timber company is subtly contrasted with the small-scale logging that "you have to hike through" to notice. References to Oregon State University's and Weyerhauser's clear-cutting operations hint at a relationship of exploitation and abuse (the mountainside bears a "scar" and the trees were mowed as if the forest were no more than a lawn for the heavy machinery of humanity). Milstein's other two dialectics, "othering-connection" and "exploitation-idealism," can be seen clearly in this essay. Connection and idealism are points of emphasis for the Sumbiotude that Nestlerode has tried to cultivate, in contrast to the exploitative othering of the timber operations:

> After a quarter of a century as the steward of this reach of Fuller Creek, I am instantly "at one" with my environment; the smell of the clean air and water is invigorating. I feel the water, cool and wet, eddying around my bared feet. Listen to the sounds of the water running over the rocks, colliding with the bank, splashing against the fallen logs. It is continuous which allows it to be powerful. (Nestlerode 2019, 11)

This recognition of water's power aligns with an observation offered by Amy Propen in her discussion of visual rhetoric, conservation and posthumanism. Propen points out the need to let go "of human exceptionalism" and challenge anthropocentrism in order to "embrace the 'betweenness' that rewilds, and thus opens the door to further curiosity about nonhuman animal life" (2018, 144). Such an approach, she argues, "understands humans, nonhumans, and matter as entangled and co-constitutive of world-making" and is compatible with "compassionate conservation" (Propen 2018, 144).

> Compassionate conservation acknowledges the interconnectedness of humans, nonhuman animals, and places; it acknowledges the need to set aside human exceptionalism and consider with curiosity the lives of our nonhuman kin. More than just seeing from the perspective of another, compassionate conservation is curious about what our fellow species might be thinking—how our gazes might intersect, and how we might communicate with one another in ways that also surrender the need to control and master nature. (Propen 2018, 144)

Taking this curious stance, Howard Grund-Clampit recalls his childhood and an expedition to find sucker-fish in the wetland behind his house in a manner that is reminiscent of Propen's call for a different kind of gaze:

> We splashed and laughed from one pool to another, and never caught a single one. But then, we started noticing other things: dragonflies, snails, water striders, and best of all, great, slimy gobs of frogs' eggs. The day was nothing like we had hoped, but full of things we loved. We were alive, vibrantly alive, surrounded and held in the full experience of that muddy, weedy place. And we were happy. (Grund-Clampit 2019, 65)

Evoking the physiological and spiritual toll of solastalgia, a "suffocating desolation," Grund-Clampit contrasts these memories with life in an urban environment: "There have been times when I stood barefoot on the nearest patch of raw earth with my eyes closed, and as the world of asphalt and cement rumbled around me I returned to the dusty paths and green fields of childhood. For those few moments, the suffocating desolation of the city was far away; my heart sheltered in safe harbor" (Grund-Clampit 2019, 65).

Describing how he and his wife, Linda, came to live on her family's farm, Howard recalls her "deep-rooted memories of the place" as an intimate relationship. Spending every other Sunday at her grandparents' farm in the "western foothills of the Willamette Valley of Oregon," the fields and orchards became treasured places. "Immersed in the fragrance of apple blossoms, she drew maps to remember the identities and layout of the trees she loved" (65). Once again, "noticing as well as counting is required to know the landscape" (Tsing 2015, 30). The passage also alludes to a deeper sense of relationship Linda had with the trees, wanting to remember "their identities," which might be different than their names. Howard calls attention to the way in which their compassionate conservation orientation has contaminated the once agriculturally oriented yet animally bereft landscape, as they planted trees, introduced earthworms, and composted all kinds of plant material:

Into the fields came more insects; then mice, voles, shrews, gophers, and moles. These in turn brought in the hawks, the owls, the coyotes, and the bobcat. Into our young forest came the deer, sleeping away the days, and drawing in the cougar. Skunks, raccoons, porcupines, possums, and snakes have each claimed their places here.

My hope is that the world of weeds and wildness will not perish—and that someday another generation of our family will take their place on this farm.

Whoever they are, they will receive a shaggy, rich-soiled place full of beasts and birds, of trees and weeds; a place that will definitely need the strong hand of a gentle, loving gardener. (Grund-Clampit 2019, 68–69)

The Grund-Clampits' land and stories offer fertility and fecundity as alternatives to purity. Howard defines "fecund" as "a richness that has the ready ability to sprout life of all kinds as easily as you or I can draw a breath . . . a happy anarchy of green" and points out the importance of allowing the land "to do those messy, unkempt things that don't seem to fit into our modern world" (Grund-Clampit 2019, 67). Compassionate contamination in the form of intentional watershed work offers one such example of where people can fit into this fecund future.

Imagine: A group of young art students and their mentors gather creekside on the Grund-Clampit farm, having walked along a marshy deer trail through tall grass, saplings, and wildflowers. We're here to cut willow, which is growing up too fast and needs to be cut back to make way for other trees and shrubs who will help stabilize the stream. The long, slender willow branches will be woven together into large basket-like pods, *stream structures*, then given to a few local farmers and ranchers to mitigate against the impacts of runoff from their fields to watershed streams. Projects such as this one undertaken by nearby university students in conjunction with the LWC are enabled by the connections watershed council members forge with local organizations and institutions.

The watershed writers and their nonhuman neighbors are living in a contested and contaminated landscape—one already irreparably altered by development, prone to flooding, unique in its forest and wetland beauty, capable of sustaining threatened and endangered species, such as Fender's blue butterfly and Western pond turtles, but only if we take care to protect their precarious habitats. The discourse of council and community members suggests that the solastalgia caused by environmental devastation can be mitigated through compassionate contamination.

What's the balance: Mac Forest, a research forest that supports significant recreation, and does save some old growth patches; Starker Forest whose signs on entry promote management for timber, fish and wildlife, a recent sign; older signs only indicate timber management; or the other owners who raze the entire watershed, show no signs of replanting; riparian areas demolished; beaver removed, etc. It is all here. And even the few patches of BLM land, with current interest in restoring native vegetation, and preserving some old growth. (Larsen 2019, 28)

As many of the stories in the collection illustrate, restoration and conservation efforts are often initiated by a desire to salvage our places of solace, to maintain the loving connection that must characterize the Symbiocene if our sense of self, so intimately tied to common spaces and other species, is not to be lost to the precarity of time and change in the Anthropocene. For Albrecht, solastalgia stems from the alteration of one's intimate relations with their environment, therefore it is clear that the human choices that contribute to solastalgia cannot continue if we desire relief from our distress. Or perhaps, as Abram suggests, "Grief is but a gate, and our tears a kind of key opening a place of wonder that's been locked away" (2010, 309).

> The name "anthropocene" registers the loss of a way of being human that is no longer sustainable. . . . We will have to relearn how to make do with less, to listen to our more-than-human kin, to find meaning in something other than narratives of progress, to respect the land on which we dwell, to understand ourselves as part of a community that exceeds the human. We will have to relearn, finally, how to reconcile our excessive power with the humbling yet necessary work of earthly coexistence, of consciously choosing to exercise restraint in a world that celebrates debauchery. The name "anthropocene" is an invitation to begin this work. (Barnett 2019, 296)

As suggested previously, I believe that the epoch that Albrecht calls the "Symbiocene" is the manifestation of that work realized, and hints of it can be found in the writings of watershed council members who have found their identities intimately entangled with the more-than-human world. Threats to that world, threats to the watershed's health, must therefore be headed off, countered, mitigated, prevented as one would seek to prevent harm from coming to any loved one. If we should fail, we risk losing something wondrous, unique, special, and irreplaceable.

The locus of the irreparable is theorized by Robert Cox in his germinal essay wherein he develops the concept in the context of environmental rhetoric. Irreparability presumes that something is unique, its status is precarious or threatened and therefore taking action is timely (Cox 1995). These themes of uniqueness, precariousness, and timeliness recur in the discourse of every environmental organization with which I've worked, and the LWC is no exception. In the case of watershed council rhetoric, and the essays in the LWC's collection specifically, the watershed is understood as holding a unique history and significance for each individual who inhabits it. There is also a common recognition of the precariousness of the watershed's future health and ecological balance (due to both natural and anthropogenic forces), and a suggestion that concerted effort is needed to maintain and strengthen the watershed (as well as the ability of inhabitants to survive the changes a watershed inevitably undergoes). "As contamination changes world-making projects, mutual worlds—and new directions—may emerge. Everyone carries a history of contamination; purity is not an option. One value of keeping precarity in mind is that it makes us remember that changing with circumstances is the stuff of survival" (Tsing 2015, 27).

The contributors to *Writing Our Watershed* do not call for immediate action in the manner of some of the "Cassandra Complex" environmental advocates critiqued by McMurry (2015) and Check (1999) as potentially ineffective. For, as Cox points out, "Loss, separation, and death, then, transform our experience of time. . . . [T]ime becomes threatening; the future becomes a source of anxiety and dread" (Cox 1995, 233). Could this very fear, and the need for certainty in the face of irreversible choices and irreparable conditions, reinvigorate the hubris syndrome so characteristic of the ideology of mastery?

In the conclusion to his 1995 essay, Cox posits that only a culture "confident of its ability to address the future" would likely find rhetorical uses for the locus of the irreparable. "Indeed," he writes, "in a culture for which the future is closed, the foretelling of loss does not function in a *rhetorical* sense at all. It is not an impetus for action, but only the fatalistic announcement of forces over which it has no control" (Cox 1995, 239). Kolodziejski, analyzing Maya Lin's *What is Missing?* online memorial exhibit, argues that a mastery perspective that frames "nature as under human care, in order to cultivate an ethic of responsibility," a perspective that uses the tension inherent in the "mastery-harmony, othering-connection, and exploitation-idealism dialectics," can also serve to "disrupt the human gaze" (Kolodziejski 2015, 432). Noting how the use of the world "vulnerable" highlights the precariousness of coral reefs and how timeliness is reinforced by the short time frame for their disappearance, Kolodziejski demonstrates how Lin's use of the locus of the irreparable can disrupt the "exploitative tendencies of the human gaze" that would objectify the reef; it does this by "framing it as a living subject worth protecting" (Kolodziejski 2015, 436).

But "vulnerable" is more than a term signifying precarity. After all, "Precarity is the condition of being vulnerable to others," writes Tsing (2015, 20). "Unpredictable encounters transform us; we are not in control, even of ourselves. Unable to rely on a stable structure of community, we are thrown into shifting assemblages, which remake us as well as others . . . thinking

through precarity makes it evident that indeterminacy also makes life possible" (Tsing 2015, 20). Master gardener and former council member Jo
Yeager describes the lessons one learns from embracing precarity:

> I have learned so much in this place. Walking up stream—that's my life.
> Carrying self-imposed burdens—that's my life. Savoring what I see, taste,
> touch, smell, hear and feel —that's my life. Learning about the things around
> me—that's my life. Relishing the recalled events of the past—that's my life.
> Trying to learn the beginnings—that's my life. Ignoring the inevitable downhill
> trip to the ocean—that's my life. There is no end to this story because I still have
> not found the beginning. (Yeager 2019, 59)

Gail Oberst, who facilitated the workshop and edited the LWC's collection
of essays, likewise describes the unpredictability of our encounters, the lack
of control we have. Yet there is also wisdom to be found in the dialogues
we have with these uncertain relations. "It strikes me, like the glancing of
sunlight from the Little Luckiamute, to stay in one place long enough to create peace; to keep returning to the watery places I know until they say what
they have to say to me" (Oberst 2019c, 39). Recalling a trip to the falls with
her son when he was a young child testing/tasting the waters, she writes, "In
these wordless joys and fears, my love for this place takes shape into words.
It takes shape in the calm waters closest to the shore, where the big rocks hold
the bank to the bed, in the rocks that emerge between falls. Here is where
I taught my son to swim. Here is where he learned the language of water"
(Oberst 2019c, 38).

THE LANGUAGE OF WATER AND DIALECTS OF TREES

This chapter offers a meditation on internatural relations but it is also partly an
appeal to the reader to seek out your local watershed council or soil and water
conservation organization, to become familiar with the work they are doing,
to lend your talents (and/or treasure), and to notice (if you do not already do
so on a regular basis) who your nonhuman neighbors are in this watershed.
An unremarkable student of natural sciences, I have come to this appreciation
late in life and am only now getting to know the flora and fauna that surround
me more intimately. If, as Abram suggests, we are to regenerate oral culture,
telling stories about and talking with the more-than-human world, we should
begin by noticing, and by knowing each other's names. Examining both the
scientific and the proper names given to the last living members of a species, termed "endlings," Joshua Trey Barnett argues that "the work of earthly

coexistence is underwritten by the discourse of naming and the practices of mourning that follow" (2018, 288). To illustrate the role of storytelling, naming, and mourning in marking both the presence and the absence in the watershed, this chapter drew upon a collection of essays "written by people who live and work in our watersheds." They are people who have learned how to listen, notice, and name those with whom they share an ecology and, as illustrated here, crafted an intimate relationship with a beloved landscape.

In a chapter titled "The Speech of Things," David Abram tells of a man he met in the Pacific Northwest who had "schooled himself in the speech of needled evergreens; on a breezy day you could drive him, blindfolded, to any patch of coastal forest and place him, still blind, beneath a particular tree—after a few moments he would tell you, by listening, just what species of pine or spruce or fir stood above him. . . . His ears were attuned, he said, to the different *dialects* of trees" (2010, 171). Numerous authors and ecologists have called for different ways of speaking and interacting with the natural world. Glenn Albrecht has a term for something I experienced in my own watershed council volunteer work—"soliphilia," or "working together with others to protect loved places" (2019, 10). Albrecht's recent book *Earth Emotions: New Words for a New World* offers a lexicon for transitioning from Anthropocene to Symbiocene. His philosophical orientation, terministic screen, and on-going conservation and advocacy efforts exemplify the kind of compassionate contamination I see as the practical corrective to anthropogenic environmental destruction. Anna Lowenhapt Tsing summarizes it:

> We change through our collaborations both within and across species. The important stuff for life on earth happens in those transformations, not in the decision trees of self-contained individuals. . . . This changes the work we imagine for names, including ethnicities and species. If categories are unstable, we must watch them emerge within encounters. To use category names should be a commitment to tracing the assemblages in which these categories gain a momentary hold. (Tsing 2015, 29)

So perhaps species are simulacra, reflecting the timeliness of an assemblage in which recognizable uniqueness and solastalgic precarity conspire to create the loci of a group's, or an environment's, irreparability. If so, are the names we use for these species a step closer to or further from the referential beings with whom we are entangled in an increasingly intimate relationship? Responding to this question, Barnett summarizes, "In some significant sense, a species comes into being only once it has been named. . . . Of course, organisms belonging to any given species physically exist whether they are named or not. . . . The act of naming delivers 'species,' which strictly speaking cannot be observed, over to us as something we can consciously consider, think about, write on, and care for" (2019, 294). To utter the known name of the other is "to begin to *safeguard* the other from total loss. Only when we are able to address nonhuman others by name can we expect to feel and know the full weight of our earthly responsibility" (Barnett 2019, 298).

Speaking the language of water and learning the dialects of trees, much like "becoming-animal," requires us to engage in rewilding projects. According to Bekoff, rewilding "reflects the desire to (re)connect intimately with all animals and landscapes in ways that dissolve borders. Rewilding means appreciating, respecting and accepting other beings and landscapes for who or what they are" (2014, 13). And it entails intentional, restorative work based on that respect and understanding. These are practices that won't just impact the regeneration of oral culture. David Abram points out that *how we write* matters, too:

> Writing of the environment in a purely functional manner "contravenes and cuts short the conviviality between our animal body and the animate earth. It stifles the spontaneous life of the senses. Our eyes begin to glaze over, our ears become deaf to the speech of tree frogs and the articulations of rain. What we say has such a profound effect upon what we see, and hear, and even *taste* of the world. (2010, 64)

I agree with Abram and see in these watershed essays bubbly narrative beginnings, the kind of fermentation that can feed compassionate contamination in the Symbiocene. To make the point even more clearly, I close with a few lines of Donna Henderson's poem "Much Raining," included in the LWC collection. In its entirety, and especially when read aloud, the poem performs the humanature relationship embedded in its similes and its surprise:

Rain like the thrumming of grouse in tall grass
Rain like a radio tuned between stations
Rain like a slash-pile on fire — that crackling
Sometimes a respite while clouds catch their breath
Meanwhile, dripsbetweenrainlike a room of clocks ticking
Rain like a woman wrapping presents in tissue
Rain like a child tearing into them later
Rain like the snap of rice spilled on Formica
Rain like the rumble of tires up a driveway
Rain like rooms full of angry fists, pounding on tables
And just when you think the rain won't end, it doesn't.

(Henderson 2019, 45)

NOTES

1. David Abram's *Becoming Animal*, from which the epigraph is borrowed (in the spirit of compassionate contamination), was adapted for the screen in 2018 by filmmakers Emma Davie and Peter Mettler, in collaboration with Abram. On their website, becominganimalfilm.com, the film is described as "an urgent and immersive audiovisual quest, forging a path into the places where humans and other animals meet, where we pry open our senses to witness the so-called natural world—which in turn witnesses us, prompting us to reflect on the very essence of what it means to inhabit our animal bodies."

2. In the summer of 2019, Oregon State University's College of Forestry came under fire from neighbors and recreational users of their McDonald Experimental Forest for allowing logging of a 420-year-old tree, in addition to many other trees between 80 to 260 years old. As a result, the College Dean issued a recommendation for a new forest management plan and "moratorium on cutting down trees older than 160 years old" (Criss 2019).

BIBLIOGRAPHY

Abram, David. 2010. *Becoming Animal*. New York: Vintage Books.

Albrecht, Glenn. 2005. "'Solastalgia:' A New Concept in Health and Identity." *PAN: Philosophy, Activism, Nature*, 3, 44–59.

Albrecht, Glenn. 2019. *Earth Emotions: New Words for a New World*. Cornell University Press.

Albrecht, Glenn. 2020. "'Sumbiotude': A new word in the tiny (but growing) vocabulary for our emotional connection to the environment." *Down To Earth*, April 27, 2020. https://www.downtoearth.org.in/blog/environment/-sumbiotude-a-new-word-in-the-tiny-but-growing-vocabulary-for-our-emotional-connection-to-the-environment-70709.

Barnett, Joshua Trey. 2019. "Naming, Mourning, and the Work of Earthly Coexistence." *Environmental Communication,* 13(3), 287–99.

Bekoff, Mark. 2014. *Rewilding Our Hearts: Building Pathways of Compassion and Coexistence*. Novato: New World Library.

Cairns, Michael. 2019. "Cool Water Bubbling Through Time." In *Writing Our Watershed: Luckiamute River and Ash Creek* (Second Edition), edited by Gail Oberst, 20–23. Independence: Luckiamute Watershed Council.

Check, Terence. "Re-thinking the Irreparable." Paper presented at the National Communication Association convention, Chicago, IL: 1999.

Cox, Robert. 1995. "The Die is Cast: Topical and Ontological Dimensions of the *Locus* of the Irreparable." *The Quarterly Journal of Speech,* 68 (3), 227–39.

Criss, Doug. 2019. "An Oregon university let loggers harvest a 420-year-old tree. The school says that was a mistake." *CNN,* July 23, 2019. https://www.cnn.com/2019/07/23/us/old-growth-trees-cut-oregon-state-trnd/index.html.

Cunsolo, Ashlee and Karen Landman, eds. 2017. *Mourning Nature: Hope at the Heart of Ecological Loss and Grief.* Montreal: McGill-Queen's University Press.

Ehrman, Terrence. 2019. "Watershed Theology." *The Irish Rover*, September 26. https://irishrover.net/2019/09/watershed-theology/.

Grund-Clampit, Howard. 2019. "Oasis." *Writing Our Watershed: Luckiamute River and Ash Creek* (Second Edition), edited by Gail Oberst, 64–69. Independence: Luckiamute Watershed Council.

Henderson, Donna. 2019. "Much Raining." *Writing Our Watershed: Luckiamute River and Ash Creek* (Second Edition), edited by Gail Oberst, 44–45. Independence: Luckiamute Watershed Council.

Kolodziejski, Lauren R. 2015. *"What is Missing?* Reflections on the Human-nature Relationship in Maya Lin's Final Memorial." *Environmental Communication,* 9(4), 428–55.

Larsen, Phil. 2019. "Biking the Soap Creek Watershed." *Writing Our Watershed: Luckiamute River and Ash Creek* (Second Edition), edited by Gail Oberst, 24–29. Independence: Luckiamute Watershed Council.

Luckiamute Watershed Council. 2019. *Writing Our Watershed: Luckiamute River and Ash Creek* (Second Edition), edited by Gail Oberst. Independence, OR.

Luckiamute Watershed Council. n.d. "Luckiamute Watershed." Accessed May 27, 2020. https://www.luckiamutelwc.org/our-watershed.html.

MacSuibhne, Seamus. 2009. "What makes 'A New Mental Illness'?: The Cases of Solastalgia and Hubris Syndrome." *Cosmos and History: The Journal of Natural and Social Philosophy,* 5(2), 210–25.

McMurry, Andrew. 2018. *Entertaining Futility: Despair and Hope in the Time of Climate Change.* College Station: Texas A&M University Press. http://ebookcen tral.proquest.com/lib/wou/detail.action?docID=5487675.

Milstein, Tema. 2013. "Banging on the Divide: Cultural Reflection and Refraction at the Zoo. In *Perspectives on Human-Animal Communication: Internatural Communication* edited by Emily Plec, 162–81. New York: Routledge.

Nestlerode. Ron. 2019. "Fuller Creek" In *Writing Our Watershed: Luckiamute River and Ash Creek* (Second Edition), edited by Gail Oberst, 10–14. Independence: Luckiamute Watershed Council.

Oberst, Gail. 2019a. "At the Ridge." In *Writing Our Watershed: Luckiamute River and Ash Creek* (Second Edition), edited by Gail Oberst, 6–7. Independence: Luckiamute Watershed Council.

Oberst, Gail. 2019b. "Little Luckiamute." In *Writing Our Watershed: Luckiamute River and Ash Creek* (Second Edition), edited by Gail Oberst, 30–35. Independence: Luckiamute Watershed Council.

Oberst, Gail. 2019c. "Between the Falls." In *Writing Our Watershed: Luckiamute River and Ash Creek* (Second Edition), edited by Gail Oberst, 36–39. Independence: Luckiamute Watershed Council.

Plec, Emily. 2013. *Perspectives on Human Animal Communication: Internatural Communication.* New York: Routledge.

Propen, Amy. 2018. *Visualizing Posthuman Conservation in the Age of the Anthropocene.* Columbus: The Ohio State University Press.

Tsing, Anna Lowenhaupt. 2015. *The Mushroom at the End of the World: On the Possibility of Life in Capitalist Ruins.* Princeton: Princeton University Press.

Chapter 4

The Trouble with Resilience

Jessica Holmes

From toxic air to warming temperatures, rising sea levels, social and political upheaval, climate refugees, food and water shortages, and threats of extinction, the state of the Anthropocene is bleak. It is no wonder that among climate writers, environmental justice advocates and environmental humanities educators, discourses of resilience have emerged to counter the eco-anxiety and climate depression brought on by the severity and scale of current global crises. In a report published in 2018, the Intergovernmental Panel on Climate Change (IPCC 2018) calculated 2030 as a deadline to reduce carbon emissions by a whopping 45 percent or risk irreversible damage that could translate into a planet largely uninhabitable for humans. Since then, global emissions have continued to rise (Global Carbon Project 2019). The steady increase has made it difficult for climate educators to be optimistic while remaining realistic and accurate. Unlike optimism, the concept of resilience seemingly allows space to acknowledge the scope of the challenge and the degree of harm while simultaneously eliciting a feeling of triumph, a recognition of strength and worth, and possibly some hope for the future; it reinforces the notion that we, humans, can overcome any obstacle, however seemingly impossible, if we are just resilient enough.

This chapter seeks to deconstruct the concept of resilience in the context of climate change and climate justice education, to evaluate its importance and consequence in the environmental humanities classroom, and to critically probe the limitations and problems with resilience advocacy in the environmental movement. Given the need for both self- and community-empowerment in tackling the climate crisis, as well as the benefits of modeling narratives of motivation, compassion, and positive transformation in our scholarship and teaching, resilience seems uniquely positioned to at once acknowledge and legitimize the vast scale of oppression and destruction and to facilitate solution-oriented forward thinking. But how might we reconcile resilience's positive capacity and value with questions of equity and inclusion, particularly given the deeply unequal and unjust distribution of climate change's impact? My contemplation of and inquiry into resilience pedagogy—that is, an applied climate education strategy that seeks to directly or indirectly build resilience among students—begins at the intersection of psychology and education. By examining examples of resilience-centered language, I pose questions about the capacity for resilience to be learned across diverse educational settings, the role that lived or embodied intimacy with environmental crises plays in cultivating resilience, as well as the relationship between climate resilience and white privilege. My critique of resilience pedagogy is in this way directly tied to broader critiques of white environmentalist and climate discourse. In the second half of the chapter, I examine the relationship of resilience to equity in three BIPOC critiques of resilience—through the lived and literary work of Tommy Orange, Terese Marie Mailhot, and the Women With A Vision (WWAV) collective as depicted by Laura McTighe. The need for such an analysis stems not only from the increasing prevalence of resilience narratives within environmental and academic circles[1] but also from my personal desire to probe the gaps and flaws within my own evolving pedagogy. As a white settler scholar and educator, I want to question the efficacy and ethical dimensions of foregrounding resilience narratives in environmental humanities courses precisely because resilience figures prominently in so much of my own teaching.

This chapter begins with a brief definitional inquiry before exploring some potential benefits of approaching climate education through the lens of resilience and evaluating several of the significant risks of and problems with resilience discourse and pedagogy. With the help of the aforementioned writers, I consider if and how it is possible to develop and teach equitable, resilience-promoting climate writing and communication courses. Ultimately, I argue that while resilience takes many forms, some of which are indispensable to navigating the climate crisis, practices and expressions of resilience are not accessible to everyone. Indigenous and black feminist critiques of resilience in particular advise those in the environmental movement to be wary of employing resilience as a stopgap solution or tool by which to satisfy white grief. By critically considering the concept of resilience, especially as a pedagogical apparatus, this chapter seeks out a resilience-informed—rather than resilience-based—environmental humanities model, so as not to perpetuate inequity and exclusion in our classrooms and communities. That is to say, it strives toward a pedagogy that engages the concept of resilience without demanding that resilience of its participants as a measure by which to judge their success.

WHAT IS RESILIENCE?

The Oxford English Dictionary defines resilience as "the quality or fact of being able to recover quickly or easily from, or resist being affected by, a misfortune, shock, illness, etc.; robustness; adaptability" (OED 2020). The word stems from the Latin *resilīre*, meaning to retreat, spring back, or rebound. The etymology of the term points to a slight ambiguity between the understanding of resilience as a passive act (that of "retreat" or "recoiling") and resilience as an active practice ("springing" or "bounding"). The former would suggest that the resilient subject emerges from difficulty unchanged or unaffected— something I argue is generally not possible within contexts of trauma such as climate crises (at least for those being directly impacted). Contemporary uses of the term seem largely to fall within the more active reverberation, touting resilience as a "rebounding" or even a bounding forward. In this more active sense, "adaptability" implies change, while "recovery" implies healing. Acclaimed neuropsychologist Rick Hanson explains:

> Mental resources like determination, self-worth, and kindness are what make us resilient: able to cope with adversity and push through challenges in the pursuit of opportunities. While resilience helps us recover from loss and trauma, it offers much more than that. True resilience fosters well-being, an underlying sense of happiness, love, and peace. Remarkably, as you internalize experiences of well-being, that builds inner strengths which in turn make you more resilient. Well-being and resilience promote each other in an upward spiral. (2018, 2)

Based on a psychological comprehension of resilience such as this—in which it is created by means of "resources"—it is important to consider the unequal distribution of resources across diverse groups. When educators talk about the unequal distribution of resources within student populations, we are often referring to those that create socioeconomic, geographic, cultural, or institutional barriers to learning, such as money, technology, safety, healthy, and freedom from discrimination based on race, gender, sexual orientation, body type, or class. These affect factors such as class size, access to textbooks, and conduciveness of classroom and study spaces to learning. But when considering resilience-based pedagogy, particularly in conversation or conjunction with mental health-promoting classroom practices, it is important to recognize that these tangible resources cannot be separated from the psychological resources Hanson identifies (such as "determination, self-worth, and kindness"). In *Resilient: How to Grow an Unshakable Core of Calm, Strength, and Happiness,* Hanson (2018) describes psychological resources as predominantly self-directed. Indeed, scientific research strongly supports the neuroplasticity of the brain and the capacity for practices like mindfulness to regulate, alter, and build neural pathways (Tolahunase et al. 2018). Still, health professionals have also illustrated the irrefutable links between, for instance, poverty and mental health, zip code and subjection to violence, and trauma and impeded academic success. If resilience is enabled by "resources" and those resources (or access to them) are unequally distributed, then it surely follows that resilience too (or access to it) is unequally distributed. Furthermore, the interrelated and cyclical nature of increased/decreased well-being and increased/decreased resilience that Hanson underscores compounds the disparity of distribution.

While resource disparities are well-known to characterize global citizens and communities at large, they are particularly evident in the example of the climate crisis. Those least responsible for the crisis and with the least available resources to combat (or "rebound" from) it are typically the most frequently and severely impacted. And yet, resilience is a term often touted not just by mental health practitioners but also by environmental justice warriors and higher education institutions; it has become a cornerstone of discourse and pedagogy for those communicating (in) the Anthropocene. The intersection between clinical understandings of resilience and those in the imaginative or public narrative opens up both opportunities and predicaments for climate educators, particularly in the environmental humanities.

Upon examining discourses of resilience within the context of the climate crisis and the Anthropocene at large, we might also consider the widespread anthropocentric function of the term. "Resilience" is by no means inherently anthropocentric in nature, only in application within certain environmental discourses. We often talk about individual, community, or human resilience, yet the resilience of the planet and the nonhumans that inhabit it are rarely discussed in the environmental humanities.[2] In particular, the "existential threat" posed by the climate crisis centers around the possibility of human extinction. Environmental discourse referencing a "dying planet" or the "end of nature," at least on the level of language, misrepresents the relationship of humans to nonhumans or more-than-humans. Nature and the planet will survive; it is humans that may not. Instead of positioning climate as a barrier to human well-being, what might an environmental humanities that regards the Earth as an example of nonhuman resilience look like? Climate change is, after all, the literal adaptation of the planet to human geophysical influence and action—a rebounding or rebalancing at the level of atmosphere. How might a reorientation of climate rhetoric to reflect a less human-centric perspective impact our understanding of climate resilience and our ability to communicate (in) the Anthropocene with greater accuracy and humility? Just as the Anthropocene narrative overlooks divides within species and suggests a sweeping disregard for the nonhuman,[3] enacting what Dinesh Wadiwel refers to as a "hierarchical anthropocentrism" (2020), normative resilience narratives similarly overlook nonhuman subjecthood, animacy, and agency, as well as disparities in access, systematic support, and well-being across communities and ecosystems.

TEACHING CLIMATE RESILIENCE

In my own experience and exploration of climate pedagogy and in speaking with fellow climate educators across multiple institutions, parallels have emerged between climate educators and frontline health practitioners such as mental health professionals, clinicians, and first responders. When it comes to students, teachers are frequently placed in the role of first responders, mental health providers, life coaches, and disaster-response volunteers, not just during extreme circumstances, such as school shootings or even fire drills, but during intimate, everyday experiences. Whether through reflective writing assignments, classroom discussions, office hours, emails, or when we notice students coming to class tired, upset, hungry, or overwhelmed, teachers often become intimately familiar with the state of mental health of our students. Mental health issues are the leading impediment to academic success, according to the National Alliance on Mental Illness (NAMI 2019). Increasing rates of diagnosable depression, anxiety, feelings of hopelessness and overwhelm, and suicide have contributed to a mental health crisis across college campuses nationwide. When combined with the potentially traumatic content presented in climate education courses, this crisis means that many teachers rightfully fear exacerbating existing mental health challenges among students and/or triggering new ones through course content. Living, studying, and communicating (in) the Anthropocene has caused mental health experts to create new terms including climate anxiety, eco-grief, pre-traumatic stress disorder, solastalgia, and apocalypse fatigue.[4] It is no wonder that resilience-based pedagogy appeals greatly to many climate educators—myself included.

My own encounters with affective student responses to climate content have motivated me to seek out resources and advice beyond the field of traditional higher education pedagogy. For instance, in a recent environmental humanities course, I used Leslie Davenport's (2017) *Emotional Resiliency in the Era of Climate Change* to develop student-led resilience training exercises and incorporate them into class lesson plans. The book is written for a clinician audience, but I found Davenport's framework to be well-suited for climate educators. She integrates clearly articulated psychological theory and research with a focus on personal stories, embodied experiences, and mindfulness practices and provides a variety of practicable worksheets and exercises that can be used directly and/or adapted for pedagogical purposes. However, despite (or perhaps because of) my relative gratification in using the text in my climate course, it is worth questioning how ethically, equitably, and effectively such a resilience resource might realistically be distributed or taught.

In discussing the effects of climate change on mental health, Davenport defines resilience as "the process of skillfully navigating through crisis with the ability to psychologically bounce back from times of high distress" (2017, 25). She adds that "resilience can be learned by virtually anyone." The question of teachability is taken up by Maria Konnikova (2016) in her *New Yorker* piece, "How People Learn to Become Resilient." Konnikova examines the research of psychologists Norman Garmezy, Emmy Werner, and George Bonanno,[5] all of who have studied the concept of resilience in clinical settings. Much of their research argues that "resilience is, ultimately, a set of skills that can be taught" (Konnikova 2016). Werner identifies a "positive social orientation" and an "internal locus of control" among children identified as resilient, meaning they were "autonomous and independent," and "believed that they, and not their circumstances, affected their achievements" (Konnikova 2016). In line with this notion of self-empowerment and control over one's life, Bonanno coined the term "PTE, or potentially traumatic event"; he argues, "Events are not traumatic until we experience them as traumatic" (Konnikova 2016).

While there is certainly substantial evidence to back up pedagogical strategies that facilitate self-efficacy and self-responsibility, when looking at the stark disparities in standards of living and rates of violence (including slow violence, systematic violence, chronic stressors, and microaggressions) across socioeconomic, racial, gender, cultural and geographic groups, as well as the gross imbalance in wealth and power between people and multinational corporations during the Anthropocene, it is very difficult to acknowledge true individual autonomy. Furthermore, the clear-cut distinction Bonanno makes between trauma and the perception of trauma seems anything but clear-cut when considering the widespread injustice and violence to which vulnerable individuals and populations are subjected. Studies of intergenerational trauma have indicated that family members' experiences of trauma can operate on a person's brain and body at the level of DNA and neurochemicals:[6] "Trauma can be passed on through generations. Experiencing trauma can lead to maladaptive ways of coping with the unresolved emotions about the event. These coping mechanisms such as hypervigilance, hyperarousal or avoidance may appear as anger, panic, isolation, anxiety or depression" (Trauma and Beyond Center 2020). Such coping mechanisms would directly prevent an individual from developing or accessing the so-called "positive social orientation" and "internal locus of control" to which Werner attributes qualities of resilience. Indeed, Garmezy's research not only identifies environmental threats such as low socioeconomic status and difficult home conditions but also distinguishes between acute threats and chronic stressors that "[exert] repeated and cumulative impact on resources and adaptation and [persist] for many months and typically considerably longer" (Konnikova 2016).

Protective factors, particularly social support and forms of intimacy, also played a role for the subjects of both Garmezy and Werner's studies. Werner granted that certain individuals deemed resilient reported elements of "luck": "A resilient child might have a strong bond with a supportive caregiver, parent, teacher, or other mentor-like figure" (Konnikova 2016). Additionally, Werner concluded that "resilient individuals were far more likely to report having sources of spiritual and religious support than those who weren't" (Konnikova 2016). These particular influences all encompass a degree of intimacy and interpersonal connection or community, an important consideration when thinking about how to implement classroom or institutional learning. Lived experiences and organically constructed communities (such as families, neighborhoods, and social circles) tend to inherently facilitate greater intimacy and connection than any given pedagogical framework. But these factors nevertheless provide cause for prioritizing interpersonal classroom relationships founded on practices like communal storytelling (through the sharing of writing, discussion, and art), which lead to the building of more authentic classroom communities.

THE (IN)COMPATIBILITY OF
RESILIENCE AND EQUITY

While psychological and pedagogical guides to emotional resilience provide many tools for climate educators, we must be careful to deconstruct the language of privilege and urgently attend to the lived realities of vulnerable peoples. Our pedagogical application of such guidelines must be governed by antiracist, antiviolent, and justice-informed knowledge. In light of an underprepared mental health system, and in the absence of clinical paradigms to address the psychological impacts of the climate crisis, Davenport offers her tools and perspectives:

> The more [resiliency] practices are engaged, the stronger and more available these resources become. A few of the many features of resiliency include accepting the reality of change, focusing on what can be done, engaging in meaningful conversations and action, nurturing creativity, encouraging flexibility and curiosity, expanding mindful awareness of the connections between thoughts, emotions, physiology, and joining with others to build community. We have the freedom to choose to live by our most sovereign values. (2017, 25)

But, if an individual has little to no access to resiliency practices in the first place, the "resources" Davenport mentions never become available. If the Anthropocene shows us anything, it is that we don't all have the freedom to choose how we live. For instance, how can one "live by [one's] most sovereign values," such as the right to safe housing and community, when whole cities are going underwater or burning to the ground? How can one vote by one's "most sovereign values" of sustainability and environmental justice when no political candidate on the ballot has committed to climate leadership commensurate with the level of crisis? How can a child experiencing poverty, abuse, or intergenerational trauma be expected to practice "flexibility" or to "nurture creativity"? Countless murders of black men and women by white officers and the militarized responses of our police force to nationwide protests for Black Lives Matter and racial justice do not allow for black individuals to "live by [their] most sovereign values." In some cases, they do not even allow for black individuals to live at all.

Recognizing this injustice, postcolonial and feminist scholar Françoise Vergès (2017) has re-dubbed the Anthropocene the racial Capitalocene; she calls for the integration of our study of "racialized policies of the environment" into an ongoing "analysis of capital, imperialism, gender, class, and race and a conception of nature and of being human that opposes the Western approach." Black feminist scholars and indigenous voices have critiqued resilience in this respect, advising those in the Western environmental movement to be wary of employing it as a stopgap solution or passive tolerance of suffering—that is, usually, the suffering of the nonwhite Other. These critiques underscore the dire need to pair climate education with antiracist pedagogy. Nowhere is this more apparent than in environmental resilience discourse. In "The Profound Emptiness of 'Resilience,'" Parul Sehgal (2015) likens resilience narratives to "classic American bootstrap logic when it is applied to individuals, placing all the burden of success and failure on a person's character." Like terms such as *diversity* and *sustainability*, resilience has been co-opted and reduced to a catchy buzzword on college campuses and in environmental studies departments. It is mostly, if not entirely, devoid of meaning, employed to make the institution or user appear culturally, racially, or environmentally attentive without having to demonstrate any accountability through actual policy or action. According to Sehgal, "Resilience is fleet, adaptive, pragmatic—and it has become an obsession among middle-class parents who want to prepare their children to withstand a world that won't always go their way" (2015). As I write this chapter amid the COVID-19 pandemic and nationwide protests against police brutality and racial injustice, I received an email from my own institution entitled, "Resiliency Planning for Autumn Quarter." It strikes me that for those struggling under the intolerable weight of oppression and injustice, sometimes resilience can be neither planned nor accessed.

When discussing any notion of shared or community resilience in the racial Capitalocene, it is vital to understand which groups or individuals are and are not treated as equal members of that community. Feminist scholar Laura McTighe offers a clear set of examples of such treatment in "Front Porch Revolution: Resilience Space, Demonic Grounds, and the Horizons of a Black Feminist Otherwise" (2018), in which she reflects upon her experiences in post-Katrina New Orleans with the black feminist collective, WWAV. After being firebombed by arsonists in 2016, the group relocated to a home "with a sprawling front porch that emptied onto North Broad Street's foot traffic" (25). Led by executive director Deon Haywood, they claimed this as a site for organizing and communing. Their gatherings began with a conversation about resilience, which had "become a catchphrase to celebrate the rebuilding of the city after the storm" (27). McTighe recounts wondering, "What exactly did resilience mean when 99,625 black New Orleanians were still displaced and thousands more were living in prison cells as a result of intensified policing?" (25). WWAV specifically resisted the erasure of black women by "working to document how the fantasy of a new, resilient New Orleans [was] being built through the evisceration of black women—that is, by isolating black women from necessary social services, blaming them for the abuse they survive[d], and then criminalizing them for this victimization" (27–8).

The WWAV porch talk underscores the very erasures too often enacted by normative discourses of resilience, however well-meaning they may be, as McTighe illustrates in her recollection of the words of WWAV member Mwende Katwiwa: "Resilience [. . . has] been used so much to . . . to paint that like 'noble Negro' story of . . . 'Oh yeah, you might be burdened but you're just so resilient!' [. . .] People always focus on the resiliency of the person versus why they need to be resilient" (2018, 31).[7] Katwiwa's description subtly urges climate educators to question their pedagogical priorities when considering whether and how to teach (or teach on) resilience. In which contexts are resilience discourses being employed to support the mental health of students (and which students?) and in which contexts are they employed at the expense of equipping students with greater knowledge of the conditions and underlying causes of injustice and environmental crisis? As educators, particularly white educators such as myself, we must do more than refrain from erasing the bodies, experiences, knowledge, and suffering of oppressed peoples; we must actively foreground and alter the conditions that enable such erasure and oppression. As Haywood put it during the porch talk, "black people been resilient for a long goddamn time. Sometimes I don't want to be resilient" (30).

McTighe's essay points specifically to the significance of front porches as historical "sanctuaries of black feminist leadership" (2018, 44); they are sites of community and organized resistance. As such, they are also threatening to those powers seeking to oppress and erase, as McTighe evidences in citing the 2016 Baton Rouge arrests of protesters on the front porch and yard of Lisa Batiste, who had invited the protesters onto the supposed safe space of her porch. According to McTighe,

> By inviting protesters onto her porch, Batiste evidenced how black feminist geographies can alter the seeming transparency of resilience space. When she called out to protesters, she revealed the absented presence of black women and black worlds in the Southern landscape. In doing so, she exposed the nascent formations of black feminist resistance that were becoming (but had not quite become) the horizons of a radical otherwise. (46)

In thinking about variations on normative pedagogical sites (i.e., an institutional classroom), the front porch provides a useful model; positioned between the domestic privacy of the home and the public space of the outside neighborhood and community, it facilitates both intimacy and transparency. Short of a literal front porch, in what ways might we adapt or reimagine our pedagogical spaces to better serve the students that inhabit them and the values we seek to further? By thinking of our classrooms as sites of community-building and organized resistance, we can better align our pedagogical strategies with goals of racial and climate justice while simultaneously attending to the lived experiences of all students.

RESILIENCE, RESISTANCE, AND HEALING

In "'Don't make the mistake of calling us resilient': Urban Indians and City Belonging in Tommy Orange's *There There*," environmental literature scholar Sage Gerson (2020) reminds white Western environmental scholars and activists that climate change and resource extraction are not just environmental issues, critiquing instances in which indigenous peoples are cast as passive environmental symbols, often of so-called resilience, such as the rebranding of indigenous sovereignty activism at Standing Rock (by settler protesters and media) as an environmental movement. Gerson cautions against the adoption of resilience discourse in environmental circles as a convenient tool by which to satisfy white grief: "The compression—of Indigeneity and environmental resilience—continues a long decontextualized and dehistoricized account of Indigeneity that disregards colonial violence, Indigenous resistance to colonialism, and Indigenous Futurisms." In thinking through white settler applications of the resilience label, Gerson directs us to the work of native novelist Tommy Orange. In *There There*, Orange pushes back against these applications by nonnative peoples:

> All these stories that we haven't been telling all this time, that we haven't been listening to, are just part of what we need to heal. Not that we're broken. And don't make the mistake of calling us resilient. To not have been destroyed, to not have given up, to have survived, is no badge of honor. Would you call an attempted murder victim resilient? (2018, 137)

Orange calls readers' attention to the way in which resilience discourse can undermine the necessary work of justice-seeking—for the realities of "attempted murder" of native peoples and centuries of ongoing violence at large—as well as the process of healing. Orange's conception of healing starkly contrasts with normative Western ideas of recovery and healing in which grief and pain are frequently pathologized, condemned, or dismissed (particularly when experienced by marginalized peoples). *There There* suggests that it is entirely possible to undertake the difficult work of healing while simultaneously rejecting identification as a "broken" or lesser people.

Orange (2018) argues for and evidences native storytelling as one component of the healing process. The polyvocal novel offers a valuable example of grief and pain that is expressed rather than diminished. Like the porch talks of the black feminist collective, the stories of *There There* are deeply intimate, but together amount to a lived history made visible and transparent to readers. In the "Interlude," Orange reflects upon the immense privilege of part-time readers of such history:

> If you have the option to not think about or even consider history, whether you learned it right or not, or whether it even deserves consideration, that's how you know you're on board the ship that serves hors d'oeuvres and fluffs your pillows, while others are out at sea, swimming or drowning, or clinging to little inflatable rafts that they have to take turns keeping inflated, people short of breath, who've never even heard of the words *hors d'oeuvres* or *fluff*. (138–39)

The image of drowning bodies is an apt, not-so-metaphorical metaphor in thinking about the disparate lived experiences of climate crisis across the globe, including indigenous communities continually being occupied, exploited, and harmed. We might liken the option to not think about history elucidated in the above passage to the option of not practicing resilience (or as Orange would prefer us to say, to simply go on existing—"To have not been destroyed, to not have given up, to have survived" [137]). Perhaps those aboard the fancy ship aren't practicing resilience because they haven't had to; perhaps practicing resilience is the act of "people short of breath" simply trying to breathe.

Many white environmentalists have never faced the prospect of loss on such a scale as the Anthropocene encompasses; the climate crisis may be the first existential crisis they have faced. This is not the case for many nonwhite people.[8] Perhaps this in part accounts for the strikingly different conceptions and expressions of pain and loss across racial lines. Terese Marie Mailhot's (2018) memoir *Heart Berries* explores native conceptions of grief and loss. In the "Afterward," she reflects on the notion of indigenous identity as "fixed in grief," explaining, "I don't feel liberated from the governing presence of tragedy. The way in which people frame our work, and the way our work exists, or is canonized—we are not liberated from injustice; we're anchored to it. . . . It doesn't limit me, or us, but limits the way we are seen and spoken about" (130). Resilience is a prime example of such a limitation in the way indigenous peoples are "seen and spoken about," especially in Western environmental discourse. Mailhot's conception of healing attributes power, not pathology, to pain:

> I think pain is presented as good for us—that we can even identify it. Before, it was a secret. In my mother's time it was a secret burden, and women were admired for their ability to ignore, to be silent, to be selfless. They were the backbone of every significant movement in our history because they were not cast to the front. Now we can speak it, and that's true healing, not a problem—to admit there is some constant pain. (135)

Just as Orange associates healing with storytelling, Mailhot accesses her private, public, and ancestral pain through language. Near the end of the memoir, she writes: "Maybe it was a hundred years of work for my name to arrive here, where I can name my pain so well that people are afraid of the consequences and power" (119). Such empowerment lays bare the gap between an expression of authentic healing and survival that has been dubbed resilience, as if to dull or accept conditioning to a "constant pain."

Those deeply in touch with environmental anxiety, grief, and loss share in the experience of another long-term pain. In her environmental studies class, Janet Fiskio aims to teach students about "not-solving" the problem of climate change. She focuses instead on "redefining the problem itself rather than searching for solutions. On an affective level, what this means is that I hold students in the presence of the unbearable grief of climate change, and I resist their attempts to break out of this 'unbearability' by turning to technological optimism or environmental education" (2017, 101).[9] Her purposeful abandonment of the language of solutions presents one possible model for relinquishing the illusion of control that normative classrooms attempt to uphold, for instance, when a teacher in a position of relative power wields tangible solutions and offers well-practiced guidance to students who, through hard work, become gratified by those answers. The "not-solving" paradigm also illuminates vulnerability, opposing the stereotypical (and potentially patriarchal) strength that characterizes the practice of resilience in the face of difficulty. Positioning vulnerability as lived human experience, rather than inadequacy, serves a threefold purpose: to de-center the human in imagining and developing climate futures, to de-center white settler voices from climate discourse (to illuminate vulnerability is to illuminate the disproportionate distribution of privilege across the human species), and to de-center pathologies of trauma as weakness.[10] The Anthropocene, despite its name and initial conception as the epoch in which humans exercise geophysical dominance over the earth,[11] is anything but an era of human control. Likewise, resilience narratives, when self-applied by white settler environmental voices, are on some level a front for exerting control where there isn't any; we are starving for it, none more pathetically than those who are used to having it.

In *Heart Berries*, Mailhot also articulates long-standing native alternatives to Western, solution-oriented pathologies of pain:

> In white culture, forgiveness is synonymous with letting go. In my culture, I believe we carry pain until we can reconcile with it through ceremony. Pain is not framed like a problem with a solution. I don't even know that white people see transcendence the way we do. I'm not sure that their dichotomies apply to me (2018, 28–29).

Resilience, as articulated in Western environmental discourse, falls far short of the reconciliation Mailhot describes here. This is not to say environmentalists should not seek out solutions to climate crises and the problems of the Anthropocene. But, resilience has been repeatedly positioned as a solution to pain from eco-anxiety, climate grief, and stress, pain that has been carried by nonwhite peoples for centuries but which now must also be borne (not quelled or dodged) by white people. Black and indigenous writers such as these show how resilience must never be weaponized to justify settler scholarship or to assuage white, Western grief—whether over our oppression and exploitation of our fellow humans or environmental losses like crumbling ecosystems, a heating planet, and the hundreds of nonhuman species going extinct with each passing day. Pain, loss, and grief must be embraced head-on, and since resilience fails to function as a solution to both grief and the oppressive conditions that have inflamed that grief and made resilience necessary, it is clear we must prioritize resistance over resilience in our movement.

NOTES

1. Examples at my own institution, the University of Washington, include a "Resilience and Compassion" grant initiative focused around environmental sustainability, a campus "Resilience Lab" promoting mental health and well-being, a series of courses on "Resilience in the Workplace," a recent webinar on "Resilience during COVID-19," and even the development of a "University of Washington Resilience Scale," intended to measure resilience in adults, particularly those with disabilities. In 2013, *Time* magazine designated "resilience" the "environmental buzzword" of the year.

2. In the environmental sciences, this is not the case. In fact, the term "climate resilience" originates from C. S. Holling's 1971 description of the capacity for relationships within an ecological system to "absorb changes of state variables, driving variables, and parameters, and still persist" (1971, 17).

3. In "The Geology of Mankind? A Critique of the Anthropocene Narrative," Malm and Hornborg critique the Anthropocene narrative for the way in which species-level conceptions of climate change overlook the "realities of differentiated vulnerability on all scales of human society. . . . If climate change represents a form of apocalypse, it is not universal, but uneven and combined: the species is as much an abstraction at the end of the line as at the source" (2014, 66–67).

4. Terms such as these are discussed in the work of Leslie Davenport (2017), Jennifer Atkinson (2018), Sarah Jaquette Ray (2020), and other climate educators. Timothy Clark refers to "Anthropocene disorder" in *Ecocriticism on the Edge* (2015, 147).

5. Norman Garmezy and Emmy Werner were developmental psychologists. Garmezy is widely credited with being the first to study resilience in an experimental setting, while Werner published a thirty-two-year longitudinal project on resilience among children and young adults in 1989. "George Bonanno is a clinical psychologist at Columbia University's Teachers College; he heads the Loss, Trauma, and Emotion Lab and has been studying resilience for nearly twenty-five years" (Konnikova 2016).

6. According to Yehuda and Lehrner, "In studies of Holocaust offspring, perhaps the most salient observation has been that most differences in offspring phenotype were associated with persistent psychological effects of parents" (2018). Additionally, "there are discussions about the impact of historical events such as colonization, slavery and displacement trauma in many cultures, including First Nations and Native American communities, African Americans, Australian aboriginals and New Zealand Maori, as well as in societies exposed to genocide, ethnic cleansing or war" (2018)

7. Bracketed omissions added.

8. Mary Annaïse Heglar makes this point in "Climate Change Isn't the First Existential Threat"; she writes, "History is littered with targeted—but no less deadly—existential threats for specific populations" (2019).

9. Fiskio draws on Judith Butler here in her use of the term "unbearability." In *Precarious Life*, Butler asks, "Is there something to be gained from grieving, from

tarrying with grief, from remaining exposed to its unbearability and not endeavoring to seek a resolution for grief through violence?" (2006, 30).

10. By "pathologies of trauma," I am referring to mental and physical health conditions (diagnosed, attributed, and/or lived) brought on by experiences of trauma.

11. Paul Crutzen proposed "the Anthropocene" as a new geological epoch in 2002.

BIBLIOGRAPHY

Atkinson, Jennifer. 2018. "Addressing Climate Grief Makes You a Badass, Not a Snowflake." *High Country News*, May 29, 2018. https://www.hcn.org/articles/o pinion-addressing-climate-grief-makes-you-a-badass-not-a-snowflake.

Butler, Judith. 2004. *Precarious Life: The Powers of Mourning and Violence*. London: Verso.

Clark, Timothy. 2015. *Ecocriticism on the Edge: The Anthropocene as a Threshold Concept*. London: Bloomsbury.

Crutzen, Paul J. 2002. "Geology of Mankind." *Nature* 415 (23): 6867. http://doi.org /10.1038/415023a.

Davenport, Leslie. 2017. *Emotional Resiliency in the Era of Climate Change: A Clinician's Guide*. Philadelphia: Jessica Kingsley Publishers.

Fiskio, Janet. 2017. "Building Paradise in the Classroom." In *Teaching Climate Change in the Humanities*, edited by Stephen Siperstein, Shane Hall, and Stephanie Lemenager, 127–35. London: Routledge.

Gerson, Sage. 2020. "'Don't make the mistake of calling us resilient': Urban Indians and City Belonging in Tommy Orange's *There There*." Paper presented at MLA Conference, Seattle, WA, January 2020.

Global Carbon Project. 2019. "Global Carbon Budget." Global Carbon Project. December 4, 2019. https://www.globalcarbonproject.org/carbonbudget/index.htm.

Hanson, Rick. 2018. *Resilient: How to Grow an Unshakable Core of Calm, Strength, and Happiness*. New York: Harmony Books.

Heglar, Mary Annaïse. 2019. "Climate Change Isn't the First Existential Threat." *Zora*, February 18, 2019. https://zora.medium.com/sorry-yall-but-climate-change -ain-t-the-first-existential-threat-b3c999267aa0.

Holling, C S. 1973. "Resilience and Stability of Ecological Systems." *Annual Review of Ecology and Systematics* 4 (1): 1–23. https://doi.org/10.1146/annurev.es.04.11 0173.000245.

IPCC (Intergovernmental Panel on Climate Change). 2018. *Global Warming of 1.5°C: Special Report*. https://www.ipcc.ch/sr15/.

Konnikova, Maria. 2016. "How People Learn to Become Resilient." *New Yorker*, February 11, 2016. https://www.newyorker.com/science/maria-konnikova/the-s ecret-formula-for-resilience.

Mailhot, Terese Marie. 2018. *Heart Berries: A Memoir*. Berkeley: Counterpoint.

Malm, Andreas, and Alf Hornborg. 2014. "The Geology of Mankind? A Critique of the Anthropocene Narrative." *Anthropocene Review* 1 (1): 62–69.

McTighe, Laura, and Deon Haywood. 2018. "Front Porch Revolution: Resilience Space, Demonic Grounds, and the Horizons of a Black Feminist Otherwise." *Signs: Journal of Women in Culture and Society* 44 (1): 25–52.

NAMI (National Alliance on Mental Illness). 2019. "Mental Health by the Numbers." National Alliance on Mental Illness. Updated September 2019. https://www.nami.org/mhstats.

Orange, Tommy. 2018. *There There*. New York: Alfred A. Knopf.

Ray, Sarah Jaquette. 2020. *A Field Guide to Climate Anxiety: How to Keep Your Cool on a Warming Planet*. Oakland: University of California Press.

OED (Oxford English Dictionary). 2020. "Resilience." Oxford English Dictionary. Oxford University Press. www.oed.com.

Sehgal, Parul. 2015. "The Profound Emptiness of 'Resilience.'" New York Times, December 1, 2015. https://www.nytimes.com/2015/12/06/magazine/the-profound-emptiness-of-resilience.html.

Tolahunase, Madhuri R., Rajesh Sagar, Muneeb Faiq, and Rima Dada. 2018. "Yoga- and Meditation-Based Lifestyle Intervention Increases Neuroplasticity and Reduces Severity of Major Depressive Disorder: A Randomized Controlled Trial." *Restorative Neurology and Neuroscience* 36(3): 423–42. https://doi.org/10.3233/RNN-170810.

Trauma and Beyond Center. 2019. "Understanding Intergenerational Trauma: Trauma Treatment Los Angeles." Trauma and Beyond Center. https://www.traumaandbeyondcenter.com/understanding-intergenerational-trauma/.

Vergès, Françoise. 2017. "Racial Capitalocene." *Futures of Black Radicalism*, edited by Gaye Theresa Johnson and Alex Lubin. London: Verso.

Wadiwel, Dinesh. 2020. "Animal Liberation After Covid-19." Lecture presented online through Animal Liberation Currents, May 27, 2020.

Walsh, Bryan. 2013. "Adapt or Die: Why the Environmental Buzzword of 2013 Will Be *Resilience*." *Time*, January 8, 2013. https://science.time.com/2013/01/08/adapt-or-die-why-the-environmental-buzzword-of-2013-will-be-resilience/.

Yehuda, Rachel, and Amy Lehrner. 2018. "Intergenerational Transmission of Trauma Effects: Putative Role of Epigenetic Mechanisms." *World Psychiatry: Official Journal of the World Psychiatric Association (WPA)* 17(3): 243–57. https://doi.org/10.1002/wps.20568.

Chapter 5

Solastalgia and Art Therapy in Climate Change

Chelsea Call

While participating in an artist residency in the Blue Mountains of New South Wales (NSW), Australia, I surveyed the concepts of *solastalgia* and *climate grief*, which led me to the conclusion that creative action can generate acknowledgment and processing of collective climate grief, fostering the continuation of human and other-than-human life.

Environmental philosopher, Glenn Albrecht, created the term *solastalgia* in 2003 to describe "the pain experienced when there is recognition that the place where one resides is under immediate assault" (Harrison 2019, 25). His term creates a conceptual framework to understand the experience of melancholia or psychological trauma, also known as place-based distress, due to environmental change. Discovering this term provided me with an integrative pathway to weave together my passions of mental health, art, and ecology. Excited to explore this concept, I submitted a proposal to the Bilpin Center for Creative Initiatives (BigCi) artist residency program in Bilpin, NSW, Australia, and was accepted.

BigCi is a small artist residency located 1.5 hours outside of Sydney on the traditional lands of the indigenous Darug peoples. Located at the edge of Wollemi National Park within the UNESCO World Heritage-listed Greater Blue Mountains, the residency introduced me to a diverse ecosystem. Here I began researching grief from an art therapist's perspective. Art therapy is a specialized field of mental health where clients are guided to create art as a means for self-expression, processing trauma, and developing insight. As the local community reeled from the recent bushfires, my creative explorations around *solastolgia* became intimate conversations with grief. I spent my days at the residency walking the recently burnt bush, witnessing the altered landscape with my camera, listening to the silent air, and recording my post-walk moods in journals.

At the time of my acceptance into the residency, Australia's devastating bushfires had not yet ignited. As my February 2020 residency date approached, the unprecedented bush fires were spreading and began to escalate to a grandiose size. As of February 15, 2020, at least 80 percent of the Blue Mountains area in NSW had burned. Upon my arrival, the fires had either been controlled or were diminished, leaving behind a new ecosystem and new psychological realities.

In studying grief, I referenced the well-known Kubler-Ross Grief Cycle, created by Elizabeth Kubler-Ross. Kubler-Ross (Hamilton 2016, 523) states there are seven stages of grief: shock, denial, anger, bargaining, depression, testing, and acceptance. While this method is not specific to climate grief and solastalgia, I believe it provides validity for conceptualizing these new ideas. Many of the community members I engaged with in Bilpin were connected to feelings of anger, depression, and sometimes acceptance.

My daily walks in the burnt bush were a process of embodiment and ritual, connecting me to the eerie silence in the forests and the visceral sensation of loss. While the trees began to expose bright new pockets of growth, the birds and mammals had yet to return. Witnessing this allowed me to acknowledge my own climate grief and provided space to process my feelings of sadness, despair, and defeat.

These walks inspired me to generate a public call for participation, asking my social media community the following questions: "When you experience grief, where do you feel grief in your body? And, what does it feel/look like?" I received over one hundred answers to both of these questions. The top three answers to the first question were chest, lungs, and stomach. The second question resulted in a wide variety of answers, notably: "My limbs feel heavy, slow, and weak." "My chest feels weighted, constricted, and hollow." And "[it is] like a forceful ripping from my body, as if you tore all my ligaments."

These humbling responses validated my hypothesis of the interconnectedness present in the feeling of grief (see figure 5.1). I used them to create a cyanotype with my body as the print. Cyanotype is an alternative photographic process using ferric ammonium citrate and potassium ferricyanide to create a blue photogram. After creating my large print, I decided to create smaller cyanotypes with local bush flora. I sewed these pieces onto my large piece, coordinating them with the places where participants noted feeling grief in their bodies. I then wrote down the corresponding answers on vellum paper and sewed this onto the opposite side of the smaller print. The culminating piece is a large mixed media installation portraying the transformative power of grief in relationship to the current environmental crisis. The human body is connected to the notion of the earth body through the cyanotype material. This creative action acknowledges the divide that has been created between

Figure 5.1   A Body-Sized Cyanotype Print with Sewn Muslin and Smaller Cyanotypes from Local Bush Flora. *Credit*: Chelsea Call.

human and other-than-humans in healing. It aims to call for integration, mitigating this false notion of separateness.

Along with this piece, I created a series of manipulated Polaroids portraying the altercation that had taken place in the landscape due to the bushfires (see figure 5.2). The Polaroid medium speaks to time, and the manipulation portrays fragility. They are my perception of solastalgia as recognition of loss, honoring the passing of a once familiar place.

Before leaving Australia, I conducted a cyanotype workshop for the students at the local elementary school in Bilpin and a workshop titled *Solastalgia and Art Therapy* for the community at the University of New South Wales. Both workshops integrated art therapy directives to assist participants in deepening their understanding of solastalgia. Mandala work, journaling, and discussion were facilitated in both to foster connectivity and

Figure 5.2 Manipulated Polaroids Portraying the Altercation that Had Taken Place in the Landscape Due to the Bushfires. *Credit*: Chelsea Call.

integration. All of the above creative processes support my belief that it is necessary to recognize the reality of climate grief and then mobilize creative actions for collective processing, fostering the continuation of human and other-than-human life. Maintaining an art therapy-inspired framework, I was able to hold space for psychological unveiling such as grief and solastalgia.

BIBLIOGRAPHY

Hamilton, Ian. 2016. "Understanding Grief and Bereavement." *British Journal of General Practice*, no. 653 (2016), 253. doi: https://doi.org/10.3399/bjgp16X687325.
Harrison, Melissa. 2019. "The Mental Pain of Climate Change." *New Statesman*, October 2019, 25–31.

Chapter 6

Living (in) Spider Webs

More-than-Human Intimacy in Installation Art by Tómas Saraceno

Katharina Alsen

"Nobody lives everywhere; everybody lives somewhere.
Nothing is connected to everything; everything is connected to something."

(Haraway 2016, 30)

From a human perspective, spiders do not exactly have the best reputation. As cultural theorist Jussi Parikka points out in his book *Insect Media*, "we hate spiders and insects together" (Parikka 2010, viii). Like almost no other animal, spiders are associated with aversion, and, more specifically, arachnophobia. Intimate relations in a more-than-human line of thought seem to be out of range. However, arachnids tend to be highly acknowledged for their natural engineering skills—in particular Araneae, the subspecies of web-building spiders. Already by the end of the nineteenth century, the *New York Times* discussed the importance of spiders by highlighting their crafting skills and workmanship. They were attributed with anthropomorphic metaphors such as "builders, engineers and weavers, hunters and mathematicians" as well as "original inventors of a system of telegraphy" (Ditmars 1897, 28). The latter referred to the capacity of spider webs to transmit information not merely by binary means of "touch" or "non-touch" but by varying factors such as the modality of movement or weight. The webs were described as sensitive communication systems which help bridging physical distance: One does not have to be physically close to cause a vibrating connection between spider, web, and external entity. Spider webs rather make possible relational and shared agency. In more recent debate, Donna Haraway has thought along similar lines by pointing out the "sympoietic threading, felting, tangling, tracking, sorting"

73

performed by arachnids (Haraway 2016, 31). Spiders thus "have much more agency than one might give them credit for, above and beyond being a figure that can push human thinking in new directions" (Moe 2019, 42).

Argentinian visual artist Tómas Saraceno (b. 1973) shares the enthusiasm about spiders and uses it to integrate their webs as both material metaphors and actual material in his installations. Saraceno's long-time engagement with living spiders and the silk structures they produce is fundamental to his research-based practice. Ongoing since 2006, he has combined a conceptual triad of art-making, biological analysis, and cultural theory. His objective is to stimulate transdisciplinary discourse and facilitate a more nuanced perspective on arachnophilia in the realms of art. My aim is to classify two different strategies by which Saraceno addresses the aesthetics, logics and materialities of spider webs, and to explore in which way they can enable more-than-human intimacy:

Figure 6.1 Tómas Saraceno, *in orbit*, 2013—Ongoing, Installation, Curated by Marion Ackermann, and Susanne Meyer-Büser, K21 (Kunstsammlung Nordrhein-Westfalen), Dusseldorf. *Credit*: Katharina Alsen.

First, Saraceno (re)creates spider web constructions of monumental scale which are made of flexible steel grids. They either produce sonic reverberations by means of human touch, or visitors can climb around in them—both following the idea of spiders as proto-architects, proto-craftsmen, and even proto-artists. That way, the natural structure serves as a model for the artist. The strategy based on mimetic reference is what I will call "spider-like" or "spider-inspired" art. Following recent scholarship in cultural animal studies, spider-inspired artworks can be understood as material metaphors: Such metaphors are meant to abandon anthropocentric view points and focus on mutual dependence of animal and human agency in cultural representations instead (Steinbrecher and Borgards 2016). Saraceno's interactive work *in orbit* (2013), a permanent aerial installation in the atrium of K21 museum in Dusseldorf, Germany, is a good example for this phenomenon (figure 6.1). The same applies to the large-scale sound landscape *Algo-r(h)i(y)thms*, presented at Gallery Esther Schipper in Berlin in 2019.

Second, Saraceno creates exhibitions of silk webs made by (and at times also presented together with) living spiders in small-scale display cabinets. In doing so, the webs are treated as high-value fragile artifacts. They are placed in dark, spider-friendly environments and are not to be touched. The theoretical framework for these works is provided by extensive studies of arachnid techniques, conducted in Saraceno's research laboratory where different species of web-building spiders are invited to occupy the building and take over space. This tactic of incorporating "real-life" spider-produced materials into installation art is what I refer to as "spiders in art" or, in short, "spider art." Saraceno's recent work *Spider/Web Pavilion 7*, exhibited at the Venice Biennial in 2019, is a typical example of this. His curatorial *Carte Blanche* for an exhibition at Palais de Tokyo in Paris, which resulted in the hybrid ecosystem *ON AIR* (2018/19), illustrates a similar approach, too: All spider webs in both nonrepresentative and exhibition rooms of the building were documented by a professional arachnologist and prohibited to be removed by visitors or (cleaning) staff for the duration of the show. Of course, one might question to what extent the exhibition of living animals inevitably leads to morally debatable exhibition*ism*. Still, Saraceno's idea of coinhabited space in which conditions are made spider-friendly and human visitors have to adapt to the needs of spiders—and not the other way around—helps induce careful attentiveness toward the animal life. A substantial degree of agency and artistry is attributed to the spiders. As an interim summary, it can be noted that both installation types described above—spider-inspired art and spider art—integrate "para-artistic" animal practices and straddle the boundary of nature and artificial (re)production. Spider webs form the conceptual and material point of departure in either case. However, the two strategies offer different perspectives on physical

proximity and (in)voluntary closeness, and thus on the potential to experience interspecies intimacy.

Looking at the above-mentioned example for spider-inspired art, this
means: Saraceno's interactive installation *in orbit* invites up to ten visitors
at a time to enter three steel mesh webs suspended at a height of twenty-five
meters above ground. The entire construction starts to vibrate when moving
along the web and its triple layers. Any kind of motion, no matter how small,
is transferred to the immediate environment. Since the communication flow
is driven by the perception of body motion and vibrational energy, it can be
framed as kinesthetic communication. Without the need of actual physical
proximity, all (animate) actors become aware of being dependent on each
other; they are sensitized to the direct effects of their bodily co-presence.
Since the notion of intimacy does not only signify interpersonal human relationships but can be seen in a broader scope (Mjöberg 2009), such a way of
radical interconnectedness unfolds the intense, potentially intimate relationality between all (animate and inanimate) actors in space. In affect theory, such
phenomena of interrelationality have been termed as "affective assemblages"
(Slaby, Mühlhoff and Wüschner 2019) and can be seen in conjunction with
Bruno Latour's actor-network-theory. To alter the Haraway quote heading
this text, one could frame this particular experience of intimate relations and
more-than-human intimacy as follows: Everything in Saraceno's *in orbit* is
connected to something, which creates the impression that everything might
be connected, yet intimately related to everything.

Beyond that, intimacy is a fragile thing. Intimacy draws on a mixture of
tension and repose and always comes along with the potential to collapse. It
is about transgressing boundaries and bears the risk of getting "too close" to
have a pleasurable experience. In *in orbit*, these ambivalent qualities of intimacy come along with an experience of fear that is triggered by entering the
steel webs at a dizzying height: The height may cause vertigo. The vibrating
environment is beyond (human) control. Not least, visitors can at no time be
sure whether they are meant to be explorers—or the (spider-inspired) prey.

Saraceno's works of the second type, spider art, also play with the ambivalence of intimate relations, although with a different focus: Visitors perform
the roles of intruders who get access to spider sites of dwelling, that is to say:
to their fragile and intimate zones. In daily human life, such constellations are
typically framed the other way around: Spiders and insects, bugs and critters
either co-exist in and co-inhabit space but go unnoticed for human actors, or
they are regarded as uninvited guests who show up unexpectedly: In general,
they are treated as "traffickers in our most intimate spaces" who undertake
"unauthorized travels into our private homes" (Chaudhuri 2013, 323). This
perspective, however, is turned around in works such as *ON AIR*, Saraceno's
Carte Blanche exhibition. There, it is the human visitor who is considered a

sneaky intruder and, in doing so, encouraged to increase their respect to spider habitats. Contrary to usual habits of eliminating spiders and their webs in human-dominated space, spider life comes first.

In total, Saraceno's art installations offer a substantial change of perspective. They open up new potentials of interspecies entanglement and experiences of more-than-human intimacy. This is what distinguishes Saraceno's approach from other spider-related works of recent art history, such as Rosemarie Trockel's experiments with living spiders in the early 1990s. For Saraceno, however, the valorization of spider life is of central importance: Arachnophilia goes art.

BIBLIOGRAPHY

Chaudhuri, Una. 2013. "Bug Bytes. Insects, Information, and Interspecies Theatricality." *Theatre Journal* 65, no. 3: 321–334.

Ditmars, R. L. 1897. "Studies of the Spider." *New York Times*, May 9, 1897, 28.

Haraway, Donna. 2016. *Staying with the Trouble. Making Kin in the Chtulucene.* Durham: Duke Univ. Press.

Mjöberg, Jessica. 2009. "Challenging the Idea of Intimacy as Intimate Relationships. Reflections on Intimacy as an Analytical Concept." In *Intimate Explorations. Reading across Disciplines*, edited by Alejandro Cervantes Carson et al., 11–22. Oxford: Inter-disciplinary Press.

Moe, Aaron M. 2019. "Holding on to Proteus; or, Toward a Poetics of Gaia." In *Texts, Animals, Environments. Zoopoetics and Ecopoetics*, edited by Frederike Middelhoff et al., 41–53. Freiburg: Rombach.

Parikka, Jussi. 2010. *Insect Media. An Archaeology of Animals and Technology.* Minneapolis: Univ. of Minnesota Press.

Slaby, Jan, Rainer Mühlhoff, and Philipp Wüschner. 2019. "Affective Arrangements." *Emotion Review* 11, no. 1, 3–12.

Steinbrecher, Aline, and Roland Borgards. 2016. "Doggen, Bologneser, Bullenbeisser. Hunde in historischen Quellen um 1800 und in Danton's Tod von Georg Büchner." In *Tierisch! Das Tier und die Wissenschaft*, edited by Meret Fehlmann et al., 151–171. Zürich: vdf.

Part II

NONHUMAN COLLABORATORS

OYSTERS, BIRDS, AND ELEPHANTS

Chapter 7

The Permeable Heart

Mindfulness in Animal-Human Communication

Peggy J. Bowers

The nearly empty shore braced itself for the soon-to-be fury of storm clouds that completely filled the expansive horizon. A fierce wind hit my face as I gazed out to sea, my toes anchored in the wet sand near the water's edge. Suddenly it seemed someone was staring at me; I looked around but saw no creature. Glancing down, I noticed a soft, slimy starfish impossibly far from the roiling waves of the receding tide. A short trail in the sand told me that it had tried to the point of exhaustion to reach the ebbing waters. Now it held one tiny arm up to me, waving, and I heard, almost synesthetically, a voice saying, "help me." Moved to compassion, I sought a way to aid its journey to the water without hurting it. Finally, I simply picked it up. It immediately stiffened between my index finger and thumb. I walked thigh deep into the surf and released it gently on the surface. It dropped instantly to the ocean floor and disappeared under the sand. A life saved; another changed. I could not shake the genuine sense of connection I felt to an organism supposedly so undeveloped nor my sense of wonder. Only much later would I learn of Gödel's incompleteness theorem, as I sought to describe a truth that could not be proven.

Experiences like these, born out of what McGinnis (2012) has termed "species loneliness," have as their prerequisite the ability simply to pay attention: to notice ourselves and others, but in a particular and focused way, similar to mindfulness, which is defined as "the power of our minds to give close, nonjudgmental attention to our experience as it unfolds" (Muesse 2011, 18). This practice of being in the present is part of human mental faculties but has been especially developed in a variety of spiritual traditions. Vietnamese monk Thich Nhat Hanh (1999) points out that our attention is always directed somewhere, but it matters where. Counterintuitively, its inward focus enables an inclusive, loving energy toward the Other. For example, observing your breath may teach you about our connectedness to the world (Muesse 2011). "We are in contact with life," Nhat Hanh (81) says, and through this, our "now heart" (the Chinese term for mindfulness) touches, nourishes, relieves suffering, and ultimately transforms. Compassion, literally "to suffer with," is based on the empathy that enables animals or people to understand the Other, and as a result brings comfort. The intimacy that humans crave between and among ourselves and with other species stems from self-compassion, whose origins lie in mindful being (Salzberg 2002). Perhaps poet Mary Oliver (1997, 32) best sums up the importance of mindfulness when she writes, "This is the first, the wildest and the wisest thing I know: that the soul exists and that it is built entirely out of attentiveness."

Remarkably, one-third of the U.S. population has displayed symptoms of clinical depression and anxiety during the COVID-19 pandemic (Berger et al.), dramatically exacerbating societal problems of loneliness, isolation, and disconnection. Mental health issues such as grief and insecurity are perhaps a mostly unseen and neglected side effect of this crisis, with lasting repercussions. The idea that contact with Nature is extremely successful at ameliorating such suffering is both well documented and more crucial than ever. Philosopher and novelist Iris Murdoch (1985) has noted that the mere observation of bird life has lifted her depression and preoccupation with the mundane. Put another way, essayist and naturalist John Burroughs (1912, 245) famously has said, "I go to Nature to be soothed and healed, and to have my senses put in tune once more." Practicing mindfulness provides one of the most valuable means to achieve this.

The accounts of soulful, connected encounters with the Animal Other are myriad and include creatures as diverse as ants, pigeons, wolves, and octopuses (e.g., Casey 2015; Montgomery 2015; Lopez 1978; Louv 2019). Citing Emerson's notion of the "common heart," Richard Louv (2019, 23) contends that this takes place in a "habit of the heart" (24). The heart, Louv explains, is a "mindful muscle" whose little-understood complexity includes the way we experience emotions (25). When we live in the moment, he claims, we are more "heartful" (26). This fragile habitat, which extends beyond self-awareness to other hearts, enables us to meet the Animal Other in a "third world" where the "connection . . . extends from within us, across the mysterious between, and into the other being" (24). These intimate encounters include awe, curiosity, compassion, serenity, existential questioning, or excitement tinged with fear, but never loneliness. Making narratives from these magical moments in liminal spaces is evidence of a life seeking attunement.

These mystical experiences, an avenue to intimate communication, are available to us if only we would live a life of mindfulness. Though almost always unexpected, they can happen to anyone who prepares. Draw the air deeply. Release your breath slowly. Be still. Simply notice and get curious about what you sense. Move gently through the world. And though words are usually superfluous, speak them softly if you must.

"Let us love the country of here below," writes Simone Weil (1973). "It is real; it offers resistance to love" (178). In so doing, we nourish this "border-defying communion" (Louv 2019, 24). The borders seem obvious; the commonalities are not always so clear. According to biologist Marc Bekoff (2007), research has shown that even unexpected species display sophisticated capacities for moral emotions such as empathy and fairness. Animals have a complex repertoire of relational sentiments as well. For example, foxes have funerals, as do elephants. Owls express gratitude (O'Brien 2008). Octopuses have unique personalities that can include a playful sense of humor, being stubborn or ornery, or enjoying a snuggle (Montgomery 2015). Wolves are loyal. Chimps laugh, kiss and make up after a fight, and play tricks on one another. Gorillas struggle with social distancing. The project of restoring our intimate bond with the natural world is worth the effort because encounters with Nature are mutually nurturing and restorative. Put poetically, "sometimes it is necessary to reteach a thing its loveliness, to put a hand on the brow of the flower and retell it in words and in touch it is lovely until it flowers again from within" (Kinnell 2002, 81). Moments of meeting the Animal Other, freely and on their terms as much as ours, cultivate a life of heartful beingness. They have lives so unlike ours, experiences so unimaginable, but they choose to approach, to connect, perhaps to wonder, and maybe to feel, as do we, less alone. These encounters are, as Barry Lopez (1978, 285) writes, "the root of fundamental joy."

The humility wrought from being chosen by another creature, who often limits its own abilities in order to enter that liminal space, creates, sometimes for only a moment, a transformational connection to that living being and more permanently to our planet, if we never forget and learn from it. We gain a sense of our place in the cosmos, poignantly captured by Henry Beston (2003, 25), who spent a year of observation and encounter on the Great Beach of Cape Cod:

> For the animal shall not be measured by man. In a world older and more complete than ours, they move finished and complete, gifted with the extension of the senses we have lost or never attained, living by voices we shall never hear. They are not brethren, they are not underlings: they are other nations, caught with ourselves in the net of life and time, fellow prisoners of the splendour and travail of the earth.

The joy, simplicity, and sanctity of that starfish meeting illuminated irrevocably the intimacy available to us with the natural world, its concomitant sense of belongingness and call to compassionate action. When mindfulness makes our hearts permeable, we become fully ourselves and are able to reveal ourselves. What a mystery: being out of the self in a moment of connection makes us whole.

BIBLIOGRAPHY

Bekoff, Marc. 2007. *The Emotional Lives of Animals*. Novato, CA: New World Library.

Berger, Miriam, Kim Bellware, Felicia Sonmez, Meryl Kornfield, Candace Buckner, Samantha Pell, Colby Itkowitz, Antonia Noori Farzan, John Wagner, and Katie Shepherd. 2020. "Surge in Anxiety and Depression Show Coronavirus Toll on Mental Health in America." *Washington Post,* May 26, 2020. https://www.washingtonpost.com/nation/2020/05/26/coronavirus-update-us/.

Beston, Henry. 2003. *The Outermost House: A Year of Life on the Great Beach of Cape Cod*. New York: St. Martin's Griffin. First published 1928 by Doubleday.

Burroughs, John. 1912. *Time and Change*. Boston: Houghton Mifflin.

Casey, Susan. 2015. *Voices in the Ocean: A Journey into the Wild and Haunting World of Dolphins*. New York: Doubleday.

Kinnell, Galway. 2002. *Three Books*. New York: Houghton Mifflin.

Lopez, Barry Holstun. 1978. *Of Wolves and Men*. New York: Charles Scribner's Sons.

Louv, Richard. 2019. *Our Wild Calling*. Chapel Hill: Algonquin Books.

McGinnis, Michael Vincent. 2012. "Species Loneliness: Losing our Sense of Place in the Machine Age." *Santa Barbara Independent,* Jan. 14, 2012. https://www.independent.com/2012/01/14/species-loneliness/.

Montgomery, Sy. 2015. *The Soul of an Octopus: A Surprising Exploration into the Wonder of Consciousness*. New York: Simon and Schuster.

Muesse, Mark W. 2011. *Practicing Mindfulness: An Introduction to Meditation*. Chantilly, VA: Teaching Co.

Murdoch, Iris. 1985. *The Sovereignty of Good*. New York: Routledge & Kegan Paul. First published 1970 by Ark Paperbacks.

Nhat Hanh, Thich. 1999. *The Heart of the Buddha's Teaching: Transforming Suffering into Peace, Joy, and Liberation*. New York: Random House.

O'Brien, Stacey. 2008. *Wesley the Owl: The Remarkable Love Story of an Owl and His Girl*. New York: Free Press.

Oliver, Mary. 1997. "Low Tide: What the Sea Gives to the Human Soul." *The Amicus Journal* 18 (4): 32+.

Salzberg, Sharon. 1995. *Lovingkindness: The Revolutionary Art of Happiness*. Boston: Shambhala.

Weil, Simone. 1973. *Waiting for God*. New York: Harper and Row, Perennial Library.

Chapter 8

Intimacy on the Half-Shell

Place, Oysters, and the Emerging Narrative of Virginia Aquaculture

Anne K. Armstrong, Richard C. Stedman, and Marianne E. Krasny

Open up a menu on the Eastern Shore of Virginia, a sandy peninsula that separates the Chesapeake Bay from the Atlantic Ocean, and you are bound to find multiple oyster-based dishes, from stew and chowder to fried and raw on the half-shell. Although some local fishers[1] still harvest wild oysters, odds are the oysters you consume in a restaurant will have been farmed. Indeed, fishers and the indigenous peoples, that came before them, have been planting seed oysters for over a century to enhance their harvests. Oysters have long been a staple of the regional economy and were even the cause of armed conflict in the nineteenth-century "oyster wars." But it is only over the last decade that industrial oyster *aquaculture* has grown significantly in economic value. Today, amid growing conflict in Virginia between waterfront property owners and oyster farmers (Finley 2017), oysters are still heralded as harbingers of place restoration, touted as cleaning the Chesapeake Bay, protecting against the floods of sea level rise, and bolstering economies all at the same time.

In this chapter, we use website text from Virginia aquaculture companies, state tourism interests, and large conservation organizations to explore how aquaculture and oysters serve as loci for intimate relations with material place, social and ecological heritage, and organizational partners. Intimacy "achieves a form of knowledge in the traffic between entities" (Farrier 2019, 19) and is a "site for the social production of knowledge and the reworking of human-nature boundaries" (Raffles 2002, 326). On an ecosystem level, shellfish are filter feeders, which, as adults, do not move far (if they move at all). They may thus come to symbolize place in ways that other marine organisms do not; they quite literally create place, which we conceive of as an intertwining of both material and social, symbolic elements. Oysters do this visibly, growing in expansive reefs that they help to create. When you eat an oyster, you eat remnants of that place—gritty sand from the substrate, salty seawater trapped inside the shell—that have been transported to your dining table. Oysters and aquaculture have come to symbolize a yearned-for intimacy with place, and yet they are also a product of the Anthropocene. They are evidence of humans' heavy hand, of the toll modern fisheries have taken on wild shellfish populations, and, increasingly, they are threatened by climate change and its impacts.

This chapter is organized as follows. First, we provide a brief overview of literature on social-ecological symbols and the intersections of place with heritage tourism and conservation. Next, we offer a background on oysters and aquaculture. Finally, we analyze and discuss texts from select aquaculture companies, Virginia tourism, and conservation websites that offer a lens through which to explore intimacy with place, intimacies across time, and intimacies among stakeholder groups.

AQUACULTURE AND SHELLFISH AS POLYSEMOUS, HYBRID SYMBOLS

Oysters and aquaculture are polysemous, hybrid symbols that combine often shared yet juxtaposing meanings. Symbols "give us the capacity to make meaning," and people may share a symbol but not its meanings (Cohen 1985, 16). A polysemous symbol has many meanings, and so a foodie, a conservationist, and an oyster farmer might all consider the oyster important, but it may mean something very different to these groups, symbolically speaking. A hybrid symbol brings together opposing elements to form new meanings (Tidball 2014a). A social-ecological symbol is a "'storage unit' containing both social and ecological meanings, and, more importantly, social and ecological interactions" (Tidball 2014b, 265). In his presentation of trees as hybrid social-ecological symbols, Tidball describes hybridity as the dual desire to connect with and separate from simultaneously. The symbol of trees and tree planting in post-Hurricane Katrina New Orleans is an "example of such a creative modality for living with difference, the differentness of a changed landscape and sense of place in the wake of disaster or war" (Tidball 2014a, 24). Like the New Orleans trees, oysters are social-ecological symbols and iconic species that have historically and continue to today shape conceptions of the places in which they grow (Krasny et al. 2014).

CREATING AND MAINTAINING PLACE THROUGH
HERITAGE TOURISM AND CONSERVATION

Before going further, we need to address the concept of place and the multifaceted ways in which people identify with, make meaning of, develop bonds with, and react to changes in place, as these phenomena underlie much of the language employed by aquaculture companies. Freudenberg and colleagues conceive of the relationship between society and the environment as a "conjoint constitution"; social processes shape physical realities, and physical realities shape social processes (Freudenberg, Frickel, and Gramling 1995). Given this assumption of conjoint constitution, we think of a place as "an aggregation of things and relationships—human and nonhuman, social and ecological—that are tangibly cohering, at least for a time" (Cannavò 2007, 20). The study of place spans disciplines, and place scholars delve into the multiple ways in which people and their physical surroundings interact. People may define themselves in terms of place and have a distinct place identity (Cuba and Hummon 1993). When the authors of this chapter self-identify with the place-based moniker "Ithacan," they do not just tell you where they live, they tell you something about who they are. The gorges and waterfalls, Cayuga Lake and its parks, the downtown square and restaurants, the majority political values and attitudes—all of these may be enfolded in that one word, "Ithacan." This is a place identity. The authors may also have a positive emotional bond with Ithaca. For the first author, this bond is deeply rooted in her love of Ithaca's forests and gorges and her experiences in these places with her family. This bond is called a place attachment (Stedman 2002). Our sense of Ithaca, or sense of place, incorporates this positive bond and the many meanings we make of Ithaca. Place meanings are descriptions of "what kind of place this is," and place attachment and sense of place are functions "of the meanings we attribute" to place (Stedman 2008, 66). Each of these elements—place identity, place meanings, place attachment, and sense of place—shape our interactions with places and people.

While people may develop a sense of place through direct experiences, the tourism industry also mediates this process by providing or capitalizing on a suite of chosen symbolic meanings. Haven-Teng and Jones write about the construction of sense of place in tourism "to exploit the unique attributes of a destination and differentiate it from competitor destinations" (2005, 71). Imagine arriving at a tourism welcome center, where you can find racks of brochures with the full range of activities available in a location. But the tourism center has a special exhibit on, say, oysters, and the "unique" activities available for experiencing the oyster culture of the region. The tourism bureau is choosing to highlight specific symbolic meanings, which mediate the way you develop a sense of that place.

Just as the tourism industry may seek to capitalize on recreating place, conservation organizations seek to protect place. This "protection" might come in the form of attempts to keep systems from changing—conserving what is here—or in the form of restoration that seeks to bring back elements of ecological systems that have been lost or are in the process of being lost. The Nature Conservancy and the Chesapeake Bay Foundation have created sanctuary reefs in the Chesapeake Bay in attempts to restore native oyster populations and rejuvenate the Bay ("Virginia Oyster Gardening" n.d.). In recreating biophysical place, conservation organizations also redefine social relationships with place and nature by prescribing which places and species should be conserved and why (Bryant 2000).

What do you do when your favorite place or your home changes drastically, even if this happens slowly over time? In Tidball's (2014b) recounting of post-Katrina New Orleans, tree planting became a way to "live with difference" brought about by a severe disturbance. Coastal communities protect their places and heritage by maintaining buildings and other infrastructure that are critical to fishers' social lives and identity and that may help attract tourists interested in heritage experiences (Khakzad 2018; Khakzad and Griffith 2016). Oyster gardeners in New York City were motivated to volunteer in part by social-ecological memories and a sense that they were restoring what had been lost, thus reducing a discrepancy in past and current place (Krasny et al. 2014). But when places change enough and for long enough, so does the sense of that place—the meanings and the nature of people's attachments (Keilty, Beckley, and Sherren 2016). In some areas of Virginia, shellfish harvesting diminished to such an extent that people who own coastal and waterside property no longer associate their place—or have memories linked to—commercial fisheries. These people have responded by attempting to limit the expansion of commercial aquaculture (Mayfield 2016). In addition to dissonant place meanings, people seek to limit aquaculture for other reasons, such as questions related to its sustainability (see last section of this chapter).

Like other coastal regions in the United States, coastal Virginia is threatened by a variety of social-ecological disturbances, from climate change and its associated ocean acidification and sea level rise, to the hypoxic, Chesapeake Bay dead zone that emerges every summer. The oyster aquaculture industry has emerged in the wake of these disturbances, and aquaculture websites, conservation organizations, and tourism have responded by presenting the oyster and aquaculture as a means of living with change. In the next section, we provide a brief introduction to oyster biology and ecology and then describe current aquaculture practices in Virginia.

A PRIMER IN OYSTER BIOLOGY, ECOLOGY, AND AQUACULTURE

Oysters are bivalve mollusks that have a profound impact on physical place. Oysters hatch from eggs as free-floating plankton, which eventually settle out of the water column as baby oysters called spat and attach to ("strike") on a substrate, preferably a high-calcium carbonate one. Over time, oysters build large, complex reefs that provide habitat to myriad species. As filter feeders, oysters remove particulate matter from the water, which increases light availability for seagrass and other vegetation (Newell and Koch 2004).

Before European explorers arrived on the Eastern Shore of Virginia, oysters were abundant and an important food source for Native American tribes (Schulte 2017). European settlers began using oysters as a food source and in a variety of other ways. Shells became lime, chicken feed supplement, mortar, and were even incorporated into railroad ballast (Schulte 2017). The oyster industry, however, did not start growing until the nineteenth century, when New Englanders and New Yorkers began looking further south to meet their oyster needs (Paolisso and Dery 2010). An 1877 New York *Sun* article describes the oyster boom in an Eastern Shore town: "Franklin City does not grow, because its sole source of income is now fully developed. Every inch of ground that can be planted to oysters is now occupied" (Spears 1877). The remaining shell piles at Franklin City are now being used as part of a shoreline restoration project ("Chincoteague Bay Field Station's Living Shoreline" n.d.). The industry peaked after the Civil War but continued to be substantial into the first quarter of the twentieth century. Starting in the 1950s and 1960s, outbreaks of two oyster diseases, MSX and Dermo, combined with overfishing to decimate the population to just 1 percent of its former size today (Schulte 2017).

With wild stocks diminished, fishers turned to harvesting hard clams (*Mercenaria mercenaria*), but those harvests also began to decline (Mann and Powell 2007). In the wake of decreased stocks of both clams and oysters, aquaculture production has increased dramatically. Oyster aquaculture expanded significantly after 2008. Now, oyster growers use two dominant techniques for rearing oysters—caged and grown on the bottom—and they both start with baby oysters ("spat") spawned in a hatchery setting. Most of the oysters grown in Virginia have an extra chromosome and are called "triploids." Triploid oysters are sterile and do not use energy to spawn, thus allowing them to grow to market size more quickly and to be sold year round. Some oyster growers run their own hatchery operations, while others purchase their seed oysters (Hudson 2019).

Oyster aquaculture is now an expanding industry that has emerged out of social-ecological disturbances and has spawned (pun intended) partnerships with other industries. For example, Virginia's commercial oyster hatcheries provide spat and larvae for restoration as well as for oyster farmers, and many of those hatcheries farm the oysters they rear and so have built a vertically integrated industry (Wallace, Waters, and Rikard 2008). And while restoring wild oysters to the Chesapeake Bay and other Virginia coastal waters is a goal in and of itself, conservation groups have also worked with aquaculture companies in a variety of ways, and state agencies and the Chesapeake Bay Program now tout oyster aquaculture as a best management practice for improving water quality in the Chesapeake Bay (Cornwell et al. 2016).

ANALYZING AQUACULTURE INTIMACIES

Discourse and symbolic language reveal place meanings (Stokowski 2002; Stedman 2003), and so aquaculture, conservation, and tourism website texts offer a trove of textual data used to investigate how these key groups are communicating about and making sense of aquaculture, oysters, and place. We conducted a qualitative, thematic analysis of website text from Virginia aquaculture companies listed in the Virginia Aquaculture Growers Directory, compiled by the Virginia Marine Products Board. Not all the growers have websites listed, and so we analyzed text from the twenty-eight companies with a website. This research started with an analysis of aquaculture companies on the Eastern Shore only and then expanded to encompass aquaculture companies throughout Virginia to confirm themes uncovered through the initial analysis. We analyzed each page on these websites. A priori concepts included materiality, place-based symbolic meanings, and ecological meanings. Other themes emerged through analysis, such as sustainability partnerships, heritage, and innovation. While the focus of this work was on aquaculture company texts, we wanted to contextualize aquaculture in terms of other oyster-related efforts in Virginia, and so we also conducted a limited review of website texts from five key nonprofit conservation organizations involved in oyster restoration and Virginia's Oyster Trail website.

  Below, we highlight the juxtaposing meanings and intimacies revealed in the website texts. We focus on oysters as symbolic of (1) intimacy with material place, (2) the entanglement of artisan craft and wildness, (3) as expressions of heritage and technological innovation, and (4) as the driver of networked sustainability initiatives. Against the backdrop of the Anthropocene, the first three themes explore how the language of aquaculture companies, tourism, and conservation organizations reveal efforts to live with change while maintaining a sense of continuity, often linked to place. The last theme underlines the basic political ecology and neoliberal structures through which aquaculture operates.

Oysters and "Merroir"

One way in which aquaculture companies portray oysters as symbolic of place is by using the language of terroir (or merroir). "After all, oysters are filter feeders," writes Rappahannock Oyster Company, "and they, quite literally, capture the essence of the region (the minerals, the grasses, the plankton) and serve it right up to you" ("Our Oysters" n.d.). Shooting Point Oyster Farm explains, "Our oysters are a direct reflection of place" ("Shooting Point Salts®" n.d.). Ruby Salts describes how their "oysters directly reflect place and take their tastes from the location where they are grown" ("The Shore" n.d.). They place their variety of oyster in a very specific geographic location: Cherrystone Creek, "on the lower Eastern Shore, where the Chesapeake meets the Atlantic" which "gives the oysters a flavor you won't forget" ("Why Choose Ruby Salts?" n.d.). The highly specific geographic information helps the company distinguish its oysters from others, and as the oyster symbolizes place, place becomes symbolic of quality and uniqueness.

Shooting Point's language around oysters and place goes even further and paints the process of eating an oyster as akin to experiencing place. The company employs the language of place poetically in its description of their oyster variety, "Shooting Point Salts":

Grown at the North end of famous Hog Island overlooking the Little Machipongo inlet these oysters define unspoiled seaside. The Atlantic tide rushing across white sand and brushed by the peat of the pristine marshes of the Atlantic Coast Reserve result in the purest form of salt oyster. Shells with honey hues, slightly sweet plump meats, and an incredible pure brine finish can only be equated to kissing the sea herself ("Shooting Point Salts®" n.d.).

While Shooting Point describes oysters as "grown," which suggests passivity, the oysters also *actively* define place. Words like "unspoiled," "pristine," "white sand," and "purest form" and the sexualized description of honey-hued shells with "slightly sweet plump meats" contribute to an sensuous portrayal of their oysters as a means not only to transport oneself to a place but to physically join with that place.

As a marketing strategy, merroir narratives elevate both the place of production and the product by mirroring language used to describe other high-status foods, such as wine. In Virginia, as in Europe, terroir narratives reveal efforts to construct regional identities that "encapsulate traditions, original values, and culture" of an area (Demossier 2016, 126) and that promise intimacy with something we perceive has been lost—such as wild nature and abundant oyster populations—through the act of eating. As Fischler writes, "food makes the eater: it is therefore natural that the eater should try to make himself by eating" (1988, 282). We would add that place makes the food, and so place *and* food make the eater.

"Heirloom hand-crafted oysters": Wild and farmed

While Virginia aquaculture narratives highlight wildness as a key quality and signifier of their product's purity, they also describe how their work and craftmanship is just as crucial for delivering a high-quality product. It is through place—the estuaries and creeks in which "heirloom" and "hand-crafted" oysters are reared—that the domestic and wild elements of the organism entangle. The H.M. Terry company describes how their "brood stock is native Virginia brood stock, selected for its growth capabilities, disease resistance, and local flavor" ("Process" n.d.). Elsewhere on their website, however, they underline that, while they are farmed, these oysters grow in the "ocean filtered . . . unique, unspoiled waters" of Hog Island Bay ("About" n.d.). This language epitomizes the oysters' symbolic hybridity as farmed and yet shaped by the "unspoiled" waters.[2] Shooting Point refers to its oysters as "hand-crafted" and "heirloom," ("Shooting Point Salts®" n.d.) two words that connote human agency and nostalgia for history rather than a wild product. These companies emphasize the oyster's status as a farmed yet wild animal, and they do not mention the fact that their oysters are most likely genetically modified triploid oysters, as 85 percent of oysters farmed in 2018 Virginia were (Hudson 2019). In other words, the oysters you consume in a restaurant are a hybrid of wild and farmed, or heritage and innovation, and, for all of their references to wild, pristine, and remote locations, aquaculture companies farm oysters, and most of the oysters that Virginia oyster farmers raise are genetically modified.

The Once and Future Oyster: Intimacy through Continuity

In this section, we explore how aquaculture companies, conservation organizations, and tourism situate oysters and aquaculture as a means through which to hold the region's past in the present while also symbolizing the future of sustainable food. The majority of oysters sold to market now come from oyster farms, and yet aquaculture companies, the Oyster Trail, and conservation groups each rely heavily on the notion that oysters and aquaculture represent continuity between the past, present, and future. Cultured oysters, in spite of their hatchery-based births and altered chromosomal count, function mnemonically to connect people to the past while also serving as a reminder of the present (Madden and Finch 2008).

One way in which aquaculture companies tie oysters to the region's heritage is by describing the colonial history of their location. Anderson's

Neck Oyster Company links their current operations to colonial oyster fisheries, describing how they are "building upon the legacy that was started at Anderson's Neck back in 1662, while we redefine what it means to be an oyster waterman" ("Anderson's Neck" n.d.). Thus, oyster farming links them via place to heritage while at the same time symbolizing the future of oyster-related professions. Chessie Seafood and Aquafarms celebrates how oysters from the York River "were demanded by British royalty during colonial days [and] are now provided by Chessie Seafood and Aquafarms" (York River Oysters n.d.), uplifting their product and the place as fit for kings and connecting consumers with Virginia's colonial past. The owners of Pleasure House Oysters on the Lynnhaven River describe how their "family operated farm strives to recreate the experience of tasting the amazing bounty of the Lynnhaven as it was experienced in the past" ("Farm" 2013), suggesting that one can taste the past by eating their oysters.

Conservation groups also play to the sense of history in the region. In its page on oyster restoration in Virginia, The Nature Conservancy begins by associating oysters with the social-ecological heritage of the Chesapeake Bay, employing John Smith's oft-quoted description of oysters laying "thick as stones" and describing how "for generations, oysters have played an important role in the Bay's economy as a food that locals, tourists and the global market love" (The Nature Conservancy 2018). Friends of the Rappahannock offers tours during which one can install shells on their restoration reef and "learn about oysters, oyster restoration, the history of the region, John Smith's journey up the Rappahannock, the seafood industry, and much more!" ("Oyster Program" 2020). Appeals to heritage are not always linked to specific historic figures or events. For example, TNC underlines how oyster restoration supports other species, such as crabs and rockfish ("Oyster Restoration in Virginia" 2018). Simply mentioning blue crabs and rockfish as benefiting from oyster restoration places oysters at a central node in a trifecta of species that symbolize history and heritage in the region (Paolisso 2007).

For the tourism industry, food products such as oysters are central to place-making, and Virginia tourism is taking full advantage of the oyster's renaissance through aquaculture by crafting a narrative around oysters and place related to heritage. In 2015, Virginia Governor Terry McAuliffe launched the Virginia Oyster Trail, capitalizing on his state's status as the nation's largest producer of both wild-caught and farmed oysters and a growing interest in the merroir of oysters. According to a video on the Trail website, tourists following the Oyster Trail will "meet the authentic watermen who for generations have been fishing the region since the dawn of our country" while also observing "water culture traditions, creativity and ingenuity that are preserving Virginia's coastal way of life" (*The Virginia Oyster Trail* n.d.). These statements highlight the paradox inherent in aquaculture's appeals to heritage; aquaculture may indeed preserve seafood-related jobs, but these jobs are inherently different than watermen's work in the past (Badger 2002).

There is, of course, the question of whose heritage is being celebrated. Historically, Black men and women were employed to shuck oysters, although the oyster industry also provided some measure of upward mobility after the Civil War, as illustrated by the story of Thomas Downing, whose parents were freed slaves and who became the "oyster king" of New York City (Guerin 2019; Anderson 1998). Today, while aquaculture provides an estimated 480 jobs in Virginia, the primary operators of aquaculture companies are white men. According to the U.S. Department of Agriculture Census, there are only two Hispanic or Latinx aquaculture operators in the state of Virginia and just four African American operators ("USDA/NASS QuickStats Ad-Hoc Query Tool" n.d.).[3] This unequal representation in the industry parallels unequal representation in the farming industry (Penniman 2018) and is rendered all the more stark by the recent protests that have erupted after the police killings of George Floyd, Breonna Taylor, and Ahmaud Arbury—all unarmed Black people.

While oysters may serve as a mnemonic for the past, through aquaculture and restoration efforts, they also symbolize technological and conservation progress. Oyster growers today use a sophisticated, often vertically integrated process that involves oyster hatcheries and nurseries before the oysters ever make it into the ocean (Hudson 2017). Ruby Salts describes the process of nurturing seed oysters in upwellers ("From Seed to Market" n.d.), and Lighthouse Oyster Company writes about their "oyster spa," a tumbling system that washes the oysters ("Home" n.d.). Certainly, acres of plastic mesh cages floating in the water do not evoke heritage but rather a modern production process, and the discovery of microplastics pollution originating from aquaculture industries complicates the notion of their sustainability (Lusher, Hollman, and Mendoza-Hill 2017). Indeed, progress toward sustainability goals and a restored Bay are much more prevalent themes in aquaculture texts than is technological innovation. In the next section, we discuss how partnerships in sustainability have emerged through aquaculture.

New Intimacies: Partners in Sustainability

The intimate relationship between water and oysters (through their role as filter feeders) is a lynchpin in partnerships between conservationists and oyster farmers. Conservation organizations work toward maintaining and restoring water quality in coastal Virginia, while oyster farmers require good water quality to operate their businesses. For many of the oyster farmers in our sample, this means actual partnerships as well as green marketing efforts to brand oysters as sustainable seafood. Rappahannock Oyster Company notes the "inspiring collective of farmers, chefs, patrons, activists, and yes, even politicians who've put purpose ahead of profit" so that the "Chesapeake once again enjoys its place among the great oyster regions of the world— this time, on a foundation of sustainability" (Rappahannock Oyster Company n.d.). Rapphannock is a large oyster farming operation and so, of course, must make a profit. But their statement highlights the extent to which oysters are a social-ecological symbol that has rallied different groups, and it situates their business as the key to restoring the Bay while continuing to make an economic profit. Ruby Salts explains, "Oyster shells are literally the foundation of [the Save our Shell] restoration efforts" ("Taking Care of the Bay" n.d.). The oysters' material, physical presence enables the aquaculture companies to create a discourse around environmental sustainability; at the same time, adherence to this discourse throughout the industry may affect practices that shape the future oyster population.

For conservation organizations like TNC, partnering with oyster farmers offers a chance to prove their worth in the region: from the first author's anecdotal experience on the Eastern Shore, residents may resent the organization's control of a substantial amount of land. TNC highlights a collaborative research project it undertook with Virginia Institute of Marine Science and four oyster growers to investigate the impacts of aquaculture on water quality in the Chesapeake Bay ("Oyster Restoration in Virginia" 2018). In an infographic developed to communicate findings from a Virginia Coastal Zone Management program, TNC situates itself as a preserver of the aquaculture industry because aquaculture "relies on conserved lands to provide clean growing waters" ("Conservation's Positive Economic Impacts for Virginia's Eastern Shore" n.d.). The Virginia Oyster Trail website focuses less on sustainability initiatives, but the Virginia Oyster Trail does tout the fact that "The Virginia Aquarium's Sensible Seafood Program lists oysters as one of the most sustainable seafood choices" (Clements n.d.).

Through an uncritical lens, these partnerships present another means of living with change as wild populations of oysters struggle and water quality remains in need of restoration—an ideal scenario in which to achieve real conservation gains while also fostering economic development in struggling coastal regions, predicated on the oyster's intimate relationship with place. Viewed more critically, these partnerships epitomize neoliberal conservation efforts that frame their work in terms of economic development, since economic value is the ultimate arbiter of whether the work is "worth" it.

THE CHALLENGES AHEAD

The effusive, place-based texts of aquaculture websites and the oysters themselves construct a sense of place and mark a "moment in the passage from memory to hope, from past to future" (Harvey 1996). But will the aquaculture

industry be able to adapt to growing threats related to climate change, chemical runoff, and plastics pollution, not to mention threats such as COVID-19?
These are large-scale challenges that transcend local processes, places, and
place meanings, and while aquaculture companies certainly employ highly
localized, place-based language to describe their product, their businesses are
yet highly impacted by nonlocal—indeed global—processes.

The COVID-19 crisis threatens oyster farmers who have lost restaurant
business and so have no place to sell their oysters. With no place to sell, they
also are unable to plant more for lack of space and may miss the mark, so to
speak, on oysters that are the right size for the half-shell market (Held 2020).
Cherrystone Aqua-Farms spins the crisis as a way for customers to order
products that are usually only sent to "top-end restaurants" but instead can be
shipped right to their home ("Cherrystone Aqua-Farms" n.d.). But adapting
to this shorter term threat may reveal little about the ability of oysters—and
aquaculture—to adapt to looming, longer term environmental threats, such as
climate change and related ocean acidification.

Ocean acidification—the decrease in the ocean's pH due to increased
absorption of CO_2—threatens oysters by decreasing the amount of carbonate available for shell-building. Larvae are particularly vulnerable. On the
Pacific coast, which has experienced greater acidification and associated
impacts on oyster survival than the mid-Atlantic, aquaculture companies have
responded by adding soda ash to water as a buffer (American Association for
the Advancement of Science n.d.). Recent research suggests the Chesapeake
Bay region will be highly socially vulnerable to ocean acidification impacts
on aquaculture because of its economic dependence on mollusk production.
Developing partnerships with Pacific coast growers with experience addressing the growing issue may build adaptive capacity in the short-term (Ekstrom
et al. 2015). In the long-term, of course, only reductions in CO_2 emissions
will mitigate ocean acidification and ensure the survival of oysters, their co-
constructed places, and their associated industries and communities.

As filter feeders, oysters' intimacy with microscopic marine particles
means that they also filter microplastics, which measure less than 5mm in
length. One microplastics-related concern is that oysters will bioaccumulate
microplastics as they filter feed, although research suggests they do so in
very small quantities (Lusher, Hollman, and Mendoza-Hill 2017). Another
concern is that the aquaculture industry's reliance on plastics makes it an
important source of microplastic (and macroplastic) pollution. Residents of
Bainbridge Island, WA, updated their Shoreline Master Plan and banned any
aquaculture activities that used nonbiodegradable plastic (City of Bainbridge
Island 2017), a move that the industry says all but bans commercial aquaculture (Schoof and DeNike 2017). Before readers condemn oyster aquaculture
for its plastics use, remember that organic food production also relies heavily
on plastic to avoid chemical pesticides, and that oceanic fisheries contribute

massively to plastics pollution in the oceans through lost and discarded nets and traps. This is not to say that plastics pollution from aquaculture is *good*—far from it. But rather to remind readers that even eating an organic, vegan diet does not allow us to escape from plastics use in food production and that, in the Anthropocene, no food choice is devoid of tradeoffs.

Aquaculture and oyster restoration also face an uphill battle in meeting sustainability and conservation goals. Mann and Powell (2007, 913) wrote that goals for oyster restoration in the Chesapeake Bay were a veritable pipe dream and that the idea that a healthy population of oysters could filter the whole Bay had "captured the imagination of a swath of readers, from ecologists . . . to politicians seeking a 'quick fix' for nutrient reduction ('it's OK, more oysters will fix it')." Interviews with NYC oyster gardeners echo this hope that oysters are the key to future environmental quality (Krasny et al. 2014). The first author once sat in on a webinar about oyster restoration goals for Long Island Sound, whose message seemed to be: "It will take a nearly impossible number of oysters to meet nitrogen reduction goals, but we are continuing to move forward with promoting oyster restoration as a nutrient reduction strategy." Meanwhile, the Chesapeake Bay Program has recently approved aquaculture as a best management practice for reaching the Bay's goals for nitrogen loads, and TNC suggests aquaculture may aid in nutrient reduction goals ("Aquaculture by Design" n.d).

Oyster aquaculture is not a silver bullet to water quality restoration or climate change adaptation but shared interest in oysters may indeed open increased opportunities for addressing long-running pollution issues in the Chesapeake Bay. In the realm of sea level rise adaptation, support for oysters facilitates living shoreline construction that enables communities to move away from traditional, hardened shoreline features, such as seawalls and jetties, which only exacerbate erosion in the long-term.

CONCLUSION

Aquaculture companies, likely without intending to do so, challenge the human-nature binary. They emphasize the capacity for material place to shape oysters and, in turn, eaters; they present oysters as the present, past, and future all stitched together; and they organize themselves into new networks based on shared interests in water quality. Understanding the meanings attributed to aquaculture and oysters and the ways in which they have come to symbolize intimacy with diverse—and even divergent—phenomena illustrates areas of opportunity for adaptive capacity and gaps in the Virginia aquaculture narrative. Oysters and aquaculture are often painted as not only the *savor*, but also the *savior*, of the Chesapeake Bay and its coastal communities. At the same time, organizations and aquaculture companies demonstrate little appetite for acknowledging on their public-facing websites the challenges they will likely face in the future, even as companies on the Pacific coast are already adapting to the effects of climate change and ocean acidification.

In a climate changed world, what meanings will we attach to oysters? We can imagine that, in a future in which ocean acidification negates the possibility of raising oysters in the open water, they might be raised fully in tanks indoors. They may become even more "boutique" should indoor aquaculture make it impossible to produce them at the scale necessary for them to be sold at reasonable prices. Would this render them devoid of place-based meanings, as they would be raised indoors, in tanks, that are both "nowhere" and "everywhere"? And might they then take on more meanings related to technological innovation? Would the emphasis on oysters' effect on water quality disappear? Would losing this important connection to place render the sustainability narrative more difficult to spin? We would not expect that this narrative of oysters would "go quietly away," however, many (e.g., Stedman 2016; Cresswell 2015) have emphasized that place-based narratives often outlast the material reality of the place itself. Most simply, this is because vested interests make an active effort to maintain these meanings: as we have shown, they can be powerfully evocative to consumers.

Ironically, oysters on Virginia's Eastern Shore may actually stand to gain habitat as sea level rises, according to modeling research (Rodriguez et al. 2014; "Mapping Portal" n.d.), although this modeling does not take into account the future effects of ocean acidification. If shoreline protection methods continue employing human-constructed oyster reefs as part of "living shorelines" in the future, and they are successful in assisting communities in adapting to and mitigation climate change impacts, the notion of oysters as hybrid creatures, embodying and built on human and nonhuman processes, might persist. Each of our envisioned futures—featuring tanks, living shorelines, and increased habitat—maintains the oyster's entanglement with human and nonhuman elements, yet the nature of the meanings related to this hybridity might vary significantly and will undoubtedly change as the Anthropocene continues to unfold.

NOTES

1. "Waterman" is the regional term for independent fishermen who harvest a variety of organisms, including finfish, shellfish, and crabs (Maryland Sea Grant n.d.). Currently, there are more waterwomen than in the past, but "watermen" remains a blanket term and women remain underrepresented in the region's fisheries (Woolever 2016). We will use the term "fishers" throughout instead of watermen to avoid gendering the profession.

2. The location of Hog Island Bay is itself symbolic of the Shore's past. Hog Island once had a town and duck hunting lodges, but coastal erosion (an inevitable feature of barrier island life, even before current rates of sea level rise) sent the entire population to the mainland in the mid-twentieth century (Tennant 2011). It may be difficult to take the claim of "unspoiled" seriously in a geologic era named the Anthropocene, but the first author's anecdotal experience on the Eastern Shore suggests that the term is employed earnestly here, especially given the relative lack of water quality problems in Hog Island Bay in comparison to other places in Virginia that are closed or have been closed to shellfishing.

3. We are unable to say how many of the operators in our sample are White because the websites offer inconsistent information about owners, operators, and employees.

BIBLIOGRAPHY

"About." n.d. H.M. Terry Co., Inc.—Sewansecott Clams & Oysters. Accessed December 11, 2017. http://hmterry.com/about.

American Association for the Advancement of Science. n.d. "A Crippled Oregon Shellfish Hatchery Spawns Better Ocean Monitoring Systems." *How We Respond* (blog). Accessed May 28, 2020. https://howwerespond.aaas.org/community-spotlight/a-crippled-oregon-shellfish-hatchery-spawns-better-ocean-monitoring-systems/.

Anderson, Harold. 1998. "African Americans on the Chesapeake." *Maryland Marine Notes*, 1998.

"Anderson's Neck." n.d. Anderson's Neck Oyster Company. Accessed May 11, 2020. https://www.andersonsneck.com/.

"Aquaculture by Design." n.d. The Nature Conservancy. Accessed April 1, 2020. https://www.nature.org/en-us/about-us/where-we-work/priority-landscapes/chesapeake-bay/aquaculture-by-design-chesapeake-bay/.

Bryant, Raymond L. 2000. "Politicized Moral Geographies: Debating Biodiversity Conservation and Ancestral Domain in the Philippines." *Political Geography* 19 (6): 673–705.

Cannavò, Peter F. 2007. "Place: Founding and Preservation." In *The Working Landscape: Founding, Preservation, and the Politics of Place*. Cambridge, MA: MIT Press.

"Cherrystone Aqua-Farms." n.d. Cherrystone Aqua-Farms. Accessed July 23, 2020. https://clamandoyster.com/.

"Chincoteague Bay Field Station's Living Shoreline." n.d. Chincoteague Bay Field Station. Accessed February 23, 2018. http://www.cbfieldstation.org/living-shoreline.html.

City of Bainbridge Island. 2017. *Shoreline Master Program Limited Amendment-Aquaculture*. https://legistarweb-production.s3.amazonaws.com/uploads/attachment/pdf/248754/Draft_Submittal_Package_Overview_Final_021717.pdf.

Clements, Leslie. n.d. "Virginia Oysters at the Heart of It All For Love or Not for Love, That Is the Question." The Virginia Oyster Trail. Accessed May 20, 2020.

http://virginiaoystertrail.com/index.php/home/blog/virginia-oysters-at-the-heart-of -it-all.

Cohen, Anthony P. 1985. "Introduction." In *The Symbolic Construction of Community*, 11–38. Ellis Horwood Ltd.

"Conservation's Positive Economic Impacts for Virginia's Eastern Shore." n.d. The Nature Conservancy. https://www.nature.org/en-us/about-us/where-we-work/uni ted-states/virginia/stories-in-virginia/vcr-land-protection-overview/.

Cornwell, Jeff, Julie Rose, Lisa Kellogg, Mark Luckenbach, Suzanne Bricker, Ken Paynter, Chris Moore, Matt Parker, Larry Sanford, Bill Wolinski, et al. 2016. "Panel Recommendations on the Oyster BMP Nutrient and Suspended Sediment Reduction Effectiveness Determination Decision Framework and Nitrogen and Phosphorus Assimilation in Oyster Tissue Reduction Effectiveness for Oyster Aquaculture Practices," 197.

Cresswell, Tim. 2015. *Place: An Introduction*. Second. Malden, MA: Wiley-Blackwell.

Cuba, Lee, and David M. Hummon. 1993. "A Place to Call Home: Identification with Dwelling, Community, and Region." *The Sociological Quarterly* 34 (1): 111–31. https://doi.org/10.1111/j.1533-8525.1993.tb00133.x.

Demossier, Marion. 2016. "The Europeanization of Terroir: Consuming Place, Tradition, and Authenticity." In *European Identity and Culture: Narratives of Transnational Belonging*, edited by Rebecca Friedman and Markus Thiel, 119–36. New York, NY: Routledge.

Ekstrom, Julia A., Lisa Suatoni, Sarah R. Cooley, Linwood H. Pendleton, George G. Waldbusser, Josh E. Cinner, Jessica Ritter, Chris Langdon, Ruben van Hooidonk, Dwight Gledhill, et al. 2015. "Vulnerability and Adaptation of US Shellfisheries to Ocean Acidification." *Nature Climate Change* 5 (3): 207–14. https://doi.org/10 .1038/nclimate2508.

"Farm." 2013. Pleasure House Oysters. February 17, 2013. https://pleasurehouseoys-ters.com/farm/.

Farrier, David. 2019. *Anthropocene Poetics: Deep Time, Sacrifice Zones, and Extinction*. University of Minnesota Press.

Finley, Ben. 2017. "Wealthy Homeowners Take on Oystermen in War for the Coast." *Associated Press*, May 1, 2017, sec. Chesapeake Bay. https://apnews.com/da5e95 2082414e38bc8c03da2f2bcf95.

Fischler, Claude. 1988. "Food, Self and Identity." *Social Science Information* 27 (2): 275–92. https://doi.org/10.1177/053901888027002005.

Freudenberg, William R., Scott Frickel, and Robert Gramling. 1995. "Beyond the Nature/Society Divide: Learning to Think like a Mountain." *Sociological Forum* 10 (3): 361–92.

"From Seed to Market." n.d. Ruby Salts Oyster Company. Accessed December 11, 2017. http://rubysalts.com/the-farm/from-seed-to-market/.

Guerin, Ayasha. 2019. "Underground and at Sea: Oysters and Black Marine Entanglements in New York's Zone-A." *Shima* 13 (2).

Harvey, David. 1996. *Justice, Nature and the Geography of Difference*. Malden, MA: Blackwell Publishers Inc. https://www.amazon.com/Justice-Nature-Geography-Di fference-Harvey/dp/1557866813.

Haven-Tang, Claire, and Eleri Jones. 2005. "Using Local Food and Drink to Differentiate Tourism Destinations through Sense of Place." *Journal of Culinary Science and Technology* 4 (4): 69–86.

Held, Lisa Elaine. 2020. "With Restaurants Closed, Oyster Farmers Need Home Cooks to Start Shucking." *Washington Post*, April 29, 2020. https://www.washingt onpost.com/lifestyle/food/with-restaurants-closed-oyster-farmers-need-home-cooks-to-start-shucking/2020/04/28/7cf0b4be-8986-11ea-8ac1-bfb250876b7a_sto ry.html.

"Home." n.d. Lighthouse Oysters. Accessed June 1, 2020. http://lighthouseoyster .com/.

Hudson, Karen. 2017. "Virginia Shellfish Aquaculture Situation and Outlook Report: Results of the 2016 Virginia Shellfish Crop Reporting Survey." 2017–7. Gloucester Point, VA: Virginia Institute of Marine Science.

Hudson, Karen. 2019. "Virginia Shellfish Aquaculture Situation and Outlook Report: Results of the 2018 Virginia Shellfish Aquaculture Crop Reporting Survey." https://scholarworks.wm.edu/reports/2017.

Keilty, Kristina, Thomas M. Beckley, and Kate Sherren. 2016. "Baselines of Acceptability and Generational Change on the Mactaquac Hydroelectric Dam Headpond (New Brunswick, Canada)." *Geoforum* 75 (October): 234–48. https://do i.org/10.1016/j.geoforum.2016.08.001.

Khakzad, Sorna. 2018. "Promoting Coastal Communities through Cultural Tourism: The Case of Fishing Communities in Brunswick County, North Carolina." *Journal of Heritage Tourism* 13 (5): 455–71. https://doi.org/10.1080/1743873X.2017.13 91272.

Khakzad, Sorna, and David Griffith. 2016. "The Role of Fishing Material Culture in Communities' Sense of Place as an Added-Value in Management of Coastal Areas." *Journal of Marine and Island Cultures* 5 (2): 95–117. https://doi.org/10.1 016/j.imic.2016.09.002.

Krasny, Marianne E., Sarah R. Crestol, Keith G. Tidball, and Richard C. Stedman. 2014. "New York City's Oyster Gardeners: Memories and Meanings as Motivations for Volunteer Environmental Stewardship." *Landscape and Urban Planning* 132: 16–25. http://dx.doi.org/10.1016/j.landurbplan.2014.08.003.

Lusher, Amy, Peter Hollman, and Jeremy Mendoza-Hill. 2017. "Microplastics in Fisheries and Aquaculture: Status of Knowledge on Their Occurrence and Implications for Aquatic Organisms and Food Safety." *FAO Fisheries and Aquaculture Technical Paper; Rome*, no. 615. https://search.proquest.com/do cview/1932298451/abstract/CB7EBEF30DCE43CFPQ/2.

Madden, Etta M., and Martha L. Finch, eds. 2008. *Eating in Eden: Food and American Utopias*. University of Nebraska Press.

Mann, Roger, and Eric N. Powell. 2007. "Why Oyster Restoration Goals in the Chesapeake Bay Are Not and Probably Cannot Be Achieved." *Journal of Shellfish Research* 26 (4): 905–17. https://doi.org/10.2983/0730-8000(2007)26[905:WORG IT]2.0.CO;2.

"Mapping Portal." n.d. The Nature Conservancy: Coastal Resilience. Accessed July 22, 2020. https://maps.coastalresilience.org/.

Maryland Sea Grant. n.d. "Watermen." Maryland Sea Grant. Accessed July 24, 2020. https://www.mdsg.umd.edu/topics/watermen/watermen.

Mayfield, Dave. 2016. "The Oyster Cage Debate: Is There Enough Lynnhaven River for Everyone?" *The Virginian Pilot*, June 1, 2016. https://www.pilotonline.com/ne ws/environment/article_a688ec2f-561e-57b0-b59f-77e69f9fa7b4.html.

National Oceanic and Atmospheric Administration. 2017. *Oysters-Edu.* Photo. https ://www.flickr.com/photos/usoceangov/23627510708/.

Newell, Roger I. E., and Evamaria W. Koch. 2004. "Modeling Seagrass Density and Distribution in Response to Changes in Turbidity Stemming from Bivalve Filtration and Seagrass Sediment Stabilization." *Estuaries* 27 (5): 793–806. https:// doi.org/10.1007/BF02912041.

"Our Oysters." n.d. Rappahannock Oyster Company. Accessed June 1, 2020. https:// www.rroysters.com/oysters.

"Oyster Program." 2020. Friends of the Rappahannock. 2020. https://riverfriends.org /oysters/.

"Oyster Restoration in Virginia." 2018. The Nature Conservancy. https://www.nat ure.org/en-us/about-us/where-we-work/united-states/virginia/stories-in-virginia/oy ster-restoration-in-va/.

Paolisso, Michael. 2007. "Taste the Traditions: Crabs, Crab Cakes, and the Chesapeake Bay Blue Crab Fishery." *American Anthropologist* 109 (4): 654–65. https://doi.org/10.1525/aa.2007.109.4.654.

Paolisso, Michael, and Nicole Dery. 2010. "A Cultural Model Assessment of Oyster Restoration Alternatives for the Chesapeake Bay." *Human Organization* 69 (2): 169–79.

Penniman, Leah. 2018. *Farming While Black.* White River Junction, Vt.: Chelsea Green Publishing.

"Process." n.d. H.M. Terry Co., Inc.- Sewansecott Clams & Oysters. Accessed December 11, 2017. http://hmterry.com/process.

Raffles, Hugh. 2002. "Intimate Knowledge." *International Social Science Journal* 54 (173): 325–35.

Rappahannock Oyster Company. n.d. "About Us." Rappahannock Oyster Company. Accessed June 1, 2020. https://www.rroysters.com/about.

Rodriguez, Antonio B., F. Joel Fodrie, Justin T. Ridge, Niels L. Lindquist, Ethan J. Theuerkauf, Sara E. Coleman, Jonathan H. Grabowski, Michelle C. Brodeur, Rachel K. Gittman, Danielle A. Keller, and Matthew D. Kenworthy. 2014. "Oyster Reefs Can Outpace Sea-Level Rise." *Nature Climate Change* 4 (6): 493–97. https://doi.org/10.1038/nclimate2216.

Schoof, Rosalind A, and Jesse DeNike. 2017. "Microplastics in the Context of Regulation of Commercial Shellfish Aquaculture Operations." *Environmental Toxicology and Chemistry*, November, 522–27. https://doi.org/10.1002/ieam .1905.

Schulte, David M. 2017. "History of the Virginia Oyster Fishery, Chesapeake Bay, USA." *Frontiers in Marine Science* 4 (127).

"Shooting Point Salts®." n.d. Accessed December 2, 2017. http://www.shootingp ointoysters.com/Shooting-Point-Salts_ep_46.html.

Spears, John R. 1877. "Built on Stilts in an Accomack Salt Meadow: Much Wealth amid Odd Surroundings—The Tide Cleans the Streets—Water from beneath the Sea--The Wild Fowl." *The Sun*, May 7, 1877. http://eshore.iath.virginia.edu/nod e/1902.

Stedman, Richard C. 2002. "Toward a Social Psychology of Place: Predicting Behavior from Place-Based Cognitions, Attitude, and Identity." *Environment and Behavior* 34 (5): 561–81. https://doi.org/10.1177/0013916502034005001.

Stedman, Richard C. 2003. "Is It Really Just a Social Construction?: The Contribution of the Physical Environment to Sense of Place." *Society & Natural Resources* 16 (8): 671–85. https://doi.org/10.1080/08941920309189.

Stedman, Richard C. 2008. "What Do We 'Mean' by Place Meanings? Implications of Place Meanings for Managers and Practitioners." PNW-GTR-744. Understanding Concepts of Place in Recreation Research and Management. Portland, OR: U.S. Department of Agriculture, Forest Service, Pacific Northwest Research Station. https://doi.org/10.2737/PNW-GTR-744.

Stedman, Richard C. 2016. "Subjectivity and Social-Ecological Systems: A Rigidity Trap (and Sense of Place as a Way Out)." *Sustainability Science* 11: 891–901. https ://doi.org/10.1007/s11625-016-0388-y.

Stokowski, Patricia A. 2002. "Languages of Place and Discourses of Power: Constructing New Senses of Place." *Journal of Leisure Research* 34 (4): 368–82.

"Taking Care of the Bay." n.d. Accessed December 9, 2017. http://rubysalts.com/sust ainability/taking-care-of-the-bay/.

Tennant, Diane. 2011. "The Eastern Shore Island Left Behind." *Virginian-Pilot*, 2011, sec. Life & Culture, Life & Culture. https://www.pilotonline.com/life/article _12b4ad24-56a8-5c60-8f4f-e98efece65b2.html.

"The Shore." n.d. Ruby Salts Oyster Company. Accessed December 11, 2017. http:// rubysalts.com/the-farm/the-shore/.

The Virginia Oyster Trail - Where Delicious Adventures Await You! n.d. Accessed June 1, 2020. https://www.youtube.com/watch?v=R-IAW0I8atA&feature=emb _logo.

Tidball, Keith G. 2014a. "Seeing the Forest for the Trees: Hybridity and Social-Ecological Symbols, Rituals, and Resilience in Postdisaster Contexts." *Ecology and Society* 19 (4): 25.

Tidball, Keith G. 2014b. "Trees and Rebirth: Social-Ecological Symbols and Rituals in the Resilience of Post-Katrina New Orleans." In *Greening in the Red Zone: Disaster, Resilience and Community Greening*, edited by Keith G. Tidball and Marianne E. Krasny, 257–96. Dordrecht: Springer.

U.S. Army/Pamela Spaugy. 2014. *140413-A-ON889-009*. Photo. https://commons .wikimedia.org/wiki/File:140413-A-ON889-009_(13894853223).jpg.

"USDA/NASS QuickStats Ad-Hoc Query Tool." n.d. Accessed December 11, 2017. https://quickstats.nass.usda.gov/results/409DB6EA-4905-3F9F-AA80-1BBF2 E6A3DC5.

"Virginia Oyster Gardening." n.d. Chesapeake Bay Foundation. Accessed May 19, 2020. https://www.cbf.org/how-we-save-the-bay/programs-initiatives/virginia/ oyster-restoration/oyster-gardening/index.html.

Wallace, Richard K, Phillip Waters, and F Scott Rikard. 2008. "Oyster Hatchery Techniques." Southern Regional Aquaculture Center.

"Why Choose Ruby Salts?" n.d. Ruby Salts Oyster Company. Accessed December 11, 2017. http://rubysalts.com/why-choose-ruby-salts/.

Woolever, Lydia. 2016. "Waterwomen." *Baltimore Magazine*, July 11, 2016. Https://www.baltimoremagazine.com/. https://www.baltimoremagazine.com/2016/7/11/waterwomen-a-handful-of-heroines-work-the-chesapeake-bay.

York River Oysters. n.d. "York River Oysters." Accessed June 1, 2020. http://www.yorkriveroysters.com/#.

Chapter 9

i am naiad

Becoming Benthic

laura c carlson

We of the Benthos
who resist impoundment
who deny all binary
We who are of nothing except each other in all things
Our softnesses entwine molecularly
Our membranes dispossess singularity
We are limestone, shell, and egg

Water nymphs known as naiads were ancient Greek immortals intrinsic to and stewards of bodies of freshwater. Worshiped by humans, naiads were protectors of water worthy of ritual sacrifice. Naiad is an epithet for freshwater mussels, water guardians themselves who filter pollutants from rivers, exhaling clarified water and nutrients—a power one might feel called to worship—all while nestled seemingly safely inside their nacreous body homes.

In ancient Greek, naiad means *to flow*. The freshwater of the Earth has flowed through the bodies of mussels for ages, tasting of the world. That taste has altered. Freshwater mussels are now one of the most imperiled families of animals in the world. Of the 300 or so species in the United States, 70 percent are endangered, threatened, or already extinct (Haag 2012).

reciprocally We cleanse shared responsibilities of being, of survival
but We cannot atone for aggregations of commercial farm pesticide runoff
—industrial chemical waste, thermal pollution, sewage
We are impounded for your domination

Figure 9.1 "i am naiad: Becoming Benthic," Performance Still, 2019. *Credit*: laura c carlson.

i am naiad: Becoming Benthic is a mythopoeic embodiment of freshwater mussels' ancient and continued stewardship of the waterways (figure 9.1). Recounting geologic time and detailing seizures of land and water from indigenous peoples and nonhumans, *naiad* acts as a proxy between humans and mussel imperilment that stems from colonial praxes of domination. *naiad* calls out the dredging, damming, extraction, and pesticide runoff that my fellow (Anglo-European) people place upon the scapes of this world, believing our right to water and land to be god-given.

—a fractured river forbids vibrancy—
they extract beneaths for transitory capital demanding passage as a
   birthright, mechanized existence a dogma of "inevitability"
they cannot discard us
existence is not a resource—they name us ecosystem
   engineers, price tag Our impact
congesting us into categories of predetermined anthro-worth

naiad's ambition is to encourage intimacy through embodiment and communication through metamorphosis. Through narrative singing, multiple histories and knowledges are forged together, acknowledging complicated pasts and heralding wondrous futures.

in Our imperiled times We stress entangled temporalities.
—the exigencies of each moment and of all instances—
each filtration is unforetold except by the auguries of possibility
that kindle among us.
It is story singing for survival
 urge listening, become Benthic.

Can I speak with and for another species? One who lacks the communicative apparatuses humans would find familiar? Am I ventriloquizing mussels or are mussels rhapsodizing through my flesh? It is only interspecies speculation.

In terms of anthropomorphism, I call for musselizing the self. Eschewing anthropodenial (De Waal 1997), I can disarm the trepidations of many simply by appearing in a paper-mâché shell shrouded in found fabrics and landscape detritus. My metamorphosis invites curiosity (figure 9.2).

Squish your toes into a lake bottom, a riverbed, the belly of a pond. This is the Benthos, all the flora and fauna which make life in the substrates of water.

to become one of the Benthos
Submerge. And reEMERGE. Coalesce.
Rework Our relations
to ancient and appended ways of being.
Attend to your breaths—as you filter oxygen through your cavities,
   allowing the air to touch your insides reciprocally.
Lull your mouths to open to a multi-sensorial world

The Benthos is both and neither terrestrial and/nor aquatic. It is a *between* and an *among*. It does not negate the seemingly binary environments but unites

Figure 9.2 **"i am naiad: Becoming Benthic," Performance Still, 2019.** *Credit*: laura c carlson.

them. The Benthos is a vesica piscus, where the circle of the named world and the circle of the unnamable, the untamable, and the unknowable can be in conversation. By becoming Benthic, we can begin to imagine the ooze and the squish of being alive.

Release. Soften your sensory organs
think with the juices of your body, decompose a dogma of self.
Sink your matter into a between world
let Us culture ourselves in the viscous malleability of the natural world.
Let Us become pulp, mush, Earth's sebum

Naiad articulates that the colonial structures impeding Benthic verve are not inevitabilities of human progress; rather, we are part of a vast and entangled cosmological system that is embedded in multiple realms of existence. How can we reperceive (in)evitability of place and time? What kind of hopeful futures can we form?

embody Our vulnerabilities—Our marshy insides mirror your flesh
think with the juices of your body in perpetual decomposition
become one body with which We can rupture verse for revelations
    outside of the myopic obscurations of Our own natures.
Decompose semiotic boundaries to be in cohesive flux with Us—
We are naiad here of Benthic spirit
give your spirit away to the great untold Benthos—in which
    our bodies disperse for interconnected self-soup.
Here it is
    the Benthos.

ACKNOWLEDGMENTS

Special thanks to my fellow artists and writers in residence and Bilpin International Ground for Creative Initiatives where this project was produced and performed. I am indebted to all those individuals who fiscally supported residency and research.

BIBLIOGRAPHY

De Waal, Frans. 1997. "Are We in Anthropodenial?" *Discover* 18 (7): 50–53.
Haag, Wendell R. 2012. *North American Freshwater Mussels: Natural History, Ecology, and Conservation.* New York: Cambridge University Press.

Chapter 10

Ada Clapham Govan and "Birds I Know"

Ecological Intimacy in a Mass-Mediated Sisterhood

Peter W. Oehlkers and Anna Ijiri Oehlkers

From 1932 to 1966, the *Boston Globe* ran a correspondence column titled "Birds I Know," featuring women writing letters to each other about their experiences with wild birds. Part of the *Globe*'s long-running "Confidential Chat," in which "sisters" using pseudonyms shared useful household tips and relationship advice, the "bird column" sustained its nature-oriented community within a framework of social support. Guiding the column for almost its entire run was Ada Clapham Govan, whose 1940 book *Wings at my Window* (composed of much column material) became a significant influence on the writing of Rachel Carson. If communication in the Anthropocene demands greater recognition of our enmeshment with nonhumans, "Birds I Know" is a landmark moment when the platform of a major newspaper, with a distinctly female perspective, created a space for communicating about everyday interactions with the more-than-human world.

This chapter looks at the column and the individual contributions of Ada Govan with special attention to their connections with the topic of ecological intimacy. "Birds I Know" stressed relational knowledge and promoted an ethic of care with respect to birds and fellow writers that was largely therapeutic. The column has a special resonance with the COVID-19 era in its exploration of the mental and emotional health benefits of connecting with wild birdlife, and its special devotion to helping "shut-ins" connect vicariously through the experiences of column writers.

This chapter is not intended as an exhaustive overview of the column but as an introduction aimed at bringing it, and Govan, back into the conversation. In preparation for this chapter, the authors did extensive searches of the

Boston Globe digital archive, logging and categorizing over 5,000 individual letters. This chapter uses extended excerpts from these letters to illustrate the themes above, with the goal of, as much as possible, presenting Govan's and other writers' voices.

OVERVIEW

The correspondence format in the *Boston Globe* dates back to 1884 (Golia 2016, 618) when the paper first introduced a Household Column and invited women readers (using *noms de plume*, or "*noms*," as they became known) to contribute letters around a range of topics from recipes to motherhood. These letters, while sometimes addressed to the general readership, were frequently addressed to individual writers, creating a virtual network of friendships. This, as has been noted (Clark and Hench 1991), was both a throwback to an earlier correspondent-based, knowledge-exchange mode of journalism and an "in-print" (Golia 2012) version of the online communities and discussion forums of today. In 1912, the *Globe* introduced the name "Confidential Chat." It had dedicated space in the Household/Women's section of the *Globe* until 2006. The feature provided a system of social support and mutual help for women who might otherwise be socially isolated.

Chat participants were drawn from the *Globe*'s broad area of circulation during this period, which included the Boston area but also significant readerships in the rest of New England. Clippings were also shared by mail and often collected in scrapbooks. By all indications, correspondents were almost entirely white, middle-class women. Male writers were not excluded (in fact, some were openly welcomed) but were expected to identify themselves. It was typical for writers to refer to each other as "sisters."

A special Chat column devoted to wild birds was first proposed by a writer from New Hampshire with the nom "Troubadour," in a letter to "Priscilla." The following excerpt provides a taste of the themes and the tone of the column to come:

> I could study, write, meditate over, hunt (just to study) forever and a day—birds. At present I have a sweet little mother chipping sparrow sitting on four little eggs in a nest built in our rose bush, directly in front of my window here. In a low shrub near a lane sits a dear little chestnut-sided warbler in her nest of four eggs. They are a dainty bird and not too shy. Then, too, a tiny chebec, or least flycatcher, is sitting on her downy soft nest in a small apple tree. Today I think I shall find a veery's nest. . . . Who else in the column are interested in birds? We have a flowers and plants department, why not one for the birds? Won't those who are interested write some of their experiences? Or perhaps describe

those they have seen, but do not know. Some of us may be able to answer questions. Let's have a bird page in our Globe book. Will you write again, Priscilla? (Troubadour 1932, 27)

Letters responding to Troubadour's proposal were published under the header "Birds I Know" starting on August 22, 1932. This header would be used for the next thirty-plus years to organize the correspondence in the Chat related to wild birds. "Birds I Know" did not have a regular publication schedule but was dependent on the volume of correspondence and the space available in the Household section. Sometimes it would appear daily, other times once or twice a month. Indeed, one of the running themes of the column was the need to bring it back to life during the lean periods. Except for a lull of activity during the years of World War II, the column ran somewhat regularly until the mid-1950s, when a new editorial policy, prioritizing shorter and more general interest contributions, took hold and the frequency and length of letters declined. The last column using the "Birds I Know" header was August 28, 1966.

A typical letter to the column would address either a specific writer, with comments about a previous letter, or address the "sisters" of the bird column as a whole. Some participants were active birders and described their bird walks and year lists. Most, however, wrote about the birds that came to their feeders and nested in their yards, often with identification queries or news about unusual visitors, such as evening grosbeaks.

One correspondent, writing under the *nom* "Of Thee I Sing," quickly became the dominant "Birds I Know" contributor. Ada Clapham Govan had been a Chat "sister" for decades under different *noms*. From 1911 to 1918, writing as "Redeemed" and then "Disillusioned," she had first-hand knowledge of the level of emotional support the column community could provide, following the deaths of her two young daughters. By the time she returned the column as "Of Thee I Sing," Govan had become a large-scale bird feeder and a prolific bird-bander, able to provide species identification support and bird-feeding advice. Her most popular contributions were the stories she told about the birds who fed and nested in the woods behind her house. Here is an early (1932) sample in a letter to "Meadowford," that combines ornithological knowledge about plumage and individual characterization, plus a bit of tragedy:

You asked about a certain goldfinch. He was a most disreputable-looking little fellow. His coat, which should have been clear gold, was mixed with faded green as though he had not properly molted, and his little black hat was shoved half over one eye. I first noticed that he preferred to sit down to his meals. Like the Romans of old, he ate reclining at ease. Then I discovered that while his feet had the power to grip a branch or the rim of the bird bath, his legs were absolutely unable to hold him upright. He fluttered from seed to seed, but could not walk. . . . "Limpy" was probably the smallest one of his mother's brood, the stronger sisters and brothers getting the main share of the food. Insufficiently-nourished birdlings suffer the consequences just as human children do . . .

"Limpy" stayed with us for several months, a happy and beloved pet. I saw a blue jay jump him one day as he sat contentedly among the seeds. I heard his wild shriek of pain and fright, saw him flutter away. Whether he died from his wound I shall never know, but we never saw him again. (Of Thee I Sing 1932, 36)

"Of Thee I Sing"/Govan became the central, guiding figure in "Birds I Know," sharing her experience and philosophy with her "Bird Sisters" until her death in 1964. Even while she was inactive in the column, which could be for years at a time, she remained a background presence and correspondents continued to address letters to her.

INTIMATE KNOWLEDGE

Govan approached her study of bird behavior with the starting assumption that birds could be considered individuals with subjectivities. Banding and sustained observation allowed her intimate access to individuals, and also warranted her use of names for individual birds, as well as the domestic dramas she told about them. She was fully conscious that her way was different from mainstream ornithology. In a 1935 letter to "A Fool There Was," she described how her writing maintained a sense of wonder that was often stifled by "experts":

I'll go my irresponsible way, knowing that father redbreast sang a lilting, lovely, good night song to the Lady of Eaves Corner, and the song was like unto no other robin's song, being hers and hers only; he loved her, and the three babies that were hers and his lay cuddled close beneath her breast. It wasn't the rousing, caroling song that a male robin sings at nightfall; it was muted and low—a lullaby and a promise: "Fear not, deary, I am near thee—standing by, my dear—never fear, my dear—cheerio—cheerio—" And those experts call that "cheery-up cheerily." Can you imagine it! How do I know the right words? Because I heard father redbreast say them myself. And I understand robinese. (Of Thee I Sing 1935, 25)

Other writers about birds have chosen this individual approach, most notably Margaret Morse Nice, in her landmark study of song sparrows, retold in narrative form in *The Watcher at the Nest* (1939). Indeed, Nice's description of her approach as "phenomenological" (Nice 1964, 2) far predates more contemporary uses of that term (such as Lestel, Bussonlini, and Chrulew 2014). But Govan's reference to understanding "robinese" makes her closer to a figure like Len Howard (1952), another amateur naturalist, whose sustained and intimate observations of birds in and around her English cottage have only recently been brought back into the conversation by Eva Meijer (2018). "Experts'" dismissals of sentimentality meant they were unable to enter the emotional space of the nonhumans they studied. As Govan and Howard understood, bird songs are not just about territory and mate attraction; they can also be used in more subtle and intimate ways.

This tension between "expert" knowledge and relational knowledge is embedded in the column title "Birds I Know" itself. On the one hand, it speaks of the hierarchical urge toward knowledge mastery that pervades the world of birding, with its identification challenges and competitive lists. This aspect was not absent from the column, but in keeping with the overall support function of the Chat, identification corrections were typically done gently, with an eye toward relationship protection, and lists were treated as achievements to be shared, not lorded over others. In a 1937 letter to "Dream Birds," Govan, who had offered an unexciting answer ("you saw a blue jay") to an identification query that was then rejected by the original author, commented,

> Now why run out on us when we all just getting nicely acquainted? You've gained an altogether wrong impression of this column. It really is for people who desire to learn more about birds. The more questions you have to ask, the better we'll all like you. What if you don't know much about birds? Come along in and you'll soon know more. Don't be sensitive regarding mistakes. Funny ones are bound to create amusement but anyone who would ridicule an honest mistake is a person you wouldn't want to know anyway. There isn't one person of that breed in this column. Sincere bird lovers are too keenly aware of their own mistakes, past, present and future, to ridicule another's. Mistakes are assets if you learn something from them. (Of Thee I Sing 1937a, 25)

On the other hand, "Birds I Know" speaks of relational knowledge, the birds one knows personally. As another prolific column writer, "Wing Flashes," wrote in a letter to "Tyro":

> There are two ways to study birds—scientifically or otherwise. I began too late for the first way, but not too late to get many happy experiences from my acquaintance with them. The doctor knows more about my neighbor than I do, but I know my neighbor better than the doctor does. So let me know my birds

as I know my neighbor and they will always be a pleasure to me. (Wing Flashes 1941, 24)

While few other column writers had the opportunity to study birds as intensely as Govan did (indeed, one enduring column trope was the writer's pause during some household task to watch the birds at the feeder) some did adopt her storytelling style. Overall, the approach worked to personalize birds and drew other readers to take the same perspective. As one long-time Chat sister, "Baltimore Oriole" asserted, in a 1939 letter to "Of Thee I Sing," "You made the birds so very understandable—so intensely interesting—that I've gone right along with you from the very first. Now my birds are individuals, and even our children know a purple finch from a chickadee" (Baltimore Oriole 1939, 26).

Govan knew that she ran the risk of being accused of anthropomorphizing birds (see Crist 1999 for a critique of this charge), but laughed it off. In a 1947 comment to "Souhegan" she wrote, "When you add that I make my birds seem like 'little people' it pleases me immensely but it makes me obnoxious to the scientific ornithologist; at least most of them. Who cares!" (Of Thee I Sing 1947, 21).

Govan's treatment of birds as individuals, enmeshed in social relationships, was key to opening up relationships between them and humans. Govan made this clear in a 1934 comment to "Snow Baby," "Remember that you must win the friendship of the birds just as you must win your human friends—by learning to know each other" (Of Thee I Sing 1934b, 24).

It was not simple "connection" to nature that Govan promoted in her stories but socio-emotional relationships—"friendships." While Govan generally did not encourage wild birds to fly in and out of her house (unlike Len Howard, who invited them to become members of the household), she would, during particularly severe weather or shrike attacks, give them access through her bedroom window.

That women might have a special ability to understand the domestic side of birdlife has long been used both to encourage the contributions of women in the field and to limit the scope of their contributions (Norwood 1993, 43). While Govan regarded herself publicly as an "inexpert" amateur naturalist, she made contributions recognized by the ornithological community via her bird banding efforts, particularly with respect to the large flocks of purple finches which visited her yard, and the rose-breasted grosbeak, five of whom she hosted as indoor companions during the last decades of her life. Her overall relationship with scientific ornithology, however, could be regarded as tense and marked with a sense of gender-based injustice. In a 1954 letter to "Woodsie One" she wrote,

Sometimes we lesser lights trot out a piece of news that is a real shock for some of the Big Boys. I have been told, politely, more than once, that I had a "vivid imagination" when the gentlemen were dying to say, "You're an unmitigated liar!" Ha! We live, learn and go right on enjoying our own discoveries even after we are slapped down. I had the satisfaction of twice making one big male eat his own words. (Of Thee I Sing 1954, 8)

The *Globe*, it should be noted, ran the last sentence as the headline with the word "never" inserted before "had," an error that Govan corrected in a subsequent letter (Of Thee I Sing 1955, 14).

Nevertheless, Govan's "friendship" approach to bird knowledge was taken up by other writers, including the Canadian nature writer Louise de Kiriline Lawrence (see Greer and Bols 2016). Edwin A. Mason, in a 1943 article about bird banding, even suggested that this approach might be the best way to expand bird knowledge, particularly during the travel-restricted war years to come, referencing this as "the less exacting realm where friendliness is the key which unlocks the door giving access to a more intimate knowledge of our bird neighbors" (Mason 1943, 244).

CARE AND THE ANTHROPOCENE

Govan repeatedly claimed that she was "saved" by the birds. *Wings at my Window* is framed by the story of a would-be invalid who gained strength through her intense focus on bird feeding, banding, and protection. In a 1936 letter to "Knocklofty Dreams," she provided some details about her salvation:

Humanity, in general, seems loaded down with gloomy forebodings. Nor is it to be wondered at, for often there seems no place left where honest decency has a chance. But always when I get that low Chicky calls me. Calls me as on that December day almost six years ago when I first saw him clinging to the railing, storm-battered and hungry, but blithely caroling "Things could be heaps worse!" Every motion was agony till I heard that voice, but somehow I threw him some crumbs which he barely sampled before he was swept away by the blizzard, leaving me in such a mental turmoil as rivaled the storm without.

For I had just resigned myself to an invalid's life—I'd be the happiest invalid that ever could be—but a burden, nevertheless. And then I heard their voices—saw them coming—Chicky! And all the relatives and friends he could scrape together on such short notice. He had only gone to call to the feast others less fortunate that they might share his bit of good fortune. (Of Thee I Sing 1936b, 21)

Helping "shut-ins" experiencing social isolation reconnect with a community had long been a mission for Confidential Chat participants. Govan's personal story resonated. This therapeutic relationship with birds could be extended via the column to those unable to leave their beds or homes. Writers self-identifying as invalids or experiencing debilitating ailments were eagerly embraced. When, for example, the Chat sister "Thru the Window Pane" became confined to her bed in 1936 writers took turns describing the bird scenes as they appeared through their own windows for her (see for example a letter from "Scarlet Tanager" (1936, 26)). Other writers testified how the column had helped them. "Calla Ann," 1947 letter wrote, "I wonder if you who write realize how much pleasure you give to us shut-ins and stay-at-homes. I enjoy my birds mostly through my windows, but I enjoy yours through the Globe" (Calla Ann 1947, 29).

In a 1942 letter Govan made it clear that her despair "went down before an intense desire to help and protect the wee bird so bravely battling the blizzard" (Of Thee I Sing 1942, 35). Sisters of the bird column should not only incorporate birds into their friendship networks but would benefit by caring for them. Other "sisters" agreed. "Warped Halo," in a 1934 letter to "Of Thee I Sing," wrote,

> I have fed them for a number of years, but never so—how shall I put it?—so thoroughly as this Winter. And this terrible Winter they certainly needed it. What a pleasure it is, too, to feel that I have helped even a few to come through the cold more comfortably. So you see that by fanning the flame of my interest you have not only helped your birds but have given me pleasure as well. And I have sorely needed something to help me bear an almost unbearable heartache. So thank you, dear lady, for helping us, the birds and me, to weather the Winter. (Warped Halo 1934, 27)

Govan's care for birds was extensive, her feeder arrays requiring hundreds of dollars a year to maintain—during the Depression. She advocated summer feeding and the building of nesting boxes as well. The practice of bird feeding, as Jones (2018) details, has become controversial in recent years, as it has become apparent that most birds don't need it, and because of disease transmission, can even be harmed by it. Anticipating the arguments of the German ornithologist Peter Berthold (Jones 2018, 91) about bird feeding as a human obligation in the Anthropocene, Govan argued that her help was necessary because "Nature" had been fundamentally disrupted by human activity. When a rare male correspondent, signing his letters "A Mere Man" criticized the popular correspondent "Knay Knay" for constructing nesting boxes (Nature did a better job), Govan responded,

Certainly no one wants to give to A Mere Man the impression that the sentimental feminists have just been awaiting a chance to gang up on him. Nevertheless I echo your surprise that anyone so well-versed in bird knowledge should remain unaware that our song birds haven't lived in a normal bird world since man introduced the alien English sparrow and the starling into this country. For these two foreigners promptly cornered the natural food and building sites of many of our most valuable and beautiful birds. Then man got busy on his own behalf. He cemented the holes in his trees and fence posts to prolong their lives and usefulness, completely forgetting that he was cutting down almost the last chance our birds had to survive in orchards and woodlots. Clearing out the underbrush and use of the poison spray gun climaxed the grand finale for several useful species that for generations had been local residents. . . . What could be a happier compromise for you than to get the birds you want, by giving them the houses they want? Indeed, the houses they need, because so many thoughtless people have remembered only their own interests, regardless of the birds whose world they have destroyed. (Of Thee I Sing 1940, 28)

About summer feeding, she wrote:

I am sure you needn't worry about spoiling the birds. For the little spoiling they get, man certainly sees to it that they pay with plenty of man-made hardships. Their natural food is sprayed with poison and birds eat the insects—and die. Their natural nesting sites are either filled with cement to conserve the life of the trees or else burned over through man's criminal carelessness. And while man expects the birds to clear his produce of insect life, how he does resent it when the birds appropriate some of the fruit they help to save! A little extra planting for the birds could largely take care of this. Birds have plenty of natural enemies, so I'm for coddling them in every way I can to make up, in part, for the extra troubles they really don't need. (Of Thee I Sing 1939, 26)

Govan was intensely concerned with larger environmental matters, directly critical of what she saw as the greed and commercialization pervading American society. While "Birds I Know" was not generally concerned with these matters, there was a consistent concern with habitat loss due to commercial development in the suburbs, as well as the possible effect of poison sprays on birdlife. These concerns were often triggered by community-wide observations that the numbers of birds visiting yards and feeders had declined. In a 1936 letter, "Of Thee I Sing" addressed her "Dear Bird Sisters,"

During the last three Winters the south has suffered severely and no doubt a heavy toll has been taken on the birds seeking sanctuary there. Droughts, floods, and gales that blow uncounted thousands out to sea, where they are drowned, have taken a terrible toll on the migrating flocks. And to crown it all, man seems to have deliberately chosen these same years for destroying brush that has always provided the natural nesting grounds for hundreds of thousands of birds—and one wonders how long it can all go on. Is this the start of an alarming and definite decline in our birds? Who else has noticed anything unusual? (Of Thee I Sing 1936a, 18)

Mary-Jayne Rust (2012), in her writing about ecological intimacy, notes that accompanying the therapeutic value of nature connection is direct exposure to its traumas. Her emotional connections with the nonhuman world left Govan vulnerable to depression when she experienced its destruction. In 1937, developers began cutting down the woods behind her house. In a letter to Chat elder "Entre Nous," she told about her experience:

March 3, I heard an ax down where my mourning doves nest and by night a dozen trees had crashed. The woodchopper told me the entire hillside was to be cleared—for house lots.

   People had assured me the woods would be safe for years to come, but last Fall I knew some danger threatened. That day of crashing trees was an unforgettable nightmare! Impossible for me to stay here listening, day after day, while my ideal went down in ruins. For those woods have long been my church, and the trees have taught me peace and understanding. They are the only religion that satisfies my needs.

   . . . For weeks I couldn't write or even think; the shock was as great as if a loved one had been destroyed before my eyes. . . . The birds and trees are a vital part of me I can't live without. . . .

   So—when the woods and old orchard go down, another sacrifice to civilization, so, too, must pass the birds of my little kingdom. They have been my solace when it seemed as if nothing could heal. (Of Thee I Sing 1937b, 26)

The supportive context of the "Birds I Know" community, however, allowed these traumas to be shared. Bird column "sisters" immediately came to her aid, offering sympathy and their own experiences. For example, "Nature Lover No. II" wrote:

I always think of the dear birds when I think of your nom. I want to tell you how very much I sympathize with you and how sorry I am that you are threatened with the loss of your bird sanctuary—the beautiful trees and homes of the birds you have cared for and loved. I hope it may be possible for you to keep at least a part of the woods for your birds.

I know so well how you feel at the possible desecration for I went through such a thing though I did not have a bird sanctuary. Seeing and hearing the woods being destroyed went to my heart, knowing too it meant the birds' houses and shelters. I would leave home for several hours whenever I could, it affected me so. And what a desolate waste—a no-man's-land as I called it, stumps and files of twigs and branches.

How can people be so ruthless not to see the beauty of a tree, not to hear, see, and know the beauty of birds? (Nature Lover II 1937, 21)

Govan eventually received material support from anonymous donors via an appeal in *Nature Magazine*, which allowed her to protect the property (it still exists as a small protected space in the Lexington, Massachusetts suburbs), but she publicly credited the sisters of the bird column for creating the conditions that allowed it to happen. The column community meant that she did not have to face the traumatic side of ecological intimacy alone.

Emotional connectedness with nonhumans also means the absence of impartiality when it comes to your "friends" and their perceived enemies (see Oehlkers and Hafen (2015) about the conflict between bird and cat-allied humans). If there is a jarring note for contemporary readers of "Birds I Know," it is the community's treatment of certain bird species. Letters frequently told about the hawks, shrikes, and even blue jays that were shot and killed to protect smaller birds at the feeders. To some extent, this was an officially sanctioned act, intended to protect birds "useful" to human agriculture (see Haraway's critique of the ecological services paradigm in Haraway, Ishikawa, et al. 2016).

Govan herself shot blue jays on occasion, though she realized that not all "Birds I Know" sisters agreed with this action. In a 1933 response to "Dorchester Bird Lover" Govan admitted:

Yes, I'm the guilty party you are looking for. Unfortunately, our blue jays don't come sailing in pairs—they come in battalions. Even so, I couldn't hit a barn door unless I was first roused to the boiling point by some jay atrocity. I'm endeavoring to make life easier for all species that are willing to "live and let live," consequently I can't turn this small sanctuary into a blue jays' Paradise. It is a refuge for the weak, and I refuse to encourage the smaller birds to come here under my protection only to turn them over to the blue jays for tidbits. . . .

There is no live and let live where the jay is concerned. He hogs everything. Many of my friends can no longer afford to put out food because the jays steal it all. . . . Don't forget that many of our song birds have been driven from their natural nesting grounds and feeding places, while, the race being to the strong, the jays have increased alarmingly out of proportion. Water is never denied the jays, and in Winter food is put on the farther side of the stone wall for them. They are given every chance to behave themselves, and I don't even seek to impose an unnatural diet on father jay's wife and family. Father is welcome to garner his egg produce wheresoever he will—save here. Otherwise it's bye-bye, blue jay. There might better be tears in the jay home than in the songbird's. (Of Thee I Sing 1933, 27)

At first glance, this violent prejudice against blue jays may seem to be inappropriately rooted in human moral standards. (Note that Len Howard (1953, 14) had a similar attitude toward magpies, which fill a similar ecological niche, and also flourish in a human-centered world.) It can be argued, however, that it was based in the very situation of ecological intimacy. Govan sympathized with the smaller, oppressed, birds in her care and related to the traumas they were experiencing. Indeed, when the blue jays themselves became victims, Govan was quick to offer her protection. In a 1934 letter to "Dusk at Sea," she wrote:

Even the blue jays look like cherubs to me now. Having lived for several months in the midst of a slaughtering pen for the maintenance of shrikes and a couple of hawks, the jays have been fed as never before. I have not allowed them in the yard but every day one to two quarts of the same food that goes to my own birds, is put on the wall for the jays. . . . Kindness can't be centered in just the things we personally love, and to kill starving creatures for raiding our feeding stations is unthinkable. (Of Thee I Sing 1934a, 25)

Compassion was the key to overruling her impulse to "run the universe." Eventually Govan would come to ("almost") pity her friends' enemy, a Cooper's hawk (Govan 1943, 97).

Govan's fellow correspondent "Wing Flashes" may have articulated the situation best for readers of the column. In a 1942 to letter to "Chirping," she remarked about the contingencies and compromises that accompany human behavior toward threats to songbirds:

Let's look this thing straight in the eye. Can we blame the cat for catching the bird and justify ourselves for eating chicken? We can't say that's different, for there's nothing different about it excepting the method of approach. And we can't say it's necessary.

If starlings or blue jays or hawks raise havoc with the plans of a favorite songbird and a rifle is in hand and our aim good, something is apt to happen, not in the raider's favor, I fear. So it is evident that individuals draw the line where ever need or interest direct. We take advantage of our dominion and establish priority in the animal kingdom according to our whims. (Wing Flashes 1942, 47)

As Linda Vance (1993, 135) suggests about ecofeminism generally, a "degree of uncertainty and disagreement" should be accepted in such matters. No absolute answer was possible or appropriate. Nevertheless as "Wing Flashes" cautioned the community, humans often fail to recognize when the protection of their nonhuman allies from would-be persecutors, such as cats or shrikes, is just another form of persecution. This kind of "care" needs to be tempered not only with compassion but with a firm eye on the power relationship between humans and nonhumans.

THE LEGACY OF "BIRDS I KNOW" AND ADA CLAPHAM GOVAN

"Birds I Know" should be regarded as a landmark in the history of mass media and environmental communication, unique in its combination of women's support network, wild bird focus, and large, general circulation platform. This chapter has tried to show how its emphasis on relational knowledge and care makes it a model for communicating ecological intimacy in the Anthropocene. Its direct legacy, however, is less clear. The "Birds I Know" column has been largely forgotten. We can find no reference to the column in either the environmental media or birding literature. When the column was discontinued in 1966, one of the explanations was that the topic was outdated, unappealing to contemporary readers who were more interested in the social issues of the day (Mass Moments 2020). In fact, as "Birds I Know" wound down in the late 1950s, it was effectively replaced by a more conventional bird column, "The Private Life of Birds," written by former managing editor, Lucien H. Thayer, who took a standard ornithological approach to his objects of study and used his own expertise to answer questions from readers. It is only been recently that the prevailing emphasis on mastery, competition, and objective observation (not to mention open misogyny) in contemporary birding has been challenged, most notably by Molly Adams and the Feminist Bird Club (Evans 2019).

Ada Govan's book *Wings at my Window* remained in print into the mid-1970s and she was the sole female contributing editor on the masthead of *The Bulletin of the Massachusetts Audubon Society* for many years. While she has been recently cited as a prominent bird feeder "during hard times" (Barker, Henderson, and Baicich 2015), her name has been largely forgotten in the birding and ornithological communities. Govan's influence on Rachel Carson (they were mutual admirers with an intense correspondence) is well-documented (Lear 1998, 127-130); Carson's resulting emphasis on "wonder" and her deliberate attempt to write in a way that appealed to a general audience is Govan's most distinct legacy (Lear 1998, 129). We hope that this chapter will help to re-establish "Of Thee I Sing" as an important voice in the history of environmental communication.

In an intellectual climate driven by concerns about the Anthropocene, more receptive to phenomenological approaches to understanding nonhumans and more supportive of an ethics of care in our relationships with them, "Birds I Know" and "Of Thee I Sing"/Ada Govan have a renewed relevance. The relatively mundane activity of watching birds at one's feeder has new meaning when viewed as a means of connecting human and bird social networks across species lines.

Indeed, in the wake of COVID-19, bird watching has emerged as a favored activity (Flaccus 2020), humans closing their social distance with nonhumans while they physically distance themselves from other humans. This activity, in turn, has become a way for people to connect via digital media. As Kirsten Schrader in her June 2020 editorial in *Birds & Blooms* put it, "In this trying time, sharing bird sightings is keeping us together even though we're working miles apart" (Schrader 2020, 6).

The popular "Birds I Know" sister, "Hope and Prayer," who eventually became one of Govan's confidants, was frequently house- and hospital-bound because of tuberculosis. Her husband built a bird feeder that extended into the house so that she could continue to observe birds and share her experiences in the column from her bed. In 1952 she wrote to "Hiawatha" about her transformation due to this experience:

> As time passes, we find that what we thought was living was merely an existence of hustle and bustle. . . . Today I am grateful for the illness that opened my heart, mind and eyes so that when health has reached its full restoration, it will be like being reborn into the same, yet a new world. (Hope and Prayer 1952, 22)

The sisterhood of "Birds I Know" can still communicate, from over half a century ago, the interwoven relationship between the restoration of personal health and the restoration of intimacy with the natural world.

BIBLIOGRAPHY

Baltimore Oriole [pseud]. 1939. Birds I Know, *Boston Globe*, June 16, 1939.
Barker, Margaret A., Carrol L. Henderson, and Paul J. Baicich. 2015. *Feeding Wild Birds in America: Culture, Commerce, and Conservation*. United States: Texas A&M University Press.

Calla Ann [pseud]. 1947. Birds I Know, *Boston Globe*, April 11, 1947.

Clark, Charles E. and John B. Hench. 1991. *Three Hundred Years of the American Newspaper*. American Antiquarian Society.

Crist, Eileen. 1999. *Images of Animals: Anthropomorphism and the Animal Mind*. Philadelphia, PA: Temple University Press.

Evans, Lauren. 2019. Birding for Social Change: Feminist Bird Club, *Audubon*. May 3, 2019. https://www.audubon.org/news/when-women-run-bird-world.

Flaccus, Gillian. 2020. Bird-watching Soars Amid COVID-19 as Americans Head Outdoors. *AP News*. May 2, 2020. https://apnews.com/94a1ea5938943d8a70fe7 94e9f629b13.

Golia, Julie A. 2012. The Column Family: Advice Communities and the Origins of Interactive Media. *American Historical Association annual meeting. Chicago.*

———. 2016. Courting Women, Courting Advertisers: The Woman's Page and the Transformation of the American Newspaper, 1895–1935 *The Journal of American History*, 103(3), 606–628.

Govan, Ada Clapham. 1940. *Wings at my Window*. New York: Macmillan.

———. 1943. Back-Yard Magic, *Bulletin of the Massachusetts Audubon Society*, 27(4), 95–97.

Greer, Kirsten and Bols, Sonje. 2016. "She of the Loghouse Nest": Gendering Historical Ecological Reconstruction in Northern Ontario, *Historical Geography* 44, 45–67.

Haraway, Donna, Noboru Ishikawa, Scott F. Gilbert, Kenneth Olwig, Anna L. Tsing, and Nils Bubandt. 2016. Anthropologists Are Talking—About the Anthropocene, *Ethnos*, 81:3, 535–564, DOI: 10.1080/00141844.2015.1105838.

Howard, Len. 1952. *Birds as Individuals*. Translated by Antoinette Fawcett. London: Collins.

Hope and Prayer [pseud]. 1952. Birds I Know, *Boston Globe*, April 20, 1952.

Jones, Darryl. 2018. *The Birds at my Table: Why we Feed Birds and Why it Matters*. Ithaca, NY: Cornell University Press.

Lear, Linda. 1998. *Rachel Carson: Witness for Nature*. Henry Holt & Company.

Lestel, Dominique, Jeffrey Bussonlini, and Matthew Chrulew. 2014. The Phenomenology of Animal Life, *Environmental Humanities*. 5(1), 125–148.

Mason, Edwin A. 1943. The Romance of Bird-Banding, *Bulletin of the Massachusetts Audubon Society*. 16 (9), 241–244.

Mass Moments. 2020. May 11, 1884. Globe Publishes First "Confidential Chat." https://www.massmoments.org/moment-details/globe-publishes-first-confidential -chat.html.

Meijer, Eva. 2018. *Bird Cottage*. Pushkin Press.

Nature Lover No. II [pseud]. 1937. Birds I Know, *Boston Globe*, August 24, 1937.

Nice, Margaret Morse. 1939. *The Watcher at the Nest*. New York: The Macmillan Company.

———. 1964. *Studies in the Life History of the Song Sparrow, Volume II*. New York: Dover Publications, Inc.

Norwood, Vera. 1993. *Made from this Earth: American Women and Nature*. University of North Carolina Press.

126   *Peter W. Oehlkers and Anna Ijiri Oehlkers*

Oehlkers, Peter and Susan Hafen. 2015. Compassionate Conservation: Across the Cat-Bird Divide between Animal and Environmental Ethics. *Conference on Communication and the Environment, Boulder, Colorado.*

Of Thee I Sing [Govan, Ada Clapham]. 1932. Birds I Know, *Boston Globe*, December 16, 1932.

———. 1933. Birds I Know, *Boston Globe*, September 20, 1933.

———. 1934a. Birds I Know, *Boston Globe*, March 21, 1934.

———. 1934b. Birds I Know, *Boston Globe*, November 21, 1934.

———. 1935. Birds I Know, *Boston Globe*, July 17, 1935.

———. 1936a. Birds I Know, *Boston Globe*, May 2, 1936.

———. 1936b. Birds I Know, *Boston Globe*, October 24, 1936.

———. 1937a. Birds I Know, *Boston Globe*, June 15, 1937.

———. 1937b. Birds I Know, *Boston Globe*, June 16, 1937.

———. 1939. Birds I Know, *Boston Globe*, June 9, 1939.

———. 1940. Birds I Know, *Boston Globe*, October 24, 1940.

———. 1942. Birds I Know, *Boston Globe*, October 30, 1942.

———. 1947. Birds I Know, *Boston Globe*, January 10, 1947.

———. 1954. Birds I Know, *Boston Globe*, December 25, 1954.

———. 1955. Confidential Chat, *Boston Globe*, January 10, 1955.

Rust, Mary-Jayne. 2012. Ecological Intimacy. In *Vital Signs: Psychological Responses to Ecological Crisis,* edited by Nick Totton and Mary-Jayne Rust. London: Routledge.

Scarlet Tanager [pseud]. 1936. Birds I Know, *Boston Globe*, May 19, 1936.

Schrader, Kirsten. 2020. Finding Joy in Birds, *Birds & Blooms*, June 2020.

Troubadour [pseud]. 1932. Confidential Chat, *Boston Globe*, June 30, 1932.

Vance, Linda. 1993. Ecofeminism and the Politics of Reality, In *Ecofeminism: Women, Animals, Nature*, edited by Greta Gaard, 118–145. Philadelphia, PA: Temple University Press.

Warped Halo [pseud]. 1934. Birds I Know, *Boston Globe*, May 9, 1934.

Wing Flashes [pseud]. 1941. Birds I Know, *Boston Globe*, October 23, 1941.

———. 1942. Birds I Know, *Boston Globe*, August 5, 1942.

Chapter 11

Dialogic Elephant and Human Relations in Sri Lanka as Social Practices of Cohabitation

Elizabeth Oriel, Deepani Jayantha,
and Amal Dissanayaka

Amid the fraught spaces of human–elephant conflict (HEC) in Sri Lanka, small-scale farmers whose standard of living are among the lowest in the country, maintain fragile relations, intimate sensorial, embodied dialogues with elephants and other species. These dialogues persist despite the modernist and capitalist land use designs that break down traditional cultivation methods and alter ontological frameworks. Traditional lifeways involved complex dialogues among humans with rain, soil, topography, plants, sunlight, and wildlife. When multispecies dialogues are thwarted by certain landscape designs, violence takes its place. The dialogues continue yet become more charged as access to land shrinks from development and as other factors such as climate change challenge food securities. In fact, the tight, highly developed landscapes bring about certain demanding intimacies for both species. Remnants of these intimacies and dialogues are worth studying and learning from as fields of social relations across species, as cohabitations.

Writing this chapter in 2020 during the coronavirus lockdown, the parallels of root causes between this global health crisis and human–elephant relations and conflict in Asia are striking. Both result from human destruction of ecosystems and wildlife habitats, industrial agriculture, and infrastructure development; the global human footprint is too large and extractive, not leaving space for the many processes that sustain living systems. Human–elephant conflict is one of the world's conservation priorities and numerous studies address the complex interconnected issues that contribute to the escalating conflict. Wildlife conservation orients around practices and discourses aimed at protecting and saving species from population declines and extinction. And yet, this chapter begins with the assumption that this approach corresponds to abstracted modernist paradigms and that wildlife and habitats are most successfully allowed to maintain resilience through multispecies socio-ecological relations.

Humans and elephants in Sri Lanka in some regions struggle daily over access to land and crops resulting from wicked and complex issues, spanning the economic, political, religious, cultural, and ecological. This complexity and the siloed nature of scholarship make these spaces difficult to comprehend and to find solutions for. This chapter can only address a sliver of this assemblage of intertwined forces and actors. For the farmers living near elephants and possibly for the elephants dealing with humans, it can feel intractable. These become spaces of multispecies trauma, poverty, loss of access and knowledge, disruption, and dependency. In this work, we apply the lens of a practice-orientation to human–wildlife issues. Sharing landscapes is a dialogue among the multispecies actors.

In these pages, we present findings on how farmers and elephants around Uda Walawe National Park in south-eastern Sri Lanka maintained a broad range of communicative approaches to sharing landscapes and how these have changed over time. Though farmers are usually the ones who harm elephants while defending their land, they also hold extensive, intimate knowledge about elephants and many say they themselves are the intruders, farming on "elephant land." This awareness of elephant terrain and loss of their rights seem an essential ingredient in the dialogue across species. These interspecies dialogues are informed by knowledge, perception, and answer Bruno Latour's question about how to be territorial. As Latour (2018) says in *Down to Earth: Politics in the New Climatic Regime*, in this time of ecological breakdown, the terrestrial is the realm of uncertainty and also the lever of change. How does one live on the earth, with the earth?—these are the central questions. We explore how farmers have lived alongside elephants, how macro forces influence these dialogues, and finally how these relations may be supported by policies and practices.

Human–elephant conflict is a territorial[1] issue, a problem of sharing landscapes with others that is part of the larger global extinction crisis, the first human-caused in Earth's history. The conflict is not an issue of problem elephants but of humans developing elephant territories, appropriating their habitat. This issue spans conservation and environmental justice, as the farmers who lose crops, livelihoods, and lives lack political voice and power. While some benefit from elephant tourism and development, those who share spaces with elephants are marginalized. The myriad ways humans and elephants react to one another and interact in Sri Lanka are responses to the past, present, and perhaps future, to myths and stories, plants, experiences, art, to dreams. Some interactions in general lead to more conflict and some to mitigating conflict.

In this chapter, we discuss changing human–elephant relations on the southern border of Uda Walawe National Park and describe characteristics of human–elephant dialogues across perception and time/space. Each of us individually research human–elephant relations and conflict in Sri Lanka, and we also collaborated in 2019 on field work; this chapter presents unpublished interview data and analysis from this collaboration. Working with a multispecies form of engaged theory (James 2006) as a lens to explore social relations across species and landscapes, our work used qualitative data drawn from semi-structured interviews and participant observation with diverse actors, such as farmers, teachers, government officials, Buddhist monks, representatives from nongovernmental organizations, and ecotourism business owners. We analyzed how the macro and micro shape human–elephant relations and how other species' agencies mediate relationalities, power dynamics, and patterns of living across time and space. Elizabeth's background in human-nature research examines marine mammals in rehabilitation centers, concepts of well-being for other species, identifying characteristics of successful cohabitation across species, and expanding the concept of personhood for other beings. Amal is a sociologist with the agrarian sector in Sri Lanka; during the last eight years, he has conducted two extensive studies on human–elephant conflict and on farmer livelihoods in the plantation sector, focusing on building interspecies coexistence. Since 2008, Deepani has researched human–elephant relations and conflict in Uda Walawe and other areas while running community projects to strengthen coexistence.

HUMAN–ELEPHANT CONFLICT IN SRI LANKA

In Sri Lanka, human–elephant conflict, taking place mostly in agricultural fields is a long-standing threat to both species, though rates of crop damage and death have increased over the last decades. Annually in Sri Lanka, approximately 70 human and 250 elephants die each year, though in 2019, 121 humans and 361 elephants died with most killed by humans (*BBC News* 2020). Approximately 6,000 now live in mostly dry regions of the island, according to official data. Farmers suffer under the mental and emotional strain of crop guarding all night, loss of livelihood (Dissanayaka et al. 2020), and widespread chronic kidney disease which in some regions impacts every household (Dissanayaka 2019). Eighty-four percent of humans harmed from human–elephant conflicts (from 2006 to 2017) are elderly males and they were mostly attacked during agricultural or related activities (data from Department of Wildlife Conservation). Elephants also likely suffer trauma as they are driven from traditional paths and lands, killed by farmers, spooked to leave a field with loud thunder crackers. As one elephant researcher says, elephants who have experienced violence and aggression become aggressive in response. This echoes Bradshaw's (2010) finding of posttraumatic stress disorder among elephants who witness or are victims of aggression.

Roots of this conflict are diverse, with many global influences deteriorating the cohabitation that traditional farmers had built over millennia. Developments erasing their historical terrain, habitat fragmentation, and forest loss are all implicated; globalization, neoliberal economic policies which have opened landscapes to extraction and foreign acquisition play into the mix. While traditional slash and burn agriculture, called *chena,* is critiqued as ecologically destructive due to fire, many studies find that rotating fields and secondary plant growth enabled elephants to thrive with nutritious plants to eat after harvest (Fernando et al. 2005; Fernando 2000; Santiapillai, Fernando, and Gunewardene 2006). The ancient tank cascade system, developed as a hydraulic water management system during the ancient kingdoms, worked in concert with slash and burn practices, oriented around sharing spaces with diverse life forms. The sophisticated tank and *chena* system allowed for crops grown in dry zones, areas set aside for wildlife needs, while the village worked collectively, sharing tasks that benefited the whole. The ancient feudal politics organized certain landscapes around centric powers, yet small villages maintained autonomies and socio-ecological balance (Handawela 2016).

While conflicts in cropped areas occurred in ancient times, Asian elephant expert Raman Sukumar (2011) describes colonialism as the major driver of HEC, with enormous alterations of landscapes into plantations, the destruction of traditional agriculture, degrading of the tank system, and with that local self-sufficiency. The 443-year period of colonial presence, from Portuguese and Dutch annexation, and then British rule, altered social relations among ethnic groups, among humans and landscapes, humans and other animals which still plays out today in extractive policies and practices of the International Monetary Fund and World Bank (Hickel 2017). With the British expulsion of elephants from the highlands for coffee, tea, cinchona plantations (Wilson 1957), they lost verdant spaces (Fernando 2000). Now they lose traditional terrain with a lack of contiguous forest in the dry zone due to large-scale dam projects, irrigated agriculture, and other developments (Tolisano et al. 1993). Postindependence development, resisting continuation of colonial rule with policies to avoid Western influence until the late 1970s, has indeed since oriented around Western modernist designs and agendas in Sri Lanka (Bastian 2018).

Loss of forest cover started in colonial times. Forest cover was 84 percent in 1880, 44 percent in 1956 and now is 25 percent, though this number includes monocultures, tree plantations, and only about 8 percent natural forest (FAO 2010). One study in India finds that HEC increases significantly when forest cover drops below 30–40 percent (Chartier, Zimmermann, and Ladle 2011); this helpful metric likely applies to Sri Lanka as well, and may speak to broader human–wildlife conflicts, supplying a landscape design feature that would support cohabitation by providing enough space for other species. The loss of forest habitats has led to the dramatic rise in human–wildlife conflict across the country with monkeys, squirrels, peacock, boar, and buffalo.

Sri Lanka with a rich and deep biocultural history finds itself impacted by the same forces shaping land-based relations globally; thus, many ontologies and relationalities mix across the island. Philosopher Freya Matthews writes that nature is the absence of abstract design or "when we or other agents under the direction of abstract thought, let things be" (Matthews 1999, 120). Abstraction is a product and producer of modernism which is a project of separation, a means of escaping the "uncivilized past." Karl Polanyi (2001) finds that dis-embeddedness occurs when economic activity separates from social spheres, thus becoming autonomous and unrestrained. In premarket societies, economic activity was held in check by other social, political, religious activities, to which we add the intimacies of multispecies dialogues. When intimacies and relationality lose their power to limit self-interest, they are often diminished through abstractions, as the ones who profit are usually far from, abstracted from the site of production, exerting foreign designs from far away. Economies are divorced from local ecological knowledge and regulation, which is apparent in the southeast where development is projected to increase by around 150,000 acres across three districts with foreign direct investments (Dissanayaka et al. 2019) and where neoliberal policies dictate socio-ecologies (Benadusi 2015). Many farmers we interviewed wait for the government to help them recover from and prevent crop loss and their expectations are rarely met, while many are indebted to agrochemical salesmen.[2] The sources of dependencies are numerous for both humans and elephants, as each are divorced from previous self-sufficiencies of communities and terrain. The dialogue among traditional and modern ways, native and foreign is key to unlocking the roots and complex realities and to equalizing actors, not letting one subsume others. Next, we discuss dialogue and dialogism's relevance to HEC.

DIALOGISM

Traditionally, farmers in Sri Lanka shared hybrid and intimate identities across other beings and maintained communication across diverse actors on and with landscapes. "The Western or naturalist form of identification . . .

is fairly different from the Buddhist and Hinduist forms of identification in Sri Lanka in which interior properties can be exchanged between human and non-human beings, such as deities, animals and plants" (Van Daele 2008, 295). These communications across diverse beings have been central to maintaining lives, survival, and sharing space. In fact, permeable identities, as Van Daele describes, imbue human and elephant relations, as historically these two species have occupied mutual spaces in cultivated fields, in sacred spaces of Buddhist temples where elephants reside, in Buddhist festivals, and in spaces of power, as kings rode celebrated elephants. These external spaces mirror internal spaces of identification and rich multispecies communications and facilitated human–elephant cohabitation (which included some conflict).[3]

The communicative groundworks for cohabitation correspond to moral philosopher Mikhail Bakhtin's dialogism, a sociopolitical corollary to biodiversity, in which multiple perspectives, meanings, voices, interests coexist without merging into one (Holquist 2002). For Bakhtin, existence is dialogic as is knowledge. The self is co-constituted with others, and this mutuality of differences is held together within dialogue. Each being has their own unique position yet is not alone, as the meeting of difference propels the creation of meaning, as each being answers to the others, and every utterance is a response to what comes before. Dialogue among multiple and diverse points of view is the praxis of democracy and diplomacy and offers a way to listen, to hear others, and to coexist across differences. The contestations are what constitute selves and world; they are existentially important, not to be nullified into one voice. In the same way, ecosystems rely on diverse beings with diverse perspectives, so do humans rely on this plurality.

In this framework, the entire world is a dialogue; this multivoiced system can be *monologic*, which is vertically oriented with one voice or perspective subsuming others as in ideologies and hegemonies, or *dialogic*, which are horizontal, inclusive systems in which many worlds and perspectives fit, such as resilient ecosystems. Dialogic relations have spatial components; the more intensified the land, the more difficult it is to share across different species and to maintain communication. Anthropocentrism, which situates human needs and interests over all others is a monologic form, driving the current extinction crisis and climate disruption. Dialogic forms of dialogue are inherently ecological, merging the biological and the communicative and social spheres. Dialogue can be considered an ecological communicative model.

FEEDING ELEPHANTS IN CONFLICT ZONES

We begin our discussion of human–elephant intimacies, relations, and conflict with the practice of feeding elephants in the Uda Walawe region in Sri Lanka.

This practice highlights many of the issues, both explicit and implicit in these interspecies intimate relations. Walking along the southern border of Uda Walawe National Park in southeastern Sri Lanka, along the reservoir's edge, and about a mile east of Uda Walawe village, twenty male elephants wait along the road, begging for food. Only one male has tusks, as most males (93 percent) of the Asian elephant subspecies in Sri Lanka are tuskless, possibly a result of genetic changes from mass hunting during British colonial rule (Kurt, Hartl, and Tiedemann 1995). They stand behind an electric fence which is not turned on, though they act as if it was electrified. Perhaps they can detect the presence of electricity with their keen vibratory perception. Bystanders approach them and offer bananas and other fruit they've bought from stalls on the road. This situation holds myriad histories, relationships, nets of human–ecological relations unraveling and re-aligning. If we were to engage in the simple act of feeding them, if we enter this relational web, it would most likely not serve these males' interests. For one, many argue their health is deteriorating from too many sweet fruits, and their dependency on humans is another issue. Yet, many assert that elephants don't have enough to eat in the Park.

Feeding elephants is now a common practice among tourists (both local and some foreign) and those on religious pilgrimage, though economies, politics, and land practices accelerate males begging on the road. Historically, during the annual *Pada Yatra* pilgrimage from Jaffna to the Hindu temple at Kataragama, some stop to offer bananas to the elephants. Near the temple, elephants now stop cars from passing until fruit is offered. Economic incentives drive the growing number of elephants begging on roadsides; they become tourist sites, driving up revenues for local vendors, echoing Milstein's "nature as performance" paradigm in Western capitalist countries (Milstein 2016). And yet, these feeding interactions and motivations are complex; many have a personal desire to interact with an elephant, along with cultural and religious incentives. These members of Proboscidea (Order of trunked mammals) hold special significance historically, culturally, religiously, and in E.O. Wilson's so-named bio-philial sense—an innate connection with other life forms.

Giving fruit to elephants is considered by some a beneficial offering; it may bring good karma and can be exhilarating to be so close to such a large and majestic animal; yet this practice contributes to crop raiding as elephants get more accustomed to and dependent on human-grown foods. Crop raiding by elephants can be viewed as a form of feeding elephants, though not voluntarily. Elephants have certainly lost their habitats repeatedly and their vegetative resources. Historically with shifting cultivation, crop remnants were accessible for elephants. Currently in Thailand, food forests are grown with diverse crops to reduce conflict with elephants, as they access outer sections (Commons 2018).

Crop raiding by elephants and humans feeding elephants are part of an interspecies enmeshed history tied to the development of a hybrid human–elephant culture on the island that has been a mutual effort. Elephants contributed through duress to building the infrastructure of Sri Lanka, in forestry, building temples, coerced to fight wars and more (Mahānāma 1908). They occupy a human–animal hybrid and limbo place, in which they are revered, while simultaneously receiving at times, brutal treatment in captive settings. Those who labor for human projects are broken, a cruel process, depriving them of food and water with beatings until they learn to rely on humans for their survival needs. Meanwhile, across Asia, one in three elephants, approximately 15,000 are captive (Campos-Arceiz 2016), though in Sri Lanka the number is around 250.

Despite subjugations, elephants have been and continue to be *cultural agents*, shaping the island's structures, landscapes, and intangible socio-cultural practices. Across the island, it is apparent that Buddhism and Hinduism wouldn't be what they are without elephant agencies, beings and lifeways, such as their frequent gentleness and their strong sociality apparent at the Elephant Gathering in Minneriya National Park, described more in a later section.

Feeding free-ranging animals in the current ecological collapse becomes a poignant practice of responsibility and hope in some regions. Although hunters historically feed or leave food for free-ranging animals to flush them out and to improve their reproduction (Tolisano et al., 1993), others feed wild animals to gain a view of them or to ensure they have enough to eat. A friend of mine (Elizabeth) in western Massachusetts feeds black bears in his yard as they've lost their forest homes, though his neighbors complain. A tribe in the Pacific Northwest, the Lummi Nation, is hand feeding Chinook salmon to highly endangered southern resident orcas in the Salish Sea who don't have enough to eat as the Chinook, their sole prey, are themselves dying out. As more and more animals lose their ability to access nutrition due to climate change, habitat loss, feeding becomes an instrument of support, survival, an act of kinship as they describe the orcas as family members. Feeding elephants is a complex mix of benefit and conflict, yet the interactions become part of the multispecies dialogues occurring in Uda Walawe.

Begging elephants are an adaptation and symptom of an unbalanced ecology of relations. In ecology and systems approaches to social relations, individuals maintain their own lives through reciprocal relations and interdependencies, each offering benefits to others (van Dooren and Despret 2018). Elephants create trails through dense, inaccessible forests that humans benefited from for centuries (Keil 2016). African elephants create water holes that other animals use (Ramey et al. 2013). Asian and African elephants fertilize soils that aid soil health for cultivation. They disperse seed and structurally modify forests and are thus called forest gardeners (Campos-Arceiz and Blake 2011). Humans grow crops that elephants have accessed for centuries after the harvest. They build water tanks that elephants utilize for their own drinking. These reciprocal relations are altered by global/local forces shaping landscapes to suit human needs.

The hybrid identities break down in the fragmented realm of politics and governance, with politicians treating land use as electoral incentives and regulation minimally implemented and monitored. Politics is the realm most readily blamed in Sri Lanka for the conflicts; it is described as an intractable realm, as intractable as HEC itself. Yet native governance has faced an onslaught of Western influences through multilateral organizations' development schemes that monetize relationships that had been social in nature. The structural adjustment programs beginning in the late 1970s required deregulation, privatization, and opened to global capitalism in order to be eligible for loans which are now astronomic debts to the Global North. These policies, enforced by the West, with foreign-owned plantations and more wreaked havoc on ecological relations of traditional practices in Sri Lanka. Attempts have been made across the postindependence decades to foster local autonomies and power sharing within development projects, though these projects often falter in the face of postcolonial structures that favor centrist power relations. Several elephant researchers call for development agencies, both governmental and nongovernmental, to take responsibility for the conflict as they are the ones responsible through vast land use alterations and concomitant changes in subjective relations to natural systems. Some of these changes are discussed next.

CHANGING HUMAN–ELEPHANT RELATIONS IN THE UDA WALAWE REGION

Here we discuss our findings on changing Uda Walawe landscape designs and logics and how these impact human–elephant relations. Relations, practices, and knowledges are a complex dialogue of traditional, animist, Buddhist, folkloric, modernist, capitalist, Western dualisms, and ecological modes. Traditional cultivation and crop guarding practices were embodied, embedded in place and performative. Prior to these development projects, this area was sporadically cultivated with traditional *chena* cultivation which is a form of slash and burn. Farmers worked closely with seasonal and climatic changes, as crops were rain fed. Up until about thirty years ago, farmers sang folksongs to protect crops from wildlife and elephants from watch huts above crops; these songs were thought to hold magical powers that maintain relations with the cosmoecological world (Ratnapala 1968). Now they use cell phones to maintain contact. Farming has been a dialogue among forces and actors on the landscape—soil, rain, wind, sun, plants, elephants, trees that store nitrogen, and topography. Village cultivation systems in ancient times were built into hillsides, and the relation of uplands to valleys was also a dialogue, one feeding the other. As an agricultural researcher described in an interview, "the upland is the husband and lowland is the wife" (September 30, 2019).[4]

The digital revolution in guarding is accompanied by land use changes, altering relations to place. One elephant researcher in the Uda Walawe area stated, "everything changed with the reservoir." The land around Uda Walawe National Park (UWNP) was part of the ancient Ruhuna kingdom and around 600 tanks dot the landscape (Molle and Renwick 2005). The reservoir, dam, irrigation, and electricity project were conceived as a postindependence development plan, designed by a U.S. engineering firm. By 1974, 60,000 settlers had come to the area; 67,600 acres were converted into irrigated agriculture—sugar cane, cotton, rice chili, and onion (Molle and Renwick 2005). UWNP was established in 1972, to create a protected area for flora and fauna, in part to compensate habitat losses from disruptions from the loss of habitat (Kotagama 2014).

The reservoir did change large swaths of landscape, in part by providing irrigation for plantation development in the region. Reservoir construction intensified use of the landscape, starting from scrubland with scattered villages and *chena* with 2000 inhabitants in the 1950s to 200,000 as of 2005 (Molle and Renwick 2005, 34). The sugar cane plantation which lies to the south of UWNP is a vast track of 54km^2, and elephants regularly cross the road to enter crops, as this plant is a favored species and the smell compels them to leave the Park. While the dam and reservoir brought electricity and some access to water, the Western (United States) design and logic of the project left behind communications and attentions that maintained ecological balance. Attempts were made at community-based empowerment through multilateral organizations, and while some made headway, descriptions of failures echo one another in this region.

With the corresponding Green Revolution in the same timeframe, with technological approaches to cultivation, gone were the shifting of crops to build soil in areas already harvested, and gone were the multiple crops grown together to prevent insects and build soil nutrition. Now one plantation grower, "the soil here is dead. There is no future in growing sugar cane. We pour chemicals on, more each year, and this cannot continue like this" (September 10, 2019). Plantations are monocultures, zones of monologue, with one crop across hundreds of hectares, and irrigation to maintain the crop throughout the year, which no longer provides elephants with crop remnants. The breakdown of ecological balance which included interspecies dialogues leads to increased conflict.

The developments of Uda Walawe region have altered elephant feeding patterns, as favored plants disappear, making crops a more necessary component of their diet. Originally, the reservoir and changing water levels from monsoon cycles brought abundant grasslands which attracted elephants. Though over time, restricting *chena* cultivation in the Park has allowed vegetation to proceed through natural succession with grasslands converting to shrub and tree layers, which is less favorable to elephants. This loss of vegetative resources is one reason they leave the Park boundaries. Around 70 percent of elephants in Sri Lanka range outside of protected areas (Santiapillai, Fernando, and Gunewardene 2006). The Park is surrounded by sixty-three villages, some of which fall within elephant ranging routes, and many cultivating with a more modernized version of *chena*. One leader of a farmer organization in Hambegamuwa said 75 percent of his crop is regularly destroyed by elephants. "Elephants don't like chili plants, but they are eating our chillis which means they don't have enough to eat" (October 16, 2018). A Department of Wildlife Conservation (DWC) ranger said that buffalo owners had illegally grazed in the Park for 30 years, from 1971 until around 2000, when the DWC took actions to stop it. "At times there were over 20,000 buffalo grazing in the Park. And the livestock owners had political support, they were powerful. The overgrazing destroyed the grass, *Panicum maximum,* which is guinea grass. When the grass all died, then the invasive species, *Lantana camera* came in and now the eastern side of the Park (near Hambegamuwa) is overrun with Lantana, which elephants won't eat" (September 10, 2019). Changing vegetative patterns are a significant feature of the changing dialogue toward monologue, as invasive species occupy the landscape.

Farmers speak of their Buddhist principles, the restrictions on causing harm.

> As a Buddhist, we don't like to harm elephants. We are not attacking them. We don't resist them. But in the meantime, we are losing our farming. We can be near them, and they don't panic. On poya day (full moon day) we were near the temple, and the elephant was 10 meters away and still didn't panic. One woman in the village does nothing to scare them away, and the elephants live in her garden and eat all the food. The rest of the village feed her. (October 16, 2018)

The intimacies of shared fields seem to habituate elephants to human presence, as this farmer's words suggest they panic less from human presence. In the past, elephants entered crop areas after harvest and ate the remains, yet now, farmers describe that "elephants eat most of my crops, and we harvest the remains" (September 22, 2019). This reversal of relationship is a result of intensified landscapes. The dialogue among climate, soil, elephants, plants, and the magical intermediaries of the folksongs is remembered today by farmers in their sixties and seventies, but younger farmers no longer use these techniques of songs and prayers or even conversations across huts. The modernist landscape design has altered these to a point where retaliation is often the only option.

One remaining dialogue is between the unofficial de facto leaders and the rest of the community for both elephants and humans who've historically sustained social networks. An elephant "celebrity" in the town of Uda Walawe named Rambo has become a kind of diplomat between the human and the elephant societies, as well as leader of male elephants near the National Park entrance. He is well-known and knows many locals; multiple conflicting accounts tell of his exploits, his personality, some claiming that he killed three people. One jeep driver describes him as a rowdy youth who led other males into rebelliousness, though he has mellowed now. These elephant leaders or diplomats are significant representatives, as they breach the interspecies divide, becoming known for their personality traits, biographies, becoming members of human communities. They are akin to human community leaders like certain school principals or Buddhist monks, who in some villages use their position to support community thriving, networks, promote higher education, and aid families dealing with human–wildlife conflicts. Hope for reducing conflicts resides with these leaders, of both species.

CHARACTERISTICS OF
FARMER–ELEPHANT RELATIONS

This section describes several perceptual and spatial/temporal choreographies that build and diminish cohabitation; these correspond to Latour's question on becoming territorial. Landscapes in Sri Lanka in elephant ranging areas are densely populated and developed spaces, with one of the highest human and the highest elephant population density in the world, straining human–elephant relations. In this developed landscape, the bodily presence of humans and elephants is one of the most successful tactics for avoiding one another, protecting one's body and crops.

The relational interspecies dialogues cohabit subjective and more external spaces, traversing states of being, thoughts, actions, and words. Farmers describe states of being that help avoid conflict, and elephants are known to avoid and prevent conflict among themselves and often among humans as well. Farmers talk about how resistance is futile. Some describe the attitude or state of being one needs to avoid problems. They say you need to surrender, and not resist. The minute you try to resist, problems start. Elephants know your feelings, they know your resistance and aggression and they will panic. And when panicked, they can trample a human quickly. So, cohabitation seems to be built on attitudes, states of being. They talk about surrender, but they do take steps to protect their crops. Surrender does not seem to apply though when one is attacked by an elephant. One farmer described suddenly coming upon an elephant at dusk on the road. He grabbed the elephant's leg and spoke to him, blaming him for any harm to come, and he survived the attack though his friend was severely injured. Farmers believe that elephants understand them when they speak, perhaps a relic of the historic songs sang to keep elephants away. Certainly, these states of being and verbal entreaties form the vocabulary of cohabitation.

Temporal Features

Cyclical time frames involve difference across the passage of repeating yet singular time. Linear time moves in a universal flow, not rooted in difference or patterns, but moving along an anonymous arrow. An alternating temporality within land use practices, tied to seasons, to cycles of monsoon, was central to human–elephant cohabitation. The monsoon acts as a landscape designer on the island and a force dictating temporalities. Elephant sociality is tied to cyclical relations across different seasonal and vegetative periods. The large annual gathering of 200–300 elephants in June/July in Minneriya National Park is a significant social event, in which they greet, play, mate, and maintain social cohesion. This event is tied to the dry season, decreasing water levels in the large ancient tank which provides fresh grass, their preferred food, and has a temporal cyclical quality.

Farmers guard crops in watch huts at night, which is when elephants enter cropped areas. Farmers in one village report that elephants arrive every day at the same time, close to dusk. In the elephant orphanage in Uda Walawe village, elephant orphans have a strong sense of time. According to staff, they come into the main area for milk every three hours like clockwork, without being told. The farmers' night-time guarding takes a tremendous toll on their health and family cohesion. Many are going blind due to lack of sleep, as they guard at night and do farm work at night; they also report marital difficulties from the grueling schedule. The conflict shrinks space and time for those on the front lines.

Time is a commodity, and time within the capitalist extractive modes of relating to the land changes ecological relationships. Plantation style agriculture, such as the sugar cane farm to the south of the Park, and foreign corporation Dole's banana plantations have shaped a temporality no longer tied to climate and seasons. Though historically, British colonial tea, coffee, rubber plantations initiated this temporal shift toward a universal unaltered time that prioritizes output over relations with the rest of the ecosystem. These changing temporalities intertwine with changing spatial patterns described next.

Spatial Features

Spaces are not voids to fill but are produced through relationalities. Spatial arrangements of the landscape are powerful drivers of human–elephant relations and conflict. The elephant is a prized commodity in the National Park where tourists pay high prices to see them browsing in the wild, while one kilometer away, in the farm fields, the elephant is a pest, leading to food insecurity, risk of injury or death, and limiting movements in communities. This spatial dichotomy is pronounced and is a way that space structures power and political dynamics; the dichotomy contributes to the divergence of farmer and elephant needs and interests which exacerbate the problems. Farmers often don't reap benefits from the large sums earned by the park and surrounding tourist infrastructure, and in contrast, their lives become more difficult from the development this tourism brings with it, as elephants have less space and crop damage increases. On the south side of the park near the National Park entrance, elephants are central to the economy, while on the north side where tourists never travel, elephants disrupt economic activity. The spatial dichotomy is both physical and conceptual, as conservation of elephants is often separated from the environmental justice issue of farmers' loss of livelihood, and the discrepancy of those who live with elephants not being the same as those who profit from their presence.

One central spatial component of human–elephant relations is the crop rotation within traditional *chena* cultivation which is gone from many fields, such as plantations with stationary crops. Rotation allowed soil to rejuvenate and allowed for elephants and others to utilize unused areas. Cohabitation in the past oriented around lifeways that humans and elephants shared, namely *movement and permeability* (Oriel and Frohoff 2020). Crops shifted fields to allow fallow times for soils to rejuvenate, while elephants are always on the move. Cropped areas were permeable spaces allowing for mutual accessibility within different time scales.

Another spatial obstacle are the electric fences between different sections of protected areas, defining those meant for elephants and other wildlife and Forest Department land. These fences are administrative boundaries, not based on ecological features, and keep elephants in spaces too small for their needs. In Yala National Park, elephant calves have been starving to death due to this fencing. Leading elephant researcher Prithiviraj Fernando said, "in Yala, for example, this problem has been occurring since 2004. The juvenile elephants are hardest hit. We see older elephants and infants but very few intervening age groups of elephants now. Elephant populations are slowly taking a crash" (Anver 2015). Electric fences around farms and villages are successful in mitigating conflict, if the community works to maintain the fences, according to Fernando. Placement of spaces, creating exclusive zones, especially large-scale fences that exclude elephants from potential habitats have enormous consequences, and are constructed without elephant biology and lifeways in their design.

Elephants have keen olfactory perception, which makes their favored crops act like magnets, luring them toward human habitats and away from forests. Sugarcane plantations are an obstacle to cohabitation in high conflict areas. Preeminent human–elephant researchers Santiapillai and Read (2010) recommend obscuring the scent of paddy fields to mitigate the conflict in Sri Lanka. "It is the elephant's sophisticated chemosensory system that may hold the key to resolving human–elephant conflict," they write (Santiapillai and Read 2010, 509). Farmers often intimately know the spatial patterns of elephants, and land use planning would improve with farmers' input. Spatially sensitive land use planning itself is one mitigation route that would benefit the entire nation, humans, and nonhumans alike.

Sounds of Dialogue

Though humans and elephants don't share a common alphabetic language, sound is a primary interspecies communicative and dialogic mode. Sound corresponds and contributes to social cohesion for elephants and also is a primary means of crop protection, as loud sounds are used to scare elephants. Elephants have more acute hearing abilities than almost all land animals. Though families are closely bonded units, individuals are in constant movement during the day, separating and coming back together (Payne 2003). They are part of a larger social dynamic called fission-fusion, a semi-fluid pattern of social composition and group size shared only by a few cooperatively hunting carnivores. They keep track of other members of the herd through seismic and acoustic communication, often using the very low acoustic range that travel long distances (McComb et al. 2003).

Elephants' greatest capacity is listening, said Katy Payne (founder of Elephant Listening Project at Cornell University) in discussion with author Elizabeth Oriel (September 14, 2010). Elephants' acoustic range is over ten octaves. They hear infrasound, which is below human hearing range, and can feel very low sounds through seismic activity, feeling vibrations with their feet. Their infrasound allows them to hear storms moving in.

In Sri Lanka, for farmers, sound is a primary means to deter elephants from entering their fields. Firecrackers, gunshots are used, though in parts of India these are banned for their negative impacts. In the past, along with folk songs to keep elephants away, farmers would play answer games back and forth across their watch huts to entertain themselves throughout the night; their voices alerted elephants to human presence, deterring their entry. According to one farming family, elephants know the difference of a human voice from an automated voice or radio voice. Now, as farmers have smart phones to stay in contact and to entertain them while in the huts, they no longer sing and pass riddles and perhaps have less success with keeping them away. Elephant sensory abilities make crop protection a continuously adapting dialogue.

Elephants' immense capacity for adaptation and learning is why physical presence is so central to crop protection. Automated systems can be quickly learned and outwitted. Electric fences around crop areas have proven successful though most communities lack necessary funds and they need meticulous maintenance to work properly. Humans possess robust intelligence and learning capacities, but it is these village farmers who can attest to the intelligence and immense adaptability of elephants. Elephants use tools, such as tree branches to outwit the electric fences, or for the few with tusks, these serve well as they don't conduct electricity. Farmers have to continually change crop guarding tactics, as elephants learn them quickly, and then know how to outwit the farmer or the device. Human–elephant relations in highly developed landscapes evolve and change quickly and both sides adapt to survive, working with perception and relations to time and space.

The sounds of dialogue have altered from and across landscapes that are more intensively inhabited, and their qualities are dependent on knowledge and experience of living with the Other. Farmers who have lived with elephants over generations tend to guard their crops more successfully with less violent means (Fernando et al. 2005). The socio-ecological relations, rooted in knowledge of territory within multispecies communities, afford a different, more nuanced dialogue across farmers and elephants.

CONCLUSION

This chapter outlines how Western and foreign designs impinge on and shrink inclusivity of dialogues across humans, landscapes, and elephants. The dialogues and choreographies of farmer–elephant relations in Sri Lanka and the roles perceptions play in this interspecies dynamic are central to cohabitation, yet are not supported in the abstracted capitalist modes of landscape extractions. What policies support these dialogues? The size of elephants and their large vegetative needs mean that land use planning must begin with elephant lifeways, even before human needs are considered. One avenue to support farmer–elephant dialogues and cohabitation is through policies that hold development agencies accountable for the conflict, recognizing the dire circumstances for farmers on elephant lands and for elephants who have lost their lands. Policies supporting these dialogues would provide farmers payments for their ecosystem services for living with elephants, possibly through ecotourism revenues while simultaneously consulting farmers who have broad knowledge of living with elephants and other complex ecological issues. Managed elephant ranges are an example of landscapes oriented around elephant lifeways and may include buffer zones that allow for seasonal cultivation that maintain grasslands (Santiapillai and Jackson 1990). Climate change already disrupts monsoon cycles and increasing impacts call for broad-scale strategies that undo abstractions of colonial and capitalist practices, re-invigorating the local, multispecies dialogues.

NOTES

1. The term "territorial" is not meant to reduce landscapes to empty spaces. Territories are complex systems and spaces, relationalities, meanings, histories for many species and forces.

2. For more on pesticide use and the economic toll for farmers, see Taylor, G.J. 1999. Pesticide Use in Sri Lanka. Environment Group, Institute of Aquaculture, University of Stirling.

3. See Guattari, The Three Ecologies for how the social, subjective and ecological spheres interconnect and mirror one another.

4. The quotations henceforth, marked solely with dates, are from anonymous sources among the authors' unpublished field work data.

BIBLIOGRAPHY

Anver, Gazala. 2015. "Sri Lanka's Starving Elephants." *RoarMedia*, September 14, 2015.

Bastian, Sunil. 2018. *Sustaining a State in Conflict: Politics of Foreign Aid in Sri Lanka*. Colombo, Sri Lanka: International Center for Ethnic Studies.

BBC News. 2020. "Sri Lanka Elephants: 'Record Number' of Deaths in 2019," January 11, 2020.

Benadusi, Mara. 2015. Elephants Never Forget: Capturing Nature at the Border of Ruhuna National Park (Yala), Sri Lanka. Capitalism, Nature, Socialism 26 (1): 77–96.

Bradshaw, G.A. 2010. *Elephants on the Edge*. New Haven, Connecticut: Yale University Press.

Campos-Arceiz, Ahimsa. 2016. "What Should We Do about the 15,000 Asian Elephants Still in Captivity?" The Conversation. Accessed May 1, 2020. http://theconversation.com/what-should-we-do-about-the-15-000-asian-elephants-still-in-captivity-64620.

Campos-Arceiz, Ahimsa, and Steve Blake. 2011. "Megagardeners of the Forest—the Role of Elephants in Seed Dispersal." *Acta Oecologica*, Frugivores and Seed Dispersal: Mechanisms and Consequences of a Key Interaction for Biodiversity, 37 (6): 542–53. https://doi.org/10.1016/j.actao.2011.01.014.

Chartier, Laura, Alexandra Zimmermann, and Richard J. Ladle. 2011. "Habitat Loss and Human–Elephant Conflict in Assam, India: Does a Critical Threshold Exist?" *Oryx* 45 (4): 528–33. https://doi.org/10.1017/S0030605311000044.

Commons, Michael. 2018. "Forest Gardening with Space and Place for Wild Elephants." Regeneration International. 2018. https://regenerationinternational.org /2018/01/15/forest-gardening-space-place-wild-elephants/.

Dissanayaka, D.M.A.C., Weerakkody, R., Buhari, R., Rathnayake, D. 2019. Causality, Nature, and Magnitude of Human-Wildlife Conflict (HWC) in Uva and Eastern Wildlife Regions in Sri Lanka. Hector Kobbekaduwa Agrarian Research and Training Institute. Colombo, Sri Lanka.

Dissanayaka, D.M.A.C. 2019. "The Relationship Between Behavioral Patterns of Sugarcane Farmers and Chronic Kidney Disease of Unknown Etiology: A Case Study of the Sugarcane Fields of Pelwatta Sugar Corporation." Master's Thesis, Colombo, Sri Lanka: University of Colombo.

Dissanayaka, D.M.A.C., Elizabeth Oriel, Rifana Buhari, Virajith Kuruppu, and Upul Sanjaya. 2020. "The Changing Role from Defenders to Challengers: In the Context of Wildlife Protection Measures Implemented in Moneragala District of Sri Lanka." *Policy Matters 2020* Special Issue on Environmental Defenders.

FAO. 2010. "Global Forest Resources Assessment 2010: Main Report." FAO Forestry Paper. Rome, Italy: FAO Food.

Fernando, Prithiviraj. 2000. "Elephants in Sri Lanka: Past, Present and Future." *Loris* 22: 38–44.

Fernando, Prithiviraj, Eric Wikramanayake, Devaka Weerakoon, L.K.A. Jayasinghe, Manori Gunawardene, and H.K. Janaka. 2005. *Perceptions and Patterns of Human–Elephant Conflict in Old and New Settlements in Sri Lanka: Insights for Mitigation and Management.* Vol. 14. https://doi.org/10.1007/s10531-004-0216-z.

Handawela, James. 2016. *Ancient Dry Zone Watershed Farming System: Hena, Wewa, and Purana Evolved by Farmers and Failed by Rulers.* Colombo, Sri Lanka: S. Godage and Brothers Ltd.

Hickel, Jason. 2017. *The Divide.* London: Penguin Random House UK.

Holquist, Michael. 2002. *Dialogism: Bakhtin and His World.* New York: Routledge.

Keil, Paul G. 2016. "Elephant-Human Dandi: How Humans and Elephants Move through the Fringes of Forest and Village." In *Rethinking Human Elephant Relations in South Asia*, edited by Piers Locke and Jane Buckingham, 243–71. Oxford: Oxford University Press.

Kotagama, Sarath W., ed. 2014. *A Pictorial Guide to Uda Walawe National Park.* Colombo, Sri Lanka: Field Ornithology of Sri Lanka.

Kurt, Fred, Günther B. Hartl, and Ralph Tiedemann. 1995. "Tuskless Bulls in Asian Elephant Elephas Maximus . History and Population Genetics of a Man-Made Phenomenon." *Acta Theriologica* 40 (October): 125–43. https://doi.org/10.4098/ AT.arch.95-51.

Latour, Bruno. 2018. *Down to Earth: Politics in the New Climatic Regime.* Cambridge, UK: Polity Press.

Mahānāma. 1908. *Mahavamsa: Great Chronicle of Ceylon.* Pali text society.

Matthews, Freya. 1999. "Letting the World Grow Old." *Worldviews: Global Religions, Culture, and Ecology* 3 (2): 119–37.

McComb, Karen, David Reby, Lucy Baker, Cynthia Moss, and Soila Sayialel. 2003. "Long-Distance Communication of Acoustic Cues to Social Identity in African

Elephants." *Animal Behaviour* 65 (2): 317–29. https://doi.org/10.1006/anbe.2003.2047.

Milstein, Tema. 2016. "The Performer Metaphor: 'Mother Nature Never Gives Us the Same Show Twice.'" *Environmental Communication* 10 (2): 227–48. https://doi.org/10.1080/17524032.2015.1018295.

Molle, François, and Mary Renwick. 2005. "Economic and Politics of Water Resources Development: Uda Walawe Irrigation Project, Sri Lanka." Research report 87. Colombo, Sri Lanka: International Water Management Institute.

Oriel, Elizabeth, and Toni Frohoff. 2020. "Interspecies Ecocultural Identities in Human-Elephant Cohabitation." In *The Routledge Handbook of Ecocultural Identities*, edited by Tema Milstein and Jose Castro-Sotomayor. New York: Routledge.

Payne, Katy. 2003. "Sources of Social Complexity in the Three Elephant Species." In *Animal Social Complexity: Intelligence, Culture, and Individualized Societies*, edited by Frans B. M. de Waal and D. L. Tyack, 57–85. Cambridge, Massachusetts: Harvard University Press.

Polanyi, Karl. 2001. *The Great Transformation.* Boston: Beacon Press.

Ramey, Eva M.,Rob Ramey, Laura Brown, and Kelley Scott. 2013. Desert-dwelling elephants (Loxodonta africana) in Namibia dig wells to purify water. *Pachyderm* 53: 66–72.

Ratnapala, Mandasena. 1968. *Sinhalese Folk Lore, Folk Religion, and Folk Life.* Dehiwala, Sri Lanka: Sarvodaya Publishers.

Santiapillai, Charles, Prithiviraj. Fernando, and M. Gunewardene. 2006. "A Strategy for the Conservation of the Asian Elephant in Sri Lanka." *Gajah* 25: 91–102.

Santiapillai, Charles, and Peter Jackson. 1990. *The Asian Elephant: An Action Plan for Its Conservation.* IUCN.

Santiapillai, Charles and Bruce Read. 2010. Would masking the smell of ripening paddy fields help mitigate human-elephant conflict in Sri Lanka? *Oryx* 44(4): 509–511.

Sukumar, Raman. 2011. *The Story of Asia's Elephants.* Mumbai, India: The Marg Foundation.

Tolisano, Jim, Pia Abeygunewardene, Tissa Athukorala, Craig Davis, William Fleming, Kapila Goonesekera, Tamara Rusinow, H.D.V.S. Vattala, and I.K. Weerewardene. 1993. "An Environmental Evaluation of the Accelerated Mahaweli Development Program: Lessons Learned and Donor Opportunities for Improved Assistance." PDC-5451-I-14-1027-00. Bethesda, Maryland: US Department for International Development.

Van Daele, Wim. 2008. "The Meaning of Culture-Specific Food: Rice and Its Web of Significance in Sri Lanka." Omertaa, *Journal of Applied Anthropology*, 292–304.

van Dooren, Thom, and Vinciane Despret. 2018. "Evolution: Lessons from Some Cooperative Ravens." In *The Edinburgh Companion to Animal Studies*, 23. Edinburgh: University of Edinburgh.

Wilson, Christine. 1957. *Bitter Berry.* London: Hurst & Blackett.

Chapter 12

ocean medicine, mother medicine, sky medicine

Michaela Keeble

ocean medicine

the only medicine
i have is
metaphor

sitting on the sand
waiting for you
to stick out
your tongue

you might do it
you might

like everything
it depends on
trust

you open your eyes
and blink

look past me
and laugh

your mouth
is a medicine bag

at the far end
of your throat choking

is a carbon
whirlpool

i stick out my tongue

all my nightmares
are intertidal

my dreams
intertidal

this is where
the damage
will be done

our children
will not grow
the bones they need

this is nothing new

Maralinga
the Marshall Islands

they even tell us Mauna Kea
will be a tool
for healers

you are laughing

we need your bitter
we need your brutal

you are laughing

we are only scientists
we are only syllables
fusing and full of
fissures

your throat is open
and you are
laughing

mother medicine

*

there are so many
rivers inside me
i may as well be
a continent

when i run
all the rivers
are running

when i tilt
this way, that way
the rivers slow down
and change direction

this continent
its infinite rivers
rests on the back
of a giant crab

the crab belongs to māui
but gave birth to māui
the way crabs do:
eggs crusting its abdomen
like slow-cooling lava

perhaps i come from
the crab

perhaps i'm treading hard
on the crab's back

*

rock crabs cringe
in the crevices

we stab at them
with spears made from
broom handles:
nails jammed in
at the ends

we pierce their shells
and drag them
from their holes
angry

i'm hunting for one of two things

proof my mother
knows me

or tools to prise open
the crab's belly

crawl back
through the volcano
into my mother's heart

sky medicine

the stars are grinding out
medicine

i am grinding it in

red stars into
rubies into
rust

compare
this seep
with soil

do i belong?
am i made
of mineral?

i want to go back
to the time my mother was

alive

was i human then?

was i a woman
who worshipped
morning sky?

today i am absent
of ancestors

i want to cut off my head
roll it back
between my legs

i want to sew my brain

into my stomach

be rid
of this division

they would have me
go shopping

but a cashcard
and a take your pick
of myths

is not the answer

i stay where i am
curled up and spinning
at speed

Part III

PLANTS AND OTHER
FAMILY MEMBERS

Chapter 13

Weirding Wellness

Mushrooms, Medicine, and the Uncanny Renaissance of Psilocybin in the Chthulucene

Josh Potter

Nearly two-thirds of the way through *Fantastic Fungi*, director Louie Schwartzberg's popular 2019 documentary on mushrooms, mycelium, and human alliance with one of nature's unsung kingdoms, there is a fleeting reference to the antiviral properties of medicinal mushrooms such as Lion's Mane. Viewed in 2020 amid the global COVID-19 pandemic, this footnote in the narrative feels like a classic "buried lede" relegating what now feels most salient about the subject to a matter of secondary consideration. It seems as though the ongoing public health crisis through which we are currently living (and others tragically passing) has come to serve as an inescapable frame for nearly every public conversation attuned to wellness, resilience, and survival, while simultaneously presenting itself as a tangible example of the larger, imminent, cascading crises of human/capital-driven ecological destruction known as the Anthropocene. It has now become difficult to have a simple conversation with neighbors, Zoom meeting with co-workers or relatives, political dialogue with allies and opponents, or write an essay on mushrooms without framing the topic in the context of present or future viral crisis.

The effect is deeply uncanny. As we sit alone-together in global quarantine, thinking about concepts like "herd immunity" and watching the precarious situation play out on a species-level register largely removed from the influence of individual actions but beholden to the coordinated efforts of communities, institutions, and governments, our shared anxieties have paradoxically engendered a kind of affective resonance and collective focus, perhaps even among those who contemptuously spurn the judgment of public health officials. This is a striking development during an age that has otherwise been marked and marred by the increasingly chaotic, fractious discourse of neoliberal gamesmanship and ethno-nationalist isolationism. In short, the one thing we seem to agree upon right now is that the world has gotten very weird and is probably getting weirder. But all that many of us can do is sit and contemplate the bizarre solitude born of our species-level vulnerability to an invisible agent and dream of what it might take to deliver us to the shore beyond our present dread.

Like viruses, fungi have long occupied a mysterious, discomfiting room in the modern psyche. Food writer Eugenia Bone says, "a mushroom is not like a vegetable or an animal; it's somewhere in between" (Schwartzberg 2019). This ontological ambiguity can elicit both fear and wonder, an affective cocktail that some hope can take us through the looking glass of our current situation. Much like the spore-dispersing mushroom caps that manifest from the vast, invisible mycelial networks pervading the earth, responsible for metabolizing once-living matter and creating the conditions for life to renew itself, mushroom narratives are rapidly dotting the popular imagination. In *The Mushroom at the End of the World* (2015), Anna Lowenhaupt Tsing encounters fungus in the scorched wastelands of capitalist ruin, existing in a state of contaminated assemblage with human curiosity and capable of teaching us about transformation—instead of progress—by showing us how "to look around, rather than ahead" (Tsing 2015, 22). Schwartzberg's film features a chorus of voices even more evangelical of the mushroom in a time of endless precarity, claiming that fungi could be nothing short of "critical to the evolution of the species."

Much of this story is not new. Both indigenous communities and modern mycologists have long known the medicinal value of certain mushroom species, and social theorists working in the spirit of Deleuze and Guattari (1980) have looked to the "rhizomatic" structure of mycelium as paradigmatic of nonhierarchical life after capitalism. Indeed, these fungal fables have long been rearing their heads within the ecological fringe, traveling through the speculative ethnobotany of Terence McKenna (1992), myco-engineering of Paul Stamets (2005), to the narrative journalism of Michael Pollan (2018). Beyond the antiviral and pollution-abatement applications for certain mushroom species, these accounts all circle a much weirder thesis focused on one outlaw variety.

Psychedelic mushrooms—specifically *psilocybe cubensis* and around 200 related species containing the psychoactive agent psilocybin—are experiencing a global renaissance as the urgency of the Anthropocene and its attendant spiritual crisis has begun razing the cultural field of a stigma that buried their serious consideration as medicine from Western discourse for the past half century. Researchers, activists, entrepreneurs, and an unlikely coalition of advocates are making the strikingly a-modern claim that this mushroom may have an urgent message for humanity in a time of global crisis, should we be humble and receptive enough to heed its call.

Renewed biomedical research has begun levying empirical evidence toward emerging psychotherapeutic techniques, in many cases explicitly validating and paying homage to modes of indigenous shamanism both estranged from and decimated by Western technoscience, while making bold claims about the medicine's psycho-social benefits. Some of the world's leading research universities are now diving headlong into psychedelic science, while grassroots activists lobby American municipalities for the decriminalization of psychoactive fungi and plants on the grounds of their natural relationship and alliance with the human species. Meanwhile, popular culture is flush with psychedelic fantasy, constellated in documentaries and TV series like *Dosed, Have a Nice Trip, Midnight Gospel, High Maintenance, The Good Place,* and even Gwyneth Paltrow's lifestyle series *GOOP*.

Hanging over this psychedelic boom—and fungal bloom—are major questions regarding psilocybin's complicated status somewhere between fungus and chemical molecule, medicine and sacrament, subject and object, an ambiguity that calls for a fundamental reconsideration of how we understand the wellness of the mind, body, spirit, community, environment, and an imperiled more-than-human world. Most compelling, the renaissance of interest in psilocybin as both medicine and perceptual catalyst foregrounds the importance of phenomenological encounter in a post-COVID world where quarantine has forced many into ascetic meditation on the uncanny dissonance between personal and global registers of knowledge, a trial that reveals the price of "mindfulness" as a radical confrontation with uncertainty and shadow. This essay joins the chorus of voices "coming out" to recall the history of modern encounters with psilocybin, charting how different configurations of shamanic and psychotherapeutic use have cycled from early anthropological intrigue and biomedical promise to what Michel Foucault—also recently outed as a psychonaut (Wade 2019)—might have called epistemological perversion, sullied by a war on drugs that has de-naturalized human relationship to a pharmacopeia of plant and fungal medicines. As this circuitous story winds its way back to the present, we find psilocybin renaissance extending its transformational tendrils into the chaotic planetary trouble Donna Haraway (2016) has usefully re-dubbed the Chthulucene to highlight the challenge of interspecies communication, kinship, coherence, and the limit of anthropocentric solutions. Following Erik Davis's (2019) recent analysis of psychedelic anomaly, this work pursues a spirit of "weird naturalism" into emerging notions of wellness, wherein healing is understood to take place beyond the mechanistic troubleshooting of disease in an individual's body-mind. Instead, this new, weird wellness follows the fault lines of an epistemic rupture that is threatening to break down default modern distinctions between the human and the natural, suggesting new ontological configurations of interspecies entanglement and the precarious fate we navigate together.

Michael Pollan's 2018 bestseller *How to Change Your Mind: What the New Science of Psychedelics Teaches Us About Consciousness, Dying, Addiction, Depression, and Transcendence* is widely considered the watershed moment in mainstreaming the psychedelic discourse. Just as *The Omnivore's Dilemma* (2006) is often credited as helping champion the farm-to-table "slow food" movement by profiling community-supported agriculture and exploring the environmental, nutritional, and labor implications embedded in dietary choices, Pollan's treatment of psychedelics has helped bring the topic of the psychedelic trip (back) to the farmers-market set. Pollan identified himself as a "reluctant psychonaut" on NPR (Kennedy 2019) who had little experience with and interest in psychoactive substances before catching wind of a rising tide in medical research into psilocybin happening at prestigious labs like Johns Hopkins, New York University, and the Imperial College of London. The story begins in 1943 in the labs of the Swiss chemical company, Sandoz, when chemist Albert Hoffman accidentally dosed himself with LSD-25, a synthetic compound originally derived from the ergot fungus. The psychiatric establishment initially embraced the potential of this new "psychotomimetic" tool for helping therapists understand the psychosis of their schizophrenic patients. What they found, however, was that, rather than a clinical definition of psychosis, what this compound "occasioned," in the language of contemporary psychedelic researcher Roland Griffiths, was more akin to the classical "mystical experience" described by scholars of religion like William James. Hence, in 1956, researcher Humphrey Osmond renamed this class of chemicals "psychedelic" for their "mind-manifesting" properties (Pollan 2018).

Laura Stark and Nancy Campbell have explored this era of psychedelic history with particular interest in the "methods of ingression" researchers pursued to understand the "ineffable" experience that psychedelic users report (Stark and Campbell 2018). These tactics were used in concert with "methods of extraction," which attempted to externalize and capture the inner subjective experience of the patient "to create evidence that seemed unmediated by language, explanation, and interpretation, and thus offered as much precision and rigor as possible" (Stark and Campbell 2018, 791). Extractive methods would later come to dominate the paradigm of clinical research as tools like the electroencephalogram (EEG) helped substantiate a brain-based model for the mind and "brain waves represented the material basis of people's psychic and sensory worlds in the form of detectable electrical activity that correlated with interiority" (Stark and Campbell 2018, 804). The practice of clinicians self-administering LSD exemplifies a moment when "clinical empathy" was considered a powerful tool in what Steven Shapin (2012) has called the "science of subjectivity," a term that Stark and Campbell note carries connotations today of both interiority and inferiority, compared to the unassailable claims of exterior objectivity (Stark and Campbell, 793). Erik Davis (2019), adopting William James's terminology, has usefully described this kind of practice as a form of "radical empiricism," which validates the subjective experience as real, *especially* insofar as it defies easy linguistic articulation and classification.

Up until 1971, when the Controlled Substances Act effectively prohibited both naturally occurring and synthetic psychedelic agents, there was a robust period of experimentation and research into the mental-health applications of these brain-chemistry tools and much of the medical literature before 2006 was produced during this era. Psychiatrists developed clinical protocols for administering psychoactive substance and facilitating the patient's experience, noticing the co-constructive effects of "set"—the patient's frame of mind—and "setting"—the ambient and social environment—on the experience occasioned by the chemical agent (Pahnke 1963). Following efforts pioneered by Czech psychotherapist Stanislav Grof (who, in 2019, published a two-volume compendium of his life's work, *The Way of the Psychonaut*), "psychedelic-assisted psychotherapy" became common among the American intelligentsia, with celebrities like Cary Grant claiming the practice had made him a "happy man" (Pollan 2018, 157).

The history more widely known is that of psychedelic prohibition, a decidedly political reflex by the Nixon administration to curtail the social upheaval similarly occasioned by psychedelic use. This was a response in large part to the revolutionary agitations of figures like Timothy Leary, who had been expelled from his post at Harvard and openly advocated the noninstitutionalized use of psychedelics. Pollan documents the lingering resentment of respected researchers like Leary's Harvard colleague Walter Pahnke for the scientific setbacks caused by the jail-breaking of psychedelics from the academy. Pahnke's most famous contribution to the literature is the 1962 "Good Friday Experiment," in which he administered psilocybin in a double-blind study to Harvard undergraduates, establishing that, with the proper set and setting, the chemical can induce mystical experience.

Pahnke's decision to test the spiritual effects of psilocybin in particular derived from his anthropological knowledge that Mazatec shamans had long been using psilocybe mushrooms as sacrament in a ceremonial context. In 1957, the banker and ethnomycologist R. Gordon Wasson published an account in *Time Magazine* of a mushroom ceremony he and his wife Valentina Pavlovna Guercken had undertaken with the Mazatec *curandera* María Sabina. The article initiated widespread interest in psychedelic experimentation, driving a countercultural pilgrimage to Sabina's small rural village that had catastrophic effects on the region's indigenous way of life, while piquing the interest of Western researchers like Pahnke, who honed in on the technoscientific value of the psychoactive molecule to cross religious traditions.

The colonial history of psilocybin's migration to the West is one that hangs heavy over the present psychedelic renaissance and still carries unresolved tensions between an indigenous relationship to the naturally occurring mushroom and the biomedical handling of a compound that has been divorced from traditional context, extracted from its fungal host, and used primarily in its synthetic form. Helen Watson-Verran and David Turnbull note how "so-called traditional knowledge systems of indigenous peoples have frequently been portrayed as closed, pragmatic, utilitarian, value laden, indexical, context dependent, and so on, implying that they cannot have the same authority and credibility as science because their localness restricts them to the social and cultural circumstances of their production" (Watson-Verran and Turnbull 1995, 115-116). Meanwhile, what has hampered Western understanding of the psilocybin mushroom experience during the decades of prohibition that followed was researchers' lack of access to the closed, indexical context of the laboratory, to which the authority of pharmaceutical research is wed, and upon which the current psychedelic renaissance has been built.

Roland Griffiths et al.'s 2006 paper "Psilocybin can occasion mystical-type experiences having substantial and sustained personal meaning and spiritual significance" broke the decades-long freeze on psychedelic research within the academy and is regarded as the beginning of the current scientific renaissance. Echoing the findings of the Good Friday Experiment, Griffiths dispelled the politicized stigma of psilocybin's harm-potential and used extensive surveying of the study's participants to demonstrate dramatic short- and long-term quality of life benefits. A statistically significant number of participants rated the experience among the most profound in their lives, comparable to the death of a parent and the birth of a child. The paper closes in stating, "the ability to prospectively occasion mystical experiences should permit rigorous scientific investigations about their causes and consequences, providing insights into underlying pharmacological and brain mechanisms" (Griffiths et al. 2006, 15).

This was a rallying cry to the scientific establishment and has given rise to the Johns Hopkins Center for Psychedelic and Consciousness Research, where Griffiths leads an army of researchers conducting studies on psilocybin's effect on treatment-resistant depression, alcohol and opiate addiction, post-traumatic stress disorder, end-of-life care, and a host of other pathologies. The measured tone and cautious scope of Griffiths's initial paper has since been emboldened by a body of research that has placed Griffiths in the vanguard of those speculating on psilocybin's long-term impact on not only human wellness but the fate of the species. "The core of this mystical experience," Griffiths says on camera in *Fantastic Fungi*, "is a mystery—the existential mystery. What are we doing here? What is the meaning of this?"

Some of the field's most interesting research has come out of the Centre for Psychedelic Research at the Imperial College of London, where Robin Carhart-Harris has expanded Griffiths's protocols to test not only psilocybin's effect on mental health but also on political orientation, nature-relatedness, and the subject's perceived position of the self vis-à-vis the world.

Carhart-Harris's research follows a model of the "entropic brain," using principles of information science to understand the extraordinary supersensitive cognitive effect of psilocybin on the serotonin 5-HT 2A/C receptor site. "The great merit of applying the measure of entropy [defined as greater uncertainty and information-content] in cognitive neuroscience is that it is uniquely adept at bridging the physical and subjective divide; mere flip sides of the same coin" (Carhart-Harris 2018, 168). While his lab employs EEG and brain-imaging techniques to make their claims about the psychedelic experience, Carhart-Harris's conception of the subjective "inside" and objective "outside" of the psychedelic experience is less rigidly dualistic than in prior research paradigms. Invoking cognitive neuroscientist Francisco Varela's notion of "neurophenomenology," Carhart-Harris's lab does not seek discrete mechanisms that engender mystical states but rather pragmatically pursues "meaningful mappings between irreducible 'mind-stuff' and intimately associated 'brain-stuff'" (2018, 170).

Fittingly, the working thesis Carhart-Harris's lab uses to understand psilocybin's principle effect is the notion of "connectedness." Moving beyond the "mystical" language of prior researchers, the principle of connectedness allows them to analyze the experience according to three general registers: connection to self, others, and the world. At the *Horizons: Perspectives on Psychedelics* conference, held October 13–14, 2019 at New York's Cooper Union Great Hall, two researchers in Carhart-Harris's team, Rosalind Watts and Ashleigh Murphy-Beiner, elaborated on the "ACE Model" used during the guided psilocybin session. Instead of suppressing challenging emotional experiences, the protocol encourages patients to "Accept, Connect, and Embody" whatever arises in the session. By moving into the entropic novelty of the psilocybin experience, participants consistently experience a higher sense of compassion, meaning in life, and gratitude, demonstrable through long-term behavioral change (including addiction recovery) and wellness (Watts and Murphy-Beiner 2019). "Post-treatment, participants referred to feeling reconnected to past values, pleasures and hobbies as well as feeling more integrated, embodied and at peace with themselves and their often troubled backgrounds" (Carhart-Harris and Erritzoe 2018, 548).

One of the most striking papers to come out of the Imperial College was a study of mostly Caucasian men with treatment-resistant depression that found "psilocybin therapy may persistently decrease authoritarian attitudes post-treatment" showing "for the first time, in a controlled study, lasting changes in political values after exposure to a psychedelic drug" (Lyons and Carhart-Harris 2018, 816). Going beyond the therapeutic treatment of the individual's sense of self, this study reveals psychedelic connectedness extending to the social organism at large and engendering a politics that is itself built on a principle of connectedness. While this assertion could be deployed to justify psilocybin's use as a political tool against the rising tide of authoritarian political regimes worldwide, Lyons and Carhart-Harris are more measured. "We are keen to avoid a value judgement," they write, "about the political changes that may (or may not) be attributed to psychedelic use," noting the vastly divergent politics that might be construed as "beneficial for society." Instead, they shift focus slightly to another major claim made in the same paper attuned to "the scale and seriousness of the problem posed by climate change" (Lyons and Carhart-Harris 2018, 817).

Along with decreased authoritarian tendencies, this study found that "psilocybin therapy increases the subjective sense of connectedness to nature 1 week after treatment, and that these effects are sustained for at least 7–12 months," associated with lower levels of anxiety and greater personal well-being (Lyons and Carhart-Harris 2018, 814). One study participant is quoted as saying, "Before I enjoyed nature, now I feel part of it. Before I was looking at it as a thing, like TV or a painting. . . . [But now I see] there's no separation or distinction, you *are* it" (Lyons and Carhart-Harris 2018, 817, researcher's insertion and emphasis). This finding has been consistent across the literature, with Griffiths noting a hallmark of the experience as the feeling "you really are connected in a meaningful way with every atom of the universe" (Schwartzberg, 2019), and NYU researcher Anthony Bossis reflecting that "nature itself is something like the substance of love" (Schwartzberg 2019).

The path to this insight, however, is not always an easy one. Watts and Murphy-Beiner use the image of the pearl diver who must leave the comfort of the boat and plunge into the darkness of the deep sea, struggling through the recesses of their consciousness to retrieve the elusive pearl. Far from panacea, Watts regards psilocybin as a "nonspecific amplifier" of psychic material, as likely to engender what Carhart-Harris calls "cognitive bizarreness" as oceanic bliss. Ninety percent of their studies' participants report the experience as one of the most "unusual" in their lives, yet EEG studies show a long-term decrease in the amygdala-based fear response of patients after only one session (Watts and Murphy-Beiner 2019). It seems as though by facilitating a direct encounter with the weird and uncanny phenomena existing in uncertain space between the individual's sense of oneself and the world, that psilocybin has the power to mitigate even one's fear of death (Schwartzberg 2019).

The language of "the uncanny" does not usually accompany clinical discussions of psilocybin therapy, but when we consider the anomalous experiences engendered by this molecule's interaction with the human nervous system, easy causal relationships between affliction and cure remain ambiguous. Rather than fitting into a mechanistic model of wellness wherein a physiological deficiency is remedied by the introduction of a healing agent, psilocybin seems to shift the default categories themselves by which we evaluate what is normative. Perhaps we should not be surprised that a pharmakon for our age should present itself in this uncanny way. As Nils Bubandt (2018, 3) writes, "the Anthropocene is a truly uncanny time, a time when the proper separation between things—between culture and nature, subject and object, human and non-human, life and non-life—is collapsing." We feel this in the dissonance between our experience of local weather patterns and knowledge of the statistics of climate change or between the dread of a sweeping viral pandemic and our relative security at home watching Netflix. While a conventional account of the Anthropocene charts human hubris to every corner of a thoroughly de-naturalized world, solutions are often recursively bound to anthropocentric agency and the default epistemologies of secular reason—or abandoned to defeat. In advancing a nonsecular understanding of the Anthropocene that aims to move beyond old notions of the "human," "nature," and even "religion," Bubandt proposes we pursue "a different kind of language and a different kind of seeing" (2018, 9).

This is the move that Donna Haraway (2016) made in coining the—fittingly unpronounceable—Chthulucene. Named less for H.P. Lovecraft's madness-inducing monster than for the chthonic powers that spread like tentacles through a more-than-human world, Haraway's "Chthulucene is made up of ongoing multispecies stories and practices of becoming-with in times that remain at stake, in precarious times, in which the world is not finished and the sky has not fallen—yet" (11). Far from solving the problem of the Anthropocene with tools that alienated the human from the more-than-human, the project for the Chthulucene, as Haraway sees it, is the renewal of kinship between diverse human and nonhuman players, composting the hubris of the human into fertile humus.

This sounds like the job of a mushroom if ever there was one. Deployed as a catalyst in what Peter Sloterdijk (2013) calls "anthropotechnics"—postreligious practices that combine the remedial project of wellness with the aspirational project of spiritual wholeness—psilocybin seems to offer a kind of multispecies collaboration in the reformation of the human subject. Erik Davis (2019) uses this idea of the psychedelic experience as anthropotechnics to gesture beyond a secular accounting of the worldview that may emerge on the other side of the uncanny. He cites Freud's original conception of the uncanny as linked to the animist worldview that regards matter as spiritually alive, noting that "it is perhaps only from the flattened and disenchanted perspective of modern subjectivity that the liveliness of the world fails to register" (Davis 2019, 14). The recent psilocybin research suggests a reciprocal possibility, that through uncanny experiences, modern subjectivity is permitted to release its vice grip on constitutive percepts and concepts, giving way to a numinous alternate paradigm.

David Abram (1996) has comfortably used the word "magic" to describe the animist perspective, defining it as "the experience of living in a world made up of multiple intelligences [and] the intuition that every form one perceives . . . is an *experiencing* form, an entity with its own predilections and sensations, albeit sensations that are very different from our own" (9-10). This couldn't be further from the underlying assumption of Western materialist biomedicine but suggests that the doorway to such an understanding could come through the radical encounter with a sentient Other. Abram's thinking channels indigenous world views, many of which place psychoactive plant medicines at the center of their cosmologies as personified entities with whom relationships must be nurtured. María Sabina herself referred to the mushrooms as her "little children" (Pollan 2018, 110). Within this relationship, the ingestion of psilocybin is less a matter of metabolizing a psychoactive alkaloid than intimately communicating with a sentient fungal ally and teacher.

Yet, as Western biomedicine warms up to the transformative potential of psychedelic experience and begins to refine protocols for guiding subjects beyond the event horizon of the modern worldview, there remains an ontological ambiguity and political tension between the chemical agent, its fungal host, and its status spanning utilitarian object, conceptual hyperobject, and collaborating subject.

In the next few years, psilocybin-assisted psychotherapy stands to fundamentally challenge certain models of mental health care, replacing long-term pharmaceutical protocols and their profit-driven rates of dependency with short-term (even single session) psilocybin treatments and new forms of talk–therapy integration. "You can't make a lot of money that way," Michael Pollan quips (Schwartzberg 2019), contrasting the profit margin of psychedelics with chronic antidepressant regimes. Yet, the promise of psilocybin has spurred a kind of gold rush, with a wide range of interests scrambling to establish contrasting for-profit, non-profit, and a community-based "pollinator" model of care that "recognizes the mutually reinforcing relationship between individual and collective wellness" (Zelner 2020).

At the center of the issue is who controls the chemical in question, which remains a federally outlawed Schedule 1 substance. All clinical research currently uses synthetic psilocybin, due to laboratory science's need for consistency and purity across chemical batches. Fearing the type of gold rush that accompanied the medical and recreational legalization of cannabis in many American states, conversations among researchers, activists, and industry figures are directly addressing the issue of how to prevent psilocybin's gross capitalization. During one especially contentious panel focused on "Economic Models for the Expansion of Psychedelics" at the Horizons conference, George Goldsmith, the CEO of UK-based pharmaceutical company Compass Pathways Ltd., was challenged for accepting money from Silicon Valley libertarian tycoon Peter Thiel to help fund new psilocybin-based healthcare protocols (Aiden et al. 2019). In January 2020, Compass controversially obtained a patent for synthetic psilocybin, a move that critics say could monopolize future therapeutic protocols and claim ownership of prior psilocybin research. An alternate approach has been taken by the U.S. nonprofit Usona Institute, which is conducting clinical trials with psilocybin it intends to make available to other researchers according to principles of "open science" (Harrison 2020).

Compass is not alone in making entrepreneurial moves into the "psychedelic space." Tim Ferriss, the venture capitalist and self-optimization guru, was interviewed by *Fortune Magazine* in February 2020 touting investment over the next five years as a "golden window" and "an opportunity to use relatively small amounts of money to have billions of dollars of impact" (O'Brien 2020). Already, psilocybin and LSD "microdosing" protocols have become de rigueur among Silicon Valley startup culture, with coders and creatives looking to access the productivity benefits of "sub-threshold" doses without eliciting a full-blown ego-shattering trip (Kelly 2020).

Some critics, meanwhile, express doubt that psilocybin treatment could ever be developed on a for-profit model, due to the political and spiritual effects cited above, clinical conclusions that the drug offers virtually zero risk of dependency, and a more existential belief about the molecule itself as a decentralizing, rhizomatic entity. This argument is bolstered by the simple recognition that control of synthetic psilocybin does not preclude access to the many prevalent, naturally occurring psychedelic mushroom species that have long been harvested and cultivated by those with a keen eye to, as Tsing says, "look around, rather than ahead."

In a gesture of postcolonial sensitivity, Watts and Murphy-Beiner have acknowledged that the protocols developed at Imperial College owe everything to indigenous mushroom healers, whom they call the "true experts." They express a longing for the day when they can legally work in the clinic with the whole mushroom itself, no doubt both to establish consistency with its shamanic legacy and so the other active compounds in the fungus can be better scientifically understood (Watts and Murphy-Beiner 2019). The consensus among researchers, however, is that it doesn't really matter if the molecule is synthetic or naturally sourced. Wasson himself reflected, "I think people who discover a difference are looking for a difference. What is important is the effect that taking the substance has on one's life and well-being, not the subtleties of this or that product" (Fadiman 2011, 247).

While Western biomedicine rushes to legitimize psilocybin as medicine, in some cases, merging its language and methods with indigenous shamanism, another tendril of the renaissance is spreading through grassroots efforts in the mycelial underground. Directly challenging the illegal status of mushroom and plant medicines (such as the peyote cactus and ayahuasca brew), the Decriminalize Nature movement has begun petitioning municipalities to eliminate the funding necessary to prosecute arrests related to possession of these species. Drawing on the emerging science as rhetorical ammunition, the movement goes beyond an argument for personal wellness and sidesteps the stigmatized language of the war on drugs, instead channeling the rhetoric of pro-immigration, anti-ICE activism ("no human being is illegal") to advocate for the legalization of the fungus itself on the grounds of its natural ecological and metabolic relationship to the human species. The group articulates its purpose as simply "To decriminalize entheogenic plants, restore our root connection to nature, and improve human health and well-being" (Decriminalize Nature Oakland 2019). Like many neo-shamanic practitioners, the movement prefers the term "entheogen" to the historically stigmatized "psychedelic," foregrounding the capacity of these plant medicines to not only manifest the human mind but "generate or inspire the divine within."

One of the rallying cries of Decriminalize Nature is to "decolonize your mind," suggesting that it is not enough to use the default modern epistemologies to think our way out of the crisis of the Anthropocene. Rather, it is only through the re-naturalization of interspecies kinship that we may learn from this persecuted Other about a course of global action.

In May 2019, the movement notched its first victory, successfully petitioning the Denver, CO, city council to suspend funding for prosecutions, with Oakland, CA, quickly following suit. As of December 2019, over a hundred other American cities were considering similar decriminalization initiatives before Covid-19 quarantine stalled most petitioning efforts (Lekhtman 2020). Nonetheless, Oregon became the first state in the nation to legalize psilocybin therapy through ballot measure 109 in November 2020.

However, during mainstream news coverage of Decriminalize Nature's early victories, Michael Pollan offered his expert testimony to caution that full legalization may not be the right path to pursue. He seemed to fear a repeat of the anarchic social moment occasioned by LSD's jail-breaking of clinical science in the 1960s and expressed the technoscientific concern that the body of medical literature be allowed to mature prior to full legalization. "Its benefits may be greater than cannabis," he said of psilocybin on NPR, "but the risks are also more serious too" (Kennedy 2019).

The comparison of psilocybin to the legal arc of cannabis is a useful one. Drug policy scholar Charlotte Walsh says that legalization efforts have often followed one of two trajectories: exemption for medical or religious use. Cannabis has taken the former route, being first legitimized as medicine for specific ailments on the state level, prior to a broader push for "adult use." Psychedelics have in some cases taken the latter route, with certain indigenous groups gaining legal rights to possess and consume peyote and ayahuasca. Noting that "to a large extent the drug experience is socially constructed," Walsh points to the general difficulties of the religious argument, given the substances' tendency to de-condition beliefs as much as instill established definitions of the "sacred." Both of these avenues restrict usage to particular constrained situations sanctioned by the state and Walsh warns that, with the medical approach, "underground psychedelic healers . . . could easily find themselves freed from prohibitive constraints, only for their tools to instantaneously be engulfed by the structures that surround Western biomedicine" (Walsh 2016, 85). The Native American Church requested in spring 2019 that Decriminalize Nature remove peyote from its project, citing the scarcity of the cacti in the American southwest and the historically hard-fought tribal access to these lands and sacrament, which might be threatened by full-scale decriminalization (Sahagun 2020). Decriminalize Nature, however, has continued to insist that full-scale decriminalization in the United States and Mexico is the best way to protect both the cactus and the various traditions that revere it from threats of ecological destruction and economic exploitation (DN Team 2020).

Most medical researchers and advocates, like Rick Doblin of the Multidisciplinary Association for Psychedelic Studies (MAPS), now endorse decriminalization as a necessary component of expanding medical use (MAPS 2019). Walsh, in fact, anticipates the incremental erosion of all narcotic prohibition and advocates the model of "cognitive liberty," which extends a classical liberal argument beyond the idea of harm reduction to the principle of benefit maximization, not only to the individual user but also to society at large. "Adopting a rights-based stance more naturally leads into the development of a new paradigm for dealing with these molecules whereby individuals can access the substances of their choosing, in the ways that they require, as is their right" (Walsh 2016, 85). She says this should be done through the "grass-roots driven promotion of ethical standards and best practices in psychedelic use, voluntarily ascribed to," resulting in a psychedelic

socio-politics "as beautifully and anarchically impossible to govern as psychedelic use itself" (Walsh 2016, 85–86).

Viewed this way, Wasson may be right that the ontological difference
between natural and synthetic psilocybin exists in the eye of the beholder.
Or rather, the conflict exists solely in abstract political discourse, not in
the human-metabolized phenomenology of the psilocybin experience itself.
Bruno Latour, a longtime critic of what he dubbed the "Great Divide" in the
modern worldview, has sought to move beyond the irreconcilable ontological categories of Nature and Society that hamper our analysis of the current
situation. He offered the "quasi-object" as one conceptual tool: "Dialectics
literally beat around the bush. Quasi-objects are in between and below the
two poles, at the very place around which dualism and dialectics had turned
endlessly without being able to come to terms with them" (Latour 1993, 55).
If we trade the bush for a fungus, psilocybin figures as a compelling example
of a quasi-object in its dual ontologies spanning naturalistic and technoscientific discourse, as well as in its pharmacological power to loosen the
dialectical strictures of the analytic mind. The colossal affective states that
dwell beyond the collapse of dialectics, however, demand less ambivalent
language. Timothy Morton's (2013) notion of the "hyperobject" attempts to
do Latour one better by identifying objects and entities of such ecological
magnitude that they altogether stretch our understanding of what might be
considered a thing.

Psilocybin may be even weirder. As a pharmacological hyperobject, this
molecule has proliferated in mycelial configurations that stretch the spatiotem-
poral comprehension of the human mind, a process that is recursively internalized when metabolized by the human body. Davis notes that the word "weird"
derives from *wyrd*, the Anglo-Saxon concept of destiny, but that it suggests a
kind of fate that is twistier than modern teleological definitions. "The weird
that enters modern English . . . suggests both the esoteric knowledge of causal
necessity *and* the perverse turn away from natural law" (12). In weirding
emerging notions of wellness, psilocybin seems to invite a new understanding
of something that may have always been the case. Modernity's desire for ontological fixity has already been scrambled by the paradoxical realities of the
Chthulucene. The path offered to modern medicine by the psilocybin experience is deeper into this tentacular entanglement of entities that are increasingly
ill-defined but might constellate in unforeseen affinities and alliances if we
can reconcile their initial alterity. To speak of a sentient mushroom, or more
generally about the possibility of interspecies communication, remains a kind
of modern intellectual heresy. But it is becoming easier to speak empirically
of the de-cohering boundaries between the self, the other, and the more-than-
human, based on the growing body of psychedelic literature. Like the fruiting
bodies of a mushroom species that pop up sporadically to remind us of the

mycelial webbing that holds the forest floor in place, reports from the psychedelic renaissance are beginning to reveal that how we fashion ourselves is inextricable from how we fashion the world. If, like the participants in these studies, we can stay with this epistemic trouble, we stand to cross the event horizon of entropic weirdness—and Latour's "Great Divide"—into a situation unencumbered by the mind-forged manacles of the modern worldview and instead open to an animistic field of plurality and reciprocity.

BIBLIOGRAPHY

Abram, David. 1996. *The Spell of the Sensuous: Perception and Language in a More-Than-Human World*. New York: Vintage Books.

Aiden, Rachel and George Goldsmith, Robert Jesse, Beatriz Caiuby Labate, James Rucker, and Bennet A. Zelner. 2019. "Economic Models for the Expansion of Psychedelics" Panel Discussion. *Horizons: Perspectives on Psychedelics*. Oct. 13, 2019, Cooper Union Great Hall, New York, NY.

Bubandt, Nils. 2018. "Anthropocene Uncanny: Nonsecular Approaches to Environmental Change." Introduction to *A Nonsecular Anthropocene: Spirits, and Other Nonhumans in a Time of Environmental Change*. AURA Working Papers, Vol. 3, 2018. N. Bubandt, ed. Aarhus University, Denmark.

Carhart-Harris, Robin L. 2018. "The entropic brain—revisited." *Neuropharmacology*. 142: 167–178. https://doi.org/10.1016/j.neuropharm.2018.03.010.

Carhart-Harris, R.L. and D. Erritzoe, E. Haijen, M. Kaelen, R. Watts. 2018. "Psychedelics and connectedness." *Psychopharmacology*. 235: 547–550. https://doi.org/10.1007/s00213-017-4701-y.

Davis, Erik. 2019. *High Weirdness: Drugs, Esoterica, and Visionary Experience in the Seventies*. Cambridge: The MIT Press.

Decriminalize Nature Oakland. 2019. Retrieved from www.decriminalizenature.org Dec. 11, 2019.

Deleuze, Gilles and Felix Guattari. 1980. *A Thousand Plateaus*. Trans. Brian Massumi. London and New York: Continuum, 2004. Vol. 2 of *Capitalism and Schizophrenia*.

DN Team. 2020. "Peyotl's Call for Unity." https://decriminalizenature.org/blog/233-peyotl-s-call-for-unity. April 20, 2020. Accessed July 23, 2020.

Fadiman, James. 2011. *The Psychedelic Explorer's Guide: Safe, Therapeutic, and Sacred Journeys*. Rochester: Park Street Press.

Griffiths, R.R. and W.A. Richards, U. McCann, R. Jesse. 2006. "Psilocybin can occasion mystical-type experiences having substantial and sustained personal meaning and spiritual significance." *Psychopharmacology*. 187(3), 268–283. https://doi.org/10.1007/s00213-006-0457-5.

Haraway, Donna. 2016. "Tentacular Thinking: Anthropocene, Capitalocene, Chthulucene. *E-flux Journal*, No. 75, September 2016.

Harrison, Ann. 2020. "Challenges to a Company's Psilocybin Patent Highlight Contrasting Business Strategies for Developers of Psychedelic Therapies." *Lucid News*, April 7, 2020. https://www.lucid.news/challenges-to-a-companys-psilocy bin-patent-highlight-contrasting-business-strategies-for-developers-of-psychedelic -therapies/.

Kelly, Jack. 2020. "Silicon Valley is Micro-Dosing 'Magic Mushrooms' to Boost Their Careers," *Forbes Magazine*, January 17, 2020. https://www.forbes.com/sites /jackkelly/2020/01/17/silicon-valley-is-micro-dosing-magic-mushrooms-to-boost -their-careers/#1a1052be5822.

Kennedy, Merrit. 2019. "Oakland City Council Effectively Decriminalizes Psychedelic Mushrooms." *National Public Radio*. June 5, 2019.

Latour, Bruno. 1993. *We Have Never Been Modern*. Cambridge: Harvard University Press.

Lekhtman, Alexander. 2020. "Pandemic Puts the Brakes on the Psychedelic Decriminalization Movement." *Filter Magazine*, April 21, 2020. https://filtermag .org/decriminalize-psychedelics-coronavirus/.

Lyons, Taylor and Robin L. Carhart-Harris. 2018. "Increased nature relatedness and decreased authoritarian political views after psilocybin for treatment-resistant depression." *Journal of Psychopharmacology*. 32(7): 811–819. https://doi.org/10 .1177/0269881117748902.

MAPS. 2019. "Statement: Considerations for the Regulation and Decriminalization of Psychedelic Substances." Posted May 31, 2019. Multidisciplinary Association for Psychedelic Studies. https://maps.org/policyreform.

McKenna, Terence. 1992. *Food of the Gods: The Search for the Original Tree of Knowledge: A Radical History of Plants, Drugs, and Human Evolution*. New York: Bantam Books.

Morton, Timothy. 2013. *Hyperobjects: Philosophy and Ecology After the End of the World*. Minneapolis: University of Minnesota Press.

O'Brien, Jeffrey M. 2020. "Business Gets Ready to Trip: How Psychedelic Drugs May Revolutionize Mental Health Care." *Fortune Magazine*, February 17, 2020. https://fortune.com/longform/psychedelic-drugs-business-mental-health/.

Pahnke, Walter. 1963. "Drugs and mysticism: an analysis of the relationship between psychedelic drugs and the mystical consciousness." PhD thesis, Harvard University.

Pollan, Michael. 2018. *How to Change Your Mind: What the New Science of Psychedelics Teach Us About Consciousness, Dying, Addiction, Depression, and Transcendence*. New York: Penguin Press.

Pollan, Michael. 2006. *The Omnivore's Dilemma: A Natural History of Four Meals*. New York: Penguin Press.

Sahagun, Louis. 2020. "Why Are Some Native Americans Fighting Efforts to Decriminalize Peyote?" *Los Angeles Times*, March 29, 2020. https://www.latimes. com/environment/story/2020-03-29/native-americans-want-mind-bending-peyote-cactus-removed-from-efforts-to-decriminalize-psychedelic-plants.

Schwartzberg, Louie. 2019. *Fantastic Fungi: The Mushroom Movie*. Moving Art.

Shapin, S. 2012. "The sciences of subjectivity." *Social Studies of Science.* 42(2): 170–184. https://doi.org/10.1177/0306312711435375.

Sloterdijk, Peter. 2013. *You Must Change Your Life.* Malden: Polity Press.

Stamets, Paul. 2005. *Mycelium Running: How Mushrooms Can Help Save the World.* Berkeley: Ten Speed Press.

Stark, Laura and Nancy D. Campbell. 2018. "The ineffable: A framework for the study of methods through the case of mid-century mind-brain sciences." *Social Studies of Science.* 48(6): 789–820. https://doi.org/10.1177/0306312718816807.

Tsing, Anna Lowenhaupt. 2015. *The Mushroom at the End of the World: On the Possibility of Life in Capitalist Ruins.* Princeton: Princeton University Press.

Wade, Simeon. 2019. *Foucault in California: A True Story—Wherein the Great French Philosopher Drops Acid in the Valley of Death.* Berkeley: Heyday.

Walsh, Charlotte. 2016. "Psychedelics and cognitive liberty: Reimagining drug policy through the prism of human rights." *International Journal of Drug Policy.* 29: 80–87. https://doi.org/10.1016/j.drugpo.2015.12.025.

Watson-Verran, Helen and David Turnbull. 1995. "Chapter 6: Science and Other Indigenous Knowledge Systems." *Handbook of Science and Technology Studies,* SAGE Publications: 115–139.

Watts, Rosalind and Ashleigh Murphy-Beiner. 2019. "Psilocybin for Depression: Introducing the ACE Model (Accept, Connect, Embody)." *Horizons: Perspectives on Psychedelics* conference presentation. Oct. 12, 2019, Cooper Union Great Hall, New York, NY.

Zelner, Bennet A. 2020. "The Pollination Approach to Delivering Psychedelic-Assisted Mental Healthcare." *MAPS Bulletin,* Spring 2020, Vol. 30, No. 1. Multidisciplinary Association for Psychedelic Studies.

Chapter 14

Multispecies Motherhood

Connecting with Plants through Processes of Procreation

Mariko Oyama Thomas

When I was little, perhaps six or seven, the backyard of my otherwise unspec-
tacular suburban dwelling presented a fertile, jubilant landscape of possibility for communication and connection. At that time, I lived in the Pacific
Northwest of the United States and can easily recall the pungent emission of
fragrance from the wet soil where I pressed my palms in the pine duff, the
underbellies of the undulating slugs somehow slick and sticky at the same
time, and the faint whisper of iris blossoms opening their feathery layers
to the rare spring streams of sunlight. Like many very young people, I was
quite positive that most of the plants around me were somehow at least dimly
aware of my presence, and at least somewhat cognizant of how life worked,
as well as busy with their own narrative arcs of love, goals, aging, eating,
love-making, and kin-making. Simultaneously, I was already intrinsically
aware of how I shouldn't speak about my animate plants and their families
in public and perceptive of the kind of social humiliation that could be easily
doled out by my seven-year-old peers or second grade teacher if I vocalized
this tiny intimate truth.

On my own time, I indulged in the dreamy possibilities of all living things
participating in complex, multilayered lives. I conceptualized flowers as fairy
creatures, and I felt constantly observed by their purple, petaled bodies. They
leaned on each other in such a way that I assumed they were family members,
baby blossoms to a velvety strong mother bloom, and I was generally torn
between the desire to capture their bodies and combine them with mine by
plucking them or eating them, and the fear that they would no longer be there
to commune with if I did, or that I might be ripping a mother from a child, a
friend from a friend.

I am by no means an anomaly of a childhood case with this anecdote, and do not consider myself any more perceptive of the more-than-human[1] world than any other child raised in the Western/ized world, even in these anthropocentric times. I share this story (rather anthropomorphic though it might be) as an example of how the possibility of relationship with and between more-than-humans seems more tangible in those years that are protected from the glare of dominant Western/ized worldviews. These ways of being that have brought Earth to its current point of precarity tend to privilege a kind of Cartesian rationalism that leaves little room for plant animacy (Hall 2011), or the possibility that as the plant queendom[2] comprises the majority of biomass on the planet (Bar-On, Phillips, and Milo 2018), and a much longer history of existence than the animal queendom let alone the human species (Morris et al. 2018), plants might know a thing or two about living, family, and procreation.

The goals of this chapter are first to explore embodied and material connections with plant-life through the lens of my experience of early motherhood. The second goal of this chapter is to ruminate on the complicated relationships between motherhood, childhood, and environmentalism in the Anthropocene and, through autoethnographic prose and poetry, bring performative moments of these to light. This chapter begins with a short summary of some of the tensions between motherhood and environmentalism, moves to some concepts that could help work through those tensions, and closes with a range of short performative writings that intimately cavort with the similarities between plant and human bodies, and the magic times and cyclic similarities of motherhood and childhood. Though this is but one reflection in one historical moment, I hope to provide some examples of ways to see commanilities between human bodies and those otherworldly green beings who are so crucial in making human lives possible.

MYTHIC CHILDHOODS

For many humans, childhood offers an era to live fully and almost mythically in the magic of place and more-than-humans (Chawla 2002), making it a more feasible time to consider sentience in plants. Childhood also allows space for children to find and make kin with forms and beings that do not resemble their own bodies. Children will often fail to discriminate between differently bodied beings and regard a teddy bear, a Barbie doll, a pet guinea pig, and themselves as able to equally participate in a raucous tea party. Young humans spend large swaths of time looking for points of relation—asking, "do ducks have belly buttons?" Or telling others assuredly "that rose looks tired and is sleeping on a leaf pillow."

Biological accuracy aside (as we may never truly know whether a rose conceptualizes a leaf the way humans consider down-stuffed pillows) the motivation to constantly connect to other beings is often blindingly present the closer to birth one is. Dominant ontologies about "nature"[3] have yet to fully infiltrate the daily imaginations of children of young ages (Herrmann, Waxman, and Medin 2010), and perhaps the rather low mastery of verbal and written speech present in youth leaves room for other possibilities and potential ways to connect.[4] Either way, early childhood exists as a space to communicate and thereby commune with trees, flowers, nonhuman animals, toy horses, and whatever is thought to exist in the dark corner underneath the bed. Whether we realized it or not at the time, this instinctual desire to comprehend the world as sensual (Abram 2012), and writhing with indelibly alive beings, is perhaps a reflection of how hugely possible ecocentric understandings of the universe are, even in adulthood, and even in Western/ized cultures.

However, while this ecocentricity is observed in youth, it is often difficult to avoid the amnesia that can occur when we learn to distinguish, categorize, compartmentalize, judge, and discriminate between like-us and not-like-us. This learned separation between human and more-than-human is rooted in industrialized and colonized societies' need to propagate an unsustainable capitalist model that relies on subjugation of more-than-humans (Naess 2006). This subjugation is woven insidiously into many parts of the fabric of Western/ized cultures. For example, as a communication scholar, it is difficult for me to ignore how most elementary words of the English language can construct boundaries between human and more-than-human. This can work to discount innate sensual knowledge of the more-than-human world, and instead promote it as something less fantastical and more disconnected. The goals of othering, and reflections of dominant anthropocentricity are hard to avoid—woven into every kind of popular culture (Sturgeon 2009), and even into children's books (Waxman et al. 2014). For example, in 2008, the Oxford children's dictionary was slated to let go of words like "catkin," "cauliflower," and "clover," and instead replace them with words like "broadband" and "cut-and-paste," prompting a legion of authors to come to the defense of those words that were no longer considered important for a child's vocabulary (Flood 2015). Nouns aside, even the use of pronouns instructs perceived separation or closeness, as choosing what may be a they/he/she versus calling a living being an "it" or "thing" has innumerable consequences toward extensions of personhood. As Kimmerer (2013) writes, young people often extend intention, compassion, and personhood to plant and animal beings until they are retrained not to, often by the adults in their lives, those persons who have lost or been coerced out of their ability to see and speak about the innate liveness of the world around them.

MOTHERHOOD REVISITED

While this focus on childhood ecocentricity is important, it is unfair to frame childhood as the only time when ecocentric worldviews can be formed, and unrealistic for current environmental goals to theorize as if there were only one time period in which innate ecocentricity is possible. While perspective shifts are (and must be) possible at any time in life, I am finding that new motherhood is a ripe potential space to re-order anthropocentric worldviews and tune-in to the more-than-human world. Through shared processes and the overall telos of making babies[5] that much of this planet shares, many points of connection emerge, despite the diverse range of ways plants, animals, fungi, and so on perform parenthood or perform body. For many, motherhood is a liminal space where identity and perspective are challenged, lost, or reinforced (Laney et al. 2015). Careers, senses of self, and relationships with other humans are often radically altered, as is environmental identity[6] or the ways in which people perceive, act, and attach to environment. This could make motherhood a fruitful time to reassess, reflect, and rework ideas or roadblocks in perception of the more-than-human world.

Over the course of this chapter, I speak through my own embodied experience of recently experienced motherhood and my sensations of the utter materiality of growing another carbon-based life-form in my womb. By writing from this space, I direly hope not to negate the expansive experiences of the concepts of motherhood, parenthood, and relation-making that are so crucial in these times. For example, I have great affinity toward the notion of "kin-making" and believe this to be a pivotal way of relating. Haraway (2016) writes, "kin is a wild category that all sorts of people do their best to domesticate. Making kin as oddkin rather than, or at least in addition to, godkin and genealogical and biogentic family troubles important matters" (2). I happen to have arrived at the perspective that prompted this chapter by the process of "godkin," however, these experiences allowed me ways to create with and bond to oddkin. There are many ways of birthing/making/creating/merging kin, out of many experiences of doing body. My entry point to kin-making just happened to be biogenetic. In the wake of anthropogenic ecological crisis and deep uncertainty and fear about the power and fallibilities of bodies amid a zoonotic pandemic and the violent oppression of not only our more-than-human kin but also our human kin, re-remembering the common bond of materiality and earthly bodies we share with so many more-than-human beings is crucial to continuing to exist together on the planet, no matter how one might engage in the concept of kin in their lives.

MAKING SENSE OF MOTHERHOOD

Though I am embarrassed to admit it, it wasn't until I found myself unexpectedly pregnant toward the end of my doctorate that I began to remember the personhood(s) of plants and my love of them as a child. This stumble into pregnancy and motherhood had unexpected consequences on my conceptualization of the world, in that I had never experienced anything that resided so relentlessly in the physical world and my material body. I could throw a full gamut of intellectual jargon, Hegelian philosophy, and critiques of media and rhetoric to frame my slowly swelling belly but at its root, the seemingly radical reality of my body existing in this Earthly realm and following an age-old trial and error filled evolutionary pattern to make carbon that makes carbon, overwhelmed the rest of my ideas. I had spent years living in a world of pure rhetoric, relying on words, and disconnected "rationality" and "logic," and I now was forced to think of myself as rooted in the soil and as simply a body in a world of bodies, with the weight of what surely resembled a small sea creature pressing into my pelvis.

As an environmental scholar, the pregnancy was intellectually complicated and confusing. Narratives that tie motherhood(s) and women in all multitudes to environmentalism can consist of tangled, painfully colonized, patriarchal motives bound up in diverse moral codes. Not only the experiences of having a female body but also the experiences of motherhood come fraught with discordant environmental discourse. As many ecofeminist scholars have scrupulously detailed, women, female bodies, and the project of motherhood have been negatively associated with "nature" for generations of humanity (Griffin 2015; Merchant 1990; Plumwood 1986; 2002). One of the philosophical moments this can be traced back to is an unfortunate proposition by Aristotle that relegated eggs in ovaries as passive and material, and female spirit as "irrational" and therefore closer to a wild and illogical "nature" that men had supposedly overcome (Merchant 1990). Historically, women were argued to live in a material realm that made them more like more-than-human animals than their male counterparts, who were argued to have transcended "nature" (Griffin 2015; Merchant 1990). The legacy of these ideas makes women's connections to birth, domesticity and the more-than-human entirely complicated for those working to subvert old oppressions, yet still wishing to engage in ecofeminist conversations and honoring the astounding possibilities of having a woman[7] body.

Currently, women, and especially mothers, continue to be positioned as beings of the domestic (i.e., material) realm, and mainstream society still has little political or economic respect for the day-to-day experiences of dealing with the material, tangible, and touchable world of domestic work and child-rearing. This has resulted in feminist movements that often eschew domesticity to participate in movements away from the material aspects of being animal-bodied beings in contact with the more-than-human world and materiality (Alaimo 2008). However, the act of separating women from the material happenings and sheer existences of their bodies also poses challenges, in that by trying to liberate women from the oppressive confines of being assumed as growers, birthers, and tenders, women are then separated from the material and physical aspects that they may choose to exercise in being born female-bodied. This includes a separation from their Earthly existences and potential connections that may ground them in kinship with the more-than-human world (Alaimo 2008; 2010). Though many feminists have fought so diligently to allow women the choice of whether they wish to use their physical bodies for procreation or domesticity, the resulting "bracketing [of] the biological body" brings severe separations, and as Alaimo (2008) writes, works to sever "its evolutionary, historical, and ongoing interconnections with the material world, [which] may not be ethically, politically, or theoretically desirable" (238).

ENVIRONMENTAL MOTHERHOOD

Mothers in Western/ized settings are not only faced with the conundrums of how to relate their bodies to the more-than-human, or ignoring being grouped into past subjugations of "nature," but also the current cultural pressures of deciding whether or not to procreate and how to keep an "environmental" household. Some environmental scholars argue that it is immoral to pose procreation as moral but overconsumption (or eco-gluttony) as immoral, the underlying message being that mainstream environmentalism is simply not enough to make the moves necessary to support the survival of other more-than-human species and spaces (Young 2001). Should women still decide to procreate under this pressure, they are still subjected to as much as 80 percent of domestic labor (Crittenden 2002)—a way of working that is often unrecognized and disrespected—and are often judged on their "greenness" or level of sustainable practices in their homes, which requires the kind of time, help, and economic privilege that not many have. As Ray (2011) writes, "with all those diapers, and commutes to soccer games and new car seats, I might as well just start hacking away at glaciers myself" (83). Ray furthers her account of the pressures of "green motherhood" (or the way that environmentalism and motherhood are intertwined) by describing the troubling tension that women are often placed in where they are expected to uphold a motherly, nurturing, close-to-"nature" affect from being born female-bodied but are also somewhat persecuted by environmental movements as the ultimate sinners in their ability and/or choice to biologically reproduce, despite the fact that males are generally needed to accomplish this. In her ruminations on motherhood and its ties to pro-environmental behavior, Ray asks for a re-evaluation as to why the labor-intensive project of being green is heaped on mothers who already run the risk of drowning in domestic labor. Here, the material labors of domestic life, women, environmentalism, and child-rearing are heaped into a messy tangle that makes it difficult to understand where and when to be what kind of woman, mother, and environmentalist.

NEW THEORIES TO APPLY WHEN THINKING ABOUT MOTHERHOOD AND ENVIRONMENT

One way to work with this tangle of motherhood, environmentalism, ecofeminism, and history could be to put a range of multidisciplinary theories in conversation with motherhood. Theories and writing surrounding the epistemological stances of animism, transcorporeality, and vital materialism offer less hierarchical ways to understand both human and more-than-human bodies, as they emphasize mutual permeability and togetherness on the planet, and often allow conversations to step momentarily away from humanist historic and current oppressions to focus more on a multispecies approach.

For example, animacy offers one potential entry point to thinking materially, as it focuses deeply on the relational aspects of co-existence (Bird-David 1999) and is less hierarchical in its positioning of different species. As described in Willerslev & Ulturgasheva (2012), animism is a horizontal relationship between people and spirits, where human-animals and more-than-human animals, life and afterlife, and death and birth, all exist in constant unison with little hierarchy. Often, animist cultures have close ties with more-than-human entities, such as the Eveny reindeer peoples' practice of pairing a reindeer with a child on birth. The reindeer guardian is charged with the task of protecting the child's "open soul" or their relatively accessible and newly transitioned spirit, and can do so by switching places with the child in the advent of malevolent spirits. In this, it is the mutual reversibility of child and reindeer that exemplifies the intersubjective relationships possible in cultures with a strong predilection toward animism. Because Eveny have no doubt that a child may embody a reindeer form and vice versa, they live in a world in which perceived boundaries between different species matter little, and personhood is possible for all.

However, theories of animacy work more for mythic landscapes and assembled and complete bodies[8] , as well as for understandings of ontological relatedness but is less effective for describing the basic similarities of being bodies made of matter. Instead, animacy relies on the expectation that all things have personhood in their own right as opposed to anthropomorphic personhood (Hall 2011). Animacy is a useful philosophical position from which to counteract the separations between objects and subjects, a division that has long placed both women and the more-than-human in the inactive/ subject area. In this sense, it could be posed as a potential feminist concern and project. As identities that has been regularly subjugated over the ages and relegated as passive, female bodies and mother bodies have much at stake in the realizations of live-ness, liveliness, and questions of agency.

Alaimo's understanding of transcorporeality and Bennett's (2010) vital materiality should also be considered as useful lenses to put in conversation with motherhood, as they put slivers of animacy in the context of current Western/ized thought and still acknowledge the relatability and permeability of having a body on a shared planet. In dominant Western/ized thought, human-"nature" separation makes it entirely easy to ignore the potential personhoods, animacies, or agencies of the more-than-human world (Carbaugh, 1996; Haila 2000) and to avoid thinking in terms of relation. For example, considering what one has in common with a sunflower or a couch as opposed to never considering these things in the same stream of consciousness or looking for similarities between them.

In Bennett's (2010) *Vibrant Matter,* she urges readers to consider the "vital materiality" that runs through all things and bodies, and the enormous environmental and political consequences of human ignorance of this. She writes, "an active becoming, a creative not-quite-human force capable of producing the new buzzes within the history of the term nature. This vital materiality congeals into bodies, bodies that seek to preserve to prolong their run" (118). Bennett suggests that humans might do well to postpone questions of subjectivity and do away with the obsession of identifying what really distinguishes human from plants or anything else, and inquires as to how anthropomorphism might be a useful tool despite many scholars' aversion to it, as, "too often the philosophical rejection of anthropomorphism is bound up with a hubristic demand that only humans and God can bear any trace of creative agency" (120).

Bennett's (2010) work helps argue against human exceptionalism, and also the concept that human bodies are special, independent, and unaffected by the world outside their skin, as she notes the ability of many seemingly inanimate items (such as food, for example) to affect the human form. Allewaert's (2013) work also touches on this, writing about colonies in the tropics and how the more-than-human world seeped into the colonizers "rationally" organized lives and bodies through mold, disease, and heat to effectively thin out the Western/ized attempts at remaining separate from their environment. Here, Bennett's (2010) work meshes well as the more-than-human and human meld in a messy permeability that belies the question of constant assembling and reassembling of animate matter to make bodies that are perhaps not our own but rather running on the same frequencies that every other "thing" on the planet runs with.

In Allewaert's (2013) and Bennett's (2010) work, they describe topics such as the agency of mold, the liveness of disease, and the inseparability of human bodies with other bodies from the environment. Feminist scholar Alaimo's (2008) work takes the concept of inseparability and suggests trans-corporeality as a term and option for addressing the material aspects and interconnections of human and more-than-human relations, writing:

> Emphasizing the material interconnections of human corporeality with the more-than-human world, and at the same time acknowledging that material agency necessitates more capacious epistemologies, allows us to forge ethical and political positions that can contend with numerous . . . realities in which "human" and "environment" can by no means be considered as separate. (239)

Transcorporeality, as she describes, is a way of imagining material bodies as constantly woven with the more-than-human world, an epistemological space that understands the utter inseparability and deep permeability of human and more-than-human corporeality. This is also an ethic, and way of being that can be applied to one's gaze of the world, and a practice on how to interact with and understand the more-than-human. It is a concept that I rely heavily on in my reflections of motherhood, both throughout this chapter and in my life outside of writing.

MOTHERHOOD MAGIC

As I write this, my infant daughter sleeps downstairs, her mouth still smeared with mud from taste-testing several varieties of gravel earlier today and her hand clamped on a leaf she has refused to let go of. It will likely end up in her digestive tract—the interaction between this leaf and her body making the two wound up in mutual permeability and similar predilections for growth. I write this after a year of letting her grow in my belly and releasing her into autonomy in a wash of blood and afterbirth on my bedroom floor, after writing my dissertation that spearheaded much of the thinking found in this essay and defending it grossly pregnant, hot, tired, and unable to escape my body or hers.

The rest of this chapter is spent on several short explorations of multispecies motherhood and the similarities and overlaps I perceived in my experiences of birthing a daughter, with those of the living, birthing, plant world. Throughout this performative autoethnographic writing, I meditate on the "material interconnections of human corporeality with the more-than-human world" (Alaimo 2008, 238) and the shared animacy and materiality that human bodies have with plant bodies. I use performative writing to muse on the discordance of gender, environment, and motherhood and as a way to sidestep the contradictory directions of scholarship on these subjects and instead focus on the intimacy of my lived experience.

The prose and poems are points of connection, empathy, and relation with plants—a deeply ignored and misunderstood part of the planet (*see* Hall 2010; Wandersee and Schussler 1999) and an experiment in using the worldview-changing time period of early motherhood in a way that momentarily shuns the deep contestation about motherhood, women, and environment, found in Western/ized culture. As methodology to guide this generative exploration, I use autoethnographic prose based on Ellis's (1999) discussion of heartful autoethnography and Pollock's (1998) articulation of performative writing. As heartful autoethnography "includes researchers' vulnerable selves, emotions, bodies, and spirits . . . and celebrates concrete experience and intimate detail" (669), and autoethnographers' work in general constantly moves from from a wide understanding of current cultural forces to the intimate and vulnerable detail of how those forces are resisted, re-inscribed, or reflected in their own lives (Ellis, Adams, and Bochner 2011), I found it particularly useful for delving into this subject matter. This undulation between outward and inward, public and private, feels apropos for writing about something as personal and universal as birth.

To sculpt the autoethnographic prose and poems, I also rely heavily on Pollock's (1998) understanding of performative writing, which as she describes it, "confounds the normative distinctions between critical and creative (hard and soft, true and false, masculine and feminine), allying itself with logics of possibility rather than validity" (81). Pollock continues, positing that performative writing "requires that the writer drop down to a place where words and the world intersect in active interpretations, where each pushes, cajoles, entrances the other into alternative formations, where words press into and are deeply impressed by the "'sensuousness of their referents.'"[9] This is an especially fecund methodology when working with the sensuous world of relating to other beings and bodies, as performative writing (especially in an autoethnographic sense) allows space to sidestep rhetorical objectivity and instead delve into my own interpretations of the lived, physical, dynamic, and deeply personal, experiences.

Ranging from interconnections between human and plant birthing, to mourning and motherhood in this time that is so perilous for every species, these performative utterances are really an interrogation into the ways that motherhood have given me permission to come back into my material and animist existence, the aforementioned childhood existence, and through this realization of what it is to have a living birthing body and form a heart-aching kinship with other mother bodies that make babies. They are also an experiment in trying to prolong the space that birthing and motherhood (despite rampant intellectual complications and contradictions) has allowed me back into, and a response to my hunch that like childhood, early motherhood is quite close to a sensual and wordless world. This writing is clumsy, and relies on imagination, phenomenological perception and interpretation, and anthropomorphism, which following the work of Bennett (2010) is still a useful starting point in perceiving connection and sameness despite scholarly wariness toward the term.

In the arrows and throes of recently birthing a human being, I have found myself able to reflect and remember much more about how I felt in my childhood ecocentricity than I used to. There are times when I can't sit still with the immense overflowing of empathy I feel toward the trees around me spreading their pollen, and the seedlings struggling to survive another unforgiving day of the New Mexico sun. Procreation, birth, and baby-rearing feel so material, so embodied, so old, and so Earthly, that I couldn't believe I had not deeply considered it as a cross-queendom connection before, causing me to sink deeply into rumination on the blindness toward interspecies connections often fostered by dominant society. True also are the similarities across plant and human worlds in watching a tiny being come to fruition. It is as if my newborn daughter, having just left a sensual, material, and instinctual place where all the world's babies are, has allowed me to be there also. In this uncertain time of anthropogenic disaster and frightening extinction, it is my assumption that if I try to understand plants as truly and vibrantly alive and animate—a ponderosa pine and I might have so much to share in the way of birth stories, and the aspens know more about making family than I will ever know.

OFFERINGS

Birthing 1

When I went into labor with her, the seedling, the spore, the tiny naked mammal, mammimal, animal, whatever you wish to call it, it was as if the earth rumbled and counting me as part of her landscape threatened to split me open in order to create a new pathway for the water that was she, to flow. I sat at dinner dressed in a wrinkled black dress and perched on an uncomfortable wooden chair through several hours of early contractions while I watched my human relations laugh and slurp wine. I sunk into my throne of tree bones and became quiet and unsure as to if what I was feeling, the deep convulsions, the shuddering ripples across my belly, were even real. Dazed, I stared as the wine seeped through their human veins and saw how powerful those grape vines were to become so delicious and so mood altering and so necessary to us, and considered my own cocktail of hormones making these convulsions happen, again so delicious, and so mood altering, and so necessary to us.

I fixed my gaze blankly at the apple tree wrapped in sparkling lights outside the restaurant and wondered what it felt like to make so many apples year after year, and if an apple blossom shifting into a fruit was felt deeply and painfully in the mother tree and if the sharp break of an apple leaving the branch and implanting in the soil reverberated in her body. My heart broke when I imagined the way a sprout curled close in its shell before bursting forth and expanding—it was just too delicate and breakable—the way the girlchild inside me was right now, head tucked to her chest and arms folded over each other in the floating universe of my body.

Most humans think of birth as a mammalian experience. Live birth is particularly valued in the hierarchies of living things, and you get even more points if your living thing comes out of your body with hair or eyes that can open. There is also no real understanding of what birth is for non-mammal bodies, and what the moment of giving birth looks or smells or feels like. Is it when the flower emerges all soft and veined or the when cone plumps up with potential or when the rhizome springs forth a sprout? When the blossoms are fertilized in a lovingly aggressive dance of stamens and ovules and bees? When the seed manages to reach the soil-womb of the forest floor? When the cotyledons[10] creep forth from their shell? When it is clear that they will survive the first spring having avoided being taken out by hungry ants, neighboring plant species, and starvation, or uprooted by record rainfall? When it no longer relies so heavily on the carbon root milk their mother nurses them with through mychorrizal networks?[11]

Later, I lay in bed trying to sleep and gave in to the gravity and truth of this seedling in me attempting to poke through the soil of my body. Nobody really knows why birth starts, it is said to be something to do with the mother's body, and something to do with the baby's body, and possibly something to do with barometric pressure, though no one can prove any of this. We are the same as plants in this vague space. A flowing mess of evolution and environment and forces that feel like magic make us bloom or birth or sprout. It is the greatest transcorporeal surrender I had ever participated in.

Later, the midwife came and pushed her hand between my legs to confirm that indeed the very framework of my anatomy was bending and swaying its way open like a willow in a windstorm and I whimpered for mercy and the invasion of her arm in my tender opening body. I thought about times I had eagerly yanked the seed casing off baby seedlings impatiently when they popped through the soil or transplanted them in a hurry, ripping their roots in the process. I promised to be more careful, more conscious, as another Earthquake shook over me.

The experience of labor and birth comes bridled with myths and stories and fear and custom and is bound tightly into the narrative of human experience and survival, yet we rarely if ever, consider the planting of flowers or strewing of cucumber seeds to be a spiritual and enormous act of helping other beings make themselves. Farmers sow their crops without attention paid to the divine act of watching life make itself, or homage to the plant mothers who entrusted their seeds to the womb of the world in hopes that just one might make it to bring her genetics to another generation. Humans say *I* give birth, and *I* raised and *made* futures for my children, but we say that "the squash sprouted," and often attribute this to a bird dropping or a windfall, giving none of the agency to eons of tree mothers slowly adapting and working together toward creating and caring for their offspring, their root-children, their kin. We have so little respect for the reproductive functions of plant-life that we haphazardly plant fields or start garden projects and forget to water them, leaving on vacation, never considering the open and exposed uterus we left behind.

When my seedling finally struggled her way into the birth canal after a day and a half of my crawling and sweating and hanging onto countertops and stair rails, I pushed her out screaming and yelling at such a volume that I vaguely heard the midwife ask someone to shut the window so not to frighten the neighbors. One push and her head emerged, eyes open and clear, turning every which way to absorb the new reality, though her shoulders were firmly stuck within me. Two pushes and she slithered to the Earth. I crouched with her, placenta still connected to her belly but no longer to mine. Like the plants, I realized I wasn't sure when she was born, and that we were all just bodies trying to make autonomy happen for our young in different stages. Was that moment when she slipped out of me the moment she was born? Or was she born two hours later when we disconnected her from the placenta, the last nutrient source I gave her so directly? Or was she born one week later when crying like the blubbering sentimental over-thinking parents we were we named her under a poplar tree? When I stop breast-feeding her? Or was she born when she first touched her toes to the body of this planet we share?

Birthing 2 (Senescence)

I spent an entire arc of the sun being more on Earth than I had ever felt and

I scratched the ground with my knees and wept and watered the soil with my eyes and begged her body to emerge from the dark cavities of mine until I descended to a dark warm world where hours meant nothing and breathing was everything.

Human birth is reduced to numbers. It takes
forty weeks for a human child to be full term
if they are born at forty weeks and a day they are overdue
if they are born at thirty-eight weeks they are branded early and
first time labor is twelve to twenty-four hours long, and contractions are
rarely serious until they are two or three minutes apart and the
entire process of our fruiting bodies is reduced to notches on a ticking
clock.
We desire it planned and scheduled but nothing this old works that way.
We share this time with plants, the green mothers,
this
liminal floating space of urges and energy this
realm of giving into the processes of body we
deem to control with Pitocin drips, slicing open lady bodies, asking for
regiment and
uniformity as if our flesh was made of something different than the
solidity and stubborn matter of the Earth around it.
Anyone who has planted a smattering of basil seeds knows that they will
burst forth at different times, perhaps they were too hot or simply not ready
deep in their cellularly dividing cores, cradled in their seed husk of a womb
here we are in the horticultural space of seasons and urges
of instincts and smells and water and sun
here we are with them, the green bodies
here they are, with us, us lost ones.

Domus

The story of Circe is most often known as the tale of a vengeful and hurt
witch who angrily turns men into pigs when they arrive on her island Aeaea.
It seems that the Odyssey rendered her the frustrated and disliked feminist
in a patriarchal world of Gods knocking up mortals. She is not meant to be
liked in this telling; she is a reflection for Odysseus's wit. However, she
is also the ultimate housewife, trapped on an island, with only the plants
and other animals for company. She must make her own life among the
more-than-humans.

When I became a mother, I became Circe. My world seized up and shrank,
then exploded in the tiny details of day-to-day domestic living, trapped on
the island of my house with only my plants and small animal baby to speak
to. I wallowed in dirt and food and diapers and simple repetitive labor. There
are meditations to be found in domus, but they are slow to learn and involve
little of the notoriety and attention the flashier parts of birthing and blooming
hold. I believe I envisioned domesticity as somewhat romantic at one time. I

thought of all the ways I could ground myself with this time at home, and pay homage to the Earth, honor the plants, provide practical magic for my family by way of feeding, washing, growing, and tending.

On the good days, I am a witch at work at her hearth, the acts of labor and craft are old, meaningful, and full of a desire to be closer to the elements around me. I am in transformation, the soil under my fingernails and knots in my hair make me meaningful and fluent in the practical spells and everyday magic of making walls and floors and overhead beams and fire and cast iron and herbs into a home and dinner. My breasts swing heavy, full of milk, and I feel I could provide for everything and everyone, I am proud in my fertility, I am grounded in my consciousness. I am a nurse log. I am an old banyan. The plants talk to me and I listen. I create microcosms of nutrients and calm. The girlchild and I move slowly through the world touching plants, doing chores, exploring facial expressions, songs, foods of this earth. I feel the sheer act of raising her among the trees and dirt and embodied chores that I am is an act of defiance. I take refuge in being like the plants, not needing the frivolous entertainments and constant motion of the industrial world.

On the less good days, the creep of household tasks threatens to strangle me and I have trouble forming sentences that sound not only like I do not have a doctorate but rather that I may never have read a book before. I cannot calm myself enough to see how the shared wordlessness I have in these moments with plants could be good. The dirt under my fingernails is disgusting and my hair works its way into a mass of unintentional dreadlocks. The weight of my breasts reminds me that I feel I roll them up to fit them into bras and there is no network of fungi and roots that is coming to my rescue. I am a solo sickly beech heading for winter. I say no spells, I feel alone.

These are the days I am also jealous of the aspens.

I had always loved these trees because they had seemed to figure out something about sitting still on a landscape, and making kin, that humans had either forgotten or had never known. Aspens grow in rhizomatic clonal colonies all hailing from a single seedling to make a giant multigenerational stand, and while individual trees only survive from around up to around 150 human years, the mass of roots can live for thousands. They seem to understand place and home and family in a way that I am still working on myself. Humans regard the freedom to leave the land of our parents as an ultimate success and show of independence and bravery, to avoid the work of maintaining home as an annoyance, but aspens are powerful in their numbers and their repetitive, dependable cycles of birth and rebirth, are strong in their knowledge of where the right place to propagate is and how to stay home and nurture and grow. They know how to be homes to so many species around them. They put in the work, and they do it slowly and surely. They are clear on the importance of ancient mychorrhizal networks the way some humans have faith and respect at being part of a bloodline. They are sure of the quiet, understated, power of home. And like Circe, and hopefully myself one day: they know they are never alone.

Transcorporeal

This year she turns one and we will bake a cake and shower her with kisses on her still-bald scalp and congratulate ourselves on keeping the tiny disaster-prone animal alive for a year.

I feel so old, because I have seen every moment of her rapidly vibrant body—

thriving in fleshy multiples putting all parts of the planet in her mouth making them part of her making herself part of them.

She loves to suck gravel and chew on grass and if I say no

she does it faster and wilder as if she vehemently opposes the possibility that these little material bodies around her were ever meant to be separate from her form

she thrives in the confidence of her mouth and her nose as the secret passage to knowing she is still more-than-human.

Every root every leaf every petal enter her form and even the acrid ones that make my tongue curl are of interest to her,

she never assumes they were ever not meant to infiltrate her belly, her nails, her pockets, her breath or

that the stuff of my breasts is any different than the stuff of this world outside of the two of us because the way

she presses to my chest and the
way she touches the ground are with such
similar urgency
and familiarity.
I want this, too. This urgent familiarity.
I now also wish to taste every leaf I see and know they probably can
taste me too.

Mourning

Now she lives here. On this side, and her umbilical cord is cut and I drink wine and I can walk away from her body and soon she will walk away from mine.

Sometimes after a dusk of avoiding the news with the pandemic, and shootings, and alarming extinction I creep onto our bed and waver my hand over the baby's tiny mouth and hold my breath until I feel the humid fog of her life on my palm and feel the immense weight of guiding her body through this perilous cartography of fear and change. I wonder if mother plants ever hold their stomata and listen for the oxygen exiting their offspring's leaves, just to be sure.

She curls asleep, mouth hanging open in an onesie printed with Redwood trees though they may as well be printed with unicorns as this is how precarious those trees feel at times.

When she is old enough to choose her own clothing how many plants on her onesies will still be here? How many will live in fairy tales about greener times how will her

kindergarten teacher choose to explain how generations of mothers didn't pay attention to this coming (this hurts, we all did, I'm sure, what we thought was best)

When I look at plant bodies I smell the loss of landscape, of familiar weather, of countless kin, I taste the sadness and difficulty of protecting one's own.[12]

How, lodgepole pines have had their skin devoured from the inside their bodies already weak from smog and drought

how they release resin and sap to try and seal the open wounds over their wooded frames how we only care because trees are

pretty

because we need the lumber.

What must it feel like to be a bristlecone pine mother?

To have watched the eons flow by and the critters of the planet make moves underneath your shade and grow up and die and to have watched some of your babies grow up and die and be slowly chopped and culled

despite all the energy given to raise them tall and strong and connect them within the web of intimately bound trees where you live,

make them good community members who share what they can with those in need,[13]

know to warn others of danger,[14]

sleep deeply and soundly through the starry nights.[15]

(Some of your babies

grow up and live long and interesting lives.)

To have felt the air and water around you change in hundreds of cycles and be quite sure your species are not personally responsible

How is it that we do not cry for the millions of cottonwood babies that cannot happen because the Rio Grande[16] is dammed or

the infant mortality rate of those flowers that now bloom before the bumblebees are there to help them or refugee roots creeping uphill to avoid the scorching summer?

How can we not weep for the monumental wooden Pietas after forest fires
who have lost the last year of seedlings? More painful than any marble statue
could convey?

How can we not sob for the verdant diaspora
migrating north, far away from all the wild beings
they once knew.

IN CLOSING: MOTHERHOOD AS A SHARED IDENTITY

When I first was pregnant, I dreamed wildly every night, perhaps from the
hormones or perhaps from the fact that procreating is really some other-
worldly stuff. I dreamed of a lettuce sprout growing in my stomach, planted
on the uterine wall, leaves waving gently in amniotic fluid. I saw my unborn
baby cradled in soil, the webs of mycorrhizae fanning around her face and
heart and feet in a fantastic weaving of nutrient-rich communication with
me, the way my blood vessels would gently pulse around the lettuce sprout.
I couldn't stop watching the more-than-human mothers. What if her progeny
was born into the soil in a year that is destined to be full of drought? Are her
tiny sprouts too close to one another so that even despite the carbon she will
nurse them on through her roots they may die? Is she essentially the birch
octomom? How much is there to learn about relation-making from more-
than-humans? How much is there to know about kin from this process?

In the gooey hormonal sea of growing someone, I felt I could be closer to
mushrooms spreading spores and ponderosas dropping seedlings and coyotes
spawning pups, in a similar way to my unquestioning acceptance of an animist world full of personhoods that I had as a child. I wanted to grow babies
that took little and gave lots to the ecosystem we live in, who looked for
more similarities than differences in our plant kin. I made a pact to consider
how tree mothers cradle their young and rhizomes make relations through
both their roots and their seeds, ever growing, with infinite possibilities for
siblings. I hoped to help her see trees as other mothers and pay close attention
to the kinships between more-than-humans and see them as no less important
than the kinship between she and I. I chose to revisit the material similarities
of my body with those of plants.

The stories surrounding motherhood, procreation, and environmental connection have several allegorical moments, and complicated and contested
representations in Western/ized culture. This can make figuring out how to
be an ecological citizen, responsible mother, moral feminist, or animist kin-
maker confusing, but as Martin Shaw (2020) says, if we have entered a story
and know the allegory of it, it fails to be a living thing and joins the ranks of
the many, many, living things are in dangerous peril of being extinct. Finding

the allegory of any of these topics or stances written about in the introduction is less important than expanding the frame for which motherhood is understood, and trusting that narratives and offerings are dynamic, and can come from all places, beings, bodies, and times, and are capable of teaching many different things.

Perhaps it is not so much what cultural narratives we tell ourselves about plants, or the more-than-human and motherhood, as how we decide to unravel them, and where we position ourselves in them. While humans certainly could do well to continue the creation of nourishing, more inclusive, more ingenious stories for this time, how might old experiences (like those of motherhood in addition to childhood) be positioned differently, reread, and reopened? How can considering the similar materiality of all things shift the way we consider personhood?

As I close this chapter, my daughter toddles around outside with pinesap smeared in her six maybe seven hairs. She has recently learned to wave and without my prompting, waves at people, chipmunks, dogs, and trees, as well as the occasional statue. It sounds insignificant, but the tiny reminder that we are, in fact, walking by many organisms in many bodies worthy of acknowledgement is endlessly helpful, as even though I currently spend quite a bit of time in commune with plants or in deep thought about them and the other bodies that make up the world, it still seems to take infinite practice. I am grateful for the experience of motherhood that offers these moments and years where empathy and relearning can be worked on, I am honored to know deeply that the birthing, breathing, mothering, world of plants and I have so much in common.

Author's Note: "Portions of this chapter were originally written as part of my 2019 dissertation, titled "Cartographies of roots: An Exploration of plant communication, place, and story."

NOTES

1. The term "more-than-human" is borrowed from Abram (2012) and while imperfect in its expression, is a critical move to avoid positioning nonhuman entities as normal and everything else as "other."

2. The use of "queendom" in place of kingdom is a conscious attempt to subvert the patriarchal language of taxonomy.

3. "Nature" is placed in quotes due to the lack of clarity on what this word actually means or refers to.

4. See Paul Kingsworth's (2020) essay "The Language of the Master" for more on this idea.

5. The use of the term "babies" is an intentional move to think of all species' young as warranting the care and affection humans generally reserve for their own babies. Additionally, in regards to the "overall telos," I am not positing that having babies is or will be necessarily normal or natural, only that most life forms as overall species re-propagate in some way or another.

6. See Clayton and Opotow's (2003) edited volume for more on environmental identity.

7. I write "woman body" and "women" throughout as opposed to womyn, womxn, wimmin, or other more inclusive words as this is the term much of my extent literature uses and the body I identify as having.

8. Meaning, bodies that are considered to be only made up of themselves as opposed to other outside matter. See Allewaert's (2013) explanation of "parahumanity" and Chen (2012) for more on this.

9. Here, Pollock (1998) uses a term by (Taussig 1989). Emphasis by Pollock (1998).

10. Cotyledons are the first leaves seedlings grow from the nutrients they have in their seed.

11. Work on tree kinship has shown that mother trees will often send nutrients to their genetically similar offspring, especially when that offspring cannot yet reach the sunlight (*see* Dudley and File 2007; Wohlleben 2016).

12. Here, the term "solastalgia" is echoed, or rather the loss of a familiar landscape (Albrecht et al. 2007; Albrecht 2006).

13. Simard et al. (1997) and Simard, Durall, and Jones (1997) showed that beech and fir trees can exchange nutrients depending on who has more to spare. Possibly, many species of plants do this.

14. Studies have shown that many plants can emit volatile chemical signals in distress that are understood by other plants (their own species and sometimes other species too) in the area so that they may increase their own defenses against predators (Heil et al. 2004; Karban et al. 2000; Karban, 2018).

15. According to Puttonen et al. (2016) study on birch trees, trees droop or "sleep" and night. Additionally, Bennie et al. (2016) work showed how artificial light pollution significantly alters the circadian rhythms of some plants.

16. The Rio Grande is an important river in the United States Southwest and Northern Mexico.

BIBLIOGRAPHY

Abram, David. 2012. *The Spell of the Sensuous: Perception and Language in a More-than-Human World*. Vintage.

Alaimo, Stacy. 2008. "Trans-Corporeal Feminisms and the Ethical Space of Nature." *Material Feminisms*, edited by Stacy Alaimo and Susan Hekman, 237–264. Indiana University Press.

Alaimo, Stacy. 2010. *Bodily Natures: Science, Environment, and the Material Self*. Indiana University Press.

Albrecht, Glenn. 2006. "Solastalgia." *Alternatives Journal* 32 (4/5): 34–36.

Albrecht, Glenn, Gina-Maree Sartore, Linda Connor, Nick Higginbotham, Sonia Freeman, Brian Kelly, Helen Stain, Anne Tonna, and Georgia Pollard. 2007. "Solastalgia: The Distress Caused by Environmental Change." *Australasian Psychiatry* 15 (1): S95–98. https://doi.org/10.1080/10398560701701288.

Allewaert, Monique. 2013. *Ariel's Ecology: Plantations, Personhood, and Colonialism in the American Tropics*. University of Minnesota Press.

Bar-On, Yinon M., Rob Phillips, and Ron Milo. 2018. "The Biomass Distribution on Earth." *Proceedings of the National Academy of Sciences* 115 (25): 6506–11. https://doi.org/10.1073/pnas.1711842115.

Bennett, Jane. 2010. *Vibrant Matter: A Political Ecology of Things*. Duke University Press.

Bennie, Jonathan, Thomas W. Davies, David Cruse, and Kevin J. Gaston. 2016. "Ecological Effects of Artificial Light at Night on Wild Plants." *Journal of Ecology* 104 (3): 611–620.

Bird-David, Nurit. 1999. "'Animism' Revisited: Personhood, Environment, and Relational Epistemology." *Current Anthropology* 40 (1): S67–S91.

Carbaugh, Donal. 1996. "Naturalizing Communication and Culture." *The Symbolic Earth: Discourse and Our Creation of the Environment*, 38–57.

Chawla, Louise. 2002. "Spots of Time: Manifold Ways of Being in Nature in Childhood." *Children and Nature: Psychological, Sociocultural, and Evolutionary Investigations*, 199–226.

Chen, Mel Y. 2012. *Animacies: Biopolitics, Racial Mattering, and Queer Affect*. Duke University Press.

Clayton, Susan D. and Susan Opotow. 2003. *Identity and the Natural Environment: The Psychological Significance of Nature*. MIT Press.

Crittenden, Ann. 2002. *The Price of Motherhood: Why the Most Important Job in the World Is Still the Least Valued*. Macmillan.

Dudley, Susan A., and Amanda L. File. 2007. "Kin Recognition in an Annual Plant." *Biology Letters* 3 (4): 435–438.

Ellis, Carolyn. 1999. "Heartful Autoethnography." *Qualitative Health Research* 9 (5): 669–683.

Ellis, Carolyn, Tony E. Adams, and Arthur P. Bochner. 2011."Autoethnography: An Overview." *Historical Social Research/Historische Sozialforschung*, 273–290.

Flood, Alison. 2015. "Oxford Junior Dictionary's Replacement of 'Natural' Words with 21st-Century Terms Sparks Outcry." *The Guardian*, January 13, 2015, sec. Books. https://www.theguardian.com/books/2015/jan/13/oxford-junior-dictionary-replacement-natural-words.

Griffin, Susan. 2015. *Woman and Nature: The Roaring inside Her*. Open Road Media.

Haila, Yrjö. 2000. "Beyond the Nature-Culture Dualism." *Biology and Philosophy* 15 (2): 155–175.

Hall, Matthew. 2011. *Plants as Persons: A Philosophical Botany*. Suny Press.

Haraway, Donna J. 2016. *Staying with the Trouble: Making Kin in the Chthulucene*. Duke University Press.

Heil, Martin, Sabine Greiner, Harald Meimberg, Ralf Krüger, Jean-Louis Noyer, Günther Heubl, K. Eduard Linsenmair, and Wilhelm Boland. 2004. "Evolutionary Change from Induced to Constitutive Expression of an Indirect Plant Resistance." *Nature* 430 (6996): 205–208.

Herrmann, Patricia, Sandra R. Waxman, and Douglas L. Medin. 2010. "Anthropocentrism Is Not the First Step in Children's Reasoning about the Natural World." *Proceedings of the National Academy of Sciences* 107 (22): 9979–84. https://doi.org/10.1073/pnas.1004440107.

Karban, Richard. 2015. *Plant Sensing and Communication*. University of Chicago Press.

Karban, Richard, Ian T. Baldwin, Kimberly J. Baxter, Grit Laue, and G. W. Felton. 2000. "Communication between Plants: Induced Resistance in Wild Tobacco Plants Following Clipping of Neighboring Sagebrush." *Oecologia* 125 (1): 66–71.

Kimmerer, Robin. 2013. *Braiding Sweetgrass: Indigenous Wisdom, Scientific Knowledge and the Teachings of Plants*. Milkweed Editions.

Laney, Elizabeth K., M. Elizabeth Lewis Hall, Tamara L. Anderson, and Michele M. Willingham. 2015. "Becoming a Mother: The Influence of Motherhood on Women's Identity Development." *Identity* 15 (2): 126–45. https://doi.org/10.1080/15283488.2015.1023440.

Merchant, Carolyn. 1990. "The Death of Nature: Women, Ecology, and the Scientific Revolution. HarperOne.

Morris, Jennifer L., Mark N. Puttick, James W. Clark, Dianne Edwards, Paul Kenrick, Silvia Pressel, Charles H. Wellman, Ziheng Yang, Harald Schneider, and Philip CJ Donoghue. 2018. "The Timescale of Early Land Plant Evolution." *Proceedings of the National Academy of Sciences,* 115 (10): E2274–E2283.

Næss, Petter. 2006. "Unsustainable Growth, Unsustainable Capitalism." *Journal of Critical Realism* 5 (2): 197–227. DOI: 10.1558/jocr.v5i2.197

Plumwood, Val. 1986. "Ecofeminism: An Overview and Discussion of Positions and Arguments." *Australasian Journal of Philosophy* 64 (1): 120–138.

Plumwood, Val. *Feminism and the Mastery of Nature*. Routledge, 2002.

Pollock, Della. 1998. "Performing Writing." *The Ends of Performance*, edited by Peggy Phelan and Jill Lane, 73–103. NYU Press.

Puttonen, Eetu, Christian Briese, Gottfried Mandlburger, Martin Wieser, Martin Pfennigbauer, András Zlinszky, and Norbert Pfeifer. 2016. "Quantification of Overnight Movement of Birch (Betula Pendula) Branches and Foliage with Short Interval Terrestrial Laser Scanning." *Frontiers in Plant Science* 7: 222.

Ray, Sarah Jaquette. 2011. "How Many Mothers Does It Take to Change All the Light Bulbs? The Myth of Green Motherhood." *Journal of the Motherhood Initiative for Research and Community Involvement,* 2 (1). 81–101.

Shaw, Martin. Interview with Emmanuelle Vaughan-Lee. "Mud, Antler, and Bone. Emergence Magazine Podcast. Transcript. Accessed July 14, 2020. https://emergencemagazine.org/story/mud-and-antler-bone/.

Simard, Suzanne W., Daniel M. Durall, and Melanie D. Jones. 1997. "Carbon Allocation and Carbon Transfer between t Betula Papyrifera and t Pseudotsuga

Menziesii Seedlings Using a 13 C Pulse-Labeling Method." *Plant and Soil* 191 (1): 41–55.

Simard, Suzanne W., Melanie D. Jones, Daniel M. Durall, David A. Perry, David D. Myrold, and Randy Molina. 1997. "Reciprocal Transfer of Carbon Isotopes between Ectomycorrhizal Betula Papyrifera and Pseudotsuga Menziesii." *New Phytologist* 137 (3): 529–542.

Sturgeon, Noel. 2009. *Environmentalism in Popular Culture: Gender, Race, Sexuality, and the Politics of the Natural*. University of Arizona Press.

Taussig, Michael. 1989. "The Nervous System: Homesickness and Dada." *Stanford Humanities Review* 1 (1): 44–81.Trewavas, Anthony. 2003. "Aspects of Plant Intelligence." *Annals of Botany* 92 (1): 1–20.

Wandersee, James H., and Elisabeth E. Schussler. 1999. "Preventing Plant Blindness." *The American Biology Teacher* 61 (2): 82–86.

Waxman, Sandra R., Patricia Herrmann, Jennifer Woodring, and Douglas Medin. 2014. "Humans (Really) Are Animals: Picture-Book Reading Influences 5-Year-Old Urban Children's Construal of the Relation between Humans and Non-Human Animals." *Frontiers in Psychology* 5, https://doi.org/10.3389/fpsyg.2014.00172.

Willerslev, Rane, and Olga Ulturgasheva. 2012."Revisiting the Animism versus Totemism Debate: Fabricating Persons among the Eveny and Chukchi of North-Eastern Siberia." *Animism in Rainforest and Tundra: Personhood, Animals, Plants and Things in Contemporary Amazonia and Siberia*, edited by Marc Brightman, Vanessa Elisa Grotti, and Olga Ulturgasheva. 48–68.

Wohlleben, Peter. 2016. *The Hidden Life of Trees: What They Feel, How They Communicate—Discoveries from a Secret World*. Greystone Books.

Young, Thomas. 2001."Overconsumption and Procreation: Are They Morally Equivalent?" *Journal of Applied Philosophy*, 18(2): 183–192.

Chapter 15

Plant Persons, More-than-Human Power, and Institutional Practices in Indigenous Higher Education

Keith Williams and Suzanne Brant

"The Anthropocene" describes the current era of the Earth's geologic history and is characterized by unprecedented human-mediated climate change, changes to landscape structure and the water cycle, and biodiversity loss (Steffen et al. 2011, 842–43). Higher education as an institution of cultural and social reproduction (Bourdieu 1973) is deeply implicated in the Anthropocene "by teaching how to most effectively marginalize and plunder Earth and human communities" (Vargas Roncancio et al. 2019, 1). Despite the existential threat posed by the changes characteristic of the Anthropocene, there are also positive social developments at this time. For example, Indigenous Peoples of Turtle Island[1] are experiencing unprecedented levels of inclusion and success in mainstream postsecondary education (Mendelson 2006, 24). The decades-long struggle for educational equality—marked by various watershed moments such as the Indian Control of Indian Education policy paper (National Indian Brotherhood 1972), the dissolution of residential schools and the findings of Truth and Reconciliation Commission of Canada (TRC 2015), and the United Nations Declaration of the Rights of Indigenous Peoples (United Nations 2007)—looks like it is finally paying off. Although Indigenous Peoples are still underrepresented in higher education, more Indigenous learners are enrolled in, and graduating from, college and university programs, and Indigenous graduate employment rates are higher than ever (Hu, Daley, and Warman 2019, 63–64; Mendelson 2006, 24). Many Canadian colleges and universities are attempting to Indigenize higher education, which essentially involves expanding the academy's conception of knowledge—including knowledge transmission and knowledge creation—to include Indigenous perspectives for transformative outcomes (Kuokkanen 2008, 2). Indigenous Peoples now have the autonomy to govern our own postsecondary institutions, for example through the First Nations University of Canada in Saskatchewan, the Indigenous Institutes in Ontario, the Tribal College system in the United States, and Intercultural University system in México and the rest of Latin America (Williams and Brant 2019, 140). The equity advances in postsecondary education suggest that society should continue following the current charted course if we want to eliminate, or continue to reduce, injustice and inequality in higher education.

However, Gaudry and Lorenz (2018, para. 7–10) suggest that most universities' attempts at "Indigenization" rely on empty rhetoric and, for the most part, involve simply hiring more Indigenous scholars and other staff without sufficient support and with the expectation that those hires will adapt to a Western cultural institution, not that the university will change its structures and processes to reflect Indigenous cultural values and practices. Ultimately many Indigenization efforts serve to reproduce the very structures that have historically served to erase and marginalize Indigenous Peoples (Gaudry and Lorenz 2018, para. 13).

Indigenous Institutes are well positioned to offer an approach to higher education rooted in Indigenous Knowledge (IK). However, from the authors' experience, Indigenous Institutes have faced chronic underfunding, lack of formal accreditation requiring program brokerage from mainstream colleges and universities, and paternalistic government intervention which have all limited the extent to which Indigenous higher education institutions in Canada have been able adequately to meet local needs (Crum, 2015; Stonechild, 2006) including the incorporation of traditional teachings and practices at all institutional levels.

This chapter proposes that a business-as-usual approach to Indigenous higher education, whether in mainstream or Indigenous contexts, serves to reproduce human exceptionalism and the human-nature dualism that is, arguably, foundational to the Anthropocene, the neoliberal project, and the inequity and oppression that Indigenous Peoples of the Americas have faced since colonization. We offer examples of ways in which IK is effectively incorporated into an Indigenous postsecondary setting at FNTI, specifically dealing with the recognition of plant personhood and enactments of more-than-human relationality, despite the challenges identified in the previous paragraph.

NEOLIBERALISM AND INDIGENOUS HIGHER EDUCATION

The modern university system—relatively unchanged in underlying structure and social intent for almost one thousand years—originated in Europe's high medieval period in response to a growing need for trained church administrators, priests, and missionaries as well as civil administrators (Axtell 2016, 1–2).

Higher education, despite remaining faithful to its medieval ecclesiastical origins for centuries, is facing significant contemporary challenges from neoliberal ideology. Neoliberalism is a distinctly economic mode of governance now insinuated in domains—including, but not limited to, postsecondary education—that had previously been framed and governed by democratic ideals (Brown 2015). As Wendy Brown (2015) points out, "Democratic state commitments to equality, liberty, inclusion, and constitutionalism are now subordinate to the project of economic growth, competitive positioning, and capital enhancement" (26). Foucault (2008) in Gildersleeve (2017, 286) describes four ways in which neoliberalism influences society: hyperindividualism, hyper-surveillance, economic determinations of productivity, and competitive entrepreneurialism.

Zygmunt Bauman's articulation of liquid modernity offers a nuanced theoretical lens through which to view the neoliberal era. Bauman's liquid modernity (2000) can be characterized by a climate of uncertainty in which citizens and other public and private-sector actors are constantly required to demonstrate their value and territory is rejected, "with its cumbersome corollaries of order-building, order-maintenance and the responsibility for the consequences of it all as well as of the necessity to bear their costs" (11). The aterritoriality associated with neoliberalism and Bauman's liquid modernity is antithetical to Indigenous ontologies that, according to Osage scholar Robert Warrior (1999, 52), are based on *topos* or territory rather than *logos* or the word or discursive reason which forms the basis of dominant European ontologies. MacDonald (2011, 260–70) and Altamirano-Jiménez (2013, 53–54) suggest that the discursive overlap between Indigenous self-determination and the emphasis on individual autonomy via marketization in neoliberal thought limits our ability to effectively critique forms of Indigenous self-determination such as various manifestations of state-sponsored self-governance and also neoliberalism more broadly. Following Warrior's (1999, 52) insight regarding *topos* versus *logos*, we suggest that institutional practices rooted in territory—either directly or indirectly—offer a productive response to neoliberalism.

The following sections describe the recognition and enactment of our relational responsibilities to the more-than-human (Whatmore 2006, 601–2), in the form of plant persons, as a place-based form of resistance to neoliberal governmentality in an Indigenous higher education context and as a productive response to the challenges associated with the Anthropocene.

PERSONALITY, PLACE, AND MORE-THAN-HUMAN POWER

As mentioned in the previous section, *topos* or territory is fundamental to Indigenous conceptions of reality (Warrior 1999, 52). The centrality of territory is further articulated by Bob Antone (2013, 168) and Vine Deloria and Daniel Wildcat (2001), who assert that everything in the universe is alive and is related through connection to place. Deloria and Wildcat (2001) summarize this understanding with the formula "power and place produce personality" (23). Following Antone (2013, 168) and Deloria and Wildcat's (2001, 23) position, we suggest that the aterritoriality associated with neo-liberalism and liquid modernity deprive us of the full expression of our personhood and the personhood of the more-than-human with whom we are entangled.

Indigenous Peoples have developed many ways to connect with what linguist Andrew Cowell (2018) calls more-than-human power (MTH power). Cowell's work among the Northern Arapaho led to the understanding that

> a person is sacred and powerful because that person literally has within them—or has access to—power derived either from the natural world or from ancestors—both of whom mediate the general MTH power of the creator, which is immanent in the world. (9)

MTH power, in the Haudenosaunee world, is exemplified by the principle of *kasasten'sera* which is variously translated as strength or power (Akwesasne Notes 2005, 34–35). Oneida elder Bob Antone describes *kasasten'sera* as the power of the collective, and the strength that comes from thought and action unified with all of creation and the cycles of life (Antone 2013, 21–22). In this chapter, we choose to translate *kasasten'sera* in English as "continuance." *Kasasten'sera*, or continuance, is the vital life-force of the human and more-than-human individual, human collectivities, and ecological communities and is a form of power derived from the unity of all matter that supports the continued existence of all creation. *Kasasten'sera*, and MTH power more broadly, differ significantly from dominant conceptions of power in Western philosophy which tend to emphasize domination (Foucault 1978; Baumann 2000) as "power over" or the inherent capacity of human agency (Arendt, 1958; Parsons 1963) as "power to." Important feminist contributions to our theoretical understanding of power include Amy Allen's notion of "power with" as the collective ability "to act together for the attainment of a common or shared end or series of ends" (1998, 35).

Another traditional Haudenosaunee principle is *ka'nikonhri:io*, or the "good mind," which occurs when the people put "their minds and emotions in harmony with the flow of the universe" (Mohawk 2010, 33). Achieving *ka'nikonhri:io* and drawing on the relationality inherent in *kasasten'sera* are necessary for becoming *Onkwehonwe* which means original, unassimilated people whose minds are inseparable from territory (Sheridan and Longboat 2006, 366). Engaging in the seasonal cycle of ceremonies and other traditional activities such as hunting, medicine plant gathering, and gardening with the Three Sisters (corn, beans, and squash) serves as a conduit to MTH power indexed to place, referenced in both the creation teachings and the lives of contemporary Haudenosaunee people. Of the Three Sisters, Haudenosaunee white corn plays a particularly significant role in the spiritual lives of the Haudenosaunee Peoples.

MTH power, including *kasasten'sera*, differs from the aforementioned Western power concepts, in that it is bound to territory and sustained through ceremonial and other traditional activities that emphasize our relationships with each other and the rest of creation (Cajete 2000, 77–83; Cowell 2018, 82). According to Nancy Turner (2014, 257–66), multiple traditional stories from Indigenous Peoples of the Pacific Northwest cast plants as central actors. For example, Skunk Cabbage (*Lysichiton americanus* Hultén and H. St. John) is personified as Skunk Cabbage Man who appears as a pot-bellied person in both Haida and Kathlamet stories as a provider of salmon and other foods. In one Nuxalk story, blueberries (*Vaccinium spp.*) are depicted as little boys who instruct a woman on appropriate berry-picking etiquette. Sword fern (*Polystichum munitum* (Kaulf.) C. Presl) is portrayed in a Kwakwaka'wakw story as a hairy faced person with dentalia earrings and cheeks colored with red ochre and with the ability to control weather (Turner and Bell 1973, 265). Devil's-club (*Oplopanax horridus* (Sm.) Miq.) is depicted by the Ts'msyen as a beautiful young woman who teaches an unlucky hunter how to improve his success by using devil's-club for purification purposes (Cove and MacDonald, 1987, 82–83). These stories typically serve as morally instructive, but they also function to maintain and transfer Traditional Ecological Knowledge (TEK) (Turner 2014, 231–34). Plants also figure as persons among some Indigenous Peoples and Mestizos of the Amazon River Basin. Luis Eduardo Luna (1984) relates several stories about "plant teachers" from Iquitos, Peru including those plants used to make the ayahuasca beverage (*Banisteriopsis caapi* (Griseb.) C.V. Morton and *Psychotria viridis* Ruiz and Pav.), tobacco (*Nicotiana spp.*), several members of the Solanaceae and Apocynaceae, and many more. According to Luna's respondents, these plants teach the shaman or traditional healer how to diagnose and cure disease, how to use other medicinal plants, and how to perform specific shamanic activities. The relational ontology implicit in these stories and traditional views of plant agency offer a radically different view of who counts as "persons" and reflects a sophisticated understanding of the profound interdependence between the elements of our natural environment, at odds with the hyper-individualism (Gildersleeve 2017) of neoliberalism and human exceptionalism characteristic of the Anthropocene (Vargas Roncancio et al. 2019). Interestingly, over the past several years, plants have been increasingly recognized as sentient and agentic by a minority of Western scholars. For example, philosopher Michael Marder offers a reconceptualization of plant agency in *Plant-thinking: A philosophy of vegetal life* (2013) and Monica Gagliano and colleagues demonstrated, through a few simple experiments, that plant awareness is significantly more nuanced and complex than previously thought (Gagliano 2018, 57–66; 79–83).

The Three Sisters (corn, beans, and squash), or *áhsen nikontate'kén:'a* in Mohawk, are central to Haudenosaunee cosmology, specifically the creation teachings. In one version of the creation teachings related by the late Seneca Chief Corbett Sundown, the earth was formed when the animals—who saw Sky Woman falling through a hole in the sky—brought soil from the bottom of the ocean and put it on turtle's back to create a soft place for Sky Woman to land. Sky Woman had gotten pregnant in the Sky World before falling to the earth, and she gave birth to a daughter. In time the daughter also became pregnant, by the west wind, and she gave birth to twins—Sapling and Flint. She died giving birth to Flint (the second twin) and the *áhsen nikontate'kén:'a*, along with tobacco and wild potatoes, sprung from her buried body. *O'nenste* (corn) grew from her breasts, *o'saheta* (beans) grew from her fingers, and *onon'onhsera* (squash) grew from her navel (Cornelius 1999, 94).

Sapling shared the Original Instructions with humanity, which included the Thanksgiving Address. The seasonal cycle of ceremonies was introduced later to remind humans about how to give thanks and to live in harmony with the natural world. The seasonal cycle of ceremonies is, as the name suggests, predicated on the natural cycles of creation. The Three Sisters play important roles in a number of the ceremonies, such as the Green Bean ceremony held in July when the green beans are ripe and the Green Corn ceremony which is held in August or September when the corn is in the milk stage (Cornelius 1999, 91–93). The Three Sisters also feature prominently in the *Ohenten Kariwatekwen*, or Thanksgiving Address, which is spoken at the beginning of important meetings to acknowledge nature and to align hearts and minds with all creation (Freeman 2015, 145–46). The Thanksgiving Address includes stanzas that pay homage to various elements of the natural and cosmological worlds of the Haudenosaunee, including (but not limited to): the people, the plants, the waters, the Three Sisters, the four winds, the earth, the four beings, and the creator. Each stanza typically praises the aforementioned element in relation to the Haudenosaunee people and ends with the refrain: "and now our minds are one." For example, the waters are praised in this version of the Thanksgiving Address delivered by Chief Jake Swamp to the Fourth Russell Tribunal, Rotterdam, The Netherlands, November 1980 (Mohawk Council of Akwesasne 2015):

> We have been given three main foods from the plant world-they are the corn,
> beans, and squash—the Three Sisters. For this we give thanks and greetings in

the hope that they too will continue to replenish Mother Earth with the necessities of the life cycle. Now our minds are one. (1)

In addition to these formal teachings, Carol Cornelius (1999, 97–101) introduces several stories in which the Three Sisters are cast as persons. In one story, Bean Woman and Squash Maiden vie for Corn Man's attentions with Bean Woman ultimately prevailing, explaining the intimate entanglement between climbing bean tendrils and corn stalks. In another story called "The Bean Woman," Bean Woman rejects a host of suitors (e.g., wolf, bear, and deer) before finally accepting Corn Man as her husband. In "The Weeping of the Corn, and Bean, and Squash People," people in an unnamed village experience crop failure for an unknown reason. One day an older woman heard weeping in the cornfield and found the Corn Spirit crying. When asked, the Corn Spirit explained that she felt neglected because the people did not plant the Three Sisters in a mound and failed to weed adequately. Squash Spirit and Bean Spirit were also there, weeping, and relayed similar grievances. The people then started to care for the Three Sisters properly. The second part of the story describes the wild animals that eat the Three Sisters (e.g., racoons and rabbits). Each of these stories cast the Three Sisters as persons with agency in direct relation to humans and in two of the cases, other animals.

The Handsome Lake Code, or *Kariwiyo* in Mohawk (which translates as "Good Word" in English), was shared with the Haudenosaunee Confederacy by the Seneca prophet Handsome Lake in 1799. Handsome Lake's message came at a time when the Haudenosaunee had endured decades of genocidal and then assimilative assault by American settlers (Akwesasne Notes 2005, 28–29; Holly 1990, 83–84). The *Kariwiyo* called upon the Haudenosaunee Peoples to revitalize traditional ways and to reject damaging aspects of Western culture such as drinking alcohol, gambling, and fiddle music (Antone 2013, 39; Johansen and Mann 2000, 286). The *Kariwiyo* was based on a series of visions received by Handsome Lake. In his last vision, a female corn spirit appears while Handsome Lake is walking in a cornfield (Lewandowski 1987, 80). Among other traditional practices, the *Kariwiyo* makes specific mention of revitalizing Three Sisters gardening and the seasonal cycle of ceremonies that spiritually contextualizes the cultivation and consumption of corn, beans, and squash (Antone 2013, 20). Recognizing and enacting our reciprocal responsibilities to the more-than-human through practices based on traditional teachings—which are rooted in relationality and territory—offer member of the FNTI community a safe-haven from the aterritoriality and lonely individualism associated with neoliberal governmentality. The following section describes the Indigenous postsecondary landscape in Canada and outlines some of the approaches we take, at First

Nations Technical Institute, to recognize and celebrate nonhuman person-hood—specifically the Three Sisters.

PLANT PERSONHOOD AND INDIGENOUS
HIGHER EDUCATION IN CANADA

In Canada, the governance of higher education is decentralized to the prov-inces which has led to a complex diversity of institutional arrangements and governance mechanisms (Jones 2014, 1). For instance, the Province of Ontario recently passed the Indigenous Institutes Act (the Act) which, among other things, recognizes the autonomy of the nine Indigenous governed and operated postsecondary institutes in Ontario that serve the education and training needs of the communities in which they are based (Indigenous Institutes Act 2017; Province of Ontario 2017). The Act, as a policy instru-ment, supports Indigenous self-determination in the sphere of higher educa-tion (Williams, Umangay, and Brant 2020, 9).

First Nations Technical Institute (FNTI)—founded in 1985 and based on Tyendinaga Mohawk Territory in southern Ontario—is an Indigenous-run postsecondary institution that offers both college- and university-level pro-gramming. FNTI serves 102 out of 129 Ontario First Nations communities through both on-site (at FNTI) and in-community training and has supported learners from 172 of 667 Indigenous communities across Canada (FNTI 2019a). FNTI's graduation rate for college-level programming (certificates and diplomas) was 94 percent during the 2018–2019 academic year. In the same time period, our university-level offerings (degrees) had a 95 percent completion rate (FNTI Marketing Department 2020). One factor potentially contributing to our success is the profoundly Indigenous ontological approach taken to all our relations, specifically recognition of the animacy of all cre-ation including the personhood of plants. The following paragraphs outline different ways in which the personhood of plants, specifically the Three Sisters, is incorporated into our institutional practices including how we run meetings and events, artwork displayed on campus or on the FNTI website, community gardening on campus, and our curriculum.

As discussed earlier in this chapter, the Thanksgiving Address was part of Sapling's Original Instructions and is typically recited at the beginning and ending of ceremonies, important meetings, or events. From the authors' expe-rience, delivery of the Thanksgiving Address brings peoples' minds together and focuses a group—at the commencement of a meeting or other important event—on relationships central to Haudenosaunee existence. When used as a closing, the Thanksgiving Address releases the minds from the ceremony, meeting, or other event. Also, while the form of the Thanksgiving Address remains static, the specific content varies depending on the speaker and the context.

With the final words of each stanza, "now our minds are one," the Thanksgiving Address inscribes a broad circle of personhood to encompass not just humans but also the Three Sisters, the waters, the medicine plants, and more. In addition to acknowledging personhood *sensu lato*, the Thanksgiving Address also contextualizes (as minor) divisive issues—that might otherwise prevent amicable consensus—so that the meeting or event can focus on important issues dealing with the fundamentals of life (e.g., clean water, healthy food). Recital of the Thanksgiving Address could be viewed as a kind of illocutionary discursive speech act (Butler 1993, 170–1) in which the speech is the act itself, the act of "bringing together minds." This performative and citational act (Hey 2006, 446–8) serves to mediate the ongoing process of recognition between people and between people and important nonhuman persons and other elements of creation. In *Undoing Gender* (2004), Judith Butler invokes "German Idealism and earlier medieval ecstatic traditions" (151) to express that relationality "simply avows that that 'we' who are relational do not stand apart from those relations and cannot think of ourselves outside of the decentering effects that that relationality entails" (151). We suggest that in the case of the Thanksgiving Address, Butler's de-centering is actually a radical re-centering, through which humans are re-situated (each time they participate) in a web of relations with the natural and spiritual world through a process of subjectification that helps us to "learn to identify with places in discourse" (Hey 2006, 446). The vitality of this citational act also creates a horizon of open futures via the variability of iterations made possible each time the Thanksgiving Address is delivered (Ruitenberg 2007, 263–64). Regular recital of the Thanksgiving Address helps us to remember, and in some cases reconceptualize, the personhood of what would be considered nonhuman or inanimate—such as the Three Sisters—by the human exceptionalism common to Western philosophical approaches and implicitly enacted in Western cultural institutions, including colleges and universities.

The Three Sisters also figure prominently in various visual elements at FNTI including a Three Sisters drawing by one of this chapter's coauthors (SB) that was made into a postcard with the illustration, on one side, and a summary of the Haudenosaunee creation teachings with a corn, beans, and squash soup recipe, on the reverse. The image (shown in figure 15.1), a *tableau vivant* that is both symbolic and literal, depicts the daughter of Sky Woman entangled with the Three Sisters all oriented toward the life-enhancing eldest brother, the sun. Or perhaps they are engaged in mutual contemplation of the fissure in the Sky World through which Sky Woman fell, inaugurating life "as we know it," on Earth? Even without knowing the creation teachings, the

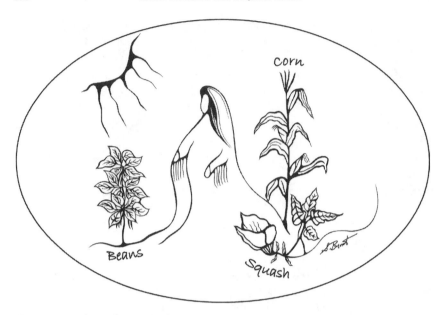

Figure 15.1   **Three Sisters.** *Credit*: Suzanne Brant.

viewer understands the profound relationality between, and animacy inherent in, the elements of this composition. The sun's rays, animatedly undulating toward the daughter of Sky Woman and the Three Sisters, are echoed by (and also echo) the corn silks and tassels, squash anthers and vine, bean tendrils, and the daughter of Sky Woman's wrist fringes, as well as the other vibrating lines that compose the various elements of this drawing. This drawing has proven so compelling to members of the FNTI community and visitors that it was uploaded on the website[2] to share with online visitors.

    Photos of corn, beans, and squash pictured together or separately are found on FNTI promotional materials and throughout the campus including posters depicting traditional Haudenosaunee varieties of corn and beans created by seed keeper Stephen McComber from Kahnawake. Ceremonial objects such as corn-husk dolls, along with the aforementioned artwork, that are found on campus provide students, staff, and visitors with familiar iconography as a reminder of the creation teachings and our responsibilities toward the Three Sisters, or those who sustain us. Affective nondiscursive representationalism manifested by visual portrayal of the Three Sisters at FNTI offers viewers the opportunity to experience the layered, complex, mysterious, and unfolding relational gestalt (Zwicky 2011) inherent in a Haudenosaunee understanding of the cosmological significance of the Three Sisters. And, as Sara Ahmed (2010) points out, affect is "sticky" in that it "preserves the connection between ideas, values, and objects" (29) and is also "contagious" between proximate bodies (Gibbs 2001, para 12–13). The contagious stickiness of affect, although unpleasant sounding, serves to reinforce norms that recognize the Three Sisters as vital and necessary persons. The act of receiving this image—in addition to affirming the importance of traditional teachings and practices associated with the Three Sisters—also creates relational bodies (human and more-than-human), informed by Three Sisters MTH power, for the dynamic and embodied interpretation of quotidian experiences at FNTI. The sticky affectivity generated by regular interactions with Three Sisters imagery, for example the image depicted in figure 15.1 actively erodes the hyper-individualism and competitive entrepreneurialism characteristic of neoliberalism by emphasizing collectivity, non-economized values, and place-based understandings. Also, the ambiguity associated with interpretation of artwork creates lacunae for highly contingent reflexivity which resists the homogenizing effects of neoliberalism's hyper-surveillance and economization of all life's domains.

FNTI's community garden, which is primarily used by staff members, has included a Three Sisters garden bed which generates produce for the FNTI community to take home and for group meals on-campus. The community garden also facilitates traditional knowledge transfer. Like the presence of Three Sister's inspired artwork on campus, gardening with—and preparing meals from—traditional crop varieties offers staff and other members of the FNTI community an opportunity for nondiscursive meaning-making via what could be viewed as an example of Carolan's (2008) concept of "more-than-representational knowledge" which is based on "sensuous, corporal, and lived experience(s)" (412). Our obligations to the Three Sisters are fulfilled by sowing, tending, harvesting them, and saving their seeds. The reciprocally relational circle is completed when we derive sustenance by consuming them. Not only does this relational reciprocity meet culturally identified axiological standards but also offers an embodied epistemology that "give(s) rise to discovery in one's body of relevant" knowledge (Diamond 2006, 59) and affords a specific configuration of sensory experiences that define embodied spaces (per Gibson 2014, 4). Like the aforementioned traditional design elements present on-campus, Three Sisters gardening in the workplace is essentially a spatializing activity that positions the work landscape as one of resistance to neoliberal norms, in which sacred responsibilities associated with ensuring life's continuance are enacted despite not aligning with economic determinations of productivity or the competitive entrepreneurialism associated with neoliberal rationality (Gildersleeve 2017).

Although curriculum and instruction are not the focus of this chapter, it would be remiss not to mention the extent to which the Three Sisters are incorporated into the curricula of the various programs at FNTI. FNTI currently offers a range of college- and university-level programming. Many of these programs, such as the Social Service diploma and the Mental Health and Addition Worker diploma, include curriculum related to the Three Sisters. Until 2017, with the introduction of the Indigenous Institutes Act, FNTI degree level offerings were all brokered through accredited Ontario universities. Under the purview of the Indigenous Institutes Act, FNTI now has degree granting status. The bachelor-level degree programs starting in 2020 include Indigenous Social Work, Indigenous Sustainable Food Systems, and Indigenous Midwifery.

Each of these programs has a suite of common courses taken during the first three-and-a-half semesters of study, prior to subject matter specialization. The common courses all focus on foundational aspects of Indigenous culture and are designed to help restore the cultural identities of our learners, all of whom has been negatively impacted by colonialism (Williams and Brant 2019). Multiple common courses include teachings related to Three Sisters, such as *Worldview and Cultural Fluency*, *Founding Values*, *Indigenous Well Being and Health Teachings*, *Indigenous Agricultural Heritage*, *Plants that Heal: An Indigenous Perspective*, *Recovering Health Sovereignty*, *Relationship to the Environment*, and *Indigenous Ecological Knowledge*. The Indigenous Sustainable Food Systems degree program also includes courses in years three and four that deal specifically with aspects of the Three Sisters polyculture. Inclusion of discussion-based and experiential aspects of Three Sisters teachings in various FNTI programs recognizes the Three Sisters as our sustainers and as persons in Haudenosaunee cosmology aligning with and reinforcing the aforementioned aspects of Three Sisters teachings that are incorporated into our pedagogic model. The inscription of more-than-human relationality as an onto-epistemological (Barad 2007) foundation in Indigenous higher education—through various institutional practices involving plant persons which draw on MTH power as *kasasten'sera*—undermines the totalizing economization and hyper-individualism associated with neoliberalism (Brown 2015; Gildersleeve 2017) and in the process offers a counternarrative to that informed by Western philosophy, which arguably unpins the Anthropocene (Vargas Roncancio et al. 2019).

FURTHER WORK

Our approach, presented here, recognizes and enacts a more inclusive relationality based on situated practices that provide access to MTH power. This is an example of an institutional-level intervention that counters neoliberal trends in the public sector which could potentially address the existential issues associated with the Anthropocene. Further research would both support the refinement of our more-than-human approach to higher education and extend this model to other contexts.

At FNTI, we plan to document the ways in which a more inclusive relationality— exemplified by our reciprocal relationship with the Three Sisters—extends to the unnamed plant persons and other elements of the more-than-human at FNTI. Also, we would like to identify other more-than-human persons, in addition to the Three Sisters, that could strengthen our decolonized approach to higher education. Garibaldi and Turner's (2004) Cultural Keystone Species concept could help to orient this identification process. Cultural Keystone Species are "the culturally salient species that shape in a major way the cultural identity of a people, as reflected in the fundamental roles these species have in diet, materials, medicine, and/or spiritual practices" (Garibaldi and Turner 2004, sect. Cultural Keystone Species, para. 1). Finally, we hope to understand, more deeply, the ways in which members of the FNTI community construct meaning through enactment of our mutual obligations to nonhuman persons.

External to FNTI, we suggest exploring the possibility of incorporating culturally relevant more-than-human persons in higher education practices in non-Haudenosaunee Indigenous contexts. For example, how can the personhood of culturally salient plants be meaningfully included in various Indigenous higher education governance models? Do Skunk Cabbage Man or the Blueberry Boys (Turner 2014, 231–34), mentioned earlier, deserve a seat at the governance table in Indigenous-run education institutions in the Pacific Northwest? Do plant teachers, such as the Ayahuasca vine (Luna 1984, 136), have something to contribute to the governance of Amazonian Indigenous Intercultural Universities? How can recognition of plant persons and the enactment of human–plant reciprocal responsibilities contribute to accessing MTH power and decentering the human in non-Haudenosaunee Indigenous cultural contexts?

Examining whether IK regarding plant persons can be equitably incorporated into Western higher education contexts is also of critical importance. If so, what is the role of IK keepers and community leaders in this process? If it is impossible to equitably introduce IK regarding plant persons in Western higher education contexts, how can these public sector institutions recognize plant persons and enact relational responsibilities to the more-than-human? Should higher education institutions look to long-forgotten Western traditions that recognize the vibrant animacy of the botanical world or should these institutions create new ways of acknowledging plant persons and enacting our relational responsibilities to the more-than-human? Engaging with the work of Indigenous thinkers (e.g., Antone 2013; Deloria and Wildcat 2001; Sheridan and Longboat 2006) and Western scholars such as Susan Ruddick (2017) and Michael Marder (2013)—who productively question human

exceptionalism and offer novel ways of conceiving of nonhuman agency—
could help the mainstream to enact a more reciprocally relational approach to
Western social and cultural institutions.

CONCLUSION

Earlier in this chapter, we introduced Deloria and Wildcat's (2001) formula:
"power and place produce personality" (23) and suggested that the aterritoriality of neoliberalism and human exceptionalism associated with the
Anthropocene both limit the full expression of our entangled humanity. In
this work, we describe a living practice—formally encoded in the institutional practices of an Indigenous-run higher education institution (FNTI)—
that re/inscribes human life within the more-than-human world exemplified
by the situated practices (Haraway 1988, 590) associated with fulfilling our
mutual obligations to the Three Sisters. This radical paradigm shift is a form
of resistance to the dominant neoliberal hegemony in higher education and is
accomplished by regularly drawing on *kasasten'sera*, or the power of life's
continuance associated with the Three Sisters, our sustainers, through embodied understandings and affective engagement with the Three Sisters, and
through performative and citational re/articulations of the dynamic relationality that characterizes our reciprocal relationships with the more-than-human.

NOTES

1. "Turtle Island" refers to North America. This term was popularized, in English,
by poet Gary Snyder in his 1974 collection Turtle Island. The name is based on the
significance of turtles in the creation teachings of various Indigenous nations (including Haudenosaunee).
2. The Three Sisters image and information can be found on the FNTI website:
https://fnti.net/mohawk-three-sisters.

BIBLIOGRAPHY

Ahmed, Sara. 2010. "Happy Objects." In *The Affect Theory Reader*, edited by Melissa
    Gregg and Gregory J. Seigworth, 29–51. Durham: Duke University Press. https://
    doi.org/10.1215/9780822393047.
Akwesasne Notes. 2005. *Basic Call to Consciousness*. Summertown: Native Voices.
Allen, Amy. 1998. "Rethinking power." *Hypatia*, 13, no. 1: 21–40. https://doi.org/10
    .1111/j.1527-2001.1998.tb01350.x.

Altamirano-Jiménez, Isabel. 2013. *Indigenous Encounters with Neoliberalism: Place, Women,and the Environment in Canada and Mexico.* Vancouver: UBC Press.http s://doi:10.1017/S0008423914000717.

Antone, Robert. 2013. "Yukwalihowanahtu Yukwanosaunee Tsiniyukwaliho: t^ As People of theLonghouse, We honor our way of life Tekal^ hsal^ Tsiniyukwaliho: t^ Praise our way oflife." PhD diss. State University of New York at Buffalo.

Arendt, Hannah. 1958. *The Human Condition.* Chicago: The University of Chicago Press.

Axtell, James. 2016. *Wisdom's Workshop: The Rise of the Modern University.* Vol. 89. Princeton: Princeton University Press. https://doi.org/10.2307/j.ctv7h0s90.

Barad, Karen. 2007. *Meeting the Universe Halfway: Quantum Physics and the Entanglement of Matter and Meaning.* Durham: Duke University Press.https://doi .org/10.1215/9780822388128.

Bauman, Zygmunt. 2000. *Liquid modernity.* Oxford: Blackwell Publishing.

Brown, Wendy. 2015. *Undoing the Demos: Neoliberalism's Stealth Revolution.* Cambridge: MITPress.

Bourdieu, Pierre. 1973. "Cultural Reproduction and Social Reproduction." In *Knowledge, Education, and Cultural Change,* edited by Richard Brown, 71–112. London: Tavistock.

Butler, Judith. 1993. *Bodies That Matter: On the Discursive Limits of "Sex."* New York and London: Routledge.

Butler, Judith. 2004. *Undoing gender.* London, UK: Psychology Press. https://doi.or g/10.4324/9780203499627.

Cajete, Gregory. 2000. *Native Science: Natural Laws of Interdependence.* Santa Fe, NM: Clear Light Publishers.

Carolan, Michael S. 2008. "More-than-representational Knowledge/s of the Countryside: How We Think as Bodies." *Sociologia Ruralis* 48, no. 4: 408–22. https://doi.org/10.1111/j.1467-9523.2008.00458.x.

Cove, John J., and George F. MacDonald. 1987. *Tsimshian Narratives.* Gatineau: Canadian Museum of Civilization.

Cornelius, Carol. 1999. *Iroquois Corn in a Culture-based Curriculum: A Framework for Respectfully Teaching About Cultures.* Albany: State University of New York Press.

Cowell, Andrew. 2018. *Naming the World: Language and Power Among the Northern Arapaho.* Tucson: University of Arizona Press. https://doi.org/10.2307/j.ctv550ctc.

Crum, Steven J. 2015. "A History of the First Nations College Movement of Canada, 1969–2000." *Tribal College Journal of American Indian Higher Education* 26, no. 3: 38–41.

Deloria, Vine, and Daniel Wildcat. 2001. *Power and Place: Indian Education in America.* Golden: Fulcrum Publishing.

Diamond, Timothy. 2006. "Where Did You Get the Fur Coat, Fern? Participant Observation in Institutional Ethnography." In *Institutional Ethnography as Practice,* edited by Dorothy Smith, 45–63. Lanham: Rowman and Littlefield.

FNTI. 2019a. *Annual Report 2018-2019.* Tyendinaga Mohawk Territory: FNTI. https ://fnti.net/photos/custom/FNTI%20Annual%20Report%202018_19_Web.pdf.

FNTI. 2019b. *First Harvest at FNTI Community Garden.* Tyendinaga Mohawk
Territory: FNTI. https://fnti.net/News/news.inc.php?ID=53andcommand=mini
ViewArticleandlang=Enads=0.

FNTI Marketing Department. 2020. *Enrolment and Graduation Statistics.* Tyendinaga
Mohawk Territory: FNTI.

Foucault, Michel. 2008. *The Birth of Biopolitics: Lectures at the Collège de France,
1978-1979.* New York: Palgrave Macmillan.

Foucault, M. 1978. *History of Sexuality: Vol. 1. An Introduction.* New York:
Pantheon Books.

Freeman, Bonnie M. 2015. "The Spirit of Haudenosaunee Youth: The Transformation
of Identity and Well-being Through Culture-based Activism." PhD diss. Wilfred
Laurier University.

Gagliano, Monica. 2018. *Thus Spoke the Plant: A Remarkable Journey of Ground-
breaking Scientific Discoveries and Personal Encounters with Plants.* Berkeley:
North Atlantic Books.

Garibaldi, Ann, and Nancy Turner. 2004. "Cultural Keystone Species: Implications
for Ecological Conservation and Restoration." *Ecology and society* 9, no. 3. https://
doi.org/ 10.5751/ES-00669-090301.

Gaudry, Adam, and Danielle Lorenz. 2018. "Indigenization as Inclusion, Reconciliation,
and Decolonization: Navigating the Different Visions for Indigenizing the
Canadian Academy." *AlterNative: An International Journal of Indigenous Peoples*
14, no. 3: 218–227. https://doi.org/10.1177/1177180118785382.

Gibbs, Anna. 2001. "Contagious Feelings: Pauline Hanson and the Epidemiology of
Affect." *Australian Humanities Review* 24, Dec. http://australianhumanitiesreview
.org/2001/12/01/contagious-feelings-pauline-hanson-and-the-epidemiology-of-af
fect/.

Gibson, James J. 2014. *The Ecological Approach to Visual Perception.* London, UK:
Psychology Press. https://doi.org/10.4324/9781315740218.

Gildersleeve, Ryan Evely. 2017. "The neoliberal academy of the anthropocene and
the retaliation of the lazy academic." *Cultural Studies ↔ Critical Methodologies*
17, no. 3: 286–293. https://doi.org/10.1177/1532708616669522.

Haraway, Donna. 1988. "Situated Knowledges: The Science Question in Feminism
and the Privilege of Partial Perspective." *Feminist Studies* 14, no. 3: 575–599.
https://doi.org/10.2307/3178066.

Hey, Valerie. 2006. "The politics of Performative Resignification: Translating Judith
Butler's Theoretical Discourse and its Potential for a Sociology of Education."
British Journal of Sociology of Education 27, no. 4: 439–457. https://doi.org/10.1
080/01425690600802956.

Holly, Marilyn. 1990. "Handsome Lake's Teachings: The Shift From Female to Male
Agriculture in Iroquois Culture. An Essay in Ethnophilosophy." *Agriculture and
Human Values* 7, no. 3–4: 80–94. https://doi.org/10.1007/BF01557313.

Hu, Min, Angela Daley, and Casey Warman. 2019. "Literacy, Numeracy, Technology
Skill, and Labour Market Outcomes Among Indigenous Peoples in Canada."
Canadian Public Policy 45, no. 1: 48–73. https://doi.org/ 10.3138/cpp.2017-068.

Indigenous Institutes Act, S.O. 2017, c. 34, Sched. 20. 2017. https://www.ontario.ca /laws/statute/17i34a.

Johansen, Bruce, and Barbara Mann. 2000. *Encyclopedia of the Haudenosaunee (Iroquois confederacy).* Westport: Greenwood Publishing Group.

Jones, Glen A. 2014. "An Introduction to Higher Education in Canada." In *Higher Education Across Nations,* edited by Kishore Mahendra Joshi and Saeed Paivandi, 1–38. Delhi: B. R. Publishing.

Kuokkanen, Rauna. 2011. *Reshaping the University: Responsibility, Indigenous Epistemes, and the Logic of the Gift.* Vancouver: UBC Press.

Lewandowski, Stephen. 1987. "Diohe'ko, the Three Sisters in Seneca life: Implications for a Native Agriculture in the Finger Lakes Region of New York State." *Agriculture and Human Values* 4, no. 2–3: 76–93. https://doi.org/10.1007 /BF01530644.

Luna, Luis Eduardo. 1984. "The Concept of Plants as Teachers Among Four Mestizo Shamans of Iquitos, Northeastern Peru." *Journal of Ethnopharmacology* 11, no. 2: 135–156. doi: https://doi.org/10.1016/0378-8741(84)90036-9.

MacDonald, Fiona. 2011. "Indigenous Peoples and Neoliberal 'Privatization' in Canada: Opportunities, Cautions and Constraints." *Canadian Journal of Political Science/Revue Canadienne de Science Politique* 44, no. 2: 257–273. https://doi.org /10.1017/S000842391100014X.

Marder, Michael. 2013. *Plant-thinking: A Philosophy of Vegetal Life.* New York: Columbia University Press. https://doi.org/10.1017/S0012217313001029.

Mendelson, Michael. 2006. *Aboriginal Peoples and Postsecondary Education in Canada.* Ottawa: Caledon Institute of Social Policy. https://maytree.com/wp-co ntent/uploads/595ENG1.pdf.

Mohawk Council of Akwesasne. 2015. *Akwesasne: A Cultural Portrait.* Akwesasne: Mohawk Council of Akwesasne Communications Unit. https://www.cerp.gouv.qc. ca/fileadmin/Fichiers_clients/Documents_deposes_a_la_Commission/P-207.pdf.

Mohawk, John and Jose Barreiro. 2010. *Thinking in Indian: A John Mohawk Reader.* Golden: Fulcrum.

National Indian Brotherhood. 1972. *Indian Control of Indian Education: Policy Paper Presented to the Minister of Indian Affairs and Northern Development.* Ottawa: Assembly of First Nations. https://oneca.com/IndianControlofIndianEduc ation.pdf.

Neruda, Pablo. 1984. *Still Another Day.* Port Townsend: Copper Canyon Press.

Parsons, Talcott. 1963. "On the Concept of Political Power." *Proceedings of the American Philosophical Society* 107, no. 3: 232–262.

Province of Ontario. 2017. "Indigenous Students—Find Out About Indigenous Institutes, Colleges and Universities, and Money to Study in Ontario." Accessed June 13, 2020. https://www.ontario.ca/page/indigenous-students.

Ruddick, Susan M. 2017. "Rethinking the Subject, Reimagining Worlds." *Dialogues in Human Geography* 7, no. 2: 119–139. https://doi.org/10.1177/2043820617717847.

Ruitenberg, Claudia W. 2007. "Discourse, Theatrical Performance, Agency: The Analytic Force of 'Performativity' in Education." *Philosophy of Education*

Archive: 260–268. https://educationjournal.web.illinois.edu/archive/index.php/pes /article/view/1471.pdf.

Sheridan, Joe, and Dan Longboat. 2006. "The Haudenosaunee Imagination and the Ecology of the Sacred." *Space and Culture* 9, no. 4: 365–381. https://doi.org/10 .1177/1206331206292503.

Steffen, Will, Jacques Grinevald, Paul Crutzen, and John McNeill. 2011. "The Anthropocene: Conceptual and Historical Perspectives." *Philosophical Transactions of the Royal Society A: Mathematical, Physical and Engineering Sciences* 369, no. 1938: 842–867. https://doi.org/10.1098/rsta.2010.0327.

Stonechild, Blair. 2006. *The New Buffalo: The Struggle for Aboriginal Post-secondary Education in Canada*. Winnipeg: University of Manitoba Press.

Truth and Reconciliation Commission of Canada. 2015. *Canada's Residential Schools: The Final Report of the Truth and Reconciliation Commission of Canada*. Vol. 1. Montreal and Kingston: McGill-Queen's Press.

Turner, Nancy. 2014. *Ancient Pathways, Ancestral Knowledge: Ethnobotany and Ecological Wisdom of Indigenous Peoples of Northwestern North America*. Vol. 74. Montreal and Kingston: McGill Queen's Press. https://doi.org/10.1111/1467 -9655.13006.

Turner, Nancy, and Marcus Bell. 1973. "The Ethnobotany of the Southern Kwakiutl Indians of British Columbia." *Economic Botany* 27, no. 3: 257–310. https://link.sp ringer.com/article/10.1007/BF02907532.

United Nations. 2007. "United Nations Declaration on the Rights of Indigenous Peoples (UNDRIP)." https://www.un.org/development/desa/indigenouspeoples/w p content/uploads/sites/19/2018/11/UNDRIP_E_web.pdf.

Vargas Roncancio, Ivan, Leah Temper, Joshua Sterlin, Nina L. Smolyar, Shaun Sellers, Maya Moore, Rigo Melgar-Melgar, Jolyon Larson, Catherine Horner, Jon D. Erickson et al. 2019. "From the Anthropocene to Mutual Thriving: An Agenda for Higher Education in the Ecozoic." *Sustainability* 11, no. 12: 1–19. https://doi .org/10.3390/su11123312.

Warrior, Robert. 1999. "The Native American Scholar: Toward a New Intellectual Agenda." *Wicazo Sa Review* 14, no. 2: 46–54. https://doi.org/10.2307/1409550.

Whatmore, Sarah. 2006. "Materialist Returns: Practising Cultural Geography in and for a More Than Human World." *Cultural Geographies* 13, no. 4: 600–609. https ://doi.org/10.1191/1474474006cgj377oa.

Williams, Keith, and Suzanne Brant. 2019. "Good Words, Good Food, Good Mind: Restoring Indigenous identities and Ecologies Through Transformative Learning." *Journal of Agriculture, Food Systems, and Community Development* 9 (B), 131–144. https://doi.org/10.5304/jafscd.2019.09B.010.

Williams, Keith J., Umar Umangay, and Suzanne Brant. 2020. "Advancing Indigenous Research Sovereignty: Public Administration Trends and the Opportunity for Meaningful Conversations in Canadian Research Governance." *The International Indigenous Policy Journal* 11, no. 1. https://doi.org/10.18584/iipj.2020.11.1.10237.

Zwicky, Jan. 2011. *Lyric Philosophy*. Kentville: Gaspereau Press.

Chapter 16

OAK

Marybeth Holleman

how many times
                    / in your life
do you sit
with your back
against the trunk
of a tree
                    / and do nothing
?
how many times
have you had
                    / the chance
?
how many times
have you
                    / taken it
?
and when you
                    / do
can you
                    / sit
can you
                    / do nothing
long enough
for the tree

         -rough bark, smooth bark-
         -scents that flow from the fissures-
         -sapstick and moss slip-
         -small flags of growth rings-
to tell you
                    / something
you did not know but
when you hear you wonder
how you have lived without
                    / knowing
this which
the tree speaks
?

Chapter 17

Objects/Ecologies

*Jardin d'Incertitude le système
écologique et l'objet technologique*

Christianna Bennett

APPROACH

Among the uncertainties lying dormant on the battlegrounds of future ecologies, there exists an unaddressed question concerning horticultural maintenance and landscape imagination: What types of kinship can we foster between plants and technological apparatuses? This includes questioning the roles and relationships of plant communities living among gardens of biological novelty and reframing ideations of invasivity.

In addition to horticultural invasiveness, there is a realm of the manufactured "other" wherein questions regarding the interaction of technologies within biological bodies and ecological systems are yet to be examined. Drones, mobile devices, and other inert yet virtually active objects have deeply permeated popular culture and visual literacy, substantially reshaping landscapes of the everyday. The idea of technology physically existing in biological beings, or being laced within the materials absorbed by live matter in ecological systems, is still largely undefined. Furthermore, the idea of artificiality pairing with biology often carries negative connotations, fueling fears of nature becoming tainted by technology.

> It was a test of a fragile trust. It was a test of our curiosity and fascination, which walked side by side with our fear. A test of whether we preferred to be ignorant or unsafe.
>
> —Jeff VanderMeer, *Annihilation*

Within the contemplative space of an imaginary garden, the *Jardin d'Incertitude*[1] described here, the following narrative and its associated visualizations offer one example of the literal entanglement of biological bodies with fabricated technologies and other crafted objects.[2] This vision proceeds from an admittedly naive, anthropocentric desire to assist in the future survival of plant life. Questions guiding this hypothetical include: Is technology another form of "invasivity" in ecological and biological settings, and what are we claiming when we distinguish "invasivity" from "nativity"? Might vegetal prostheses assist in the climate transitioning of biota? And, finally, will fabricated prosthetics pair with living plant matter productively? If so, what will the responses of the plants be in forced entanglements with the artificial?

Proceeding from these points, the *Jardin d'Incertitude* posits one uncanny aesthetic of a speculative Arcadia.[3] In the otherworldly space of this "paradise," a willow tree (*salix x niobe*) is outfitted with prosthetic limbs, leaves, and branches by human caretakers. As human visitors move through the surreal verdure, they are confronted with potential discomfort and confusion upon discovering examples of live, filigreed technological devices nesting and burrowing within the biological.

Through its inert materiality, *Incertitude* demands that viewers consider future climatic scenarios and the complications of vegetal adaptation in an increasingly hot, wet, and unruly planet. The ground is the first indication of conflict with ideas of idyllic stability that visitors encounter upon entering this place (see figure 17.1). Islands of terrain appear and disappear under the surface of accumulating and dissipating water bodies at the bounds of the

Figure 17.1 **Section through the *Jardin d'Incertitude* Water Gardens with Weeping Willow Shown among Purple Loosestrife, Zebra Mussel Terrain, and Prosthetically Armored Wetland Grasses.** Illustration by Christianna Bennett, Rachael DiChristina, and Madeline MacDonald, 2018.

garden. Nostalgic images of pristine wilderness are interrupted by the immensity and agency of water bodies and the odd practices of the garden's caretakers. Momentarily dry terrain is lined with dense, aggressive plants often perceived as invasive species. Looking closer, one will realize the garden is filled with another form of invasivity—instances where technological devices and plants manifest in increasingly strange and entangled ways.

As one manifestation of the future interactions of technological interfaces paired with living matter, *Incertitude* offers the surgical introduction of prosthetic limbs for vegetation in the interest of prolonging the survival of individual species. Plant prostheses are spliced by humans into tissues of verdure to assist vegetation in enduring unrestrained, aperiodic temperatures and atmospheres.

ENTER

Jardin d'Incertitude: le système écologique et l'objet technologique
Pour autant que nous sachions . . .

In *Jardin d'Incertitude*, "invasivity" manifests in ecological and technological forms. A transmutation of organic authenticity is constituent with how far into the site a visitor finds herself, coinciding with the vector of maintenance, as it is completed by the garden's caretakers. The further a visitor wanders inward, the more the examples of normative biological invasivity fall away and entirely manufactured prostheses begin to appear. Nowhere exactly the same, the fabricated biology pairs with live plant matter according to a diversity of adaptive devices. Even the ground is made from a diversity of materiality, from layers of crushed zebra mussels to fragments of disposed manufactured objects, with the edges of dry land tightly lined by communities of plants with prosthetic armor.

Hybridized vegetal limbs—plant prostheses—are present on many individual specimens in the garden and to varying degrees of intensity. Fearing the swell of a long-anticipated climatological demise, caretakers splice prostheses into the tissues of their verdant progeny, offering a relatively instantaneous upgrade in lieu of millennia of adaptation. Horticultural agency is observed by the gardeners as the plants respond physically to their newly acquired limbs and leaves. Through exertions of force, collaboration, or rejection of the prostheses, the vegetation expresses their desires over time.

Water commands the succession in this place, requiring a response from both the plants and their caretakers. The provision of predetermined paths for uncomplicated human appropriation is not present here. Nor is any assurance of optimal terrain for seedlings. A dynamic chemistry that dictates the interactions between the living and the inert generates a constant ambiguity

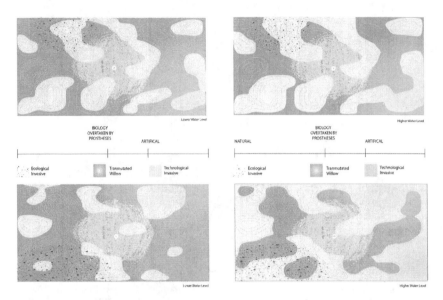

Figure 17.2 Series Images Demonstrating Temporal Relationships between Soil Topographies and the Garden's Waterbodies in Plan. Illustration by Christianna Bennett, Rachael DiChristina, and Madeline MacDonald, 2018.

and unpredictability for all forms of life (see figure 17.2). Inhabitants must navigate unique, erratic, enigmatic landscapes with little or no ability to forecast future security.

From a distance, an idyllic image of unrequited nature surrounds a single willow tree, commanding the centermost space of the garden. Direct lines-of-sight are blocked in all directions by the assertive canopy of the Weeping Willow. This results in a forced physical interaction with the willow's limbs while walking through the terrain. One cannot avoid pushing aside the branches of the tree to arrive at opposite sides of the garden. The commanding extremities of the *salix* forces physical closeness with its branches, preventing any straightforward movement along the watery gardens or the passage of smaller species lining the water's edges (see figure 17.3). Biological invasives block movement into certain territories as they clamor for ideal conditions. Lining the fertile edges of the water-filled ponds, the biological invasives frame views of the distant, and seemingly bucolic, through a barrier of the "unwanted," forcing consideration of the uncertain authenticity of the garden's "naturalness."

DEPART

When one exits the *Jardin d'Incertitude*, they re-enter a space of relatively authentic biological legibility. In this environment, individual plants persist

Figure 17.3 View of Weeping Willow Blocking Visual Access to the Further Reaches of the Garden. Illustration by Christianna Bennett, Rachael DiChristina, and Madeline MacDonald, 2018.

unadulterated by human tools or touch. The battles of climate and storm are fought with soft limb and tissue alone. In periods of extreme heat, extremities are burned and break off. When there is too much water, veins swell and suffocate. In this realm, caretakers withhold additional outfitting in order to witness genuine healing-in-action. In which domain will the anthropocentric urge to aid and care for plant life prove worthwhile despite critical blindness to the sensitivities of our companion biota?

NOTES

1. *Jardin d'Incertitude* meaning "Garden of Uncertainty." The garden was first sited in Montreal and therefore first imagined and named in the French language.

2. It is worth noting exemplary artists and gardeners whose innovative practices have shaped vegetal grafting techniques and methods of pairing fabricated materials with growing plants. These individuals include Gilles Clément, Philip Beeseley, Mel Chin, Hans Haacke, Sandra Voets, Laura Stein, and Bridgitte Raabe, among others.

3. Arcadia is invoked here to refer to the speculative atmosphere of an imaginary, utopian landscape. This is in reference to the Edenic wilderness of ancient Greece known as Arcadia, or Arcady, recognized as simultaneously a physical location and a mythological territory belonging to the gods. *Jardin d'Incertitude* is likewise an entirely fictional garden, though it is imagined as not entirely outside of the realm of a near-future reality.

BIBLIOGRAPHY

Beesley, Philip. 2010. *Hylozoic Ground: Liminal Responsive Architecture.* Cambridge, ON: Riverside Architectural Press.
Clément, Gilles, Sandra Morris, and Gilles A. Tiberghien. 2015. *"The Planetary Garden" and Other Writings.* Philadelphia: University of Pennsylvania Press.
Nemitz, Barbara. 2000. *Trans Plant: Living Vegetation in Contemporary Art.* Ostfildern-Ruit, Germany: Cantz.
VanderMeer, Jeff. 2014. *Annihilation.* New York: Farrar, Straus and Giroux.

Part IV

NONHUMAN AGENCY, ACTIVISM, AND LEGAL PERSONHOOD

Chapter 18

If the Ocean Were a Person

Jenny Rock and Ellen Sima

If the ocean were a person, what would they be like? Before you read further, answer that yourself. And consider, if we recognized their personhood what could *we* be like?

As an exercise in agency, our grammar will now recognize Ocean with the pronoun they/them. How do you know Ocean, and what is your relationship with them? What do they provide for you and vice versa? The fact that your eye probably stumbled in reading this is telling.

Recently, the personhood of bodies of freshwater has been recognized, like New Zealand's Whanganui River. As Te Awa Tupua, all its physical and spiritual elements as an indivisible and living whole are conferred with innate value and rights as a legal entity. Recognizing the connectivity of water, fed by a complex catchment of many tributaries from headwaters to estuary mouth, we ask: Can we extend personhood to Ocean?

Humans have a long relationship with Ocean, arguably as long as forever, given how many of our cultures hold Ocean as the origin of all things. Aztec and Greek gods were born of water, and Peruvian, Mexican, North American, Indian, and Scandinavian mythologies all see Earth as generated from Ocean. Simultaneously, as a force of nature, we have long associated the physical power of Ocean with cruelty and danger. In many belief systems, extreme marine forces such as storms, floods, and tsunamis were the vengeful acts of Nature or of irate deities who employed these forces to express their rage. Furthermore, from early explorers to fairly recent scientists, Ocean presented a vast and impenetrable frontier of physical breadth and extreme depth. This inaccessible Ocean was perceived as disconnected from human activities and permanent settlement, a space without the necessary human culture, politics, art, and sociability from which history is made. Through our terrestrially biased lens, Ocean was considered unimportant and largely empty of life.

Even midway through the twentieth century, institutionalized science still believed Ocean's deeper realms to be immune to the effects of dumping human waste.

The juxtaposition of Ocean as life-giving, destructive, and unknowable/untouchable means they could at once evoke positive emotional responses in us and remain sublimely hostile. And yet, over recent decades, new opportunities to explore and study Ocean through technological and scientific advancement have radically changed our understanding, revealing them as full of life but suffering from human impact. No part of Ocean is currently unaffected by human influence; we increasingly understand their living resources as over-exploited and their ecosystems as degraded (figure 18.1). In contrast to the vastness and emptiness in past conceptions, today's Ocean is imbued with science and industry. But do we know them now in a different way? Is the influence of science shrinking Ocean's space, and, in making them more comprehensible, do they become less threatening? Or does their sublime mystery and dominance remain?

We asked ninety-two New Zealanders with a range of background knowledge about marine science to reflect on the value of Ocean and its future prospects and to describe an embodied Ocean: "If the ocean were a person, what would they be like?" Nearly half described an entity that was large, physical, and tangible, in continuous, connective motion and alive with energetic force. Thematic analysis of participants' rich and varied anthropomorphic descriptions of a personified Ocean revealed personal, gender-related, and behavioral and physical attributes. These attributes included those imbued with intentionality (e.g., "nurturing," "violent," "hiding secrets"), as well as human activities or attitudes (e.g., "monk," "garbage man," or "passionate," "multifaceted," "capable of great emotion") and physical attributes (e.g., "long, flowing hair," "azure blue eyes").

Clearly, Ocean meant many things in tandem, as they always have. The most obvious theme to emerge was that of variety and even contradiction between attributes, reflecting a character of complexity and ambiguity. Positive behavioral attributes painted the picture of a kind, patient, and reliable character ("nice," "friendly," "approachable"), while antonymous descriptions referenced one that was "volatile" and "raging" with "fierce" tendencies, "prone to outbursts," and "pissed off." Some even overtly described a bipolar character with "split personalities, sometimes fun, sometimes violent," or with "anger management issues." Indeed, the most commonly offered singular descriptors were "moody" or "unpredictable," indicating that Ocean was still perceived to oscillate between states of malevolence and benevolence, at once terrifying us with violent power and inspiring our love and protection.

What emerged from our analysis as new was the simultaneous vision of Ocean as a vast physical entity that was far from empty of life or immune

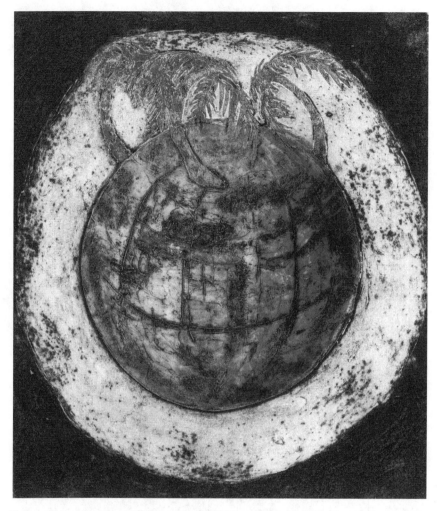

Figure 18.1 *Warming Cell*, **Jenny Rock, 2018, collagraph, 23 × 21 cm.** *Credit*: Jenny Rock.

to human actions. This dichotomy, while beholding Ocean as "majestic," "wondrous," and "colossal," also depicted "a sensitive giant," who was associated with "waste," as "exploited," "dying," and "polluted." Different from the traditional dichotomous conceptions of Ocean as good (life-supporting) or evil (destructive), the destructiveness embodied in the new dichotomy comes from human impact rather than from Ocean themself. While the good remained in what we receive from Ocean (participants suggested a multitude of their material and nonmaterial ecosystem services),[1] the evil now sat with human exploitation and environmental destruction.

Figure 18.2 *Pushed Off the Ends*, Jenny Rock, 2018, collagraph, 23 × 17 cm. *Credit*: Jenny Rock.

Our values, beliefs, and cultural understanding are integral components of conservation management, shaping our interactions with Ocean as much as our scientific knowledge and technical remediation skills. As we continue our anthropogenic assault on the world with progressive severity, it is vital to revise our contemporary relationship with a continuously life-giving Ocean. Although personification is not a requirement for recognizing more-than-human personhood, it may serve as an initial step for many of us to begin considering the characteristics, attributes, and values we find in Ocean. Anthropomorphic representations can assist us in empathizing, and granting recognition of an entity worthy of respect and stewardship. Such personification might provide points of connection for us to develop proenvironmental (empathetic) behavior toward the nonhuman world that is critical to confronting climate change impacts (figure 18.2) and marine ecosystem collapse.

NOTE

1. For a full account, see "Waterlines: Confluence and Hope through Environmental Communication," presented at the Conference on Communication and Environment, Vancouver, Canada, June 17–21, 2019. https://theieca.org/conference/coce-2019 -vancouver/papers/if-ocean-was-person-what-would-they-be-gauging-perceptions.

BIBLIOGRAPHY

Rock, Jenny, Manon Knapen and Ellen Sima. "If the Ocean Was a Person, What Would They Be Like: Gauging Perceptions of the Ocean through Personification." Presented at the Conference on Communication and Environment, Vancouver, Canada, June 17–21, 2019. https://theieca.org/conference/coce-2019-vancouver/ papers/if-ocean-was-person-what-would-they-be-gauging-perceptions.

Chapter 19

Personal Affairs

Litigating Nonhuman Animal Personhood in the Anthropocene

S. Marek Muller

The law is, at its core, a judgment of how intimate and entangled relation-ships form and should function in a social world. Arguments about how the law should function and whom it should protect can "be understood as determinations about who counts and how we should take account of them" (Matambanadzo 2012, 43). So, what is the nature of the law—specifically, of *animal* law—in the Anthropocene, and how could/should it address social relationships in a "more-than-human world" (Abram [1996] 2012)? In this chapter, I assess the rhetorical formulations through which morality, legality, and ideology intertwine in arguments about nonhuman animal personhood. To do so, I critique the rhetorical strategies and tactics deployed by Steven Wise, a leading voice in the U.S. Animal Rights Movement. Through a rhetorical analysis of Wise's Nonhuman Rights Project, I assess the moral and legal value of extending the category of "person" to nonhuman animal subjects. I further explore the intersecting matrices of domination that func-tion to oppress human and more-than-human subjects through the discursive construction of legally pertinent similarities and differences. Taking seriously the pursuit of multispecies liberation and the intimate ecological connections of everybody and every *body*, I critique "speciesism" (Singer 1975) under the law and warn against using "cognitively ableist" (Carlson 2001) methods to combat de jure speciesism.

As the author, I position myself as an unyielding advocate for human and nonhuman animal rights and liberation. This chapter therefore employs critical animal studies, critical legal studies, and critical disability studies. Critical animal studies is a theory-to-activist discipline that critiques the pernicious role of speciesism in environmental degradation. Its prescriptive goal is "total liberation"—the pursuit of multispecies equality through the dissolution of speciesism and all other oppressive -isms through engaged scholarship and activist activities (Best 2009). Accordingly, critical animal studies takes influence from anarchist studies of state oppression through de jure and *de facto* animal exploitation, rendering it a useful partner for critical studies of the legal system. The law is, after all, not so much an apathetic, objective "science" as it is a rhetorical systematization of moral frameworks (Hasian, Condit, and Lucaites 1996). Deconstructing the function of human supremacy through legal discourse is crucial to the dissolution of speciesism (Francione 1995).

Critical animal studies deploys intersectional analyses of oppressive systems. Taking speciesism as a root cause of many human-centered oppressions such as racism or sexism (for instance, the assertion that certain humans are inherently "less" human than others or should be "dehumanized" through "animalization"), the field rejects "single-issue" critiques of animal exploitation (Best et al. 2007). Instead, scholars assess how a particular animal's liberation is always and already intertwined with liberation across species lines. Thus, it is a useful partner with critical disability studies, which decries "medical models" of ableism that render disabled bodies as less-than-human, in need of medical or state interventions to "fix" them or eliminate them from society. Employing a "social model" of disability in which disabled bodies are understood primarily through societal mechanisms that are themselves disabling, critical animal and disability studies dissect how the role of the idealized human body functions in discourses regarding equity and justice (Shakespeare 2006).

Methodologically, I invoke ideological rhetorical criticism. Whereas the term "rhetoric" is often used as a pejorative to describe artful and deceptive language, the academic study of rhetoric can be understood as the study of arguments. Rhetorical studies examine persuasion—communication from one party resulting in attitudinal or behavioral change in another party. The purpose of studying rhetoric is to learn the most effective modes of persuasion in response to specific exigencies in order to become a more effective and ethical participant in civic life. To accomplish this task, ideological rhetorical criticism identifies and critiques ideologies embedded in rhetorical texts. Ideology is "a political language, preserved in rhetorical documents, with the capacity to dictate decision and control public belief and behavior" (McGee 1980, 3–4). It is ultimately a rhetorical creation constituted and reconstituted through discourse. Critics assess not only what is in a text but also what is absent from a text, for when dealing with historical and contemporary conflicts, stakeholders often disregard alternative choices that should have been considered (Wander 1983).

Like critical animal studies and critical disability studies, ideological rhetorical criticism is both descriptive and prescriptive. Critics assess what is persuasively effective or ineffective about a text and critique its under-girding ontological and/or moral principles to help create a better world. In my assessment of nonhuman animal personhood and arguments on how to achieve it, I adhere to the notion that ideological critics of the Anthropocene have an "ethical duty" (Cox 2007) to determine if not the best tactic, then at least the most morally consistent tactic through which to secure nonhuman animal liberation. Both "the rhetoric of those activists who champion 'animal' rights, or welfare, or liberation, or abolition" and those "who argue that humans should be permitted to use 'animals' must be examined," in particular for their "failures, assumptions, and exploitations, if we are ever to have an honest debate about the relationship between humans and other animals" (Goodale and Black 2010, 7).

I contend that Wise and the Nonhuman Rights Project make strategically sound and rhetorically coherent points about the need for expanding the moral and legal boundaries of the "person" in the Anthropocene. In an era of environmental devastation and mass extinction, privileging the homo sapien as the sole member of the moral community—and thus the sole species entitled to legal rights under the law—is a manifestation of speciesism that must be dissolved. Thus, the fight to afford legal personhood to nonhuman animals is legitimate. However, Wise's self-described emancipatory stance is riddled with moral inconsistencies in need of resolution. Both Wise's and the Nonhuman Rights Project's guiding rhetorical tactic is inconsistent with their purported strategic goal of dissolving de jure speciesism. Their sustained emphasis on "practical autonomy" privileges an anthropocentric—more specifically, a cognitively ableist anthropocentric—standard of cognition. Wise's master rhetorical argument from "sufficient similarity" (an analogical argument connecting subjects x and y to prove that both parties ought to receive the same treatment) has potentially detrimental consequences for disabled human bodies. Furthermore, it discriminatorily favors the few charismatic megafauna whose cognitive traits most closely resemble an idealized, able-bodied human subject. Therefore, whereas the notion of legal personhood for nonhuman animal subjects is an important step toward decentering human privilege, similar precedential arguments do not liberate animal bodies inasmuch as they manifest how cognitive ableism *is* intimately intertwined with speciesism in the rhetorical construction of personhood.

PERSONHOOD AND THE ANIMAL QUESTION

Contrary to its vernacular usage, "person" is not necessarily a synonym for "human." Personhood is a complex moral and legal category embedded in rhetorical constructions of rights, justice, and the greater good (Black 2003;

Rose 1988). Philosophically, a person refers to a subject inherently deserving of certain rights and privileges. Persons are members of the moral community and thus entitled to some degree of ethical consideration in public deliberations over the development of rules and policies.

In other words, moral community members are entitled to protection from undue harm. Protection most often occurs under the law; legal personhood codifies membership in the moral community. If moral persons are inherently entitled to certain treatment, one cannot violate those moral rights without breaking the law. A legal person, then, refers to a person whose rights ought to be protected through legal codification and precedent. More specifically, "legal personhood is a creation of law, whose role is to identify the subjects of certain rights and obligations, and grant legitimacy to actions realized pursuant to those rights and obligations" (Quintana Adriano 2015, 118). In scenarios in which a person's rights or interests conflict with those of a nonperson, the person (being more morally valuable than the nonperson) is more likely to come out on top. Ergo, groups aiming to extend the definition of personhood to nonhuman environmental subjects are engaging in a legal *and* moral battle over who matters most and how that "who" should be protected.

At many moments, both vernacular and institutional, particular humans have not been defined as people. The most obvious example is designating certain humans as chattel, as occurred during the transatlantic slave trade. More recently, during the 2020 coronavirus outbreak, U.S. senator Rand Paul made national headlines by suggesting on the Senate floor that undocumented immigrants should not get tax credits: "If you want to apply for money from the government through the child tax credit program, then you have to be a *legitimate person*" (quoted in Brody 2020). In contrast, nonhuman organisms, such as corporations, have at times been granted personhood status in various capacities. In *Citizens United v. FEC* (2010), the U.S. Supreme Court ruled that first amendment protections extend to corporations. This ruling was applied to *Burwell v. Hobby Lobby* (2014), which declared that corporations were in fact people, capable of exercising religious liberties. Nonhuman animals have also been granted personhood in limited capacities. For instance, in 2013, India's Ministry of Forest and Environments decreed that "dolphins should be seen as 'non-human persons' and as such should have their own specific rights" (Coelho 2013). Natural objects, such as forests and rivers, have also been named persons. In 2017, the New Zealand Parliament decided that the Wahangui River was an indivisible, living whole that henceforth possessed "all the rights, powers, duties, and liabilities" of a legal person (Warne 2019). In other words, not all humans are necessarily treated as persons, and not all legal persons are necessarily human.

Arguments about who constitutes a person and the rights to which a person is entitled are only rhetorically powerful within their ontological systems.

Unfortunately, the Anthropocene's prevailing ontological framework is anthropocentric, wherein *homo sapiens* are the sole members of the moral community and thus at the center of the moral universe. In an anthropocentric ontology, the interests of human beings are always and already more important than the interests of the more-than-human world. Environmental and animal rights arguments that decenter human supremacy are thus at an argumentative disadvantage from the start. For example, if one argues that dolphins ought to be named as persons and afforded legal rights on the basis that they are *sentient* (a common argument in animal rights circles, which largely follow a sentientist ontology), this argument only makes logical sense if sentience, not species belonging, is the premier quality of a person. If only humans are people, and only people have rights, then arguing for dolphin rights and personhood due to dolphin sentience is akin to arguing for dog personhood on the basis of their ear shape. The argumentative backing simply does not follow. The naming of more-than-human subjects as persons is thus an intensely complex rhetorical battle that has worked in precious few cases but, more often than not, falls short.

At the crux of debates over personhood are the qualities that define a subject as a person to begin with. Classical rights theorists often assert that nonhuman animal persons have "inherent value," a natural importance and predisposition to rights independent of one's personal beliefs on the matter (Regan [1983] 2004). Some ecocentric arguments highlight one's membership in a "biotic community" (Leopold 1970). Still others assert that rights ought to stem from a being's sentience (Francione 2012). And, in an anthropocentric ontological framework, a person's value is embedded in *species membership*. However, because the *homo sapien* species segregates itself through systems of domination such as colonialism, racism, sexism, ableism, and so on, members of dominant economic and social groups are able to qualify the "ideal" *homo sapien* subject. Thus, in an inherently unequal and anthropocentric world, the most valuable person who deserves the most rights is the one whose being most closely resembles the humans with the most social and economic capital (see Wynter 2003).

If, on a basic existential level, human wants and needs are greater than more-than-human wants and needs, then rhetors arguing for multispecies liberation must either (1) frame their arguments within the prevailing hierarchical anthropocentric system in order to show that other species are sufficiently similar to ideal human subjects or (2) attempt to overhaul the system altogether and replace it with another. As the following sections will show, Wise and the NhRP attempt to do the first through their arguments regarding practical autonomy and sufficient similarity. However, because of the inherently oppressive nature of prevailing cognitively ableist anthropocentric systems, their arguments ultimately fall short in the pursuit of nonhuman animal liberation. Even through the second method is inherently more challenging than the first (overhauling a system is tougher than tweaking an existing system), I demonstrate how arguments regarding nonhuman personhood that work within domineering ontological and axiological frameworks ultimately damage the pursuit of human and more-than-human flourishing in the Anthropocene. In other words, despite Wise's solid grasp of courtroom politics and genuine belief in nonhuman animal personhood, his reification of oppressive speciesist-ableist systems risks perpetuating violence against the vast majority of subjects existing in a more-than-human world.

CONTEXT: STEVEN WISE AND THE NONHUMAN RIGHTS PROJECT

On March 16, 2017, Wise told a New York's First Judicial Department that two chimpanzees, Tommy and Kiko, should be considered legal persons under the law. His appeal was in response to the Third Judicial Department's ruling that Tommy and Kiko were not eligible for personhood because they could not bear duties or responsibilities. Citing New York's habeas corpus statute, Wise asserted that they should be released from captivity to live the rest of their lives at an animal sanctuary. Wise commented to multiple media outlets that the decision was "biased and arbitrary" and "not backed up by science" (quoted in Fermino 2017). He answered judges' queries as to why, after so many failed appeals, he and his legal clinic (the NhRP) continued suing on behalf of their animal clients. Unfortunately, two months later, the appeals court ultimately ruled against Tommy, Kiko, Wise, and the NhRP. The judges unanimously asserted in their legal opinion that despite the plaintiffs' "laudable" goals, Tommy and Kiko "lack sufficient responsibility to have any legal standing" (quoted in Brown 2017). Unfazed, Wise retorted that he would be appealing the decision yet again.

Wise, a longtime animal rights activist and lawyer for forty years, thanks Peter Singer's *Animal Liberation* for steering him toward animal law. Since reading the book, he has published four books on animal rights law, written multiple articles for law reviews, and even produced an animal rights documentary shown at the Sundance Film Festival. He has also partnered with other famous animal activists such as primatologist Jane Goodall and served as a lecturer at Harvard University. Overall, Wise argues, great apes, elephants, and cetaceans living in captivity have a "fundamental right to bodily liberty" and, as "autonomous beings, they have the right to be released from captivity and sent to an appropriate sanctuary" (2017).

Wise founded the NhRP in 2007, originally calling it the Center for the Expansion of Fundamental Rights. The goal of the group is to sue on behalf of nonhuman animal plaintiffs in captivity in order to secure their freedom from unjust imprisonment. By citing the legal precedent of habeus corpus, the group seeks to not only prove that their clients are being treated unjustly but also set a legal precedent that would secure nonhuman animal personhood writ large, thus opening a door for future cases involving animal rights. The NhRP lists five central argumentative objectives on their official website: (1) to change the legal status of great apes, elephants, dolphins, and whales from "things" to "persons"; (2) to better define the qualities sufficient for the recognition of nonhuman personhood; (3) to develop grassroots campaigns at the local, national, and global level; (4) to build a broad-based coalition of individuals and organizations interested in secure legal personhood and rights for nonhuman animals; and (5) to view the concept of "justice" from larger social, historical, political, and legal perspectives (NhRP n.dc.).

Wise explains that his plaintiffs must be dubbed legal persons to secure legal rights—specifically, the right to either sue or have a third party sue on their behalf. Furthermore, Tommy, Kiko, or Minnie must secure a private right of action in which a person is legally entitled to enforce their rights under a statute. Ideally, once these protections have been secured, the NhRP's clients will have secured legal standing: the ability to show that a person has a stake in the outcome of a suit and is thus entitled to show the court how they have been harmed in the case at hand. Nonhuman animal standing assures that "a chimpanzee confined to a tiny cage or injected with a deadly microbe . . . has a clear stake in the controversy" (Wise 2014, 11). Since nonhuman animals remain mere things under the law, the NhRP hopes to open the door to nonhuman animal personhood (and subsequently legal rights, private right of action, and legal standing) "for every appropriate nonhuman animal" (11).

The NhRP has received international attention for its efforts. Multiple philosophers have aided in composing briefs on behalf of the organization. Acclaimed animal activists Peter Singer and Jane Goodall each sit on the board of directors. Journalistic outlets ranging from *Wired* to *Science* to *Al Jazeera* have reported on the group's suits. *Gizmodo's* George Dvorsky upbraided the court's decision to deny Tommy and Kiko their rights: "The court's reasons for refusing to recognize chimps as persons was flawed; this decision won't stand the test of time" (2017). Meanwhile, famous scholars such as Richard Epstein have condemned Wise and the NhRP, fearing the potential consequences of extending the rights of personhood to nonhuman animals. In an interview for *Harvard Magazine,* he stated "We kill millions of animals a day for food. . . . If they have the right to bodily liberty, it's basically a holocaust" (Feinberg 2016). Regardless of one's opinion on Wise and the NhRP, which cites bodily liberty and integrity as the foremost rights entitled to their clients, their increasing attention and influence cannot be discounted.

Chimpanzees Tommy and Kiko are only two of the NhRP's nonhuman animal clients. Tommy, explains the NhRP, lives alone and caged in a shed in New York. As Tommy's "owner" Patrick Lavery argues, "He likes being by himself" (NhRP, n.db.). Kiko similarly was found in a New York cage. A former animal "actor" in the film *Tarzan in Manhattan,* her on-set beatings rendered her partially deaf. Photos of Kiko show him with a steel chain and padlock around his neck (NhRP, n.db.). Currently, the project is focused on two elephant clients: Happy, at the Bronx Zoo, and Minnie, at the Commerford Zoo. Minnie's two elephant kin died at the zoo due to inhumane treatment. Two of the group's former clients, chimpanzees Hercules and Leo, are now living at a wildlife sanctuary. While Wise was unable to win their case, the nonstop litigation was almost certainly a factor in the two research animals being "retired" and sent to live out their lives in peace.

Despite Wise and the NhRP's lack of legal victories thus far, their tenacity appears to have had some effect on judicial statements over time. The more they appeal, the more judges' written opinions have suggested a potential shift in both social and institutional opinion on nonhuman animal person-hood. When the New York Supreme Court rejected the NhRP's plea to make Hercules and Leo legal persons under the law, Judge Barbara Jaffe wrote in her legal opinion that "not very long ago, only Caucasian, male, property-owning citizens were entitled to the full panoply of legal rights under the United States Constitutions" (quoted in Grimm 2015). Similarly, after Tommy and Kiko's failed 2017 appeal, Judge Eugene M. Fahey issued a legal opinion on the failure of the Court to seriously consider the moral and legal conundrums raised by the NhRP:

> [It] amounts to a refusal to confront a manifest injustice. . . . To treat a chimpan-
> zee as if he or she had no right to liberty protected by habeas corpus is to regard
> the chimpanzee as entirely lacking independent worth, as a mere resource for
> human use, a thing the value of which consists exclusively in its usefulness to
> others. Instead, we should consider whether a chimpanzee is an individual with
> inherent value who has the right to be treated with respect. (quoted in NhRP
> n.da.)

Although Judge Fahey concurred with the Court's decision to deny the NhRP's appeal on behalf of Tommy and Kiko, he stated in his legal opinion that "I continue to question whether the court was right to deny leave in the first place" considering that "it speaks to our relationship with all life around us. While it may be arguable that a chimpanzee is not a 'person,' there is no doubt that it is not merely a thing" (NhRP n.da.). Wise and the NhRP assert that opinions such as Jaffe and Fahey's have "opened the door to nonhuman animal personhood in New York and throughout the United States" (Wise 2018).

The slow and steady shift in judicial opinion may be a sign of upcoming legal victory. A victory for Wise, however, would involve dismantling the "Great Legal Wall" that has "divided every other species of animal in the West" (Wise 1999, 61). On one side of this wall, every human is a "person" with legal rights; on the other, every nonhuman is a "thing" with no legal rights. Whether sentient or not, existing in legal "thinghood" renders a being "invisible to civil judges for their own rights" because "only legal persons . . . can be legally seen" (2010, 1). Therefore, "every animal rights lawyer knows that this barrier must be breached" (1999, 61). Being legally seen under the law entitles one to genuine protections through rights, which "act like a suit of legal armor, shielding the bodies of natural persons from invasion and injury" (2010, 103).

In keeping with the fight against speciesism, Wise deconstructs species itself as a prerequisite to moral, and subsequently legal, consideration, liberty, and rights. A species "is just a population of genetically similar individuals naturally able to interbreed" (241). Naming *homo sapiens* as the sole bearer of personhood makes zero sense in terms of moral consistency; after all, "no one suggests that it is the human ability to interbreed that justifies our legal personhood" (241).

Wise and the NhRP are extremely careful in their legal strategies and tactics. Instead of following the lead of other animal rights organizations such as People for the Ethical Treatment of Animals, which has sued organizations like SeaWorld by citing the thirteenth amendment and casting captive orcas as "slaves," the NhRP is more cautious. They only file suits in jurisdictions they deem most hospitable to nonhuman animal personhood, a judgment based on what Wise calls "a hierarchy of common law American state jurisdictions according to their perceived hostility to certain key legal arguments" (10). Fully aware of the rhetorical power of judicial opinions in influencing future court decisions, Wise explains: "If these early cases are brought at the wrong time, in the wrong place, or before the wrong judges, they may strengthen the Great Legal Wall" (1999, 68). Wise and the NhRP do not have a flair for the dramatic. Rather, they believe in a slow and steady approach to securing nonhuman animal personhood that, rather than unraveling speciesism in one fell swoop, will set a legal precedent and create a "domino effect" for future animal lawyers. Wise explains:

> One of our initial litigation goals is to encourage judges to begin to think about the injustice of the de facto legal thinghood, the abject rightlessness, of all nonhuman animals in the United States, for we believe that to think about this

injustice will inevitably lead fair-minded judges to condemn it. The real, more complex story is that we persist, undeterred, secure in the knowledge that our approach to securing recognition and protection of the fundamental rights of nonhuman animals is legally, morally, factually, historically, and inevitably correct. (2018)

Whereas some animal liberationists might see this incremental approach as ineffective, Wise advises:

The necessary foundation for the legal rights of non-human animals does not yet exist. Do not expect a judge to appreciate the merits of arguments in favor of the legal personhood of any non-human animal the first time, or even the fifth time, she encounters them. While a sympathetic judge might be found here and there, no appellate bench will seize the lead until the issue has been thoroughly aired in law journals, books, and conferences. (1999, 66)

Ergo:

Our strategy has long been grounded upon the assumption that fair-minded judges persistently exposed to the existing overwhelming expert evidence of the complex cognition and autonomy of our nonhuman animal clients, coupled with powerful mainstream legal arguments, will struggle in good faith to overcome any implicit negative biases to arrive at the legally and morally correct decision that at least some nonhuman animals deserve legal personhood and those fundamental rights that protect their fundamental interests. (2018)

The remainder of this chapter does not question the speed of Wise and the NhRP's litigation. On the contrary, since the "law" is a rhetorical construction composed in part from mass cultural shifts throughout time, space, and place, the notion that incremental legal opinions might someday lead to a groundbreaking ruling on animal personhood seems valid. Given the increasing numbers of vegans in the United States, the increasing questions on the personhood of nonhuman entities such as corporations or technology sporting artificial intelligence, and the threat of mass extinction that has become omnipresent in the Anthropocene, the NhRP's slow tread toward a new legal precedent is encouraging.

What I *do* critique, however, are the ideological mechanisms undergirding Wise's legal arguments. Since legal decisions set legal precedents, and since legal precedents set the foundation for future legal rulings, it is important that decisions regarding nonhuman animal rights embrace the rights of nonhuman animals. The previous sentence may seem repetitive, but upon closer examination of the NhRP's strategies and tactics, it becomes clear that their premier arguments about personhood status ultimately exclude the majority of nonhuman animals from moral consideration. By drawing upon a cognitively ableist standard of "practical autonomy" as a precursor to rights and personhood, Wise and the NhRP not only stress the same ableist premises used to deny certain human subjects their rights but also integrate ableist standards *with* speciesism. The following section reveals how "practical autonomy" is not a liberatory rhetorical tactic through which to achieve nonhuman animal rights, but is in fact an anthropocentric rhetorical construct that reifies the violent boundaries of personhood that the NhRP claims to want to fight against.

CRITIQUE: "PRACTICAL AUTONOMY" AS COGNITIVELY ABLEIST ANTHROPOCENTRISM

I do not doubt that Wise and the NhRP genuinely wish to secure personhood and subsequently liberty for their clients. However, the ideology underlying their primary legal tactics is more anthropocentric than they would like to think. The law functions as a rhetorical conversation between institutions and publics. Once morality is codified into the law, the public is likely to accept that moral as valid. Similarly, the more a public comes to agree upon a specific vision of morality, the more likely it is that legal institutions might finally bend and encode that moral into legal precedent. Thus, merely finding a way to secure personhood for the likes of Tommy, Kiko, Minnie, and other "smart" nonhuman beings is an insufficient tactic through which to secure animal liberation. Were the NhRP to succeed in freeing their clients through arguments from sufficient similarity, it would set a legal precedent that would continue excluding most bodies from moral consideration. Personhood that is based on practical autonomy does not decenter the human, but rather recenters it. Specifically, premising nonhuman animal personhood on practical autonomy idolizes the able-bodied human subject. It is not only a rehash of the argument from marginal cases (which puts disabled human subjects at risk) but also a manifestation of the ableist-speciesist nexus. Constructs such as practical autonomy ultimately deny the majority of species membership in the moral community due an unjust, cognitively ableist ideology.

Wise relies upon the "argument from marginal cases" to make his case for legal rights for nonhuman animals. The "argument from marginal cases" is a common argumentative trope in moral philosophy and legal rhetoric, particularly in regard to the rights of nonhuman subjects. The structure of the argument is as follows: if human beings extend rights on the basis of certain species characteristics, but not all human beings have those characteristics, then the argument is invalid. In particular, since the speciesist argument against animal rights typically asserts human superiority in areas such as intelligence, rationality, or self-consciousness, Singer and other like-minded act-utilitarians point out the multiple human bodies that do not conform to those normative standards of humanness—in particular, infants, the critically injured, and the cognitively disabled. Just because an infant does not demonstrate superior intelligence does not mean that adults treat them as a legal thing. Or, to be macabre, a human baby's lack of rationality does not entitle other humans to farm and eat baby flesh. Singer famously summarized his version of this argument from marginal cases by asserting the following:

> The catch is that any such characteristic that is possessed by all human beings will not be possessed only by human beings. For example, all human beings, but not only human beings, are capable of feeling pain; and while only human beings are capable of solving complex mathematical problems, not all humans can do this. (1974, 106, 111)

Arguing for the rights of human beings on the basis of superior human intellect or other cognitive qualities is thus contradictory, disingenuous, and speciesist. If human bodies were truly the sole persons in the universe, they would need to have some uniquely human quality separating them from the billions of other species in existence. Since the primary categories used to espouse human superiority—for example, intellect, rationality, language, and self-consciousness—do not actually apply to all human subjects, one of two things must occur: *either* infants, the critically injured, and the cognitively disabled should be denied personhood and rights, *or* the speciesism inherent in those arguments should be disbanded and personhood/rights extended across species lines.

However, there are multiple critiques of the argument from marginal cases, especially when applied to nonhuman animal rights and personhood. These critiques tend to come from two camps: animal rights activists and disability rights activists. Some of Wise and the NhRP's rival animal rights activists have a problem with naming intelligence or other mental capacities as prerequisites to rights and personhood, preferring sentience as the sole precursor to moral consideration. Animal rights lawyer and self-proclaimed "vegan abolitionist" Gary Francione has called this moral framework a "similar minds approach" to animal liberation. As he excoriates: "To the extent that we link the moral status of animals with cognitive characteristics beyond sentience, we continue the humanocentric arrogance that *is* speciesism" (2012).

The idea of "being 'smart'" is important for Francione only insofar as it might qualify someone for a scholarship to a university, but it should not gauge "whether we use someone . . . as a nonconsenting subject in a biomedical experiment" (2012). A college student who scores low on a math test is not punished by being forced to become a test subject for a new pharmaceutical drug. The similar minds approach to animal rights merely celebrates species qualities that are sufficiently similar to human beings. The only difference is that instead of species membership as a precursor to personhood and rights, being "smart" is substituted as an equally anthropocentric human characteristic in need of emulation. Worse still, according to Francione, the similar minds approach invokes "a game that animals can never win. They'll never be enough 'like us'" (2012). Whereas a lawyer might argue that an animal's ability to learn sign language makes it sufficiently human, a judge might argue that its inability to use the *English* language is the mode of intelligence that matters most. Ultimately, the similarity of one animal's mind to a human being's is restrictive at best, incoherent at worst.

Furthermore, disability activists have long taken issue with the argument from marginal cases on the basis that it pathologizes disabled bodies. One critique is blatantly speciesist—that is to say, the notion that a comparison of human bodies to nonhuman animal bodies is inherently wrong. Such a stance is often based on traumatic personal or cultural experiences (e.g., being called a "brute" in the history of colonial oppression. But, from a rhetorical perspective, prima facie rejection of such analogical argumentation is ideologically premised upon the notion that human bodies are inherently superior to others (Armstrong 2002). However, there is a critique of the argument of marginal cases that deserves more substantial attention. Comparisons of human bodies to animal bodies are not inherently problematic, but absolutely can be when they perpetuate institutions such as ableism. The argument from marginal cases in particular invokes a medical model of disability wherein cognitive disability is "arrogantly conceived as misfortune, impairment or temporary embarrassment" (Donaldson and Kymlicka 2015, 238). Susan Donaldson and Will Kymlicka explain the crux of the issue undergirding the argument:

> The burden of the [argument from marginal cases] is to call for consistency in the way we deal with these "marginal" cases, so that whatever moral status we accord to "deficient" or "unfortunate" people with [cognitive disability], we should do so as well for animals with comparable cognitive capacities. . . . It perpetuates a deeply problematic conception of neurotypical human cognition as defining the core of moral status, and treats other forms of subjectivity as somehow deficient bases of moral status. (238)

Thus, if the total liberation of species is to be achieved, then any arguments about nonhuman animal rights and personhood must be assessed for its potential consequences for human subjects embedded in historic systems of oppression. In other words, people like Wise's overarching moral *strategies* (that is to say, his vision of an equitable future) and therefore ought to be consistent with his rhetorical *tactics* (how that future is to be achieved vis-à-vis legal argumentation and court rulings).

In keeping with Singer and other proponents of the argument from marginal cases, Wise has long asserted that "as long as society awards personhood to non-autonomous humans, such as the very young, the severely mentally retarded, and the persistently vegetative," then it must, as a matter of equality, award basic rights to animals (2002, 785). Noting that infants and disabled human subjects are entitled to "immunity rights" such as bodily integrity, Wise continues: "Thank goodness for that, as it is the weakest humans who are in most need of legal protection from exploitation" (2002). Specific to Wise and the NhRP, however, is their emphasis on granting rights and personhood to animals possessing what they dub "practical autonomy." Wise explains his central objective in choosing clients and litigating on their behalf: "What facts can we prove in court, if we're claiming that autonomy is a sufficient condition for personhood?" (quoted in Keim 2013).

What, then, is practical autonomy? In a court of law, Wise specifies that practical autonomy constitutes any living subject "for whom we think we have sufficiently powerful data that shows they are autonomous beings" (quoted in Keim 2013). More specifically, Wise asserts that practical autonomy comprises "a minimum level of autonomy," including but not limited to "the abilities to desire, to act intentionally and to have some sense of self" (2002). These characteristics specifically entitle a subject to "basic rights." Cetaceans, for instance, often spend their whole lives in one singular family unit and "have social sensitivities as pronounced as our own" (quoted in Keim 2013). Gorillas have in the past been able to learn human sign language. Cognitive ethnologists have discovered that many nonhuman animals have morals and principles in their social communities (Bekoff and Pierce 2009).

In the case of chimp and bonobo plaintiffs, Wise cites the nonhuman animals' possession of "primary consciousness" (wherein subjects like Tommy and Kiko can feel pain, suffer, and be aware of that pain and suffering in the present moment). He further cites their "secondary consciousness," in which clients possessing practical autonomy "derive sophisticated cognitive, emotional, and social capabilities; immense and powerful intellects; and an ability to anticipate the future that qualitatively differ little from the capabilities of human beings" (1996, 184). Imprisoning autonomous species for the purposes of human entertainment or betterment (be it a roadside zoo or a lab) is not only cruel, but a means to "*strip them of their culture*." Unjust imprisonment is analogous to human imprisonment insomuch as it deprives us "of a substantial portion of what gives meaning to our lives" (185). Indeed, "We don't enslave people or deprive them of their right to bodily integrity because we think we will benefit if we do" (2002).

Perhaps more interesting than what practical autonomy *does* include is what is does *not*. Wise and the NhRP advocate for the "precautionary principle" in its application under the law. If a human or nonhuman animal subject can be *reasonably certain* to possess practical autonomy, then it ought to be granted liberty. However, Wise concedes, "under the moderate application I urge, African grey parrots and African elephants are entitled to basic rights. Based on what is known, dogs and honeybees are not. But who knows what exciting breakthroughs tomorrow's research may bring?" (2002). That is to say, while Wise does not rule out rights for all nonhuman animal species, his incremental approach to legal personhood relies upon first proving that his clients possess practical autonomy; specifically, a version of practical autonomy that is sufficiently similar to a normative human subject. Referring to an alligator versus a chimpanzee, Wise explains: "When I look into the eyes of an alligator, I don't get anything except I'm lunch. . . . When I look at them, I get a very different feeling than I do looking at a chimp . . . we're very far apart from each other" (quoted in Kaufman 2016).

It is in moments like these that Wise reveals a concerning aspect of his and the NhRP's undergirding ideology. Not only do they apply the argument from marginal cases in a manner that medicalizes cognitively disabled human subjects, they do so in a manner that pathologizes "unintelligent" nonhuman animal subjects. In other words, the NhRP lays bare the interweavings of speciesism and ableism, where the former is not confined to nonhuman animals and the latter to humans. On the contrary, nonhuman animals can be just as impacted by ableist ideas as disabled human subjects. In this particular instance, Wise and the NhRP employ a rhetoric of "cognitive ableism," defined by Licia Carlson as "a prejudice or attitude of bias in favor of the interests of individuals who possess certain cognitive abilities (or the potential for them) against those who are believed not to actually or potentially possess them" (140). Ultimately, it is "the tendency to essentialize cognitive disability" as well as "the failure to address adequately the nature of cognitive privilege" (Carlson 140) that perpetuates this discriminatory stance within and across species lines.

One should notice how, in this instance, Carlson does not equate "individual" with "human." Whether an individual is human or nonhuman animal, "without attending to the specific nature and history of a particular classification, there is the risk of reducing the individuals therein to prototypes" (Carlson 141). She warns how a prototype "can be constructed according to a prevailing stereotype, where the 'cognitively disabled' are defined by a simple, unproblematic set of characteristics that are assumed to be fixed and inherent" (141). Carlson further identifies the inherent nonsense of cognitive ableism since, as she explains, the "boundaries of disability as a category are permeable, and though we may not be members now, we are all 'temporarily able'" (141).

The law functions through precedent. It is a constant conversation occurring across time, space, and place. Thus, a legal decision from 1810 still has potential impact on a legal decision in 2020. It is therefore of utmost importance to evaluate the potential consequences of what a victory for Tommy, Kiko, Minnie, or one of the NhRP's other clients might mean for future nonhuman animal subjects in need of help. Wise has made clear that he is unsure of the potential for rights and personhood for those nonhuman animals who do not display cognitive features that are sufficiently similar to humans. This is an issue, since legal decisions are based upon prior legal cases that are also sufficiently similar to the case at hand. Thus, were Tommy to be freed on the basis of his intelligence, and were other chimpanzees able to use this same argumentative premise to secure basic rights and liberty, then a being's *intelligence* would gain far more legal capital than it already has under the law. One need only look back to Supreme Court cases such as *Buck v. Bell,* which legalized the forced sterilization of cognitively disabled human subjects, to see the harm of using such problematic constructs on nonhuman animal subjects under oppression. Perhaps Tommy and other chimpanzees would acquire personhood, but the precedential power of intelligence would deny the vast, vast, *vast* majority of other nonhuman animal subjects the possibility of moral consideration. Why? Because "intelligence" too is a rhetorical construction premised upon cultural valuation of what makes an ideal mind (Serpell 1994). And construction is both speciesist and ableist at its core.

Ultimately, claims Carlson, "the question of what it might mean . . . to examine our own cognitively able and privileged identities presents perhaps the deepest challenge to the philosophical tradition and its assumptions regarding reason, cognitive ability, and personhood" (142). And, despite the obvious differences between what it means to exist as a neurodivergent human subject versus a nonhuman animal subject, the mechanisms through which to deny both categories of beings their rights and personhood remain intertwined. Advocating for legal personhood only for those human and nonhuman animal subjects in whom the lawyers and judges can "see themselves" is not a radical rhetorical move. Rather, it entrenches the same speciesist mentality that denied nonhuman animal personhood in the first place. As such, while the group claims to fight against legalized notions of the "Great Legal Wall" dividing human and nonhuman animal subjects, their arguments actually *reify* this notion and, subsequently, rhetorically damage the legal battle for nonhuman animal rights. Wise and the NhRP's emphasis on practical autonomy and sufficient similarity entrenches anthropocentric and cognitively ableist constructions of cognition, ultimately demonstrating how the total liberation of species cannot function when the speciesist-ableist nexus is left uninterrogated.

CONCLUDING REMARKS

Wise's NhRP reveals how speciesism and ableism intersect in moral and legal debates over nonhuman animal personhood in the Anthropocene. In particular, Wise and the NhRP make manifest the speciesism inherent in the legal system and how such speciesism must be dissolved through an exploding of the moral/legal category of the "person." Doing so requires a dissolution of the "Great Legal Wall" that relegates *most* human subjects as persons and *nearly all* nonhuman subjects as things. Since the law is a codification of morality, achieving legal personhood is a necessary prerequisite to nonhuman animal rights and liberation. But, despite Wise's shrewd use of legal norms and systems to further his and the NhRP's cause, I argue that the potential consequences of their success outweigh the benefits. The cognitive ableism undergirding the NhRP's argument from practical autonomy not only makes manifest the problematics of the utilitarian argument from marginal cases, but also recenters the human subject as the premier model of personhood. The only difference is that, in this new manifestation, that human subject must also meet arbitrary standards of cognitive prowess.

I do not mean to simply "trash" Wise and end this chapter. Such scholarship is, much like anthropocentrism, petty, cruel, and far too easy. Rather, I conclude by offering a series of probing questions and potential ontological alternatives to defining personhood and emancipating animals in the Anthropocene. Specifically, I advocate for the "cripping" of nonhuman animal personhood—that is to say, a deployment of personhood arguments that takes seriously the existential intersections of speciesism and ableism. The arguments about moral and legal personhood in these assumptions impact the more-than-human world. But admission of inherent differences between subjects need not equate to an admission of inferiority. That every being has rights to be recognized and revered and that every being is *intimately connected* to every other being is an entry point for revolutionary bilateral legal relations in a more-than-human world. In particular, I draw upon the advice of Sunaura Taylor (2017), who asserts that "caring across species and ability" and "cripping animal ethics" requires pivoting from emphases on sufficient similarity to able-bodied human subjects toward the acknowledgement and valuation of species alterity. Taylor asserts that in the battle for total liberation in the Anthropocene: "We could recognize our mutual dependence, our mutual vulnerability, and our mutual drive for life. We could also start listening to what those who need care are communicating about their own lives, feelings, and the care they are receiving . . . we could recognize that we are all citizens of shared communities" (2017, 218). In other words, constructions of a moral community need not be dependent on what subjects all have in common. Constructions must be based on recognized *existential intimacy.*

Since every being is different, the only similarity of moral importance is
a shared existence in the world, wherein "all of us exist along a spectrum
of dependency (210). Cripping "animal ethics" must involve a cripping of
"rights," which must involve a cripping of the "person," which must at the
same time involve a cripping of "subjectivity" itself. In the Anthropocene, a
move toward nonhuman personhood involves asking: "How we can develop
a sustainability movement that includes more bodies and more radical value
systems" (173). It further requires viewing all bodies as interconnected, interdependent, and intimately related.

One example of an alternative methodology for procuring nonhuman
animal personhood is Earth Jurisprudence, or "Wild Law." This ecocentric
school of legal thought takes seriously the Leopoldian notion of the biotic
community and invokes a systems approach to personhood. Humans, nonhuman animals, and natural objects such as rivers and stones all have their roles
to play in the maintenance of sustainable life on Earth and thus are entitled
to rights and personhood. After all, "Human Law" is merely a supplement to
"Great Law," which is the ecological rules governing the maintenance of life
on Earth (Burdon 2011; Maloney and Burdon 2014, 7). This jurisprudential
system is also imperfect—were it flawless, nonhuman animal personhood
would be a forgone conclusion.

Nonetheless, as Wise himself explains, rights are "the least porous barrier against oppression and abuse that humans have ever devised" (2014,
236). Where Wise and the NhRP maintain the nonporous barriers of rights
personhood, Earth Jurisprudence explodes those boundaries by reimagining
rights for an entire earth community, with specific rights for humans, nonhuman animals, and natural objects. Christopher Stone, for instance, famously
argued that trees should have legal standing and rights (2010). Not every
being has the same rights because not every being needs the same rights, but
every being matters by virtue of its existence *as* matter in a biotic community.
Practitioners of this ecocentric legal approach, such as the Center for Earth
Jurisprudence in Orlando, Florida, demonstrate how there *are* means through
which to defy anthropocentrism under the law without excluding the vast
majority of bodies from moral consideration. If put into conversation, perhaps
Wild Law and the NhRP might better one another.

There already exist a slew of alternative methodologies through which to
procure nonhuman animal personhood. None are perfect. Some are in conversation; some wildly contradict the others. What they have in common is
the desire to expand the moral community by exploding the category of the
person morally and legally. I do not pretend to know for certain which method
is guaranteed success. What I do know is that anthropocentrism and neuro-
ableism are pernicious systems. They must not be allowed to contaminate
the battle for total liberation in the Anthropocene. While Wise and the NhRP

demonstrate the importance of nonhuman animal rights in the battle for total liberation, a model of justice premised upon exclusion is doomed to fail.

BIBLIOGRAPHY

Abram, David. (1996) 2012. *The Spell of the Sensuous: Perception and Language in a More-than-Human World*. Reprint, New York: Vintage Books.
Armstrong, Philip. 2002. "The Postcolonial Animal." *Society & Animals* 10 (4): 413–19.
Bekoff, Marc, and Jessica Pierce. 2009. *Wild Justice: The Moral Lives of Animals*. Chicago: University of Chicago Press.
Best, Steven. 2009. "The Rise of Critical Animal Studies: Putting Theory into Action and Animal Liberation into Higher Education." *Journal for Critical Animal Studies* 7 (1): 9–52.
Best, Steve, Anthony J. Nocella, Richard Kahn, Carol Gigliotti, and Lisa Kemmerer. 2007. "Introducing Critical Animal Studies." *Journal for Critical Animal Studies* 5 (1): 4–5.
Black, Jason Edward. 2003. "Extending the Rights of Personhood, Voice, and Life to Sensate Others: A Homology of Right to Life and Animal Rights Rhetoric." *Communication Quarterly* 51 (3): 312–31.
Brody, Sam. 2020. "Rand Paul: Non-people Shouldn't Get Federal Tax Credit." *Daily Beast*, March 18, 2020. https://www.thedailybeast.com/rand-paul-says-non-people-shouldnt-get-federal-tax-credit.
Burdon, Peter, ed. 2011. *Exploring Wild Law: The Philosophy of Earth Jurisprudence*. Kent Town, South Australia: Wakefield Press.
Carlson, Licia. 2001. "Cognitive Ableism and Disability Studies: Feminist Reflections on the History of Mental Retardation." *Hypatia* 16 (4): 124–46.
Coelho, Saroja. 2013. "Dolphins Gain Unprecedented Protection in India." *DW*, May 24, 2013. https://www.dw.com/en/dolphins-gain-unprecedented-protection-in-india/a-16834519.
Cox, Robert. 2007. "Nature's 'Crisis Disciplines': Does Environmental Communication Have an Ethical Duty?" *Environmental Communication* 1 (1): 5–20.
Donaldson, Sue, and Will Kymlicka. 2015. "Rethinking Membership and Participation in an Inclusive Democracy: Cognitive Disability, Children, Animals." *Disability and Political Theory*: 234–62.
Dvorsky, Greg. 2017. "Appeals Court Says Chimps are not Legal Persons—Here's Why They're Wrong." *Gizmodo,* June 9, 2017. http://gizmodo.com/appealscourt-says-chimps-are-not-legal-persons-heres-w-1795959514.
Feinberg, Cara. 2016. "Are Animals 'Things'?" Harvard Magazine, March-April 2016. https://harvardmagazine.com/2016/03/are-animals-things.
Fermino, Jennifer. 2017. "Nonhuman Rights Project Argues for Chimpanzees' Rights, Release to Sanctuary in New York Appellate Court." Nonhuman Rights Project. March 16, 2017. https://www.nonhumanrights.org/media-center/03-16-17-nonhuman-rights-project-argues-for-chimpanzees-rights/.

Francione, Gary. 1995. *Animals, Property and The Law*. Philadelphia: Temple University Press.

———. 2012. "Only Sentience Matters." *Abolitionist Approach* (blog). August 12, 2012. http://www.abolitionistapproach.com/only-sentience-matters/.

Goodale, Greg, and Jason Edward Black, eds. 2010. *Arguments About Animal Ethics*. Plymouth, UK: Lexington Books.

Grimm, David. 2015. "Judge Rules Research Chimps Are Not 'Legal Persons.'" *Science,* July 30, 2015. http://www.sciencemag.org/news/2015/07/judge-rules-rese arch-chimps-are-not-legal-persons.

Hasian Jr, Marouf, Celeste Michelle Condit, and John Louis Lucaites. 1996. "The Rhetorical Boundaries of 'The Law': A Consideration of the Rhetorical Culture of Legal Practice and the Case of the 'Separate but Equal' Doctrine." *Quarterly Journal of Speech* 82 (4): 323–42.

Ikaheimo, Heikki. 2007. "Recognizing Persons." *Journal of Consciousness Studies* 14 (5–6): 224–47.

Kaufman, Anthony. 2016. "The Lawyer Fighting for Animal Rights in 'Unlocking the Cage' Asks: What Kind of Being Are You?" *Los Angeles Times*, June 24, 2016. https://www.latimes.com/entertainment/movies/la-et-mn-unlocking-the-ca ge-feature-20160617-snap-story.html.

Leopold, Aldo. 1970. *A Sand County Almanac: With Other Essays on Conservation from Round River*. Ballantine Books. First published in 1949 by Oxford University Press.

Maloney, Michelle, and Peter Burdon, eds. 2014. *Wild Law-In Practice*. New York: Routledge.

Matambanadzo, Saru M. 2012. "Embodying Vulnerability: A Feminist Theory of the Person." *Duke Journal of Gender Law and Policy*, no. 20, 45–83.

McGee, Michael Calvin. 1980. "The 'Ideograph': A Link between Rhetoric and Ideology." *Quarterly Journal of Speech* 66 (1): 1–16.

Nonhuman Rights Project. n.da. "Client, Kiko (Chimpanzee)." Nonhuman Rights Project. Accessed May 19, 2020. https://www.nonhumanrights.org/client-kiko/.

———. n.db. "Client: Tommy (Chimpanzee)." Nonhuman Rights Project. Accessed May 19, 2020. https://www.nonhumanrights.org/client-tommy/.

———. n.dc. "Who We Are." Nonhuman Rights Project. Accessed May 19, 2020. https://www.nonhumanrights.org/who-we-are/.

Quintana Adriano, E. A. 2015. "Natural Persons, Juridical Persons and Legal Personhood." *Mexican Law Review* 8 (1): 101–18.

Regan, Tom. (1983) 2004. *The Case for Animal Rights*. Reprint, Berkeley: University of California Press.

Rose, Nikolas. 1988. *Inventing Our Selves: Psychology, Power, and Personhood*. Cambridge, UK: Cambridge University Press.

Serpell, Robert. 1994. "The Cultural Construction of Intelligence." *Psychology and Culture*, 157-163.

Shakespeare, Tom. 2006. "The Social Model of Disability." *The Disability Studies Reader*. 2nd ed. Edited by Lennard J. Davis. New York: Routledge, 197–204.

Singer, Peter. 1974. "All Animals Are Equal." *Philosophic Exchange* 5 (1): 102–16.

———. 1975. *Animal Liberation.* New York: Random House.

Stone, Christopher D. 2010. *Should Trees Have Standing?: Law, Morality, and the Environment.* Oxford: Oxford University Press.

Taylor, Sunaura. 2017. *Beasts of Burden: Animal and Disability Liberation.* New York: New Press.

Wander, Philip. 1983. "The Ideological Turn in Modern Criticism." *Communication Studies* 34 (1): 1–18.

Warne, Kennedy. 2019. "A Voice for Nature." *National Geographic,* May 2019. https://www.nationalgeographic.com/culture/2019/04/maori-river-in-new-zealand-is-a-legal-person/.

Wise, Steven M. 1996. "Legal Rights for Nonhuman Animals: The Case for Chimpanzees and Bonobos." *Animal Law,* no. 2: 179–86.

———. 1999. "Animal Thing to Animal Person—Thoughts on Time, Place, and Theories." *Animal Law,* no. 5: 61–69.

———. 2002. "'Practical autonomy' Entitles Some Animals to Rights." *Nature* 416 (6883): 785.

———. 2010. "Legal personhood and the nonhuman rights project." *Animal L,* no. 17: 110.

———. 2014. *Rattling the Cage: Toward Legal Rights for Animals.* Boston: Da Capo.

———. 2017. "What Chimpanzees Deserve: Attorney who Represents Tommy and Kiko Makes the Case for their Legal Personhood." *New York Daily News,* March 16, 2017. http://www.nydailynews.com/opinion/chimpanzees-deserve-article1.2999345.

———. 2018. "Letter #2 from the Struggle for Nonhuman Animal Rights: January 2018 to September 2018." Nonhuman Rights Project. September 27, 2018. https://medium.com/@NonhumanRights/letter-2-from-the-front-lines-of-thestruggle-for-nonhuman-rights-january-2018-to-september-2018-c84f5e581d4f.

Wynter, Sylvia. 2003. "Unsettling the Coloniality of Being/Power/Truth/Freedom: Towards the Human, After Man, Its Overrepresentation—An Argument." *CR: The New Centennial Review* 3 (3): 257–337.

Chapter 20

Tahlequah's Internatural Activism

Situating the Body and the Intimacy of Grief as Evidence of Human-Caused Climate Change

Madrone Kalil Schutten

Grief is the glue of community. "Showing up" in the vulnerability brought to bear by grief is one of the most intimate acts experienced during earthly lives. In the aftermath of a wound, a community grows through a transformative change that binds it together. Distinct from sadness, grief "arises when something is lost irretrievably, or when a death occurs" (McLaren n.d., para. 2). Grief demands the difficult action of asking what must be mourned and what must be released completely (McLaren n.d.). As such, the action of grieving should be seen as a process, a ritual or practice, a rite of passage, a journey we know we will take and yet are rarely prepared to experience. Witnessing the intimate grieving process of another being is an honor. "Grief, like love, remains a deeply intimate experience and the modes of 'dealing' with it are perhaps as varied as the number of sufferers" (Pribac 2016, 198). Human beings are not the only beings who experience grief. During the summer of 2018, Tahlequah, a mother orca from the endangered Southern Resident pod in the Pacific Northwest, called on the world to witness her grieving process as she carried her dead baby for 1,000 miles over the course of seventeen days in what became known worldwide as the "Tour of Grief."

In what follows, I argue that Tahlequah's intimate grief functioned as a form of public protest, wherein she situated the body of her calf as evidence of human-caused climate consequences. The trifecta of lack of salmon due to damming, toxin accumulation (e.g., polychlorinated biphenyls (PCBs) in mother's milk), and vessel noise disturbing hunting for orcas presents undeniable proof of climate destruction. Anthropogenic activities such as these have altered the earth, and thus we find ourselves in a cycle of complicity, realizing our implications and striving for a new coherence paradigm (Plec 2013) as we adapt and try to change the environmental consequences humans have brought on the planet and all its beings. This process of realization is painful, frustrating, and can lead to much grieving. Because humans can empathize with these three states, Tahlequah's mourning quickly gained attention around the world, creating a space that pulled humans into the emotional performance of her death rites. Moreover, working through complicity and implication in witnessing Tahlequah's grief offers the opportunity for humans to move into the coherence paradigm. Shifting to this paradigm is key for humans to understand, appreciate, and see themselves as a part of an interconnected biotic community. Engaging the concept of "internatural activism" (Burford and Schutten 2017), our job now is to understand the actions of more-than-humans, like Tahlequah, as more profound, rhetorically salient, performative, and politically motivated.

This chapter will creatively play with voice, using a "strategic anthropomorphism" (Schutten and Shaffer 2019) and internatural performatives that focus on the intimate entanglements of humans and more-than-humans in the Anthropocene. In what follows, I take up these concepts to actively work toward challenging the status quo and the binaries between human-nature and human-more-than-human. Therefore, the voice in this piece also reframes the traditional academic voice. Reflectively engaging in the process of re-imagining our interdependent voices through performatives is part of the internatural movement to shift humans toward a more coherent paradigm. Intimacy with our language and emotions is an integral part of this shift.

SETTING THE STAGE

In order to arrive at a place of connection with more-than-humans' grieving, it is important to set the stage through an exploration of relevant terms and ideological worldviews. First, I want to remind us of the reason to use the term "more-than-human" (Abram 1996). More-than-human as a "term is not meant to reverse hierarchy and imply that more-than-humans are better than humans. Rather, it simultaneously recognizes that humans are animals and acknowledges that it is not just humans who are capable of communication, intersubjective relationships, and agency" (Endres 2019, 4). Within the field of environmental criticism, the study of more-than-human rhetoric is seen as one of three foundational aspects (Endres 2019). Recognizing that discourse generated from the more-than-human world "counts" means exploring alternative symbol systems, or in the case of Tahlequah, grief rituals, as significant rhetorical practices that are indeed communication—something more than pure instinct.

Next, it is key to acknowledge that more-than-humans are not simply machines operating on instinct alone. More-than-humans are more than capable of having interconnected intimate relationships, and thus grief when those relationships end. Many people consider the awareness of mortality to be unique to humans, and so the idea that other animals grieve their dead is hard to perceive (Yeoman 2018). In fact, the denial that more-than-humans have such awareness, and the separation of humans from more-than-humans, has been used to justify many unethical and inhumane practices, such as experimental research and factory farming (Adams [1990] 2003). Yet a growing number of scientists are now challenging the human species' "monopoly on grief" (Yoeman 2018, 34). In discussing long-lived social mammals (e.g., whales, primates), biologist Robin Baird states, "There's no doubt in my mind that these animals have strong bonds with other individuals. In cases like that—the behavior of animals toward the premature death of their own offspring—it would be hard for me to imagine that it could be anything other than exhibiting grief" (quoted in Yoeman 2018, 34).

Tahlequah was not the first cetacean to be seen carrying the remains of her young (Yoeman 2018), but she did so for an exceptionally long amount of time. "Killer whales are known to carry their deceased calves for a few days in their grief, just as elephants and gorillas mourn their dead" (Knoth 2019, 61). It is also important to note that "the expression of grief does not depend on the relative brain size or cognitive power alone. The capacity to form intimate relationships is emerging as a significant, separate factor in determining which species mourn their losses" (King 2019, 2). These are just a few examples of scientific studies that legitimize the grieving practices of more-than-humans in a world that has held up the Cartesian reality of human exceptionalism as a worldview to further solidify the nature-culture binary. The experience of grief presumes intimacy exists with more-than-human beings.

Lastly, I turn briefly to the academic view on anthropomorphism in disciplines that study human and more-than-human relationships. "The newest area of marine research is anthrozoology—the study of the relationships between human and non-human animals" (Knoth 2019, 3). Explicitly, anthrozoology "encompasses anthropormorphism of animals as a research theme" (3). Knoth argues that "anthropormomphism can be used as a powerful tool in promoting conservation considerate behavior by highlighting research that promotes animals as being similar to humans" (38). Akin to anthrozoology, environmental animal communication scholars have been wandering into the wilder sides of "internatural communication" lenses (Plec 2013) by offering opportunities to explore communication alongside more-than-human animals. Internatural communication "includes the exchange of intentional energy between humans and other animals as well as communication among animals and other forms of life. It is at its core, as is the study of communication generally, about the construction of meaning and the constitution of our world through interaction" (6). It is noteworthy that internatural communication adds to the study of intentional energetic exchanges between humans and other animals, specifically exploring how these relationships function to co-construct meaning in our worlds. In short, internatural communication moves beyond species-specific relationships and includes interspecies intimate relationships. The process of moving through complicity, realizing our implications, and shifting into a coherence paradigm are some of the stages humans grapple with in order to view internatural communication as a legitimate form of discourse between beings.

Anthropomorphism is one important aspect of shifting to a coherence paradigm where humans can recognize internatural activism among more-than-human species. Understandably, there has been some trepidation toward accepting anthropomorphism in environmental criticism. In discussing zoo'd animals as captive classes, Schutten and Shaffer (2019, 4) put forth the idea of a "strategic anthropomorphism" in order to end the "paralysis that diminishes, erases, and disempowers voices from the natural world." For example, anthropomorphism can help humans have empathy toward more-than-human grief. This in turn helps humans relate to other entities and teaches them about alternative experiences of grief. Human intuitive knowing often precipitates this intimate experience, prompting us to move beyond our human-centeredness and engage with more-than-human performances to "go deeper." In discussing captive more-than-humans and human intuition, Schutten and Shaffer comment:

> One reason captive classes are often ignored is because meaning-making does not include sense-making capabilities like intuition, embodied response, and emotion, which are all examples of non-reasoned discourse. Because reason is valued over intuition, our intuitive knowing is questioned. Intuition and embodied knowing is what allows us to comprehend resistive communication from zoo'd animals. (4)

Similar to captive classes (zoo'd animals), sharing the grief of free-living more-than-humans ultimately helps us to see the disorder in our human order, thus seeing interconnectedness vs. separateness.

Strategic anthropomorphism helps bring communication forward as a primary element to heighten human understanding, which in turn helps amplify our awareness of connection beyond the human realm. As such, more-than-human beings are leaving a significant trail, marking out a prominent role in communication studies as they emerge to humans as communicative beings in a process of, as Abram (1996) notes, becoming with. In a practice of becoming with the more-than-human world, performance is used to engage and stimulate intimate environmental discussion exploring metaphorical "humananimal" wisdoms (Milstein 2013). Having a feeling of and intimacy with the more-than-human is an important method of creating a solid stewardship ethic in a re-imagined democratic world that values humans as interconnected with the free-living environment.

A strategic anthropomorphism privileges intuition over reasoned discourse allows for "alternative symbolics" (Schutten and Rogers 2011) as forms of civic action and "acknowledges human transcorporeal experience with more-than-humans" (Schutten and Schaffer 2019). Taken together, strategic anthropomorphism and alternative symbolics help humans identify aspects of internatural activism. Alternative symbolics are different ways of knowing that promote and acknowledge new symbolic endeavors that are inclusive of the relationship between humans and more-than-humans (Schutten and Rogers 2011). In writing about the resistive qualities of zoo'd animals, Schutten and Shaffer (2019, 9) noted that "what makes symbols persuasive is the ability to affect some sort of embodied experience between those in relation." Therefore, the performance of Tahlequah's grief ritual presents as an intimate, embodied, alternative symbolic, creating a bridge for human and more-than-human communication. This is consistent with other examples of internatural activism. In an earlier work, a colleague and I explored the murders of the captive orca named Tilikum as a form of resistive discourse, finding that "Tilikum's actions disrupt complicity and implication . . . creating a breach that bridges the divide of human/orca communication by illustrating alternative symbolics" (Burford and Schutten 2017, 2). Furthermore, this piece also illustrated the importance of placing "equal value on more-than-human 'voices' in anti-captivity rhetoric even when the 'symbols' are not linguistic" (2). As such, part of the project of identifying alternative symbolics aligns with the recognition that a variety of discursive symbols are important for environmental communication. One way to continue in this vein of thinking and deepen our reflection as related to Tahlequah is to consider the rhetorical implication of "mother," which I will discuss later in this chapter.

In this re-imagined world, where more-than-humans have a voice and alternative symbolics are valued, creaturely rhetoric matters in the democratic process. It is vital to stretch our understanding to recognize new forms of political environmental discourse in which more-than-human animals can comfortably be at the forefront. The post COVID-19 world makes this even more evident as disease transmission due to climate disruption becomes more prominent. In an article about how coronaviruses jump to humans, Bodin (2020, para. 4) cites Margaret Wild, an expert in wildlife diseases and professor at Washington State University: "These diseases don't transmit to humans often, and when they do, it's typically when we push natural systems by destroying animal habitat or crowding different species together with people in a marketplace." Bodin goes on to explain that "*habitat erosion, in fact, may be one of the biggest factors in how viruses have begun breaking down the walls* between us and the animals that originally carried them" (para. 4; emphasis mine). As such, we must count the discourses of Tahlequah as sincere and legitimate communication, illustrating the consequences of habitat disruption and destruction for Southern Resident killer whale pods. We are in conviviality with these Others. Our bodies are tied to theirs.

We have discussed the importance of strategic anthropomorphism and alternative symbolics as they relate to internatural activism and the intimacy of grief. I turn now to the grounding of my reflection for this chapter. I situate my perspectives by using the theoretical lenses of performance studies and autoethnography.

INTIMACY OF PERFORMANCE AND THE PERFORMANCES OF INTIMACY

This section lays out some of the theoretical grounding for this chapter related to the self-reflexive (read intimate) aspects of performance studies and autoethnography. These theories offered me a lens for sense-making beyond my humanness and are important to advancing international movements for environmental change. I have been writing about the plight of orcas in captivity, as well as their diminished wild habitats, for some time now. I first began writing about Tilikum, a captive Sea World orca, in 2014. Captured at the age of two, he died on January 6, 2017, after thirty-three years of captivity. I wept. I wondered how I could have such depth of emotion for a being I never met. This grief that I experienced felt not only reflected but also magnified upon observation of the world's reaction to the death of Tahlequah's baby. In "Grieving at a Distance," Teya Pribac (2016, 194) defines the concept of grieving at a distance as "the grief experience by humans for animals whom they don't personally know and which includes but is not limited to vicarious grief." In my own experience of grieving at a distance, I had engaged in perspective-taking with Tilikum for so long that I did feel a relief at his dying. My tears were tears of liberation for his release from suffering, through death, as a "captive class" (Schutten and Shaffer 2019). About a year after the death of Tilikum, another orca captured my heart and mind, and I found myself writing a performance piece about J35, otherwise known as Tahlequah.

Tahlequah's Tour of Grief offers us a text illustrating the ways the body is both the site of lived experience and also offers citational "evidence" of truth(s) experienced by that body. Watching, imagining, or being exposed to the death rites of Tahlequah as a mourning mother brings forth intimate experiences of death. In this way, seeing Tahlequah's deceased baby is evidence of the truth of global climate change and the human-caused impacts responsible for this *body of evidence*. As I began writing the performance, I saw Tahlequah's body as a site of intimate grief and pain. Her pain would not be denied as the intimate act of carrying her dead calf was elevated to a place where humans paid attention. As a result, human discourses began raising questions about their own complicity and how they were/are implicated in the lived life cycles of these beings. The crafting of spoken word for this performance piece was modeled after a speech style called program oral interpretation, which includes some combination of prose, poetry, and drama.

In addition to program oral interpretation, this work also takes some of its character from theories of autoethnography. In *Body, Paper, Stage: Writing and Performing Autoethnography*, Tami Spry (2011, 121) writes:

> Opening up to the ways in which we are all connected to one another causes us to become aware of our own social conditioning and a system of power relations that we are part of due to race, gender, size, etc., and which causes us to experience the world differently. As well as ourselves, this kind of critical perspective may make others uncomfortable.

I offer the addition of more-than-humans to this "opening up" as a way to nudge us into the uncomfortable, unknown place that is essential for the growth of ethical, equal environmental stewardship. Perspective-taking with more-than-humans, especially in their most intimate moments, may present a challenge, but this is necessary in order to turn toward a new paradigm that values all entities as having intrinsic worth. Moreover, in our willingness to be uncomfortable, we may come to see more-than-humans—in this case grieving orcas—as having something valuable to say about the current state of climate destruction.

Through opening up, we can bear witness to what Phaedra Pezzullo (2007, 146–47) writes: human beings are "trained to overlook" and in turn "risk identification with the fate of other people, places, and events." Extending the concept of witness to include the fate of more-than-humans opens us to engage in alternative symbolics or different ways of knowing as having value and meaning. Importantly, Pribac reminds us that "to *see* is to bear witness. Once you see, you cannot *unsee*. Seeing brings about personal change" (2016, 193; emphasis in original). Tahlequah's Tour of Grief was indeed an event that caused many humans, in their witness, to identify with her calf's death. This set in motion attention to the climate change implications for such a premature fatality, which ultimately led to policy changes.

Not only did her performance inspire policy changes, but the language used to speak about the action and the emotions evoked became an integral part of the attempts to shift audiences toward a coherence frame. Therefore, the inclusion of my own voice represents human reflexivity and intimacy as I check my own complicity in what has harmed Tahlequah's pod. I do this in an attempt to challenge my vulnerabilities to the same degree Tahlequah did during the summer of 2018. However, I recognize that the death of this calf is not equivalent to my engagement with this story. My expressed vulnerabilities here do not compare. This artistic choice exemplifies the process described by Spry (2011, 124), who writes: "Your autoethnographic scholarship is an opening into the complex negotiations of meaning making with others for the purpose of adding alternatives to the single story; all personal experience is in concert with the political." In order to read the rhetoric of Tahlequah as internatural activism, her action needs to be viewed as part of the meaning making and as adding an alternative interpretation to the story she was telling via her Tour of Grief. As Spry reminds us in the quote above, "all personal experience is in concert with the political" (124), including the entire narrative from all perspectives—both human and more-than-human. I will therefore take liberty with voice and interpretation and recognize that these identification processes can also contribute to systems of power-over while simultaneously knowing the power of a strategic anthropomorphism for conservation and ecological citizenship. I do this strategically in order to center the agency and actions of free-living orcas like Tahlequah. As mentioned earlier, this part of the project enlists a strategic anthropomorphism in order to center the voice of more-than-humans in the internatural movement and as a participant in the democratic process. In short, what you will read below will sometimes sound theatrical or conversational, which is the intended effect.

PAINTING A PORTRAIT OF TAHLEQUAH'S POD

In studying orcas, and specifically the Southern Resident population who inhabit the Salish Sea off the coast of Washington State and British Columbia, it is impossible not to see their interdependence with humans. It is also clear to anyone who spends time in or studies this landscape that human-caused climate change is a significant factor in these interconnections. The birthing process is long for orcas, with a gestation period of up to 18 months (Knoth 2019). They are also considered slow reproducers (Knoth 2019), complicating the environmental stressors on their habitat. At the time of Tahlequah's Tour of Grief, Robbins (2018, para. 1–2) wrote:

For the last three years, not one calf has been born to the dwindling pods of black-and-white killer whales spouting geysers of mist off the coast of the Pacific Northwest. Normally four or five calves would be born each year among the urban population of whales—pods named J, K and L. But most recently, the number of orcas has dwindled to just 75, a 30-year-low in what seems to be an inexorable, perplexing decline.

Endangered and struggling, one can imagine the excitement and joy the pod must have felt at the birth of this new baby. Orcas have strong familial bonds, with all members of the family helping to care for the young. Aunts and young males in the pod will watch the calf while the mother hunts, and they bring her food if she is struggling. They will also do this to help any whale that has fallen behind or is sick (Knoth 2019). It is clear to the scientific community that orcas have complex social behaviors. In fact, "findings show the portion of killer whale brains that deal with language are incredibly similar to humans, while the part that deals with emotions is 3x larger in killer whales and far more complex than in humans" (53). Given these many similarities, it is difficult not to anthropomorphize orcas, yet it is important to also recognize that orcas have their own sovereign lives (Knoth 2019).

In addition to the linguistic and emotional similarities to humans, orca habitats are also interdependent with human choices. Orcas were listed as endangered in 2005 and are essentially starving because their food source is the endangered Chinook salmon, a fish more than forty inches long and the largest species of Pacific salmon (Robbins 2018). Unlike other orcas that are considered "transient" and have other, more varied diets, these orcas only eat this one type of salmon. This particular orca hunting ground is suffering from intense noise pollution as a consequence of the multimillion-dollar whale-watching industry, commercial vessel traffic, and recreational boating (Robbins 2018). Unfortunately, their most preferred foraging spot, as Hanson explains, "is essentially a big rock ditch where sound bounces off" (quoted in Robbins 2018, para. 15). This is thought to interfere with echolocation, making "it harder for the whales to find their prey and to communicate prey location among themselves," and can create hearing loss (Robbins 2018 para. 16). The news articles written about Tahlequah's performance illustrate that people were beginning to realize their own complicity via the implication of tourism (e.g., whale watching) at the continued expense of these orcas. This fits with Plec's (2013) first two stages. Similarly, "in the 1970s and 1980s, theme parks such as Sea World captured nearly four dozen orcas from the region, possibly shrinking the pods' gene pool" (Robbins 2018, para. 7). This, combined with toxins, has gravely challenged their ability to populate their species, as only two males have fathered half of the calves in the past three decades (Robbins

2018 para. 7). All of these human impacts were amplified by Tahlequah's internatural activism, illustrating a realization of complicity and implication.

These whales are often considered "urban" because they live off the coast of Tacoma, Seattle, and other cities creating municipal and industrial waste (Robbins 2018 para. 20). As such, they carry some of the highest levels of pollution of any marine mammal. Chemicals that are now banned, such as DDT, PCBs, and PPDE, which are used frequently in flame retardants throughout the world, accumulate in the salmon they eat. They stay in their fat and the females transfer large amounts of contaminant to their offspring (Robbins 2018 para. 22). The reality of interconnected toxic exchange causing disease and weakened immune systems for orcas further implicates humans in their endangered status.

I now invite the reader to take a deep dive into the imagined world of Tahlequah and her pod family. Briefly lean into the intimate experience Tahlequah shares of grieving her baby. Allow yourself to open up to the prospective emotions and feelings of the more-than-human world as they struggle to survive the climate changes made manifest by the Anthropocene. The following creative writing is designed to highlight the entanglements of humans and more-than-humans by blending prose, climate facts, and anthropomorphized caricatures. A consequence of this play with story and narrative is that your view may become messy or distorted and in turn help you to re-imagine your connections with more-than-humans. In this way, we have the opportunity to realize how we are complicit and implicated. Only then can the human species begin the environmental projects needed to shift into an interconnected, coherent paradigm.

WITNESS: IMAGINING INTO THE GRIEF

Imagine witnessing a large, magnificent, black-and-white orca mother keeping her dead baby afloat.

> She had just given birth, following a nearly year-and-a-half long gestation period. It was her second offspring, a daughter, and the first live birth in the declining Southern Resident community in three years. But 30 minutes after birth, the calf died. J35 [Tahlequah] would not let her baby go. With great effort, she swam with the tiny body on her head and made deep dives to retrieve it when it slipped off. Other members of her pod registered her distress: at one point, a group of females gathered in a tight circle around J35, an act of apparent emotional attunement that lasted at least two hours. Seventeen days and 1,000 miles passed before J35 finally released her daughter's corpse for good. (King 2019, para.1)

Virtually attending the viewing of this deceased calf, carried by her grieving mother, brings our attention to the plight of the endangered Southern
Resident killer whales. It is emotional. I feel angry, sad, and have environmental fatigue for all that is going on in the natural world and our place in
this web. Is this what it takes to get our attention: a twenty-one-year-old
orca mother whale parading her dead orca baby's body around for over two
weeks? This is evidence of the truth that humans are the polluters; we are the
climate destroyers.

TESTIMONY: TAHLEQUAH'S PLIGHT,
AN ORCA TESTIMONIAL

Life has been hard. I hear stories from my kin about how it used to be before
these impossibly loud boat creatures with two-legged beings standing on
them were constantly watching us. I have toxins such as PCBs in my blubber
and in my milk, which are released into my bloodstream when I am stressed
or hungry—which is a lot, if not all of the time now—making me continually
susceptible to disease and poisoning my children (Sandstrom 2018). I don't
always feel the best either. We have been living with and in this pollution and
trying to adapt for years now. It is not working.

I am an acoustic being. I rely on sound to find and catch my prey, and
to communicate with my family. You humans did a study that found the
Southern Residents lose five-and-a-half hours of foraging time every day
due to noise and disturbance from commercial vessels, specifically whale-
watching boats (Sandstrom 2018). It does not matter how many salmon are
here in these waters if I cannot hear to find them.

Back in the day, between 1976 and 1998, our pod grew to 100 in number;
it was as if we were protected. I hear about those days, as I was born in 1997.
Guess I missed those glory days because now the boats just keep coming
(Ragen 2018). My aunt has lost her hearing due to these boats, so she can no
longer fish for herself. We help her, of course, but she is not old enough for
this to be happening to her. We are overwhelmed by these floating noise creatures. If only they would leave us be so we could hunt and hear properly, perhaps then we could have some break from this suffering and thrive once again.

TESTIMONY: COMPLICITY AND
IMPLICATION—A HUMAN'S CONFESSION

I have a confession to make. I myself took a whale-watching boat out twice to
see Tahlequah's family. I didn't know her then and the story of her grief that

would later receive international attention and coverage hadn't yet happened. I still did not understand how I was, how humans are, implicated in her story. This was the conversation as it unfolded in my mind: "I love the beauty of the sea. I love these beings." I allowed myself to be selfish. The crew assured us that there were distance guidelines in place to keep us away from the orcas. This helped me feel like it was OK. This particular whale-watching group is known for their conservation and sensitivity to the beings from whom they make their livelihood. "After all," I thought to myself, "they only stay on the water for two hours, no matter what. I hear that the other boats will follow the whales for longer times." This helped me rationalize the experience, to be complicit. "This industry is conscious and cares for more-than-humans, right?"

I ask no further questions. I do not inquire. "There they are! J and K Pod!" My heart is pounding. "I am able to share the same space with these ancestors of the ocean. Breathe the same air and hear them breathing." I take a moment and look around. I see many boats circling to get a good look at the orcas—to watch nature's show (Milstein 2015). "This feels wrong," I think, "I would not appreciate this if I were them. This feels like objectification." But I remain complicit, I brush this concern off. I ignore it for my own pleasure and perceived connection to the Other.

Even as whales are dying in front of us from toxins, starvation, and noise pollution, the number of whale-watching boats continues to grow; there is no limit to the number of boats and trips per day or length of time they can stay with the whales. In peak season, May through October, dozens of boats follow these orcas like paparazzi all day, every day, throughout the Salish Sea. The whale-watching boats and the recreational boats they attract form a kind of floating coral reef from which the whales cannot evade, escape, or hide (Sandstrom 2018). Remind me again how this is better than visiting Sea World? How many boats were on the scene when this calf was born? Science, often ignored in our times, tells us that the most effective thing society could change to help these whales recover in the short term is to turn down the volume of boats in the Salish Sea.

TESTIMONY: THE GRIEVING PUBLIC

I've resisted this eulogy. I don't want to think it through. I want the baby to fall to the bottom of the ocean and for life to go on. I don't want to sit with the horror of extinction. But, it is day 17 and there is only grief. Bottomless, endless grief. And Tahlequah won't quit until we look, until we REALLY look at what we've done to her baby.

We've dammed the rivers, we've poisoned the ocean, we've turned their home into a zoo. We've run our barges loaded with the imported goods we bought off #Amazon right through their hunting grounds, creating so much noise pollution they can't hunt and they can't communicate with each other. Now Canada will run the #KinderMorgan #TransMountain pipeline into their neck of the Salish Sea. There will be more barges and more oil spills until no life is left. The mansions that sit on the coast of the San Juan Islands will have first-rate views of a dead ocean. There will be no whales, no sharks, no salmon, no starfish, no kelp, no oysters, no life. The #SouthernResidentKillerWhales are the keepers of this sacred place. They are the people who live underwater. They are smarter than us. By a lot. With brains four times our size. The media wants to make this a story of scientific discovery: Tahlequah's mourning is proof that animals have complex emotions! Are you fucking kidding me? Tahlequah's mourning is proof that humans have self-serving, simple-minded, self-destructive brains incapable of the complex emotion required to be truly intelligent beings. Today it is Tahlequah's baby. Tomorrow it will be your baby. And you don't want to see it, but it's all right there. We must look. We must. We are barreling towards a dead ocean and a burned planet. I know you feel helpless to change it. We all do, but we must. We must act now. We are running out of time. (Psychic Sister 2018)

TESTIMONY: DIRECTOR OF THE WHALE TRAIL

My name is Donna Sandstrom and I am the director of The Whale Trail, a nonprofit headquartered in Seattle, and a member of Governor Jay Inslee's task force on Southern Resident killer whales.

Two weeks ago I was at Lime Kiln Point State Park when we heard that J Pod was heading our way. People lined the cliffs and crowded the rocky shore. We could see the orcas on the horizon. Our visual senses engaged. First their blows, then their dorsal fins came into view. It was like waiting for Christmas! As the whales approached, we could hear them breathe. Phwoosh! The sound of their exhalations carried across Harro Strait. Now we have the sense of hearing and there is something so profound in hearing them breathe. It feels other-worldly and yet there is some connection. Some people clapped, and some people cried. The sea glowed orange, reflecting a fiery sky. "How lucky are we!" a man said to his kids. The whales continued north, their blows backlit in the setting sun. Three huge whale-watching boats stayed with them even as they disappeared into the dark. (Sandstrom 2018, para. 11)

Humans are striving to connect. I have stood at Lime Kiln Point and seen the pod swimming out to sea. I know the feeling of hearing breath from a whale and the profound awe it inspires. We are *inter*dependent. Sadly, it seems that humans are loving these whales to death.

WITNESS: NATIVE NATION ATTEMPTS
LIFE-SAVING INTERVENTIONS

Sadly, there are others, other babies on the edge of death. "For the Lummi Nation, the orca, also known as the blackfish, are family members—relatives under the sea" (Mapes 2018a, para. 1). Julius, the Lummi chairman, is attempting to feed fish to a starving 4-year-old-orca (Mapes 2018a). This crisis is personal for them. The fish could help hydrate and feed the young whale, who is so emaciated that her cranium is visible (Mapes 2018a). She looks like a ghost of herself. These are apex predators, indicator species relaying important information about the health of these waters, and it is not good. As hereditary Chief Bill Jams bemoans, "It is off balance. We need to remember everything is alive. The water. The fishes. Everything, and we are here to respect it, and not just the almighty dollar" (para. 18). Julius tells the tale of his interconnection to this orca: "We are both fishing creatures; we both live for the salmon. And in our community, we come together when someone is hurting. We come together when someone needs help. It is the same with the Salish Sea, and with the orcas. She is part of the web that connects us all" (para. 20).

WITNESS: IMPLICATION AND COHERENCE
IN WASHINGTON STATE

As the tribe works with the National Oceanic and Atmospheric Administration to decide the best course of action, the governor of Washington has decided on several measures to help orcas in peril. One is to put a temporary three-year ban on watching southern orca residents (Mapes 2018b). Another is to increase the viewing distance from 200 to 400 yards (Mapes 2018b). A third is a new seven knot (or less) go-slow zone for all vessels within a half-nautical mile of the orcas (Mapes 2018b). People will likely complain. Humans want to get closer, to touch what is other-worldly to us.

Introducing the governor of Washington, Jay Inslee: "I thought a lot about this and concluded the general approach was a safe and prudent one that errs on the side of survival. . . . This is a relatively small inconvenience to give them a break. . . . Someone who is starving should not be scrambling for that last morsel that can keep them alive" (Mapes 2018b, para. 29, 33). *Someone who is starving should not be scrambling for that last morsel to keep them alive.* He said "someone."

OUR INTIMATE CONNECTIONS AS GATEWAY TO INTERNATURAL ACTIVISM

I ended the performative writing above with a comment on the governor speaking of orcas as "someone." This is significant because it indicates that the orcas have agency. Not that they are people, but that they are "some-ones." And if they are "someones," they are indeed beings that experience the breadth of life from joy and play, as well as emotions such as grief with expressive performatives, like Tahlequah's Tour of Grief, that demand action. Looking at "humanimal" relationships like those of humans and free-living orcas raises awareness about the ways communication can transform intimacies between humans and more-than-humans (Milstein 2013). Below, I point to two areas that help illustrate Tahlequah's internatural activism. Both are constructions that create emotive responses aiding our understanding of alternative symbolics and helping us recognize them as internatural activism. The first illustration deals with perspective-taking with the Mother Archetype and the second relates to Tahlequah's transference of grief used for political ends.

Turning to the first example, it is clear that the symbolic meaning of Mother is important to Tahlequah's rhetorical power. After discussing strategic anthropomorphism in this chapter, it is not a far reach to argue that the intimate bond between mother and child, and thus the Mother Archetype, was an important aspect of this image event. Whether Tahlequah was performing grief for her pod or the human onlookers does not matter. It was a form of spectatorship that made it hard for us to distance ourselves from what was happening. Humans understand the concept of mother and what that means or at the very least what we want it to mean. Quite often the death of a child is private. We give the grieving mother time away and we are careful with someone in this understandably vulnerable state. However, Tahlequah made this intimate and private moment extremely visible. In turn, this visibility made orca whale suffering more obvious by our leaning-in to watch, and in a sense, needing to witness her suffering. In this way, it was environmental voyeurism facilitating the perspective-taking of imagining, for just a moment, what it would be like if we held our dead baby in our arms, as well as what would be our intense yearning and helplessness to change the outcome. Here, strategic anthropomorphism is much more than simply spectacle because it goes deeper than just viewing an event. It internalizes and shifts the performance from entertainment to intimacy. For example, in a study of grieving women who miscarried, one woman commented, "The doctor said the babies were too young to survive when they were born. They lived for a short time and died. I was heartbroken and felt very helpless because I wasn't able to help them. I didn't want to let go of them but I knew I had to let go" (Kalu 2019, 5). Tahlequah, acting in the same way as this human mother, was making transparent for spectators the similarities between more-than-human and human animal families. She demanded our attention as a sentient being via her public protest. Our subsequent empathetic identification with orca mothers and "vicarious bereavement" highlights "interspecies equality" (Pribac 2016). Additionally, Jessica Knoth's (2019) study of Tahlequah, anthrozoology, anthropomorphism, and marine conservation draws out several themes of anthropomorphism from news articles. One article discussed readers responding with stories of their own grief and loss while empathizing greatly with Tahlequah as a mother whale. Another said, "She literally is pushing her baby to connect with it and, hope against hope—hoping that it will take a breath, which it will never do". (69).

Tahlequah's death rites expose important narratives for humans. As discussed above, the intimate act of birth and of becoming a parent rise to the surface for humans incensed by Tahlequah's story. However, her actions also point to the challenge of facing death as "the natural conclusion of love" (Williams 2001, 207). In discussing human abuse of the land and each other, Terry Tempest Williams writes, "Could it be that what we fear most is our capacity to feel, and so we annihilate symbolically and physically that which is beautiful and tender, anything that dares us to consider our creative selves?" (108). Intimacy requires a close familiarity and love with another. I contend that Tahlequah's dead baby acted as a foil for humans, illustrating the annihilation of beauty in the world and our bracketing off of any feelings related to our sustained environmental destruction. In short, the loss of our intimate connection to the earth is almost too much to bear, and so it is sadly ignored. Yet, Tahlequah's performance with her daughter's *body of evidence* makes it clear that we have been complicit in the death of this baby. Quite literally, the calf's body and Tahlaquah's grieving performative body demonstrate as well as evoke intimacy with humans. Moreover, how can humans create a connection to the natural world if they do not see themselves as inextricably linked to free living beings? The tender relationship between mother and child exposes the callous nature of humans toward more-than-human entities in this community. In fact, the denial of this interconnectedness spotlights the human-caused imbalances in the oceanic world.

In this way, Tahlequah's death rituals express our climate change grief, which has been disenfranchised through minimization and denial. Put another way, there is so much climate destruction and anthropogenic violence that it is hard to pinpoint which tragedy to put our energies into, and Tahlequah's plight gave us one place to focus. Grieving the destruction of the natural world is not something seen by all as "legitimate," although it makes sense that as human-animals, we would be in tune with and feel the consequences of these changes in various ways (changes in landscape and climate—e.g., dryer, hotter, wetter, etc.—new health conditions, outbreaks, etc.). Taken together, Tahlequah's story is an example of our climate change grief; her performance points to the larger systemic issues that led to her baby's death. She becomes the connector between this grief and the reasons for grieving, illustrating our interconnections and making it difficult to compartmentalize or avoid human implication. In this cultural moment, Tahlequah's dead baby provides evidence of the truth that humans are the polluters and climate destroyers.

This is an important recognition for creating environmental citizen action because "we never in fact mourn the unknown; we always mourn the known" (Pribac 2016, 195). Moreover, this has been an issue for the climate change movement because unless there is a trauma or disaster, humans tend to not believe something is real without proof via experience. Tahlequah, her deceased baby, and the entire Southern Resident pod gave us this opportunity. In sum, her actions as a mother, intimately raw in the grieving of her dead calf, created a call-to-action to help her family because "family" is an important concept for humans as well. This call-to-action is an act of internatural activism. She literally put her body and the body of her calf on the metaphorical protest line, demanding action.

Also key to internatural activism is seeing the events brought to the surface through the experience of Tahlequah's grief rituals as legitimate action. I wrote in the beginning of this chapter that grief demands the difficult practice of asking what must be mourned and what must be released completely. Yes, Tahlequah needed to release her baby and mourn her death, and yet, her ritual compels us to suspend our disbelief for a moment and ask: Is it possible that she knew she would draw attention and that this attention could point to her dead baby as a consequence of the changes to her environment? Is it too far of a stretch to imagine that her actions were alternative symbolics where she was essentially screaming to the onlookers, "This has happened because you have come in droves!" Could it also point out that what needs to be released is the unsustainable climate consequences of a rogue human species? To this end, Ken Balcomb from the Center for Whale Research comments:

It's a little bit of anthropomorphism, but I think she was letting everyone else know she was grieving. . . . They're very intelligent. They know people are out there: I've seen them look at boats hauling fish out in nets. I think they know that humans are somehow related to the scarcity of food. And I think they know that the scarcity of food is causing them physical distress, and also causing them to lose babies. (quoted in Yong 2018, para. 15)

If orcas, dolphins, and whales are as smart as we are (on a human intelligence scale), how could they not understand that boats are creating noise that impacts their hunting? Why should we assume that the parading of this body by Tahlequah was not an image event that created a "mind bomb" designed to both allow her to grieve and to "shake us up" about climate change consequences (DeLuca 1999)? In this way, the image event was for us and not just her pod. We could witness and engage with her agency. She may not have thought, "Oh that's the *Seattle Times* over there," but she knows, as Balcomb points out, that since these "entities" (read boats and humans), have come to her home, the babies are few and far between and they often die.

In a very real, material way, Tahlequah's international activism resulted in legitimate political changes in policy for Washington State that directly affected her livelihood and that of her family pod. Her activism shifted many toward a coherence paradigm as evidenced by their intimate use of language and emotion describing their understanding of her death ritual. Following Burford and Schutten (2017, 10), "coherence necessitates that audiences take orca communication seriously and acknowledge them as key players in shaping public policy and participating in environmental social movements." Examples like Tahlequah's provide opportunities to identify forms of rhetorically salient international activism.

What spectators across the world witnessed during those seventeen days that Tahlequah swam with her dead baby was not simply a being with complex emotions. Laying the dead body of her daughter bare as spectacle to illustrate the consequences of androgenic actions was significant communication. This helped humans internalize her performance, shifting it from entertainment to intimacy. In this way, she demanded liberation and emancipation from us, the climate destroyers that put her in this situation with her offspring. Witnessing the intimacy of her grief was the entry into interconnection, offering us an opportunity to dialogically engage in the performance, which in turn enabled us to put ourselves in her place. We can see ourselves expressing emotions like hers, and thus her Tour of Grief offered the watcher an opportunity to experience and reflect on their own complicity and implication in the Southern Resident pods' plight. We know that these two self-reflexive states of being were embodied by the public because actualized changes to policy that affect orcas and their habitat occurred. These changes moved us toward coherence. The body of this baby was the site of the evidence that we deny, which ultimately affects our body and being. We cannot let the corpses of destruction be marginalized, devalued, erased, or ignored anymore; our very existence depends on it.

AUTHOR NOTE

On September 6, 2020, *The New York Times* reported that Tahlequah became a mother once again.

AUTHOR ACKNOWLEDGMENTS

I would like to thank Jonny Gray for helping me from my early thoughts about this chapter and Ashleigh Day for reading a more evolved draft. I would also like to thank Suzanne Pullen for dreaming the conference panel that first inspired my thinking about Tahlequah.

BIBLIOGRAPHY

Abram, David. 1996. *The Spell of the Sensuous: Perception and Language in a More-Than-Human World*. New York: Vintage Books.

Adams, Carol. J. (1990) 2003. *The Sexual Politics of Meat: A Feminist-Vegetarian Critical Theory*. New York: Continuum.

Bodin, Madeline. 2020. "Coronaviruses Often Start in Animals—Here's How Those Diseases Can Jump to Humans." *Discover*, April 2, 2020. https://www.discovermagazine.com/health/coronaviruses-often-start-in-animals-heres-how-those-diseases-can-jump-to.

Burford, Catilyn, and Julie "Madrone" K. Schutten. 2017. "Internatural Activists and the 'Blackfish Effect': Contemplating Captive Orca's Protest Rhetoric through a Coherence Frame." *Frontiers in Communication* 16 (1): 1–11. https://doi.org/10.3389/fcomm.2016.00016.

DeLuca, Kevin M. 1999. *Image Politics: The New Rhetoric of Environmental Activism*. New York: Guilford.

Endres, Danielle. 2019. "Environmental Criticism." *Western Journal of Communication*, 00 (00): 1–18. https://doi.org/10.1080/10570314.2019.1689288.

Kalu, Felicity A. 2019. "Women's Experiences of Utilizing Religions and Spiritual Beliefs as Coping Resources After Miscarriage." *Religions* 10 (3) 1–9. http://doi.org/10.3390/rel10030185.

King, Barbara J. 2019. "The Orca's Sorrow." *Scientific American*, March 2019. https ://www.scientificamerican.com/article/the-orcas-sorrow/.

Knoth, Jessica M. 2019. "Anthrozoology, Anthropomorphism, and Marine Conservation: A Case Study of Sothern Resident Killer Whale, Tahlequah, and Her Tour of Grief." Master's thesis, University of Washington. ProQuest (13899852)

Mapes, Lynda V. 2018a. "Feeding a Wild Orca: Inside the Practice Run to Save the Ailing Killer Whale J50." *Seattle Times*, August 6, 2018. https://www.seattlet imes.com/seattle-news/environment/hand-feeding-a-wild-orca-inside-the-practice -run-to-save-the-ailing-killer-whale-j50/.

———. 2018b. "Gov. Jay Inslee Wants $1.1B to Help Save Puget Sound's Critically Endangered Orcas." *Seattle Times*, December 13, 2018. https://www.seattletimes. com/seattle-news/environment/gov-jay-inslee-wants-1-1-billion-to-help-save- puget-sounds-critically-endangered-orcas/.

McLaren, Karla. n.d. "Grief: The Deep River of the Soul." Karla McLaren (website). Accessed April 23, 2020. https://karlamclaren.com/grief-the-deep-river-of-the-soul/.

Milstein, Tema. 2013. "Banging on the Divide: Cultural Reflection and Refraction at the Zoo." In *Perspectives on Human-Animal Communication,* edited by Emily Plec, 162–181. London: Routledge.

———. 2015. "The Performer Metaphor: 'Mother Nature Never Gives Us the Same Show Twice.'" *Environmental Communication* 10 (2): 1–22 http://dx.doi.org/10 .1080/17524032.2015.1018295.

Pezzullo, Phaedra C. 2007. *Toxic Tourism: Rhetorics of Pollution, Travel, and Environmental Justice*. Tuscaloosa: University of Alabama Press.

Plec, E. 2013. *Perspectives on Human-Animal Communication: Intematural Communication*. New York: Routledge.

Pribac, Teya B. 2016. "Grieving at a Distance." In *Mourning Animals: Rituals and Practices Surrounding Animal Death*, edited by Margo DeMello, 193–199. East Lansing: Michigan State University Press.

Psychic Sister. 2018. "I've resisted this eulogy." Facebook, August 9, 2018. https:/ /www.facebook.com/thepsychicsister/photos/ive-resisted-this-eulogy-i-dont-want -to-think-it-through-i-want-the-baby-to-fall/1330013743768498/.

Ragen, Tim. 2018. "Yes to Whale-Watching Moratorium: Cut the Engine Noise, Save the Orcas." *Seattle Times*, December 11, 2018. https://www.seattletimes.com /opinion/yes-to-whale-watching-moratorium-cut-the-engine-noise-save-the-orcas/.

Robbins, Jim. 2018. "The Northwest's Orcas are Starving and Disappearing. Can They Be Saved?" *News Tribune*, July 12, 2018. https://www.thenewstribune.com/ news/local/article214589010.html.

Sandstrom, Donna. 2018. "Cut the Toxins and Boat Noise, and Boost Salmon, So Orcas Can Survive." *Seattle Times*, August, 10, 2018. https://www.seattletimes.com /opinion/cut-the-toxins-and-boat-noise-and-boost-salmon-so-orcas-can-survive/.

Schutten, Julie K., and Richard A. Rogers. 2011. "Magick as an Alternative Symbolic: Enacting Transhuman Dialogs." *Environmental Communication: A Journal of Nature and Culture* 5 (3): 261–280. http://doi.org/10.1080/17524032 .2011.583261.

Schutten, Madrone K., and Emily Shaffer. 2019. "Tails from Captive Classes: Interspecies Civic Action at the Contemporary Zoo." *Frontiers in Communication* 4 (35): 1–11. http://doi.org/10.3389/fcomm.2019.00035.

Spry, Tami. 2011. *Body, Paper Stage: Writing and Performing Autoethnography.* Walnut Creek, CA: Left Coast Press.

Williams, Terry, T. 2001. *Red: Passion and Patience in the Desert.* New York: Pantheon Books.

Yoeman, Barry. 2018. "When Animals Grieve." *National Wildlife.* https://www.nwf .org/Home/Magazines/National-Wildlife/2018/Feb-Mar/Animals/When-Animals -Grieve.

Yong, Ed. 2018. "What a Grieving Orca Tells Us." *Atlantic*, August 14, 2001. https:/ /www.theatlantic.com/science/archive/2018/08/orca-family-grief/567470/.

Chapter 21

Never the Same River Twice

How Legal Personhood of Rivers Affects Perceived Stability of Policy Solutions

Carie Steele

Public policy is motivated, designed, and implemented as a reflection of societal ideas, while also shaping societal actions in the future. It connects our ideas to actions and connects people to one another and their world. Landmark environmental policies during the 1960s and 1970s were motivated by the rise of the environmental movement and designed to protect resources that humans relied upon. Those policies have shaped American ideas about how to protect natural resources. Decades later, humans face new and pressing environmental problems. Finding viable policy options requires revisions to humans' understanding of our relationship with nature and innovative policies.

One policy innovation has been extending legal rights to natural resources. Around the world, various bodies of water have been accorded legal rights that are meant to resemble personhood. Australia, Bangladesh, Colombia, India, and New Zealand have all attempted to give some measure of legal standing to one or more rivers within their borders. Similar efforts have been less successful in the United States. In September of 2017, a lawsuit was filed in Colorado to give the Colorado River legal rights. The motion was later withdrawn. In 2019, the city of Toledo passed the Lake Erie Bill of Rights, which was struck down by an Ohio judge in 2020.

The creation of legal rights for nature is due to the inability of existing policies to deal with the new and evolving environmental problems. In the Anthropocene, interconnected, rapidly changing system-level problems require a more intimate understanding of the natural world and more dynamic and responsive policy approach. As new challenges arise, the value, interpretation, and scope of existing policy is reviewed and revised to better reflect the interconnectedness of humans and the natural world. These changes enable further innovation and often require greater intimacy between communities of humans as well as between humans and nature.

PATH DEPENDENCE AND THE CLEAN WATER ACT

In 1972, the Clean Water Act (CWA) became the preeminent federal water protection law. It was one piece of a generation of early environmental laws. Now, nearly fifty years later, the CWA not only remains the foundation of water protection in the United States, but it also primes thinking about how to design water policies and shapes policy outcomes.

The CWA requires a permit to be issued prior to dredging, filling, or discharging pollutants into "navigable waters" and focuses on the protection of fishable and drinkable water sources.[1] Yet, in practice, identifying protected waters is complicated. The EPA's initial rules identified "navigable waters" as "traditional navigable waters and the core tributary systems that provide perennial or intermittent flow into them" (EPA 2020). This definition excludes waterways that contain water only after precipitation events, as well as wetlands disconnected from traditional navigable waters.

In 2015, under the direction of President Obama, the EPA issued the Clean Water Rule, attempting to address and clarify these definitional problems.[2] Under the Clean Water Rule, numerous streams and wetlands were identified as essential to the integrity of navigable water. In addition, the Clean Water Rule extended protection to key wetlands including Texas Coastal Prairies, pocosin wetlands, and prairie potholes.[3]

The Clean Water Rule was an attempt to expand the policy's protections by reconstructing the definition of protected waters to better reflect the interconnection of the hydrological system while also incorporating a more diverse understanding of the value of water in all its forms. In its first iteration, the CWA identified the value of water in terms of human consumptive use. The Clean Water Rule attempted to extend protection to bodies of water that had limited consumptive value.

In February of 2017, President Trump signed an executive order directing the EPA to repeal the Clean Water Rule.[4] The Clean Water Rule was replaced by the Navigable Water Protection Rule in June 2020. The new rule reduces protections, particularly those for wetlands that do not directly abut traditional navigable water.

The CWA was part of a collection of ground-breaking legislation that signaled a dramatic change from previous policy, which left much of environmental policy in the hands of states (Kraft 2017; Sale 1993). The resulting pieces of legislation, although victories at the time, continue to shape the American imagination with regard to environmental policy design and enshrine ideas from the time about the value of nature and humans' relationship to it—the same anthropocentric ideas that have contributed substantially to the creation of the Anthropocene. Continued definitional wrangling illustrates how the CWA remains the key mechanism for regulating pollution on lakes, rivers, and streams in the United States. It has provided much needed protection, yet it also serves as the touchstone for water policy in a path-dependent policy world.

Path dependence is the dependence of future outcomes on past events (David 1985; Page 2006, 87). In the field of policy analysis, the concept of path dependence articulates the importance of historic policy actions in shaping ideas about policy problems and design. Essentially, the policies designed in the current moment make some future policies more or less likely (Freeman and Jackson 2012, 137). Efforts to protect water in the United States are constrained by the CWA's existing structure. Moreover, most efforts at new policy solutions continue to design those policies almost exclusively in the CWA's image.

The CWA model is not unique. Many countries have devised policies that fit this model to regulate the use of natural resources. However, in the time since the CWA and other policies like it were created, our understanding of environmental problems has changed. New problems connect ecological, political, economic, and social systems, cross-jurisdictional boundaries, and defy simple policy solutions. Policies like the Clean Water Act—that focus on consumptive value and regulate specific behaviors—are proving inadequate in addressing these new issues. As pressure on water resources grows, so does pressure on water policy. As a result, people and governments are seeking out innovative technical, behavioral, and institutional policy responses.

One such innovation has been the creation of legal rights for nature and the granting of personhood—a dramatic and nonincremental policy shift (Carlson 1998; Bertagna 2006). Existing policy solutions are intended to produce sustainable limitations on human activities. Legal personhood for nature moves policy away from defining acceptable uses and instead enables judicial review and limitation of all uses depending on how those uses affect nature and natural systems (Daly 2012). Not only does the extension of legal rights to nature enable environmental protection against a broader range of threats and identify values in nature beyond its use in human consumption, it also challenges typical Western thinking about our relationship to nature and may signal a seismic shift in thinking about how to design effective environmental policy (Maganalles 2015).

Nonhuman legal standing for nature requires environmental policy to evolve beyond managing nature based upon the benefits the resource produces for humans. Such changes necessarily include adapting to and accepting dynamic natural processes, valuing complete and healthy ecosystems and the services they provide, and acknowledging the interconnection of resources we have traditionally tried to manage as separate and unconnected. It requires communities to share knowledge and to be inclusive with visions of human-nature relationships. Ultimately, expanding legal standing and granting personhood to nature requires a willingness to rethink and ignore the artificial line between civilization and nature. Once put into practice, such policies have the potential to transform our perception of problems and policy solutions and to increase our intimate connections to the world around us.

INSTITUTIONS, LEGAL PERSONHOOD, AND PUBLIC POLICY

The fields of political science and policy analysis focus on how the rules and institutions of decision-making affect how problems are defined, how competition over policy is conducted, and the likelihood and viability of different policy solutions. Much like the rules of athletic competition, political institutions and decision-making rules determine who the relevant players are, the actions available to different players, the boundaries of the field of competition, and acceptable means of interaction (North 1990, 4). As a result, the rules of the game influence which strategies are likely to be used and successful in policy competition. While foundational documents (e.g., constitutions) establish the initial framework for competition, the creation of new policies often redefine the competition. For example, the U.S. Constitution did not originally define who could vote but rather left states to define voting rights.[5] Over time, a variety of laws and amendments standardized voting rights and expanded the franchise.[6]

Like laws that have expanded the franchise, laws and policies that provide rights to nature require a change in societal thinking. These laws redefine relationships among participants. Just as the Nineteenth Amendment to the Constitution of the United States redefined women from subjects to voters and changed the political relationship between men and women, granting legal rights to nature changed societal dynamics between those who held rights previously and those who are newly included in those rights (McConnaughy 2013).

Most people rarely consider how political institutions and decision-making rules shape the society in which they live, often thinking about these structures as permanent, immutable fixtures of society. Yet, rules governing political competition are also subject to change and revision. Modifications to these rules and institutions can cause dramatic changes in how policy competition is conducted, as well as what policies are produced.

Among the rules that have the most impact—both procedurally and heuristically—are rules that define personhood, legal standing, and rights (Carlson 1998; Bertagna 2006). Political rules and institutions determine which actors are entitled to take which actions. For example, in the United States, universal suffrage does not mean that every citizen can vote. The rules of participation limit some citizens' participation—children and, in some states, felons. Similarly, the rules that govern the judicial system limit which actors can take which actions within the judicial process. Holding legal personhood is an essential criterion for having access to the powers and protections of the judicial system.

Personhood grants an individual or entity specific rights, duties, and responsibilities. Legal personhood includes three key elements: legal standing or the right to sue or be sued in court, the right to enter and enforce legal contracts, and the right to own property (Naffine 2003; O'Donnell and Talbot-Jones 2017, 160; O'Donnell and Talbot-Jones 2018, 8). Although extending legal personhood to a nonhuman entity may seem unusual and extreme, it is hardly unprecedented. Corporations have long enjoyed legal personhood in many countries, including the right to enter into legal contracts and sue or be sued separate from the human beings associated with the firm.[7] In the United States Supreme Court case *Citizens United v. Federal Election Commission*, the majority opinion went farther, granting corporations first amendment rights similar to those of individuals and recognizing their right to contribute to political campaigns.[8]

POLICY COMPETITION AND POLICY CYCLE

The institutions and laws of a country or a state create the rules regarding how policy competition can take place. The policy cycle is a set of stages or steps that happen in the process of the creation and continuation of policy (Anderson 2011; Smith and Larimer 2009; DeLeon 1999; Brewer and DeLeon 1983). Different authors have suggested different numbers and names of stages but most agree on at least five components: problem definition, policy formulation, policy adoption, implementation, and evaluation. It is useful to think of it as circular, where the completion of one cycle feeds into another because the evaluation process provides many opportunities to change or repeal the policy.

Problem definition is the process by which a problem is identified as a societal problem requiring public societal action. The way problems are identified and defined affects whether or not policy action is needed, what policies designs are acceptable or feasible solutions, and so on. Any given problem could be defined in multiple ways. Agenda-setting is the process by which a single problem definition is selected, framed in a way that makes the problem subject to policy action and selects the venue most appropriately responsible for responding to the problem as defined. Each policy problem will have multiple possible solutions and multiple possible venues (local, state, national government, legislative body, court, bureaucracy, etc.). In the policy formulation stage, a single policy solution is identified and designed to fit the problem that has been defined. The proposed policy then proceeds through an adoption process through which it is accepted or approved. After a policy is adopted, it is implemented. Finally, after some time, the impact and effectiveness of a policy is re-examined. This includes scheduled reviews of outcomes, internal evaluations and reports by the implementing agents, reauthorization requirements, as well as legal challenges by those affected by the policy. Political rules and institutions establish the channels by which policy can be made, determine which actors have the power to affect policy in each of these stages, and specify which forum for competition is used in each of these stages.

STANDING AND RIGHTS OF NATURE IN THE POLICY CYCLE

The judicial process has been essential to environmental protection and policy. In the United States, most environmental law—both legislative and judicial decisions—has focused on establishing sustainable limits for resource use or creating unique protections for specific resources or features. A vast majority of environmental law intended to reduce degradation is driven by human interest in protecting consumption and monetary valuation of natural resources (Gunningham 2009, 179–80; Doremus 2002, 327; Stallworthy 2008, 24; O'Donnell and Talbot-Jones 2018, 8). Granting rights to nature is a monumental change in how nature is viewed in the policy cycle.

The extension of nonhuman legal personhood to nature impacts each stage of the policy cycle differently. The most obvious impact is seen at the evaluation stage. Standing, as one of the rules that determines how competition can happen in the judicial system, determines which entities can rely on the courts for recourse. Extending legal rights to nature—in whole or part—is intended to provide access to the judicial process as a means of suing for damages and enforcing legal contracts (O'Donnell and Talbot-Jones 2018, 8–9)

In most countries, standing requires a legally designated person to demonstrate harm. In the case of environmental law in the United States, individuals and organizations can file suit as a third party on behalf of the environment, but only if they can demonstrate material harm to themselves as a third party. This severely limits the types of cases that can be filed. For example, in *Sierra*

Club v. Morton, the Sierra Club organization brought a suit for an injunction against the National Forest Service's approval of a ski development by Walt Disney Production near Sequoia National Forest. The court determined that the organization did not "have a direct stake in the outcome" and thus did not have legal standing.[9] Lack of legal standing for nature makes it nearly impossible to bring grievances regarding ecosystem health to the judicial system. As a result, it is difficult to challenge policies that only protect resources viewed as valuable for human consumption.

Legal personhood also enables citizens, activists, and politicians to frame problems as a threat to nature or ecosystems, regardless of their impact on humans, much the same way they frame other issues as a threat to other entities, like small businesses. Likewise, granting legal personhood would affect which policy solutions and designs are considered viable. The threat of future legal action would improve the negotiating position of environmental interests while providing additional protection and recourse for policies that do not protect the ecosystem as a whole.

MOVING TOWARD LEGAL RIGHTS FOR NATURE

Considerations about how to design legal rights for nature have been underway for several decades. This movement has become more urgent as we seek solutions to complex environmental problems associated with climate change. Legal provisions recognizing the rights of nature now exist in Australia, Bangladesh, Bolivia, Colombia, Ecuador, India, Mexico, New Zealand, and the United States, as well as several international efforts, notably the 2010 World People's Conference on Climate Change and the Rights of Mother Earth and the 2020 United Nations' Harmony with Nature Initiative (Kauffman and Sheehan 2019).

The key questions about extending rights and legal personhood to nature focus on the source of the legal designation and how the environment could be represented in court. Current provisions that recognize the rights of nature identify those rights as stemming from three different sources. The first is national constitutions. Ecuador's 2008 constitution grants legal rights to nature, including the right to exist, flourish, and evolve. It also empowers "all persons, communities, peoples, and nations to call upon public agencies to enforce the rights of nature."[10]

The second source of legal rights for nature comes from passage of new laws. In 2010, Bolivia created legal rights for nature with the passage of the *"Ley de Derechos de la Madre Tierra"* or "Law of Mother Earth." Similarly, some of the most successful environmental initiatives in the United States in the last fifteen years have been the creation of local laws that articulate and protect the rights of nature. In 2010, the city council of Pittsburgh, Pennsylvania, unanimously adopted the Pittsburgh Community Bill of Rights in response to concerns about fracking and state efforts to preempt municipal authority (Troutman 2014). The law created enforceable rights of citizens to clean air and water, and, in language that reflected the Ecuadorian Constitution and Bolivia's Law of Mother Earth, included the right of nature to exist and flourish.

The third source of legal rights for nature has been legal decisions. In India's Uttarakhand province, a judge issued a unilateral ruling identifying the "sacred" and "revered" nature of the Ganges and Yamuna rivers and granting them legal personhood (Earth Law Center 2017).

Explicitly recognizing the legal rights of nature also requires the representation of the interests of nature in court. Solutions to the representation problem focus on the designation of an entity to represent the interests of nature (Bertagna 2006, 415; O'Donnell and Talbot-Jones 2017, 160; O'Donnell and Talbot-Jones 2018, 9–10). Because these entities necessarily include humans, the process of creating a representative board or agency for nature often serves as a key mechanism through which humans gain greater intimacy and understanding of nature across groups. Representation of nature's interest in court requires not just an understanding of consumptive values but of different communities' relationships with nature and a deep appreciation for its role and needs.

These initiatives illustrate a continuing policy cycle that incorporates growth, evolution, and hybridization in human thought. In many cases, laws that grant rights to nature reflect the incorporation of indigenous thought into colonial Western governance systems. The success of these efforts relies heavily on strong cooperative relationships among communities. Legal personhood for nature honors multiple visions of human relationships with nature and makes the interconnection of ecosystems an essential component of any policy action.

In addition to requiring a person or group to act as the representative of nature, granting legal rights to nature, either in part or whole, requires a change in expectations around policy stability. Policy incrementalism has meant that once landmark environmental policies are made, changes in policy from year to year are nonexistent or relatively small. Granting legal rights to nature would inevitably lead to tensions with existing environmental law.

Efforts to secure the rights of nature have taken many forms. These varied approaches all lead to differing levels of connection between humans and nature. To explore the interconnection between legal rights, human intimacy with nature, and policy change, I will examine four case studies that reflect these different approaches. Three of these cases—Australia, New Zealand, and Colombia—represent relatively successful bids to create meaningful legal rights for nature. The fourth case—the Colorado River in the United States—specifically examines how a lack of connection may doom an effort to create meaningful legal rights for nature. I've selected these cases because each case relates to freshwater resource management but varies on other key features, including the type of contestation, the source of legal rights, and the scope of legal outcomes.

PERSONHOOD FOR RIVERS: CASE STUDIES

Case 1: Victoria, Australia

Australia provides an interesting case for several reasons. First, as a country that comprises an entire continent, it has no cross-border issues in river management. However, like the United States, Australia is a federal state. This means that it has a central or federal government that coexists with regional, state, provincial, or territorial governments. Within a federal system, the division of power is split and, in some cases, shared between the central and regional governments. This division of power and responsibility poses unique challenges and strengths for environmental policy. For example, in Australia, as in the United States, regional governments are historically responsible for water resource management. Each has its own water rights laws that fit within a national policy framework (Gardner, Bartlett, and Gray 2009, 34; Kildea and Williams 2010, 596).

Victoria is a state located in Southeast Australia. The management of Victoria's rivers, lakes, and estuaries is guided by a collection of laws, among which the Environmental Protection Act of 1970 and Victorian Water Act of 1989 are most crucial. The Environmental Protection Act of 1970 outlines which resources need to be protected and which human activities should be limited to provide that protection.[11] The Victorian Water Act of 1989 is the framework that guides the allocation of water rights for commercial and irrigation uses.[12] The decisions regarding water use under the Victorian Water Act of 1989 have a tremendous impact on the volume of water available in the region's rivers and estuaries. These two pieces of legislation formed the foundation of water policy in Victoria at the turn of the century.

From 2001 to 2009, Southeastern Australia, including Victoria, experienced its worst drought since 1900. The Millennium Drought had a profound impact on human communities in the region, placing restrictions on irrigation and household water, reducing agricultural production and allocations of water for urban environments, and creating the need to pipe water directly to some communities (Sohn 2007; Herberger 2011). In addition to the human costs, thirty-three wetlands were disconnected from source rivers to increase the supply of water for human use. Lakes began to dry up, exposing acidic soils, and the salinity of the Coorong River increased to five times saltier than sea water (Government of South Australia n.d.). Later studies found that over-reliance on surface water as well as high levels of surface water diversion during the drought had lasting effects, including the deterioration of riparian ecosystems and reduction of groundwater resources (NWC 2010; McKernan 2010; van Djik et al. 2013). As a result, the continued use of the Murray-Darling Basin was put in jeopardy.

The severe ecological consequences of the Millennium Drought increased demand for water policy that incorporated the needs of ecosystems. In 2007, the Victorian State agreed to refer some of their water management powers to the Commonwealth, enabling the passage of national water reform legislation (COAG 2008). The new legislation focused on the creation of an environmental water reserve, the establishment of sustainable limits for river diversion, and the investment in river recovery through the creation of water purchasing programs. The subsequent Environmental Water Reserve protected a holding of water used to maintain minimum flow rates in rivers and streams. To do so, the legislation made water rights more exclusive— more like private property—and the national government was responsible for purchasing water from entitlement holders to meet minimum flow rates for environmental protection (O'Donnell 2012, 74–75).

However, with the increase of extreme climate-related events, such as drought, flood, and wildfire, the minister for environment drew increased political pressure regarding water rights decisions (O'Donnell 2012, 74). As the Commonwealth changed water rights to make water more like private property, it became clear that nature and ecosystems were unable to assert legal claims to water as a private property. Recognizing that market and climate pressures might motivate a roll-back of environmental rights protection, the Victorian State restored some of its water management powers and decision-making responsibilities through the creation of the Victorian Environmental Water Holder (VEWH) in 2010 (O'Donnell 2012, 76–77; O'Donnell and Talbot-Jones 2018, 9).

The Environmental Water Reserve provides a key legal provision that outlines the environment's legal entitlement to water (Foerster 2007). The VEWH was created as a corporate entity to fulfill the provisions of the Environmental Water Reserve and to represent the legal rights of nature. Specifically, the Reserve is intended to maintain minimum stream flows in Victoria's rivers through the use of on-stream dams and limitations on human water rights. Like a corporation, the VEWH was created to be a legal person, representing the interests of the environment, with the legal power to sue and be sued and to hold property—in this case, water. In addition, the VEWH took over legal responsibility for deciding on water entitlements for human use in the state (VEWH 2013). The minister for environment remains responsible for water policy more broadly but is unable to direct the use of environmental water in Victoria in a given year.

As one of the first attempts at establishing legal rights for nature, this case illustrates three key factors. First is the importance of problem definition and framing. The Environmental Water Reserve played an essential role in framing water policy reform as not only about human consumption. In establishing nature's right to water—in addition to propertizing water—the Environmental Water Reserve established the necessity of creating an entity like the VEWH. The creation of purchasing programs and policies that treat water as a private good could easily have excluded nonhuman interests in the Western market and legal system. The rights of nature framing provided a different collection of potential policy designs, including ones that would not have been possible without this preexisting framing.

Second, the Environmental Water Reserve and the VEWH both emphasize the interconnection between humans and nature. Their very existence codifies scientific understanding that human health and well-being is intimately tied to the health and well-being of the environment. The Millennium Drought provided a powerful illustration of how anthropocentric policies that focus on maintaining human consumption at the expense of ecosystems may further endanger human consumption. The development of policies that attempt to account for nature's right to exist demonstrates a tremendous shift in thinking.

Among the alternative policy designs that the rights of nature framing provided is the creation of a legal entity comprised of humans but representing nature. The commissioners who serve on the VEWH have wide latitude to manage resources and allocate water rights according to what best serves the natural ecosystems. Instead of relying on human consumption to determine how much water is left for nature, the VEWH enables nature equal legal footing. In other provinces, water entitlements are determined by market forces. Under the VEWH, nature holds entitlement to water despite not participating in the market system.

Finally, granting rights to nature not only adds responsibility but leads to more flexible and measured responses to political pressure. Anthropocentric public policies created and exacerbated climate change. The negative effects of climate change increase political pressure for more anthropocentric and extractive public policy. Understanding and acknowledging the connections between ecosystem health and human prosperity enables communities to prioritize the needs of nature over human consumption. Granting nature itself rights reflects a more nuanced understanding of human well-being while also enabling wiser, more measured decisions, as well as the construction of policy options that incorporate the needs of ecosystems and better mitigate the effects of climate change.

Case 2: Whanganui River, New Zealand

The Whanganui River, on New Zealand's North Island, is the third longest river in the country. The River used to serve as an important route to the interior of the island. Just as in the previous case, it does not cross any national boundary. The government of New Zealand has held primary ownership of the River since 1873. However, for as long as the government has claimed ownership, the indigenous Maori have disputed this claim.[13] The Whanganui River has historically been one of the primary areas of settlement for Maori. While national government has largely managed the River for commercial and consumptive purposes, it is an essential piece of cultural landscape for the Maori. Due to its importance to their cultural identity, the Maori view the River as having a distinct personality (Hsiao 2012, 371; Magallanes 2015).

The dispute over ownership illustrates how differing ideas about the relationship between humans and nature leads to different definitions of problems and potential policy solutions. The government's view of the River as a resource that is owned and managed leads to a variety of policy solutions that include ensuring Maori access to the River, extending water entitlements to the Maori, licensing fishing rights, and so on. By contrast, the Maori understanding of the River as a distinct person rebukes these conceptions of ownership.

In 2012, the government and the Maori reached an agreement that would grant the River legal personhood. This was later formalized in 2017 with the Te Awa Tupua Act, or the Whanganui River Claims Settlement Act, after eight years of negotiation (Magallanes 2015). The agreement was noteworthy for several reasons. First, unlike the Australia case in which nature was entitled to a resource, in this case, the Whanganui River itself was granted rights as a legal person. A legal guardian is intended to represent the whole person that is the River (Magallanes 2015; O'Donnell and Talbot-Jones 2018, 10). This was one of the first instances in which a natural feature was not just given legal rights but legal personhood.

Second, the granting of personhood at the time was not only a unique policy solution but also extremely pluralist. The real source of disagreements over the River sprung from differing understandings of ownership. Environmental regulation in New Zealand relies entirely on the mechanism of ownership. The government's definition of ownership conferred rights to use the resources as desired. In contrast, Maori definitions of ownership confer responsibility to protect the resource (Hsiao 2012, 372). Once there was clear understanding of where disagreement lay, the two parties could begin to design a policy that addressed these differing definitions. Granting rights to nature was a uniquely powerful means of doing this. The 2017 treaty specifically incorporates the Maori worldview and grants the River rights as a whole legal person. The agreement prioritizes the well-being of the river for its own sake.

In addition, the agreement establishes a legal guardian to represent the river in court should it be necessary. The creation of a legal guardian enabled the river's protection through the same legal system on which other environmental regulations rely. The legal guardian, Te Pou Tupua, consists of two individuals—a representative of the government and a representative of the Maori—who must act as one to represent the River. The legislation also establishes a group consisting of representatives of stakeholders to advise the guardian. The group acts as a collaboration mechanism that enables stakeholders to actively engage in the development, approval, implementation, and review of strategy documents regarding river protection and management (Tschirhart et al. 2016).

With this agreement, New Zealand became a pioneer in environmental policy. Granting legal personhood to the River fundamentally changed the way people think about and relate to the river. By granting the river legal personhood, management decisions were required to prioritize the well-being of the River. Moreover, the well-being of the River was no longer defined by its usefulness to humans. The establishment of a legal guardian and advisory group enabled the construction of a clear personality for the river while empowering stakeholders to actively participate in learning about the River's personality. Perhaps most importantly, when communities disagree about the management of the River, the legal guardian is able to use the legal system to protect the interests of the River without consideration of human consumption.

The case is a clear demonstration of flexible and innovative problem solving. It reflects a willingness to learn by incorporating multiple legal perspectives and worldviews into a single policy solution. In addition, the development of a legal guardian for the River, consisting of both an indigenous and a governmental representative who must act as one in the interest of the River, makes it clear that the policy solution was based on intimate knowledge and understanding of the River and the people. The representatives are tasked with developing intimate knowledge about the River, but the agreement clearly relies on collaboration between two human communities as a key component to developing such knowledge.

Case 3: Atrato River in Colombia

The Choco region of Colombia is found along the Pacific Ocean in the northwest of the county. It is one of the most biodiverse regions on the planet. It is also a region of agricultural value with large quantities of arable land and rich mineral deposits. The Atrato River and its tributaries account for nearly

60 percent of the region's water resources. It is an essential part of the rainforest ecosystem and the third most navigable river in the country. Mining and extractive industries have been present in the Choco region since 1550. Today, the impact of extractive industries and large-scale agriculture poses a serious threat to the Atrato River as well as the communities that live in its basin (Calzadilla 2019, 4).

The Atrato River is essential to the small-scale farming and traditional lifestyles of indigenous and Afro-Colombian communities in the Pacific region. Both indigenous and Afro-Colombian communities have made historical claims to territory, which the Colombian state has generally disregarded. Indeed, in the case of Afro-Colombians, the government and society at large have historically denied their very existence in Colombia (Minority Rights Group International 2008). During the Colombian Civil War, both indigenous and Afro-Colombian communities suffered repression and violence as well as land seizures at the hands of both the government and rebel paramilitaries (Andrews 2004). After the Civil War, the Colombian government attempted to make amends by providing new protections for disadvantaged ethnic communities. Law 70 was ratified into the Colombian Constitution, which specifically identified Afro-Colombians as a distinct ethnic group and provided for the defense of their territorial rights, much like numerous indigenous communities (Wade 1995). In addition, the Colombian government has developed decrees, ordinances, and directives around *consulta previa*—indigenous communities' rights to consultation on projects within their territory—which Afro-Colombians, in theory, could leverage (Menendez-Montalvo 2014).

This special designation among Afro-Colombian and indigenous communities provides a unique legal basis for efforts at environmental protection. Yet, these legal protections have done little to stop land seizures and environmental degradation due to mineral extraction. In 2011, after years of failed consultation efforts, local communities petitioned the national government to halt mining activities and prevent further environmental degradation.[14] Although the National Mining Agency intervened, by 2014 the *Defensoria del Pueblo* declared a state of human and environmental emergency in the Choco region (Margil 2017, 27).

In 2015, frustrated by the lack of governmental response, community organizations, including *Tierra Digna*, filed a motion for protection in the Administrative Court of Cundinamarca, which quickly decided against the protection order. The plaintiffs then brought their case to the Sixth Circuit Constitutional Court. In November of 2016, the Constitutional Court ruled that the Atrato River Basin was to be granted legal personhood with the rights to "protection, conservation, maintenance, and restoration."[15] The ruling relies on provisions of the 1991 Colombian Constitution, which guarantee the protection of cultural diversity, biodiversity, and the environment.[16]

The deciding opinion specifically acknowledges the deep and inexpressible connection between indigenous communities and the environment in which they live:

> The so-called bio-cultural rights, in their simplest definition, refer to the rights that ethnic communities have to administer and exercise sovereign autonomous authority over their territories—according to their own laws, customs—and the natural resources that make up their habitat. Their culture, traditions, and way of life are developed based on the special relationship they have with the environment and biodiversity. In effect, these rights result from the recognition of the deep and intrinsic connection that exists between nature, its resources, and the culture of the ethnic and indigenous communities that inhabit them, all of which are interdependent with each other and cannot be understood in isolation, argued that the river played an essential role in the cultural rights of indigenous and Afro-Colombian citizens in the Choco region. According to the judge, this combination of constitutional guarantees and biocultural importance of the river to communities Colombia entitled the Atrato River to rights and protection of a legal person.[17]

As a result of the ruling, the Court required the creation of a commission of the Guardians of the Rio Atrato, as well as a restoration plan and commission to oversee it—giving specific roles to civil society organizations. In addition, the ruling also established required actions and responsibilities of the government to the indigenous and Afro-Colombian communities in the Choco region.

Although the decision to grant the Atrato River legal personhood reflects the interests of specific ethnic communities, and is therefore similar to the New Zealand case, the Colombian case differs in some key ways. First and foremost, the decision was not a negotiated outcome between the government and the indigenous population. Unlike the New Zealand case, in which communities worked together to devise an innovative solution, in the case of the Atrato River, the granting of legal personhood and the other requirements were decided upon and designed by a single judge. However, that decision relies on key legal documents, including Colombia's own Constitution, that illustrate revolutionary societal thinking (even if only aspirational) about the relationship between government and people as well as between human communities and nature.

The Court's decision relies primarily on portions of the Colombian Constitution that was ratified in 1991. The Constitution is an essential piece of the rules of the game. It establishes which political players can take which actions, what their responsibilities are, and provides criteria for appropriate interactions. The incorporation of environmental protection into the

Constitution established expectations that the government would be responsible for some aspects of environmental protection and opened an entire
universe of potential policy designs to ensure that those responsibilities were
being met. Similar legal protections for ethnic groups allowed the court to
easily couple ethnic territorial and environmental claims.

Interestingly, the Court's decision not only confers personhood to the river
but also requires the restoration of the ecosystem and identifies the governments' responsibility to communities within the basin to help recuperate
traditional lifestyles. In comparison to the New Zealand case, in which a
representative of the Maori community was to act as legal guardian with the
responsibility of protecting the River, this case suggests a broader conception
of the entity that has been granted rights. Specifically, the River and its basin
include indigenous and Afro-Colombian communities as part of the broader
biotic community that was granted personhood.

The ruling also seems to recognize the flexibility and adaptability that will
be required given the establishment of personhood for the River. If the rights
of nature are to be the foundation for management, an inclusive and dynamic
managerial approach is necessary—one that includes checks on activities
that violate the rights of nature, opportunities for coordination among the
communities in the river basin, and mechanisms for the continual evaluation
of the needs of nature. There is no single stable policy that can manage this
level of interconnection.

In line with this, the ruling also gives civil society organizations, including
the Humboldt Institute and the World Wildlife Federation, specific roles in
the planning and restoration efforts. Unlike the New Zealand case, in which
two groups negotiated and agreed to a shared intimacy in order to represent
the legal rights of the River, the disputing parties in Colombia are not brought
together and the decision is not a result of negotiation. Given the antagonistic
relationship between local communities and the government, it is unsurprising that the court decided to appoint a third party to act as supervisor to these
processes. It also suggests that this case is unique, in that the key threat to the
River's personhood is actions, or rather the lack of action, by the government.
This suggests that in cases where government actions threaten the rights of
nature, there may be a need to develop additional institutional protections of
those rights.

Case 4: Colorado River, United States

The final case is a failed attempt by an environmental group called Deep
Green Resistance to create legal personhood for the Colorado River in the
state of Colorado in the United States.[18] The United States, like Australia, is

a federal country in which each state has some decision-making power with regard to water rights. The Colorado River is an important water source for seven western states in the United States—Arizona, California, Colorado, Nevada, New Mexico, Utah, and Wyoming. Competition over access to and use of the Colorado River has required substantial policy effort, resulting in the Colorado River Compact. The Colorado River Compact provides for the division of water rights among the compact states while also seeking to establish the relative importance of different types of uses of the River. Under the Colorado River Compact and other minor agreements, two large dams have been built on the River: the Glenn Canyon Dam, which led to the creation of Lake Powell, and the Hoover Dam, which led to the creation of Lake Meade. The dams changed the natural cycles of seasonal floods, draining and diverting such a large portion of the River that the Colorado River Delta, where the river meets the Pacific Ocean, ceased to exist.

In 2017, a lawsuit was filed by Denver attorney Jason Flores-Williams along with representatives from several environmental organizations in response to these and countless other damages inflicted upon the Colorado River ecosystem. Specifically, the suit sought injunctive relief from state actions that violated the River's "right to exist, flourish, regenerate, be restored, and naturally evolve."[19] In addition, the pleadings cited cases from Ecuador, Colombia, and New Zealand, as well as the recognition of corporate personhood, to argue for personhood rights for the Colorado River ecosystem. The plaintiffs' arguments focused on the near-infinite collection of relationships that make up the Colorado River ecosystem. Because the River is reliant on water sources ranging from snowpack in the mountains to groundwater springs, it ties together a wide range of human and biotic communities. The plaintiffs argued that to appropriately protect the river, the river should be granted personhood as a way to encompass all these connected relationships (Miller 2019, 369).

The intent of the lawsuit was undoubtedly rooted in a deep understanding of the interconnected relationships between the River, the humans who use it, and the environment around it. If the lawsuit had been successful, it would have provided an important first step toward protecting a key water source for humans that has been rapidly depleted under current anthropocentric policy. It also would have opened the door for other personhood and rights of nature cases for a variety of other natural features. However, the case was resisted strongly by the state of Colorado and later withdrawn by the plaintiffs under threat of sanction for bringing a frivolous or vexatious complaint.

Despite the plaintiffs' exploration of the River's connection to a broad range of human and natural communities, the case failure was largely a result of a lack of connection in the policy cycle. First, unlike in the Australia and New Zealand cases, where the basis for legal personhood came from negotiations and the creation of law, this lawsuit sought to force a legal decision from a judge, like in Colombia. But, unlike the Colombia case, there is no underlying constitutional principle to form the basis for such a decision. Although there has been some local-level success in establishing rights for nature, there was no existing state- or federal-level law under which personhood might obviously fit. Moreover, in the U.S. judicial process, plaintiffs must be able to demonstrate harm to have standing. Much like *Sierra Club v. Morton*, the plaintiffs' approach did not demonstrate harm to the third party representing nature, and thus the case did not offer reasonable grounds for standing.

Second, unlike the New Zealand and Colombia cases, in which specific ethnic groups' claims formed an important basis for protecting river and ecosystem health, the Colorado River lawsuit was filed without consultation with indigenous groups. This is particularly puzzling, given that several indigenous nations have water rights on the Colorado River. These groups not only make up a substantial portion of stakeholders along the River but previous rulings have given indigenous nations high priority when allocating water rights. Moreover, indigenous knowledge, cultural legacy, and mythology are strongly tied to the Colorado River. Incorporating indigenous views of an interconnected river community, as was done in New Zealand, would seem to be a natural fit for this lawsuit. The failure to work with the broader human community seems like an oversight.

Third, the Colorado River is one of the most important rivers in the American West. The River and its tributaries are key sources of water for seven different states. While the lawsuit sought legal personhood, its consideration of how that person should be legally represented was less clear. There is tremendous uncertainty around how one acts as the legal guardian of a river that crosses into other states that have not recognized the legal personhood of the river.

Ultimately, this effort failed because of a lack of connection between the case, the broader community around the River, and the existing conceptualizations of the River and its ecosystem. Although granting personhood rights changes the way we think about environmental policy problems, communities must first be willing to imagine a more complex relationship with nature for this to be a viable option. Evidence of that change is generally found first in the establishment of some constitutional or other statutory law regarding responsibilities to the environment. Nothing in the management efforts of the Colorado River prior to this case suggested that there were any such shifts that might make establishing personhood through a court ruling possible. In many ways, the failure of the case was driven by a failure in agenda-setting, choosing to use the judicial process rather than another option.

LIVING IN THE ANTHROPOCENE AND
LIVING AS PART OF NATURE

As we move deeper into the Anthropocene and grapple with the complex new problems created by anthropocentric policies, we have also begun to shift in our thinking about humans' relationship with nature. For centuries, much of environmental policy has focused on enabling human consumption of natural resources. Underlying these policies was the idea of humans as separate from and ruling over nature. But, as we face the consequences of climate change, we have begun to broaden our view of viable policy options. Among the most innovative is the recognition of the rights of nature.

The successful cases examined here illustrate how the willingness of communities to change their view of nature and embrace interconnection results in a closer relationship with nature and with each other. In two of the cases in which rivers are given legal personhood, the policy change is rooted in previous law or policy that reflects changes in societal thought that are already underway. In the Australia case, this initial policy change is an attempt to respond to disaster. In the Colombia case, the Constitution provides environmental protection that is not directed specifically at a river. In the New Zealand case, the shift in societal thought is more abrupt and the result honoring cultural differences.

Each case in which a river is successfully granted legal personhood also illustrates how the act of granting rights to nature changes humans' relationship with it. In the cases of Australia and New Zealand, humans not only recognize the right of nature to exist but also establish entities whose sole purpose is to defend the well-being of nature within human governing structures. In contrast, in the Colombian case, the ruling by the Constitutional Court essentially designates indigenous and Afro-Colombian communities as part of the River and its biotic community. Although the Colorado River case focuses on the failure to gain legal rights for the river, it also illustrates the necessity of interconnection. No single person or group can leverage the entire policy cycle alone. The proponents failed to connect the numerous groups that could have supported the effort and ultimately withdrew their case.

These cases also illustrate how extending personhood to nature requires a more flexible and adaptable understanding of how to manage that relationship. Human institutions—the rules of the political game—rely on procedures and processes requiring human involvement. As we realize and appreciate how human well-being is inextricably tied to environmental health, we must find ways to advocate for the needs of nature within these same institutions. Those solutions may include the provision of environmental rights in constitutions, laws recognizing the right of nature to exist and thrive, the creation of legal entities that speak on behalf of nature, all of these, or others not explored here. Our ability to understand the needs of nature and develop ways to advocate for those within our own limited institutions are skills that will be invaluable in the more volatile era of the Anthropocene. Ultimately, this shift in thinking, nascent as it is, represents a promising evolution for both us and the environment. Through it, we can learn to see ourselves as part of a larger biotic community. Acting on it, we can see old rivers renewed.

NOTES

1. Federal Water Pollution Control Act Amendments of 1972, 86 Stat. 816, 33 U.S.C. § 1251 (Clean Water Act).
2. Clean Water Rule: Definition of "Waters of the United States," 80 Fed. Reg. 37,054 (June 29, 2015) (codified at 33 C.F.R. pt. 328; 40 C.F.R. pts. HO, 112, 116, 117, 122, 230, 300, 302, and 401). 33 C.F.R. § 328.2.
3. The Navigable Waters Protection Rule: Definition of "Waters of the United States," 85 Fed. Reg. 22250 (April 21, 2020) (codified at 33 C.F.R. pt. 328; 40 CFR pts. 110, 112, 116, 117, 120, 122, 230, 232, 300, 302, and 401).
4. Exec. Order No. 13778, 82 Fed. Reg. 12,497 (February 28, 2017).
5. U.S. Const. art.I, § 2.
6. U.S. Const. amend. XV; U.S. Const. amend. XIX; U.S. Const. amend XXVI; An Act to Establish an Uniform Rule of Naturalization, 1 Stat 103 (1790).
7. *Trustees of Dartmouth College v. Woodward*, 17 U.S. 518 (1819)
8. *Citizens United v. Fed. Election Comm'n*, 558 U.S. 310, 342 (2010).
9. *Sierra Club v. Morton*, 405 U.S. 727, 740 (1972).
10. Ecuador Const. of 2008, ch. 7, art. 71.
11. Environmental Protection Act of 1970, Victoria, Australia act n. 8056/1970.
12. Water Act of 1989, Victoria, Australia act n. 80/1989.
13. Waitangi Tribunal, "The Waitangi Tribunal's Inquiry into Historical Claims: A New Approach." Wellington: Waitangi Tribunal, 2001.
14. Decree 4134 (2011).
15. Republic of Colombia Const. Court (sixth district). Case T-622 2016. Proceeding T=5.016.242.
16. Art. 7 and art. 79.
17. Republic of Colombia Const. Court Case T-622 2016, 35.
18. *See* Am. Compl., *Colo. River Ecosystem v. Colorado*, 2017 WL 9472427, No. 17-cv-02316-NYW (D. Colo. Nov. 16, 2017).
19. *Id.* ¶ 81.

BIBLIOGRAPHY

Anderson, James E. 2011. *Public Policy Making*. 7th ed. Boston: Cengage Learning.
Andrews, George R. 2004. *Afro-Latin America, 1800–2000*. London: Oxford University Press.

Baumgartner, Frank R. and Bryan D. Jones. 2002. *Policy Dynamics*. Chicago: University of Chicago Press.

Bertagna, Blake. R. 2006. "'Standing up' for the Environment: The Ability of Plaintiffs to Establish Legal Standing to Redress Injuries Caused by Global Warming." *Brigham Young University Law Review* 2006 (2): 415–71.

Brewer, Garry D., and Peter DeLeon. 1983. *The Foundations of Policy Analysis*. Homewood: Dorsey.

Calzadilla, Paola V. 2019. "A Paradigm Shift in Courts' View on Nature: The Atrato River and Amazon Basin Cases in Colombia." *Law Environment and Development Journal* 15 (0): 3–11.

Carlson, Ann E. 1998. "Standing for the Environment." *UCLA Law Review* 45 (April): 931–1004.

COAG (Council of Australian Governments). 2008. *Agreement on Murray-Darling Basin Reform*, July 3, 2008. https://www.coag.gov.au/sites/default/files/agreem ents/Murray_Darling_IGA.pdf.

Crawford, Sue E.S. and Elinor Ostrom. 1995. "A Grammar of Institutions." *American Political Science Review* 89, no. 3 (September): 582–600.

Daly, Erin. 2012. "The Ecuadorian Exemplar: The First Ever Vindications of Constitutional Rights of Nature." *Review of European, Comparative & International Environmental Law* 21, no. 1 (April): 63–66. https://doi.org/10.1111/j.1467-9388 .2012.00744.x.

David, Paul. 1985. "Clio and the Economics of QWERTY." *American Economic Review* 75, no. 2 (May): 332–37.

DeLeon, Peter. 1999. "The Stages Approach to the Policy Process: What Has It Done, Where Is It Going?" In *Theories of the Policy Process*, edited by Paul A. Sabatier, 19–34. Boulder: Westview.

Doremus, Holly. 2002. "Biodiversity and the Challenge of Saving the Ordinary." *Idaho Law Review* 38: 325–54

Dorsey Jones, Charles O. 1997. *An Introduction to the Study of Public Policy*. 3rd ed. Boston: Wadsworth.

Earth Law Center. 2017. *Universal Declaration of Rights of Rivers*. https://static1 .squarespace.com/static/55914fd1e4b01fb0b851a814/t/5c93e932ec212d197ab f81bd/1553197367064/Universal+Declaration+of+the+Rights+of+Rivers_Final .pdf.

EPA (Environmental Protection Agency). 2020. "Navigable Waters Protection Rule." EPA. April 20, 2020. https://www.epa.gov/nwpr/final-rule-navigable-waters-prote ction-rule.

Fisher, Douglas Edgar. 2010. *Australian Environmental Law: Norms, Principles and Rules*. Sydney, Australia: Thomson Reuters.

Foerster, Anita. 2007. "Victoria's New Environmental Water Reserve: What's in a Name?" *Australasian Journal of Natural Resources Law and Policy* 11 (2): 145.

Freeman, John, and John E. Jackson. 2012. "Symposium on Models of Path Dependence." *Political Analysis* 20, no. 2 (Spring): 137–45.

Gardner, Alex, Richard Bartlett, and Janice Gray. 2009. *Water Resources Law*. Chatswood, Australia: LexisNexis Butterworths.

Government of South Australia, Department of Energy and Water. n.d. "Millennium Drought." South Australia (website). https://www.environment.sa.gov.au/topics/river-murray/about-the-river/millennium-drought, accessed July 10, 2020.

Gunningham, Neil. 2009. "Environmental Law, Regulation and Governance: Shifting Architectures." *Journal of Environmental Law* 21 (2): 179–212.

Herberger, Matthew. 2011. "Australia's Millennium Drought: Impacts and Responses." In *The World's Water: The Biennial Report on Freshwater Resources*, ed. Peter Gleick. Island Press/Center for Resource Economics.

Hsiao, Elaine C. 2012. "Whanganui River Agreement: Indigenous Rights and Rights of Nature." *Environmental Policy and Law* 42 (6): 371–75.

Kauffman, Craig M., and Linda Sheehan. 2019. "The Rights of Nature: Guiding Our Responsibilities through Standards." In *Environmental Rights: The Development of Standards*, edited by Stephen Turner. Cambridge: Cambridge University Press.

Kildea, Paul, and George Williams. 2010. "The Constitution and the Management of Water in Australia's Rivers." *Sydney Law Review* 32: 595–616.

Kingdon, John W. 1984. *Alternatives, Agendas, and Public Policies*. Boston: Little Brown.

Kraft, Michael. 2017. *Environmental Policy and Politics*. 7th ed. New York: Routledge.

Lindbolm, Charles E. 1979. "Still Muddling, Not Yet Through." *Public Administration Review* 39, no. 6 (November-December): 517–26.

Magallanes, Catherine J. 2015. "Nature as Ancestor: Two Examples of Legal Personality for Nature in New Zealand." *Vertigo—La revue electronique en sciences de l'environment*. https://journals.openedition.org/vertigo/16199.

Margil, Mari. 2017. "Court Decisions Advance Legal Rights of Nature Globally." In *Rights of Nature and Mother Nature: Rights-Based Law for Systemic Change*, edited by Channon Biggs, Tom B.K. Goldtooth, and Osprey Orielle Lake. San Francisco: Movement Rights.

McConnaughy, Corrine. 2013. *The Woman Suffrage Movement in America: A Reassessment*. Cambridge, UK: Cambridge University Press.

McKernan, Michael. 2010. "Coming to Terms with the Reality of a Land Burnt Dry." *The Australian*, November 12, 2010. https://www.theaustralian.com.au/national-affairs/coming-to-terms-with-the-reality-of-a-land-burnt-dry/news-story/45e772910aa3e2e7f61d26e1604b1a52.

Menendez-Montalvo, Myriam. 2014. "*Consulta Previa: A Defining Issue for Latin America*." *Equals Change* (blog), Ford Foundation. August 14, 2014. https://www.fordfoundation.org/ideas/equals-change-blog/posts/consulta-previa-a-defining-issue-for-latin-america/.

Miller, Matthew. 2019. "Environmental Personhood and Standing for Nature: Examining the Colorado River Case." *University of New Hampshire Law Review* 17 (2): 355–78.

Minority Rights Group International. 2008. *World Directory of Minorities and Indigenous Peoples - Colombia: Afro-Colombians*. n.p.: Minority Rights Group International. https://www.refworld.org/docid/49749d3cc.html.

Naffine, Ngaire. 2003. "Who are Law's Persons? From Cheshire Cats to Responsible Subjects." *Modern Law Review* 66, no. 3 (May): 346–67. https://doi.org/10.1111/1468-2230.6603002.

NWC (National Water Commission). 2010. *Impacts of Water Trading in the Southern Murray—Darling Basin: An Economic, Social, and Environmental Assessment.* Canberra: Australian Government.

North, Douglass C. 1990. *Institutions, Institutional Change and Economic Performance.* Cambridge: Cambridge University Press.

O'Donnell, Erin. 2012. "Institutional Reform in Environmental Water Management: The New Victorian Environmental Water Holder." *Journal of Water Law* 22, no. 2 (January): 73–84.

O'Donnell, Erin, and Julia Talbot-Jones. 2017. "Legal Rights for Rivers: What Does this Actually Mean?" *Australian Environment Review* 32 (6): 159–62.

———. 2018. "Creating Legal Rights for Rivers Lessons from Australia New Zealand, and India." *Ecology and Society* 23 (1): 7. https://doi.org/10.5751/ES -0954-230107.

Page, Scott E. 2006. "Path Dependence." *Quarterly Journal of Political Science* 1 (1): 87–115. http://dx.doi.org/10.1561/100.00000006.

Sale, Kirkpatrick. 1993. *The Green Revolution: The American Environmental Movement, 1962–1992.* New York: Hill and Wang.

Smith, Kevin B. and Larimer, Christopher W. 2009. *The Public Policy Theory Primer.* Boulder: Westview.

Sohn, Emily. 2007. "The Big Dry: Prolonged Drought Threatens Australia's People, Wildlife, and Economy." *Science News* 172 (17): 266–68.

Stallworthy, Mark. 2008. *Understanding Environmental Law.* London: Sweet & Maxwell.

Stone, Christopher D. 1972. "Should Trees Have Standing? Towards Legal Rights for Natural Objects." *Southern California Law Review* 45: 450–501.

Troutman, Melissa. 2014. "Rights of Nature Report: Pennsylvania Ecosystem Fights Corporation for Rights in Landmark Fracking Lawsuit." *Public Herald,* December 10, 2014. https://publicherald.org/grant-township-speaks-for-the-trees-in-landma rk-fracking-lawsuit/.

Tschirhart, Céline, Jayalaxshmi Mistry, Andrea Berardi, Elisa Bignante, Matthew Simpson, Lakeram Haynes, Ryan Benjamin, Grace Albert, Rebecca Xavier, Bernie Robertson, Odacy Davis, Caspar Verwer, Géraud de Ville, and Deidre Jafferally. 2016. "Learning from One Another: Evaluating the Impact of Horizontal Knowledge Exchange for Environmental Management and Governance." *Ecology and Society* 21 (2): 41. http://dx.doi.org/10.5751/ES-08495-210241.

van Djik, Albert, Hylke E. Beck, Russell Crosbie, Richard de Jeu, Yi Y. Liu, Geoff M. Podger, Bertrand Timbal, and Neil R. Viney. 2013. "The Millennium Drought in Southeast Australia (2001–2009): Natural and Human Causes and Implications for Water Resources, Ecosystems, Economy and Society." *Water Resources Research* 49, no. 2 (February): 1040–57. https://doi.org/10.1002/wrcr.20123.

VEWH (Victorian Environmental Water Holder). 2013. *Reflections: Environmental Watering in Victoria 2012–13.* Melbourne, Australia: State Government of Victoria.

Wade, Peter. 1995. "The Cultural Politics of Blackness in Colombia." *American Ethnologist* 22, no. 2 (May): 341–57.

Chapter 22

The Titans at the Heart of the Anthropocene

Diving into the Nonhuman Imagery of Leviathan

Patrícia Castello Branco

This chapter considers the film *Leviathan* (Castaing-Taylor and Paravel, 2012), an experimental documentary filmed aboard a fishing trawler departed from Newport, Massachusetts—once the whaling capital of the world, made famous in Herman Melville's (1851) *Moby* Dick—which the directors used as their base of operations and observations. The film is an intimate portrait of a specific human practice—fishing—which here allows for an encounter with otherness: to see how the fishes see, to dive into the raw materiality of steel, to break with all types of humanism. In this manner, the film provides a sensory journey beyond the limits of human perception and understanding.

Leviathan begins with a black screen and strident metallic noises accompanied by the sounds of the wind and the sea. Slowly, light strokes begin to appear in silvery flashes on the darkened background. We catch glimpses of motion in blue and yellow and a stretch of indistinct green shapes. As the disoriented camera continues on, it shows fish and steel chains, a yellow shape, and bright foam against the black of the night sky. From these abstract colors and shapes, figurative forms begin to resolve: the yellow gives way to a man in rain gear and the blue motion becomes a glove pulling nets through the dark waters. As the camera situates the action aboard an industrial fishing trawler, viewers come to understand that the images they have just seen are fishing gear ruthlessly facing the fury of the natural elements. For the next eighty-four minutes, the cameras are caught with the fish inside the nets, accompany the flight of the seagulls, dive with the shoals, and travel inside the killing machinery of the fishing vessel. In the absence of any apparent order, guidelines, establishing shots or perspectives, they offer close and intimate snapshots of nonhuman bodies and matter. The resultant cinematic experience disorients points of view, confounding night and day and under-water and areal perspectives. Everything in *Leviathan*, as the title suggests, is grand, violent, hallucinatory, and strange.

In this chapter, I will examine *Leviathan*'s aesthetic framework through philosophical perspectives on the Anthropocene, nonhuman and multispecies encounters, and Heidegger's ideas on the essence of modern technology. My aim is to demonstrate that the film aligns with nonanthropocentric and nonhu-manistic aspects of experience, evoking the sensory understandings of other species that emerge from the convergence of two very specific materialities: the technological devices of image and sound recording and the bodies and matter they encounter (in this case, everything to do with the sea and the action of fishing, including fish, seagulls, raw fishing machinery, nets, and steel). At the core of the documentary, I argue, is the relationship between nature and technology and the human and the nonhuman. As we witness an attempt to see the world from within the intimacy of bodies and matter, we explore a new sensorium that functions as a kind of eco-criticism of the Anthropocene and its philosophical frameworks.

The chapter begins by exploring how the film's formal structure creates a "haptic way of seeing" that liberates images from a strictly human perspec-tive and allows for the illusion of a pure encounter with matter. In section 2, it probes into the way that encounter questions the philosophical perspectives of the Anthropocene, mainly its nature-culture divide. Section 3 brings technol-ogy into the analysis of the film's philosophical critique, considering the way it complicates the nature-culture divide by appearing as a hybrid, or even as an ally, of nature against culture. Section 4 continues to analyze the issue of technology in an attempt to demonstrate that, as a whole, the film is a visual demonstration of the essence of technique as *Ge-stell* (Heidegger), disclosing the dominant logic of the Anthropocene, which views nature as a permanent standing reserve (*Bestand*). Section 5 then explores *Leviathan*'s oscillation between a view of technology as the "supreme danger" and as "that which saves"—*Ereignis*—demonstrating how, from the depths of the technological ordering of the world, a *turn* can occur (*die Khere*, in Heidegger's words). In this film, such a *turn* is dependent on overcoming Heidegger's strictly human-centered phenomenological perspectives toward a material concep-tion of cinema as nonhuman perception. This latter idea will be addressed in section 6, where we briefly track its genealogy, focusing on the works of Dziga Vertov, Jean Epstein, and Siegfried Kracauer, among others. Departing from the film's underlying philosophical perspectives, this chapter concludes by exploring how the haptic experience of intimacy with matter can function as a form of eco-criticism, creating a new sensorium and urging nonanthro-pocentric ways of seeing and relating to the world.

PRODUCING DE-ANTHROPOMORPHIZED
IMAGERY THROUGH A HAPTIC EXPERIENCE
OF INTIMACY WITH THE MATERIAL WORLD

A De-anthropomorphized Imagery

Leviathan is a difficult work to categorize within the conventional genres of cinema. It can, nonetheless, be described as an experimental documentary, associating two seemingly contradictory terms.[1] On the one hand, like a documentary, the film focuses on something that pre-exists and is created neither by the imagination nor by the intellect of its authors. It is not a work of fiction. On the other hand, it is an experimental piece that largely discards all cinematographic conventions. In particular, *Leviathan* explores the full mobility and portability of the GoPro and miniature DSLR cameras used to film it. To capture the unconventional viewpoints and angles noted earlier, cameras were affixed to the heads, chests, and wrists of fishermen's bodies; underwater poles; and fishing nets that were repeatedly submerged and pulled from the water. They were thereby able to follow schools of fish and capture diving seagulls from an underwater perspective, with a few birds even hitting the cameras. The GoPros were also set on the top of the ship's mast, where they surveyed crewmembers working on a narrow deck and even accompanied an exhausted fisherman in a confined shower.

The action of removing the cameras from the standard, eye-level point of view liberates the film from the human perspective and creates de-anthropomorphized imagery. The formal options seem to acknowledge that the multiplicity of species and of (living and nonliving) entities in this ecosystem necessarily have different points of view. As the cameras take various perspectives, they refrain from privileging any one species in particular. All beings have the same status, are treated in the same way, and are given the same importance. This is confirmed by a detail at the end of the film; as Pat Dowell observes, "in the credits *Leviathan* lists not only the fishermen, unnamed in the course of the film, but also each bird species, the moon ('Luna'), the sea ('Mare'), and every fish species" (2013). By de-centralizing the points of view of human characters, the narrator, and directors, *Leviathon* inverts the conventional parameters of cinema. The holders of the point of view are not the human characters, the narrator, or even the directors. As Bégin notes, referring to the use of GoPro cameras in *Leviathan,*: "The GoPro camera is a recording device that emancipates the sensitivity of human and non-human bodies from the intelligible discourse normally expressed on their subject by an interpreter's gaze" (2016, 112). This radical shift away from human perspective is what we see in the first moments of the film, when we struggle to make sense of the myriad of light and sounds referred to in the introduction. The focus on sensorial experiences urges an abandonment of all attempts at rational interpretation of the pro-filmic material, creating an eminently haptic experience.

Riegl's "Haptic Functioning of the Eye" as a Centering on Matter

Before turning to the many characteristics of the haptic experience in *Leviathan*, let us briefly define the haptic and explain its conceptualization throughout the history of the visual arts. In *Late Roman Art Industry*, first published in 1901, Alois Riegl (1985) uses the term in contrasting a haptic to an optical perception. For him, the haptic or tactile refers to the lack of perspective or depth in Egyptian art, which he attributes not to the artists' lack of awareness of the mathematical rules of perspective, but to their lack of interest in the presentation of empty space. Egyptians considered space a mere absence of materiality, or emptiness. Since for them space connoted an absence—of bodies and matter—they didn't see the relevance of representing it. Rather, (deep) space was an obstacle to understanding the absolute individuality and materiality of an object. For this reason, Egyptian artists ignored depth, representing objects in a way that repressed foreshortening and shadows in what Riegl called a tactile perception (1985, 25). Focusing on the tactile would allow viewers to grasp separate entities in their material inviolability and presence. Touch, not sight, provided information about the closed surface of objects. From here, Riegl concludes that ancient art was predominantly tactile, engaging the eye to work like the hand, as exemplified in the Egyptians' bas-reliefs, which, according to Gilles Deleuze, Riegl describes as follows: "Bas-relief brings about the most rigid link between the eye and the hand because its element is *the flat surface*, which allows the eye to function like the sense of touch; furthermore, it confers, and indeed imposes, upon the eye a tactile, or rather *haptic,* function; it thereby ensures, in the Egyptian 'will to art,' the joining together of the two senses of touch and sight, like the soil and the horizon" (2005, 85). In other words, the haptic establishes a link between the eye and the hand, training the eye to behave like a hand.

In opposition to haptic art, Riegl describes optical art of the late Roman period. Optical art seeks to inscribe objects within an infinite and unified space. Governed by geometrical and mathematical rules, this space is abstract and deprived of materiality. Rather than emptiness, optical art sees space as the frame that organizes the relationship between objects. While haptic art focuses on the concrete, unique materiality of objects, optical art is more preoccupied with abstract rules and seeing from a distance (1985, 67). More specifically, it tends to home in on a single, object-independent space, equal in all circumstances and internally consistent, in which entities stand in their proper relationships. Riegl further explains that haptic vision emphasizes touch while optical vision minimizes it (1985, 26). His contrast of haptic versus optical art articulates the objective-abstract binary that goes on to govern his analysis.

Based on Riegl's pioneering analysis, the notion of the haptic has been further developed by Walter Benjamin (1935) in relation to the tactile quality of cinema, Gilles Deleuze (2005) through his concept of the "logic of sensation," and, more recently, Laura Marks (2000; 2002). It has been used to define a kind of perception that subverts optical-spatial organization, including that facilitated by Renaissance perspective, camera obscura, and photographic optical devices with linear coordinates and exterior and fixed viewpoints that offer a distant view.[2]

Erwin Panofsky (1991) and Maurice Merleau-Ponty (1964) have offered analyses of the Renaissance perspective that relate to the rediscovery of the haptic and its critique of modernity. Panofsky argues that because the optical *mimesis* based on Alberti's perspective was founded on an eminently mathematical model, it acquired the status of truth. He explains that perspective mathematized visual space and, in doing so, raised art to the status of truth, establishing the paradigm of both visuality and *mimesis* that would last for almost five centuries. During the Renaissance, the image of visual space was fully rationalized on a mathematical level. The era succeeded in accomplishing what had not previously been possible—a unitary and noncontradictory spatial construction of infinite extension in which bodies and intervals of empty space were united according to certain laws. Through Panofsky's argument, we can infer that by raising representative images to the status of "truth," the fifteenth-century visual model opened the door to the coronation of vision. The eye was treated as infinitely richer, more opulent, more magnificent—and above all, more "real"—than any other sense. In the Renaissance, the Enlightenment's equation of vision with reason (the eye and the rational mind) was already anticipated (1991, 29–31).

Following Panofsky's critique of the Renaissance, phenomenologist Maurice Merleau-Ponty (1964) views the construction of the image according to perspective rules as a tendency to replace "lived-space" with a mathematical, dematerialized, geometric, logical visual simulacrum. Rather than "naturalness," Merleau-Ponty associates these efforts with a cyclopean eye that is completely detached from the senses and the sensible world. Merleau-Ponty's criticism extends to Alberti's *construccione legittima* and to the Cartesian conception of space (1964, 50). Both seek to transform "lived space" into a network of relationships between objects seen by an external witness or a geometer that reconstructs them from a distance. The fixity, immobility, organization, continuity, and spatial uniformity that we find in Renaissance images legitimates the fantasy of omnivision and the illusion of the existence of a single point of view according to which the perceiving subject can relate to the objective world, which is neutrally detached from the subject and stands as an object or thing. In this manner, the fifteenth-century optical image prefigures modern objectivity.

Leviathan's Haptic Experience as a (Re)union with Matter

The haptic qualities of *Leviathan* rely on the consistent use of disorienting close-ups, taken as the GoPro cameras literally dive into matter, immersing themselves in the material entities. Impregnated with matter, the filmic angle establishes relationships with the entities (human and nonhuman) it encounters, embodying their movement and rhythm. The eye functions like the hand, "touching" the material entities and developing a strong proximity to the pro-filmic world. The viewer experiences the boat moving at an accelerated pace, the fish swimming swiftly, the nets ripping the animals from the sea, and the relentless slicing and cutting of the machines. In this manner, at its core *Leviathan* is an insubordinate celebration of flow, disorganization, and material existence. In addition to these elements, the film's hallucinatory montage offers an experience of fragmentation, as the editing dispenses with any external *logos* according to which images might be organized. Diverse points of view proliferate through the constant shift in perspective.

Christopher Pavsek stresses the extent to which *Leviathan* puts Castaing-Taylor's "visceral distrust of words or discursivity, a *logophobia*" into filmic practice (2015, 4). This logophobia, argues Pavsek,

> appears in Castaing-Taylor (and Paravel's) interviews in terms very familiar with 'Iconophobia'; as a distaste for, variously, propositional knowledge, narrative voiceover, the preresearched and the pretextualized, the false clarity of explanation, and didacticism more generally (5).

The "logophobia" that Pavsek discovers in *Leviathan* is manifest not only in the quasi-total absence of words but also in the film's annulment of the very logic that structures and allows for discursive thinking. In the place of such logic, or *logos*, it offers unfamiliar images filmed through disorientating perspectives and chaotic movements. The hegemony of the interpretive subject as the structuring basis of cinema gives way to a configuration centered neither on ideas, plot, dialogue, nor rational organization of any kind but on the presence and movement of bodies. We are left with physical sensations, disintegrated perceptions, flashes of light, and glances of movement that reunite the spectator with the material world.

Through the haptic qualities of *Leviathan*, viewers are called to abandon their usual, optical ways of seeing. The film proposes neither a set of ideas about industrial fishing nor even an appreciation of the clash provoked by the invasion of nature by human activity but rather something much deeper: it invites us to embark on a sensory journey beyond the human gaze. Paravel (2013) confirms that it was an anthropological imperative for her that the footage be created without anyone looking through the viewfinder of the camera. This allowed the film to be "embodied," as though "the body is the eye, basically" (2013).

That said, although it is true that the film addresses the "body as eye," the perspective of the cameras does not completely overlap with that of the fish or with the fisherman's body. Nor does it coincide with the body of the waves or of the boat. The cameras have a material body of their own. In this light, the nonhuman images are not simply "embodied." As technological material entities in their own right, the cameras offer their perspective on encounters with other entities, the most fascinating and vigorous of which occur at border crossings, such as the perspectives of the fish or the entanglement of the cameras with the flow of the fishing nets. Through the role of the camera, cinema provides a constant reminder of the role technological agency plays in configuring our worldview. Through its own form of embodiment, the camera in *Leviathan* eschews the imposition of an outside and abstract subject that assumes authoritative knowledge of the pro-filmic world and its ocular-centric conventions. It immerses itself in matter through technology, demonstrating that cinema is not merely a tool but a body in its own right. The resultant haptic experience is not simply one of embodiment but one of encounter, proximity, or intimacy among bodies taken as pure material entities.

THE GODS AND THE TITANS AT THE CORE OF THE ANTHROPOCENE

The film's title, *Leviathan*, refers simultaneously to a biblical maritime monster of fearful proportions, to the sea and its sublime features, and to the great Hobbesian Titan composed of human powers and governed by the logic of domination through force. But it also designates the film itself, as the technological devices of cinema function like a titan toward which spectators are sensorially dragged and submerged. As Scott MacDonald argues: "The film's title seems to be a reference to the Biblical Leviathan, a large sea monster or whale, but the leviathan in *Leviathan* is the film itself" (2013, 299). Like the Titans of Greek mythology, the biblical Leviathan is in conflict with the spiritual forces of culture. The reference confirms the way the film's entanglement with the natureculture divide places it in dialogue with one of the most important pillars of Western culture: the belief that there is an irreducible difference between culture and nature and an ongoing conflict between the two. This conception and its role in the Anthropocene's dominant worldview has been much debated.[3] As Donna Haraway observes: "The distinction between nature and culture has been a sacred one [in Western culture]; it lies at the heart of the great narratives of salvation history and their genetic transmutation into sagas of secular progress" (1997, 60).

In particular, Greek cosmogony conceived of the world as a continuing war between the Titans (natural forces) and the spiritual gods of Olympus. The latter are the founders of the very same culture that was delivered to humans by Prometheus's fire. In its turn, the Judeo-Christian religion is based on the idea that humans are different from the rest of creation. God, having created the universe and all living things, also created the masterpiece that is the human being, made in his image. It posits humankind as an exceptional species among the rest of creation and urges humans to uphold spirituality over their natural side, *animalitas*, which is frequently regarded as a source of evil and menace.

With the dawn of modernity, the difference between culture and nature began to rely on a distinction between humans and nonhumans, opposing what the latter lacks (spirit) and the former retains (reason). The Cartesian cogito, or Kant's transcendental subject, developed into an idea of human reason as a pure subject that relates to the world taken as a pure object. As such, modernity's idea of progress rests on the belief that nature, deprived of spirituality, is a stable and constant standing reserve upon which humanity can exercise its domination and power. Juxtaposed to this conception of human exceptionalism is the idea that nature is "without world." As Bruno Latour highlights, since nature and things have no world, they are also conceived of as being without agency:

> Most of the social sciences and most of philosophy since Kant have been without a world. Things do nothing. What you learn at the beginning of sociology, especially if it's continental theory, Bourdieu or Frankfurt, is precisely that things do not act. Are we so naive as to think that things act? No, we know very well that it's the projection of our own society and value onto things which do nothing. (2003, 79)

Because nature has no world, it is considered a pure object, a mere setting without agency, spirit, or *logos*. As Derrida writes in his reflections on the use of the word "animal":

> Animal is a word that men have given themselves the right to give. These humans are found giving it to themselves, this word, but as if they had received it as an inheritance. They have given themselves the word in order to corral a

large number of human beings within a single concept: 'the Animal', they say. And they have given it to themselves, this word, at the same time according themselves, reserving for them, for humans, the right to the word, the name, the naming noun (nom), the verb, the attribute, to a language of words, in short to the very thing that the others in question would be deprived of, those that are corralled within the grand territory of the beasts: The Animal. All the philosophers we will investigate (from Aristotle to Lacan, and including Descartes, Kant, Heidegger, and Levinas), all them say the same thing: the animal is deprived of language. (2008, 32)

Leviathan unfolds within this worldview, revolving around the encounter between the human and the nonhuman, which takes the form of a series of confrontations between the ocean and the boat's hull; the fish's living bodies and the serial-killing machines on-board the trawler; and the flight of the seagulls and the industrial treatment of living matter. The resultant imagery illustrates the disruption caused by the intrusion of industrial fishing devices in the ocean and their encounter with the material bodies (living and nonliving) in the sea's natural ecosystem.

The montage of images in the film also facilitates a cinematic enquiry into the possibility of multispecies encounters. Castaing-Taylor explains that the film's main aim was to question "where to situate humanity in the cosmos we were constructing." As he continues,

For all of the inherent anthropomorphism of cinema, we had a kind of posthumanist ambition to relativize the human in a larger physical and metaphysical domain of both interspecies bestiality and of animate-inanimate promiscuity, one in which humans, fish, birds, machines, and the elements would have a kind of restless ontological parity. (MacDonald 2013, 327)

He further explains: "We still wanted to create this multiplicity of perspectives that would relativize the human," perspectives that

would make the spectator rethink humanity's relationship to nature, in relationship to a plethora of other beings, of other animals, of other kinds of inanimate objects—the elements, the earth, the sky, the sea, the boat, mechanization, fish, crustaceans, starfish—everything that is involved in the ecology of what's going on in industrial fishing today (Castaing-Taylor and Paravel 2013).

TECHNOLOGY AS A THIRD ELEMENT IN
THE NATURE-CULTURE BINARY

Throughout the eighteenth and nineteenth centuries, technology acquired a profound emancipatory meaning, on the one hand, liberating humankind from hard labor and, on the other, guaranteeing its increased sovereignty over the natural world. It became the great ally of the human project of dominating nature. As a result of this framework, in Western cultures, humans have come to see culture as unmistakably separate from nature and "progress" as the development of the technological and scientific knowledge that guarantees their continued supremacy over the natural world. In *Leviathan*, this very conception reveals some of its most brutal features. At first, technology seems to be on the side of culture in conquering the natural world. As the film unfolds, however, that perspective begins to weaken. The camera aligns itself more with a nonhuman point of view, stressing the violent yet sublime sides of the technological enterprise, which, in this sense, parallels the force of the ocean. It shows that an act like fishing is not only violent from the perspective of nonhuman entities but that the humans involved are also technologically mobilized and forced to adjust to the very same willingness that invades the natural environment.

In this vein, the film also oscillates between showing technological agency as a human activity (which is manifest in its portrayal of industrial fishing machinery), and stressing its overwhelming power as a force that transcends humans. It emphasizes that humans themselves are deeply technologically ordered and managed, situated within a logic where their actions are enmeshed with those of industrial machinery. As filmic techniques level the distinction between humans and other objects, they become an integral part of a gear that transcends human subjectivity. It is here where the film stages its critique of the role that technology plays within the Anthropocene's nature-culture divide, giving rise to the questions: Is technology in fact a mere instrument in the hands of humanity for dominating nature? Or does it hide other attributions, other essences, other agencies?

Ernst Jünger's conception of technology as a manifestation of the "natural will to power," which he borrowed from Nietzsche, can help us further interpret the role technology plays in the film. Jünger (2017) believes that technology, like a storm, is a natural force committed to power, not an instrument of human culture. Rather than create new technological forms, he argues that the pursuit of technological "progress" brings natural forces, which have been unveiled by science, into the cultural realm. In this manner, technology becomes a tool or a "Trojan horse" by which nature, in the passionate will to power at work in all of life, conquers culture (2017). Applied to *Leviathan*, Jünger's insights underlie the experience of technology as a natural force or a nonhuman potency, which are echoed by Martin Heidegger's conception of modern technology both as "the supreme danger" and as "that which saves" (1977, 28).[4] Interpreted through Heidegger and Jünger's theories on technology, the film seems to endorse the view that "modern technology is no merely human doing" (Heidegger 1977, 19). But, what exactly does this mean? What does it mean to say that modern technology is "no merely human doing," and how does this idea apply to *Leviathan*?

THE TECHNOLOGICAL DETERMINATION OF THE ANTHROPOCENE AS THE "SUPREME DANGER"

According to Heidegger, the question "What is technology?" usually results in one of two answers: "One says: technology is a means to an end. The other says: technology is a human activity" (1977, 4). The former corresponds to the instrumental conception of technology, the latter to the anthropocentric. Both endorse all of the misinterpretations of the humanistic/modernist project of ruling and dominating the natural world. In addition, Heidegger argues that the essence of technique (*techné*) has changed since the advent of modernity: it is characterized not by production or making (*Her-stell*) but by enframing (*Ge-stell*).

In German, the term *stell*—common to all kinds of *techné*—denotes making; in the Heideggerian context, it therefore takes on the meaning of disclosure, bringing into presence, or putting into work, and acquires a provocative, violent connotation when applied to technology. While nature is forced to release or supply its energy, the energy of *Ge-stell*, or modern technology, is a "violent setting-upon, in the sense of a challenging-forth" (Heidegger 1973, 479). It is a "provocation" in which all that is disclosed is forced to take a predeterminate configuration: "Nature, made available to provide energy, now appears as a '*reservoir*' of energy." If nature supplies its energy, man is forced (*gestellt*) to respond and correspond to the energies that are produced, to the point that we can say: "The greater the provocation of nature, the greater the provocation to which man himself is subjected" (1973, 480). It's important to stress that the disclosure carried out by modern technology does not simply produce, it provokes. It thus denotes an ordering (*Bestellen*)[5] and a provocation (*Herausforderung*). We see this combination in the term *Herausfordern*, which comprises the verb *fordern* (to provoke, to intimidate, to demand) and the prefixes *her* (to here) and *aus* (out, uncovered). It literally means to demand the exit (the appearance) here. What does this mean? What precisely does it mean to say that modern technology does not produce but rather provokes? According to Heidegger, modern technology orders in the double sense of the verb "to order": it commands, and therefore necessarily intimidates, and it puts things in a specific organization. Everything it discloses is automatically framed in a previous configuration. There is no space for the unexpected or for the indeterminate; there is no production in which entities are simply allowed to disclose or unveil themselves freely. Rather, humans enter a field in which entities are violently forced to disclose what is hidden according to a previous frame. The provocation is maximal.

In *Leviathan*, Heidegger's description of modern technology is evoked through the ordering of all entities according to the external logic of industrial fishing: the ocean is reduced to a mere standing reserve; the serialized fish-killing machines serve as the frames within which all entities are filtered, organized and put in order; and the cinematic devices capture the world and rearrange it according to a pre-given structure. All beings in the film thus appear under the aegis of technological ordering and provocation. Through the recurrent shots from inside the fishing nets, animals are forcibly removed from the vast, fluid habitat of the ocean and placed into serial production machines, where their bodies are cut according to the logic of industrial organization. The provocation and ordering of fish then extends to all entities in this environment. The ocean, waves, seagulls, and even humans and their fishing gear all appear under what Heidegger would describe as *Bestand* (standing reserve),[6] which refers to the way entities are disclosed under technological *enframing*. As stressed, Heidegger argues that with modern technology, humans (who are the agents of provocation toward the world) are also strongly provoked. Thus, he argues that *Ge-stell* is the "reciprocal provocation of man and being for the calculation of what is calculable" (1991, 146). With modern technology, entities are provoked to disclose what is hidden in them in a nonharmonious way, nullifying any other possibilities of disclosure.

Having already analyzed the meaning of the term *Stellen* in this context, the key to further understanding this process is an analysis of the prefix *Ge-* in the term *Ge-stell*. Heidegger (1973, 479) clarifies that the *Ge-* in *Ge-stell* serves as a concentration of all modes of *stellen*. It strives to express the gathering of all forms of setting upon and disclosing, the assembling of all possibilities of configuration into a single point. Thus, *Ge-stell* aims to denote a specific constellation in which all other forms of making disappear. As explained, in modern technology, everything is standardized, ordered, and provoked. This explains why the *Ge-stell*, or the essence of modern technology, is seen as the "supreme danger," annihilating any other possibilities of *stellen*.[7] As a result, the provocation carried out by technology also entails the total closure of the Real. Only that which occupies a pre-given position in a previously established structure is disclosed; only that which fits on the informative grid of the Real can be unveiled. Thus, the *Ge-stell* is "the danger" because it obliterates any other forms of disclosing. It also hides itself as a form of unveiling, disguising its essence under the cover of "instrumentality" to appear instead as an instrument of progress, a tool for the inevitable drive of culture toward development, power, and domination over nature.

As we have seen, the attributions of modern technology as the "supreme danger" are clear in *Leviathan*. The film vividly embodies the essence of modern technology as *Ge-stell*. However, *Leviathan* also affects a rupture, perhaps opening the door to what Heidegger, borrowing from Hölderlin, would designate as "that which saves." As Heidegger theorizes later in his career, the "saving power" emerges from within the ever-growing danger in modern technology. Whereas in *The Question Concerning Technology* (1977), Heidegger first described the main characteristic of *Bestand* as a "stable position," fifteen years later he believed that this "stable position" was in a process of deep transformation. He came to view the main characteristics of *Bestand* as consisting of "permanent availability" and *Eretzbarkeit*, or the "fact that each entity becomes essentially replaceable, in a generalized game where everything takes the place of everything" (1973, 456). As technology develops, the stable position becomes more of a "permanent availability," where things lose all identity. Thus,

> *Bestand's* ontological determination (of the entity as standing reserve) is not *Beständigkeit* (stable position), but *Beistellbarkeit*, the constant possibility of being commanded and commanded, that is, of being permanently available. In *Bestellbarkeit*, the entity is presented as fundamentally and exclusively available—available for consummation in the global calculation (1973, 456).

This reformulation of the characteristics of the standing reserve is concomitant with the development of new electronic and digital technologies as opposed to mechanical ones. But it is also dependent on a strategy that is internal to the very development of Heidegger's thought. For Heidegger, overcoming the "supreme danger" corresponds to the "emergence" of a new stage in the relationship between man and being and is theorized in the idea of *Ereignis*.[8]

Overcoming Phenomenology: Multispecies Encounters and the Intimacy of Bodies, Materials, and Sensorialities

As Heidegger posits later in his life, technology also introduces disruptive elements in relation to modernity's logical-scientific thinking. Through technological agency, a new fluidity replaces the objectivity characteristic of modern thought. Liberating the fixed, stable attributions of objects, *Ge-stell* sets forth an impulse that dissolves objects into an indistinct mass, the standing reserve, that combines object and subject, nature and culture, natural beings and artifacts, and the pro-filmic world and that created by cinematic devices. Modern technology is thereby part of a process of endless disintegration, redistribution, and re-aggregation. Dreyfus and Spinosa describe the Heideggerian dissolution of subject and object as "a corollary of the rapid changes in identity and technologically assisted multi-perspectivism in this post-human era that can also be an announcing sign of 'that which saves'" (1997, 173). Stressing that Heidegger's diagnosis of modern technology is thus not totally negative, they write that it "free[s] us from having a total fixed identity so that we may experience ourselves as multiple identities disclosing multiple worlds is what Heidegger calls technology's saving power" (173). In the same vein, Arthur Kroker (2004, 33–73) posits that what he terms a "hyper-Heidegger" would help us see that contemporary "hyper-technologies" can, through a permanent deconstruction of the realm in which they move, open the door to a new type of relation to the world.

It is this type of relation that comes forth in *Leviathan.* Through Heidegger, we can understand the film's technologically assisted multi-perspectivism as what makes possible the multispecies encounters, nonanthropocentric views, and haptic experience. The decentralization of the senses that occurs during the viewing experience uncouples perception from the hegemony of the eye's abstract and logocentric liaisons. Analyzing the extent to which the particular ordering and provocation brought by the technological fishing activity becomes visible and can be recognized as such, as Heidegger envisages, would allow us to more precisely locate the *Ereignis* in the film. It is clear that the entire film is a visual demonstration of the essence of the technique as *Ge-stell* that addresses nature as a permanent standing reserve (*Bestand*). It relies on raw images of violent encounters between living beings and machinery, disclosing the predatory logic of industrial fishing from a nonhuman perspective. Deprived of all anthropocentrism, what stands out is the brutality of the provocation directed against all beings in that environment. In this case, technology ceases to hide its essence as *Ge-stell,* which Heidegger describes as a first step toward radical change, a *turn.* The brutal logic of the *Ge-stell* that we experience cannot leave us indifferent. Its titanic dimensions appear as a "supreme danger" to both human and nonhuman beings.

The idea that the *Ge-stell* can bring about its own overcoming is embodied in this film, not only through the unveiling of technology's essence, but also through the dissolution of the division between object and subject, or nature and culture. The immersion into nonhuman points of view brought on through the film's haptic imagery initiates an abandonment of the anthropocentric, pointing toward a way out of modernity's thinking and toward a new relationship to nature and other species. Nonetheless, it remains important to stress that even as *Leviathan* incorporates much of Heidegger's critiques of technology (and some of his hopes), it distances itself from key Heideggerian views—mainly from his accounts of animals as being wordless, understood as a deficient mode of human existence. In this sense, the film's main aspiration is not a Heideggerian project of reencountering the Anthropos but of overcoming it. Seen in this way, *Leviathan* embodies the way in which modern technology can transform and pervert not only ocular- and logocentrism but also anthropocentrism, as images expand beyond the limits of the human body and human "unveiling."

FILM AS NONHUMAN PERCEPTION: A SENSORY JOURNEY BEYOND THE LIMITS OF THE HUMAN AND A NEW SENSORIUM

Leviathan demonstrates the extent to which film has the capacity to create nonhuman images that emerge from the convergence of two materialities: the technological devices of image recording and editing and the bodies and matter they encounter in the process. This idea is not new to the long history of cinema. Early film theorists of the 1920s and 1930s, including Dziga Vertov, Jean Epstein, and Siegfried Kracauer, all posited that the technological essence of cinema allows us to see and hear beyond the human eye and ear. All three located cinema's most important quality in its ability to uncover features of reality that are otherwise invisible to human perception. Vertov famously summarizes this idea through his description of film as a "mechanical" or "kino-eye":

> I am a kino-eye, I am a mechanical eye. I, a machine, show you the world as only I can see. Now and forever, I free myself from human immobility. I am in constant motion. I draw near, then away from objects. I crawl under, I climb onto them. I move apace with the muzzle of a galloping horse, I plunge full speed into a crowd, I outstrip running soldiers, I fall on my back, I ascend with an airplane, I plunge and soar together with plunging and soaring bodies. . . . Free from the sixteen-seventeen frames per second, free of the limits of time and space, I put together any given points in the universe, no matter where I've recorded them. My path leads to the creation of a fresh perception of the world. I decipher in a new way a world unknown to you. (1984, 17–18)

The GoPro cameras and other filming and editing devices in *Leviathan* indeed function as a "kino-eye," making visible aspects of the world that the stable human point of view cannot grasp.

Epstein, along with other filmmakers of the first French avant-garde, shared Vertov's premise through the idea of the "intelligence of the machine" (2014). Epstein saw film in particular as a thinking machine, or an eye outside of the eye, whose power to see both surpasses and adds to

the power of the human eye. By showing us the world from a nonsubjec-
tive, nonhuman perspective, film becomes a "revelatory medium."[9] Both
the mechanical eye of the camera and cinema's ability to highlight motion
contribute to this capacity, since they can capture the mobility of reality, as
opposed to the human tendency to immobilize through perception. Epstein
summarizes these theories in the concept of *Photogenie*, which he considers
to be "the purest expression of cinema" (1924, 6). During the first decades
of cinema, *photogénie* was defined as a relationship involving the mediation
and transformation of the Real through the camera, editing, and the screen. It
acquired a quasi-magical quality that rendered previously unknown visions—
inconceivable without the technological union of the lens and reality—and
offered nonhuman visions and perspectives. Epstein's *photogenie,* more
specifically, condenses the pro-filmic world with the mechanical (camera,
editing, and projection) and the filmmaker's subjectivity, summarizing film's
revelatory quality: "Cinema can get a new power that, renouncing the logic
of facts, engenders a sequence of unknown visions—inconceivable outside
the union of objective and the mobile film" (1924, 6). *Photogenie* offers a
pleasure that the viewer can neither describe verbally nor rationalize cognitively. It permits the association of film with the experience of the irrational
and incommensurable, facilitating access to realities and dimensions that
did not exist prior to the encounter between the lens, celluloid, light, and
the object being filmed. Germaine Dulac also famously used the term *photogénie* to summarize the potential of cinematographic technological devices
that fuse the technological with "reality" through "the shot and the shooting
angles, the fade, the dissolve, superimposition, soft focus, and distortions"
(1924, 306). Rather than eliminating reality, Dulac's version of *photogénie*
transforms it into something completely new (Delluc 1920).

In the same line of thought, and more than a decade later, Siegfried
Kracauer will criticize modernity's emphasis on abstractions, for which science is the main responsible (1997, 50), and will praise cinema's capacity
to address and deal directly with matter. Bresson will also refer to: "That
which no human eye is capable of capturing, any pencil, brush, feather of
fixing, your camera captures without knowing what it is and fixes it with the
scrupulous indifference of a machine" (1986, 26). He further explains: "Your
camera catches not only physical movements that are inapprehensible by
pencil, brush or pen, but also certain states of soul recognizable by indices
which it alone can reveal" (97).

In the same spirit, almost a century later, *Leviathan* finds a nonhuman perspective through the mechanical eye of the GoPro. Liberated from a human
perspective, a fluidity forms in the material dimensions of the world, allowing
for a surfacing of the nonhuman presence in what seems hostile and foreign.
While understanding that the nonhuman can never be entirely integrated into

subjectivity or human meaning, *Leviathan* aims to situate it into a particular expression of life that unfolds independently of human perception.

The film, in this sense, is an aesthetic experiment that questions the extent to which it is possible to access the nonhuman world without reducing it to an inhumane humanity or glorifying it as a kind of underlying structure whose connection to the human can be found in embodied perception. The constant dismemberment of images, the successive temporal and spatial collapses, and the dizzying visual and sound montage all contribute to the film's aim of resisting anthropocentric thinking. The filmic experience struggles permanently against the urge to settle into a fixed viewpoint, concept, or interpretation, looking for meaning beyond the physicality of matter. It achieves this through the dual process of creating the imagery with the GoPro cameras and organizing the images and sounds in editing. It is via these two levels that the film effectively "touches" the spectator and provides him or her with the uncanny sensory experience of being beyond the human. In this manner, the visuality of *Leviathan* conditions the possibility of encounters between the human and the nonhuman. Its haptic experience functions as the place in which bodies—technological devices, the vessel, the sea water, the human bodies of the spectators, and the marine bodies of the ocean animals—can resonate without being reduced either to each other or to the Anthropos.

CONCLUDING REMARKS:
RE-FRAMING ECOLOGICAL PERCEPTION THROUGH
ECOLOGICAL CRITICISM AND A NEW SENSORIUM

In opposition to erudite art forms, which foster the optical perception that accepts the authoritarian "aura" of an object, Benjamin (1935) allows us to view the tactile possibilities of popular cinema that initiate a haptic viewing experience. Through "tactile perception," the contemplative value of optical art is replaced by a use value that inhabits a work of art. The audience becomes involved in the work, playing an active role in the interpretation of meaning and, in the process, acknowledging the lack of a pre-given reality or natural order. In other words, the process of viewing a film facilitates the realization that "reality" and "meaning" are constructions, created in tandem by filmmakers and spectators. Even if not fully aware of the process, a state that Benjamin describes as "absent-minded," audiences produce interpretations and criticism continually as they watch a film (1935, 19). They are not passive viewers but active players whose perception of reality is being challenged through perceptive shocks even if they are not aware of the critical embodied processes they are performing (1935, 17). Cinema's spectator,

Benjamin stresses, integrates criticism in the very act of perception. The perception of film's perception is critical in itself.

Before Benjamin's theory on film, this idea was already an important aesthetic value in Dadaism, which aimed to generate moral shocks that would challenge social, political, and cultural values. Futurism viewed "perceptive shocks" as signs of a new era dominated by mechanistic relationships and machines. Movements like the Bauhaus in Germany, De Stijl in the Netherlands, and Constructivism in Russia all thought that technological shocks accompanied the development of modern technology and could be instruments of social liberation. Influenced by these ideas, experimental filmmakers believed that cinema held a privileged position when it came to questioning old conceptions and views. As a medium of the senses, it works directly on the nervous system, creating physical disruptions and a new kind of viewer. It is able to produce not only moral shocks but also physical ones. In this sense, avant-garde artists anticipated (and likely inspired) Benjamin's ideas about the physical disruption produced by cinema and its tactile dimension. All of these strategies are closely connected to the exploration and development of the technological aspect of cinema and its facilitation of a nonhuman vision.

Following in the vein of the nonhuman, post-anthropocentric perspectives such as that of *Leviathan* undermine the notion of humans as "unique, isolated entities," drawing us instead, as Robert Pepperell argues, "towards a conception of existence in which the human is totally integrated with the world in all its manifestations, including nature, technology, and other beings" (quoted in King and Page 2017, 164). Because *Leviathan* dwells in human and nonhuman encounters, it leads to an understanding of human culture according to a model of distributed agency that transcends divisions between the human and the nonhuman. It reminds us that humans are not outside observers of the world. Nor are "they simply located at particular places *in* the world; rather, we are part *of* the world in its ongoing intra-activity" (181). Due to its experimental features, *Leviathan* raises deep questions on the subject of perception, offering real possibilities beyond the usual ways of interpreting the world and the images that prompt perceptual shocks. The film struggles to disrupt our usual perceptions by challenging our viewing habits and expectations. In doing so, it contributes to our wider ecological awareness, grasping a new ecological sensorium that will be able to question the Anthropocene at its very heart, that is, in its own perceptual and cognitive relation to the nonhuman.

As we have seen, *Leviathan*'s aim of de-anthropomorphizing our point of view leads us to abandon the human *logos*, overcoming ocularcentrism and moving within a haptic visuality that promotes immersion, proximity, intimacy, nonhuman points of view, and the abandonment of anthropocentric relations to the world. The abandonment of *logos* is achieved not only through focusing on the haptic but also through the succession of physically disturbing experiences. Loud noises, clashes of images, hallucinatory montages, the confusion of day and night, and disorienting points of view all prompt the total abandonment of reflexive thinking, welcoming a subversion of orientation. The film thereby demonstrates that in our careful distinctions between nature and culture, there exists another seemingly contrary phenomenon: the entanglement of technology and nature, of humans and nonhumans. As images and sounds proliferate, the prospect of keeping nature and culture (the two Leviathans in the film) in separate chambers becomes increasingly unlikely. We experience a new kind of bodily entanglement. As such, what *Leviathan* ultimately offers is a new challenge to an art form that has the capacity to reveal the connections between matter, providing a glimpse into a post-Anthropocene era.

NOTES

1. On the relation between documentary and experimental film, see MacDonald 2015 and Unger 2017.

2. On the relation between the optical visuality, Renaissance perspective, modernity, and the ocular devices of cinema and photography see Panofsky 1991; Merleau-Ponty 1964; Crary 1990; and Levin 1993.

3. See, among others, Latour 1993; Descola 2013; and Viveiros de Castro 1996.

4. On Jünger's influence on Heidegger's thoughts on modern technology, see Zimmerman 1990, 66–75. The quotations given in the text are related to Heidegger's phrase: "But where danger is, grows the saving power also" (1977, 28).

5. I here follow W. Lovitt's translation, using *bestellen* for "*to order.*" See Heidegger 1977, 51.

6. *Bestand* usually denotes a store or supply that is standing by. It carries the connotation of the verb *bestehen*, with its dual meaning of *to last* and *to undergo*. Here, I follow W. Lovitt's translation of *Bestand* as "standing reserve." See Heidegger 1977, 16.

7. *Die Gefahr* (The Danger) is, in fact, the title of an essay which, along with *Das Ding* (The Thing), *Das Ge-stell* and *Die Kehre* (The Turning), complete a set of four lectures that Heidegger delivered in December 1949 under the title *Einblick in das, was ist*. Tracing these helps understand why Heidegger considers modern technology to be the "supreme danger."

8. *Ereignis* literally means "event," "chance," "occurrence." According to Heidegger, "the word *Ereignis* is taken from natural language. *Er-eignen* (to happen) originally means: *er-äugnen*, that is, to discover with the eye, to awake with the eye, to appropriate. . . . The word is now used as *singulare tantum*. What it designates only occurs in the singular" (1991, 145).

9. On the issue of Epstein's conception of film as a revelatory medium, see Turvey 1998; Turvey 2008; and Wall-Romana 2013.

BIBLIOGRAPHY

Bégin, Richard. 2016. "Go-Pro Augmented Bodies, Somatic Images." In *Screens: from Materiality to Spectatorship—A Historical and Theoretical Reassessment*, edited by Dominique Chateau and José Moure, 107–15. Amsterdam: Amsterdam University Press.

Benjamin, Walter. 1935. *The Work of Art in the Age of Mechanical Reproduction*. In *Illuminations*, edited by Hannah Arendt, translated by Harry Zohn. New York: Schocken Books, 1969.

Bresson, Robert. 1986. *Notes on Cinematography*, translated by Jonathan Griffin. London: Quartet Encounters.

Castaing-Taylor, Lucien and Véréna Paravel. 2013. "Leviathan: The Fishing Life, from 360 Degrees." Interview by Pat Dowel. *NPR*, March 16, 2013. https://www.npr.org/2013/03/16/174404938/leviathan-the-fishing-life-from-360-degrees.

Castro, Viveiros de. 1996. "Os Pronomes Cosmológicos e o Perspectivismo Ameríndio." *MANA* 2 (2): 115–44.

Crary, Jonathan. 1990. *Techniques of the Observer: On Vision and Modernity in the Nineteenth Century*. Cambridge, MA: MIT Press.

Deleuze, Gilles. 2005. *Francis Bacon: The Logic of Sensation*. Minneapolis: Continnum.

Delluc, Louis. 1920. "Photogénie." In *Photogénie*. Paris: Editions de Brunoff.

Derrida, Jacques. 2008. *The Animal that Therefore I Am*. New York: Fordham University Press.

Descola, Philippe. 2013. *Beyond Nature and Culture,* translated by Janet Lloyd. Chicago: University of Chicago Press.

Dreyfus, Hubert L., and Charles Spinosa. 1997. "Highway Bridges and Feasts: Heidegger and Borgmann on How to Affirm Technology." *Man and World* 30, no. 2 (January): 159–77. https://doi.org/10.1023/A:1004299524653.

Dulac, Germaine. 1924. "Les procédés expressifs du cinema." *Cinémagazine*, July 4, 1924. Translated in *French Film: Theory and Criticism, 1907–1939*, vol. I, organized by Richard Abel, 305–14. (Princeton: Princeton University Press, 1988).

Epstein, Jean. 1924. "Ce quelques conditions de la photogénie." *Cinéa-Ciné pour tous,* August 15, 1924, 6–8.

———. 2014. *The Intelligence of a Machine*, translated by Christophe Wall-Romana. Minneapolis: Univocal Publishing.

Haraway, Donna.1997. *Modest Witness@Second Millenium.FemaleMan_Meets_ OncoMouse. Feminism and Technoscience*. London: Routledge.

Heidegger, Martin. 1958. "La Chose." In *Essais et Conférences*, translated by André Préau, 194–218. Paris: Editions Gallimard.

———. 1973. "Séminaire de Zähringen." In *Questions III et IV*, 4, translated by André Préau, 69–488. Paris: Gallimard.

————. 1977. "The Question Concerning Technology." In *The Question Concerning Technology and Other Essays*, translated by W. Lovitt, 3–36. New York: Harper & Row.

————. 1977. "The Turning." In *The Question Concerning Technology and Other Essays*, translated by W. Lovitt, 36–49. New York: Harper & Row.

————. 1991. "O Princípio da Identidade." In *Heidegger,* 137–47. São Paulo: Nova Cultural.

Jünger, Ernst. 2017. *The Worker: Domination and Form*, translated by Bogdan Costea and Laurence Paul Hemming. Evanston: Northwestern University Press.

King, Edward and Joanna Page. 2017. *Posthumanism and the Graphic Novel in Latin America*. London: UCL Press.

Kracauer, Siefried. 1997. *Theory of Film, the Redemption of Physical Reality*. Princeton: Princeton University Press.

Kroker, Arthur. 2004. *The Will to Technology and the Culture of Nihilism: Heidegger, Nietzsche, and Marx*. Toronto: University of Toronto Press.

Latour, Bruno. 1993. *We Have Never Been Modern*, translated by Catherine Porter. Cambridge, MA: Harvard University Press.

————. 2003. "A Strong Distinction between Humans and Non-humans Is No Longer Required for Research Purposes: A Debate between Bruno Latour and Steve Fuller." *History of the Human Sciences* 16 (2): 77–99.

Levin, David Michael. 1993. *Modernity and the Hegemony of Vision*. Berkeley: University of California Press.

MacDonald, Scott. 2013. "Conversations on the Avant-Doc: Scott MacDonald Interviews." *Framework: The Journal of Cinema and Media* 54, no. 2 (Fall): 261–330.

————. 2015. *Avant-Doc: Intersections of Documentary and Avant-Garde Cinema*. Oxford: Oxford University Press.

Marks, Laura. 2000. *The Skin of the Film*. Durham: Duke University Press.

————. 2002. *Touch: Sensuous Theory and Multisensory Media*. Minneapolis: Minneapolis University Press.

Merleau-Ponty, Maurice. 1964. *"The Film and the New Psychology."* In *Sense and Non-Sense,* translated by H. L. Dreyfus and P. A. Dreyfus. Evanston: Northwestern University Press.

Panofsky, Erwin. 1991. *Perspective as Symbolic Form*. New York: Zone Books.

Paravel, Véréna. 2012. "An Interview with Véréna Paravel and J. P. Sniadecki." By Patricia Alvarez Astacio. *Society for Cultural Anthropology*, December 17, 2012. https://culanth.org/fieldsights/an-interview-with-verena-paravel-and-j-p-sniadecki.

Pavsek, Christopher. 2015. "Leviathan and the Experience of Sensory Ethnography." *Visual Anthropology Review* 31, no. 1: 4–11.

Riegl, Alois. 1985. *Late Roman Art Industry*. Rome: Giorgio Bretschneider. First published 1901.

Turvey, Malcolm. 1998. "Jean Epstein's Cinema of Immanence: The Rehabilitation of the Corporeal Eye." *October* 83 (Winter): 25–50.

————. 2008. *Doubting Vision: Film and Revelationist Tradition*. Oxford: Oxford University Press.

Unger, Michael. 2017. "Castaing-Taylor and Paravel's GoPro Sensorium: Leviathan (2012), Experimental Documentary, and Subjective Sounds." *Journal of Film and Video* 69, no. 3 (Fall): 3–18

Vertov, Dziga. 1984. *Kino-Eye: The Writings of Dziga* Vertov, translated by Kevon O'Brian. Berkeley: University of California Press.

Wall-Romana, Christophe. 2013. *Jean Epstein: Corporeal Cinema and Film Philosophy*. Manchester: Manchester University Press.

Zimmerman, Michael. 1990. *Heidegger's Confrontation with Modernity: Technology, Politics, Art*. Bloomington: Indiana University Press.

Chapter 23

Listen to the Lake

Nature as Stakeholder

Kathy Isaacson

How can salmon have a voice when policy-makers consider genetically modifying their species? Rather than considering salmon a commodity like other factory-farmed animals, how can they be included as stakeholders when considering the future of food (Seibert 2019)? Communication plays an essential role in constructing human-nature relations. Ecocultural communication explores the misconception that nature is a simple set of resources for human use, inviting stakeholders to engage with the interconnectivity of humans and the natural world (Parks 2020).

Stakeholders, those who have a "stake" or an interest in the outcome of an issue, are increasingly wondering if nature can be engaged as an equal participant. In Yosemite National Park, there is a grove of 2,000-year-old Sequoia trees surrounded by aging park infrastructure. A three-year restoration project did consider the trees a stakeholder: "At each stage of the project, the team asks: Is this in the best interest of the trees?" (Bishel 2019). They saw a moral obligation to respect that interdependence (Haigh and Griffins 2009).

Various strands of environmental communication invite the communication discipline to change the conceptualization of *internatural* communication—interactions "among and between natural communities and social groups that include participants from what we might initially describe as different classifications of nature" (Plec 2013, 5–6). Yet in practice, changing the dynamics of these relationships is difficult, and practitioners can often feel stymied, not knowing how to "listen to a lake." An ecocultural perspective, where communication becomes both a lens and a tool for human-nature relationships, suspends the discourses that see nature as an entity separate from humans (Milstein et al. 2011). These four progressive steps are starting points to engage with nature as a stakeholder.

Listen to local stories. Oral traditions and local stories about the natural environment speak of the world as "full of active entities with which people engage" and demonstrate nature's expressive character (Cajete 2000, 27). Learning about these stories not only offers culturally specific understandings of nature as animate but also can model different ways that nature and humans communicate. In the Athapaskan and Tlingit oral traditions, glaciers are sentient beings that listen, pay attention, and respond to human behavior. Listening to glaciers through the stories of local people gives a layer of richness and substance to issues of climate change (Cruikshank 2005).

Develop a grammar of animacy. Once we become familiar, through local stories, with the ways in which nature might communicate, we can begin to develop a grammar of animacy that honors the ways in which nature is part of our ongoing conversations. Such a grammar respects nature as perceptive, feeling, and expressive. Referring to our natural world inhabitants as "he," "they," "she," or even "kin" (brother or sister or grandmother) expresses the aliveness of our stakeholder partner (Kimmerer 2007). Direct engagement implies an attending to, a concern for, and a focused engagement with another.

Appreciate silence as a resource. Learning to speak with nature also requires privileging the role of silence in internatural interactions. Silence can be understood to be a means of communicating our co-expressive existence with nature (Milstein 2008). "Speaking," as we think of it, can privilege human forms of communication. When seeking to comprehend nature's language, silence might allow us to attend to the forms of communication preferred by nature. When botanist Robin Wall Kimmerer (2013) listens to plants, she first asks permission of the plant and then listens in silence with both sides of her brain. The analytic left-brain looks at empirical signs while the intuitive right hemisphere approaches the encounter with openness and curiosity: "Plants tell their story not by what they say, but by what they do. What if you were a teacher but had no voice to speak your knowledge? Wouldn't you act it out? In time, you would become so eloquent that just to gaze on you would reveal it all" (128–29). A primary way to engage with silence includes listening and gathering insights with all of our senses and aspects of ourselves: "In indigenous ways of knowing, we understand a thing only when we understand it with all four aspects of our being: mind, body, emotion, and spirit" (47).

Represent Nature as Partner. Once stakeholders become aware of and more comfortable with nature as a partner, they can begin to represent those interests in conversations and decision making. Stakeholders can represent the natural environment, asking generative questions, such as What is in the best interests of the lake? If the lake were to join in this conversation, what do you think she would communicate? How has the lake communicated his interest in this issue thus far? Stakeholders can address the interests of the lake by using a variety of creative processes including interviews, focus groups, worksheets, dialogue, creative art, and murals.

In a multiyear dispute in Catron County, New Mexico, between loggers, ranchers, the Forest Service, and environmental groups, little progress occurred until the stakeholders went out to the trees. Stakeholders gathered around the trees, measured the trees, leaned against the trees, and began to consider the trees as stakeholders. Previous enemies shook hands among the trees, built trust, and made plans for moving forward. When conflicting stakeholders engaged with this shared natural resource, they took a critical step toward getting past gridlock. Listening to a lake or a tree might take a while. What nature wants to contribute may be "shy like owls who don't like to be seen during the day. It seems that intuitive listening requires us to still our minds until the beauty of things older than our minds can find us" (Nepo 2012, 8–9).

If we can suspend the discourses that see nature as an entity separate from humans and expand the definition of stakeholder to include other-than-humans (Milstein et al. 2011), we can create futures that are more holistic, creative, collaborative, and ethical (Starik 1995). Let's privilege forms of inquiry and communication that construct sustainable futures. Let's listen to the lake.

BIBLIOGRAPHY

Abram, David. 2010. *Becoming Animal: An Earthly Cosmology.* New York: Pantheon Books.

Bishel, Ashley. 2019. "Caring for Giants: Preserving Sequoia Groves By Balancing Needs of Tourists and Trees." Project Management. February 15, 2019. https://www.projectmanagement.com/articles/573011/Caring-for-Giants-Preserving-Sequoia-Groves-By-Balancing-Needs-of-Tourists-and-Trees.

Cajete, Gregory. 2000. *Native Science: Natural Laws of Interdependence.* Santa Fe, NM: Clear Light.

Cruikshank, Julie. 2005. *Do Glaciers Listen? Local Knowledge, Colonial Encounters, and Social Imagination.* Vancouver: UBC Press.

Gergen, Kenneth J. 2014. "From Mirroring to World-Making: Research as Future Forming." *Journal for the Theory of Social Behaviour* 45 (3): 287–310. https://doi.org/10.1111/jtsb.12075.

Haigh, Nardia, and Andrew Griffiths. 2009. "The Natural Environment as a Primary Stakeholder: The Case of Climate Change." *Business Strategy and the Environment* 18 (6): 347–59. https://doi.org/10.1002/bse.602.

Kimmerer, Robin Wall. 2013. *Braiding Sweetgrass.* Minneapolis: Milkweed.

———. 2017. "Learning the Grammar of Animacy 1." *Anthropology of Consciousness* 28 (2): 128–34. https://doi.org/10.1111/anoc.12081.

Leopold, Aldo. 1949. *A Sand County Almanac: And Sketches Here and There.* Oxford: Oxford Univ. Press.

Milstein, Tema. 2008. "When Whales 'Speak for Themselves': Communication as a Mediating Force in Wildlife Tourism." *Environmental Communication* 2 (2): 173–92.

Milstein, Tema, Claudia Anguiano, Jennifer Sandoval, Yea-Wen Chen, and Elizabeth Dickinson. 2011. "Communicating a 'New' Environmental Vernacular: A Sense of Relations-in-Place." *Communication Monographs* 78 (4): 486–510. https://doi.org /10.1080/03637751.2011.618139.

Nepo, Mark. 2012. *Seven Thousand Ways to Listen: Staying Close to What is Sacred.* New York: Simon & Schuster.

Parks, Melissa. 2020. "Explicating Ecoculture: Tracing a Transdisciplinary Focal Concept." *Nature and Culture* 15, no. 1 (Spring): 54–77.

Plec, Emily, ed. 2013. *Perspectives on Human-Animal Communication: Internatural Communication.* New York: Routledge.

Seed, John, Joanna Macy, Pat Fleming, and Arne Naess. 2007. *Thinking Like a Mountain: Towards a Council of All Beings.* Gabriola Island, BC Canada: New Catalyst Books.

Siebert, Margaret Markham. 2019. "Genetically Modified Salmon and the Future of Food: A Qualitative Content Analysis of Twitter." PhD diss., University of New Mexico. ProQuest (AAT 2308191776). Retrieved from http://libproxy.unm.edu/ login?url=https://search-proquest-com.libproxy.unm.edu/docview/2308191776?a ccountid=14613.

Starik, Mark. 1995. "Should Trees Have Managerial Standing? Toward Stakeholder Status for Non-Human Nature." *Journal of Business Ethics* 14 (3): 207–17. https:// doi.org/10.1007/bf00881435.

Chapter 24

The Geo-Doc

A Proposed New Communications Tool for Planetary Health

Mark Terry

In these precarious times, it is essential to keep the lines of communication open while ensuring that the information travelling through those lines is trustworthy. We often say that the first casualty in any war is the truth.

This pandemic is a war between us and an unseen enemy, an enemy that is its own lethal weapon. Thankfully, our lines of communication are still open and nonfiction film is being recruited for active duty. Televised news reports are watched more than usual on various platforms including social media, where the consumer often serves as the producer, casting a shadow on the authenticity of the news being reported.

As our living environments become compromised, so too do our digital environments. For global issues that impact all of us, a remediation of the nonfiction film—the documentary—is required to better represent the truth as it exists in providing visible evidence of the issue around the world. Why the documentary? Because when used responsibly, the documentary film can indeed present truthful depictions of actuality, in some academic circles referred to as "factuality." Indeed, the film genre has a long history of laying claims to the truth, including those demonstrated by *Kinopravda* (1922), *Cinéma Vérité* (1961), and *Visible Evidence* (1992).

The Geo-Doc is a proposed digital form of the documentary that endeavors to serve this purpose. It is both a technology and a methodology of producing and curating visible evidence in words and images that address global issues that impact all of us, such as planetary health. The Geo-Doc is a multilinear, interactive database documentary film project presented on a platform of a Geographic Information System (GIS) map of the world. It is designed to incorporate not only documentary film content and nonfiction footage of a global issue but also equally reliable metadata related to that issue. GIS technology affords the Geo-Doc producer a limitless amount of data accessible online within each of its pins. Valuable relational dimensions like time and space afford the user a framework that reveals new data when compared to those housed within other pins.

In my book *The Geo-Doc: Geomedia, Documentary Film, and Social Change*, I use as a case study a geomedia project called the *Youth Climate Report*, a database of documentary films first conceived in 2011 as a feature-length montage of climate research reported by youth aged eighteen to thirty worldwide. It was adapted to the Geo-Doc format in 2015 and presented at the United Nations Framework Convention on Climate Change (UNFCCC) in Paris. Using GIS as an exhibition platform allows for countless more video reports than the mere five or six in the feature-length linear film format of only sixty minutes. The first incarnation of the Geo-Doc showcased 181 video reports and metadata from all seven continents. Delegates and policymakers used the prototype during the Paris Climate Summit and praised it for its comprehensive representation of climate research worldwide within an easily accessible digital space.

The Paris conference requested more videos for the following year's conference in Marrakech. The UNFCCC established a competition—the *Global Youth Video Competition*—together with *Television for the Environment* and the *Youth Climate Report*. From this competition, documentary film reports of climate research around the world produced by the global community of youth are submitted and curated. The top videos provide content for this Geo-Doc project. Today, the *Youth Climate Report GIS Project* showcases more than 420 films and related metadata and is in service to the policymakers of the United Nations.

At the subsequent Climate Summit in 2016, UNFCCC Communications Director Nick Nuttall announced that the Geo-Doc project had been officially adopted as a partner program under its Article 6 mandate for education and outreach (UNFCCC 2016a). In his public address at the COP16 press conference, Nuttall spoke to the value of video as a unifying medium in advancing climate change policy:

> It is fantastic to see the enthusiasm and commitment of young people working on concrete ways to reduce greenhouse gas emissions and to adapt to the impacts of climate change. The many videos we received from around the world, placed . . . on this global, easy-to-use map, are testimony to this commitment. The videos help underscore the fact that governments, regions, cities, businesses, and investors are all stepping up to the plate to jointly tackle climate change and create a greener, safer and more sustainable future for themselves and the world. (UNFCCC 2016b)

In 2018, then-executive director of the United Nations Environment Program, Eric Solheim, described the project and its format as a valuable method of bridging the gap between science and policy:

> It comes down to a need to find the best methods for communicating science. The most important thing to remember is that the decision-makers are not scientists. Certainly, they have a grasp of the basic concepts, but politicians and civil servants are also generalists. Data visualisation in the *Youth Climate Report GIS Project* is one of the incredible tools available to get the science and the data across. (Interview 2016)

As an instrument of social change, the Geo-Doc works as a communications tool and data delivery system for those charged with creating progressive policy. The structural components—both theoretical and practical—represent the proven approaches to documentary filmmaking when it successfully speaks truth to power and yields measurable social change. Granted, these occasions are rare and usually identifiable only when the policymaker directly acknowledges the influence of the documentary film, but when it does work, we can isolate the methodology at play and use it for future productions with activist goals.

Two such approaches are the Participatory Mode and the Direct Approach. First identified by Bill Nichols in 2001 as one of six modes of documentary filmmaking (the others being Poetic, Observational, Reflexive, Expository, and Performative),[1] the Participatory Mode engages the profiled community in the filmmaking and storytelling process. This ensures an accurate depiction of the social issue being presented rather than its (mis)interpretation by the filmmaker who is reporting on the issue from the outside.

An extension of this mode is the Direct Approach, not to be confused with the Direct Cinema movement of the early 1960s. What I call the Direct Approach is related more to exhibition than to production. If a change in policy is the goal of an activist documentary film project, the process is expedited when the film is presented directly to the policymaker and, on top of that, made in collaboration with the policymaker. Many activist documentaries instead choose to tell their own stories and present them to audiences comprising the general public, frequently asking them at film festivals—or within the film itself—to act as surrogates and demand new laws from the policymaker.

There are examples when this approach has worked (*The Newfoundland Project* [1967]; *Sin by Silence* [2009]; *The Polar Explorer* [2010]), but the key factor is collaborating with the policymaker before, during, and after production to ensure the required data and related information, such as personal testimony, are represented in the documentary film. This is preferred in much the same way the Participatory Mode values the perspective of the community members over that of the outsider. The colonial gaze of the well-intentioned but self-righteous activist filmmaker does a relative disservice to the cause when the community members are excluded from the filmmaking process.

Other structural components of the Geo-Doc include the semiotic story-telling techniques of ecocinema, multilinear narratives, and a database documentary framework. The unique methodologies employed in ecocinematic documentaries (time distortion, irony, and anthropomorphism, among others) are best used as a means of providing implicit narratives that underscore the messages of the explicit narratives in a process-relational approach designed to make viewers connect better with the world they see on the screen and the world in which they live.

Ecocriticism theorist Adrian Ivakhiv (2013, 12) best articulates this style and its intent in his book *Ecologies of the Moving Image: Cinema, Affect, Nature*:

> It is a model that understands the world, and cinema, to be made up not primarily of objects, substances, structures, or representations, but rather of relational processes, encounters, or events. As we watch a movie, we are drawn into a certain experience, a relational experience involving us with the world of the film. In turn, the film-viewing experience changes, however slightly, our own experience of the world outside the film.

This relational process is extended to the use of multilinear narratives in a manner unique to GIS technologies. The Geo-Doc contains multiple film units geo-located across a digital map of the world. Each film unit is a stand-alone documentary that offers a variation on the project's foregrounded theme. In the case of the *Youth Climate Report*, for example, the theme is climate research, impacts, and solutions.

The film units within the Geo-Doc framework can be compared with each other together with the provided metadata in any number of ways but, most significantly, through the lenses of time and space. For example, if documentary film units examining glacier retreat in the Arctic are related to those made in the Antarctic during the same year, we might uncover different rates of decline leading to a discovery that one polar region is warming faster than the other. The explicit narratives of each film do not convey this data, yet when they relate to each other temporally and spatially, implicit narratives—and new data—can be revealed.

The virtually unlimited amount of film units in a Geo-Doc project constitutes what is known as a database documentary. These cinematic structures are often seen to be living documentaries, since new contributions can be made continually, indefinitely enhancing the narratives—both explicit and implicit—of the Geo-Doc. It is important to note, however, not to prioritize "collection over selection" (Druick 2018, 401), as film scholar Zoë Druick so eloquently puts it, and only to contribute film units and their related data from reliable sources and collected using the Participatory Mode.

This is the basic framework of a Geo-Doc. Extensions and enhancements to this construct vary with each project's theme and its content collection parameters. The global nature of a Geo-Doc project and its use of proven documentary theory and practice make it a useful communications tool in bridging the gap between science and policy in matters of planetary health, both for Earth's environment and Earth's residents.

NOTE

1. In 2017, Nichols added a seventh mode—Interactive—in the third edition of his book *Introduction to Documentary*.

BIBLIOGRAPHY

Druick, Zoë. 2018. "A Wide-Angle View of Fragile Earth: Capitalist Aesthetics in The Work of Yann Arthus-Bertrand." *Open Cultural Studies* 2, no. 1 (Dec. 13, 2018): 396–405. https://www.degruyter.com/view/journals/culture/2/1/article-p396.xml.
Ivakhiv, Adrian. 2013. *Ecologies of the Moving Image: Cinema, Affect, Nature.* Waterloo: Wilfrid Laurier University Press.
Klaus, Olivia, dir. 2009. *Sin by Silence*. Orange, CA: Quiet Little Place Productions.
Low, Colin, dir. 1967–1968. *The Newfoundland Project* (aka *The Fogo Film Project*). National Film Board of Canada.
Nichols, Bill. 2001. *Introduction to Documentary*. Bloomington: Indiana University Press.
———. 2017. *Introduction to Documentary*, 3rd ed. Bloomington: Indiana University Press.
Solheim, Erik. 2018. "Interview with Erik Solheim," by Mark Terry. *Youth Climate Report* (April 2018). http://youthclimatereport.org/?p=2428&preview=true.
Terry, Mark, dir. 2010. *The Polar Explorer*. Toronto: Polar Cap Productions II.
———, dir. 2011–2015. *The Youth Climate Report*. Toronto: Neko Harbour Entertainment.
———, dir. 2015–2020. *The Youth Climate Report GIS Project*. Bonn, Germany: United Nations Climate Change. https://drive.google.com/open?id=13sPbdm hKOFINj9WsPllhmN_rAaHdhncV&usp=sharing.
———. 2020. *The Geo-Doc: Geomedia, Documentary Film, and Social Change.* London: Palgrave Macmillan.

UNFCCC (United Nations Framework Convention on Climate Change). 2016a. "Lights, Camera, Marrakech." Marrakech, Morocco: UNFCCC, November 9, 2016. https://unfccc.int/topics/education-and-outreach/events--meetings/global-yo uth-video-competition/2016-global-youth-video-competition-on-climate-change
———. 2016b. "See Inspiring Climate Action." Bonn, Germany: UNFCCC, October 19, 2016. https://unfccc.int/news/see-inspiring-climate-action-entries-to-global -youth-video-competition.

Part V

GENDER, EARTHLY INTIMACIES, AND OTHER TROUBLE

Chapter 25

Intimate Dwelling and Mourning Loss in the (m)Anthropocene

Ecological Masculinities and the Felt Self

Todd LeVasseur and Paul M. Pulé

THE INTIMACY OF PLANETARY CALAMITY: A GENDERED PROBLEM?

We dwell in intimate relations. Intimate relations dwell in us. From the holo-biont of our primate intestinal track to our sympoietic dwelling as primates in co-evolved ecosystems, we are enmeshed in and with life.[1] And also with death. It is to the latter that we turn our primary attention throughout this chapter. As we contemplate our species' destruction of the living systems in which we are immersed, we question the gendered character of the pull toward death and away from what sustains us. Through a critical analysis of men, masculinities, and Earth, we offer an alternative, ecologically inspired way forward, facilitating a greater understanding of what it is that has kept us from adequately maintaining our habitat on Earth. In particular, we frame our discussion on the notion of ecological masculinities,[2] a concept that leads to a deepened awareness of gender and capacity to care for all of life (Hultman and Pulé 2018).

The intimacy of our dwellings requires us to honor great losses, as much as we celebrate wonderous becomings, in that inevitable dance of death begetting life. Our intimate care for Earth, others and self has entered a time of deep mourning. Accordingly, we, as scholar/activists, co-create this chapter with a view to offer some resolution to the mourning we feel, both person-ally and professionally, for social and ecological calamities that are upon us. In doing so, we acknowledge our positionalities as hetero-cis-gendered men and dedicate a response steeped in broader, deeper, and wider care, in support of a planetary hospice for the unraveling of the Holocene. We do so by recognizing that we have entered the (m)Anthropocene (Di Chiro 2017; Raworth 2014).

The following musings are then a blend of heart and rigor. Here, we present both self-explorations and analyses of Earthen solidarity from our subjectivities as men and in consideration of masculine social constructions. Our intent is to educate others and ourselves about the impact of emotional antiphons on the tragic planetary unfoldings of our times. These incursions into the "felt self" present intentionally contra-traditional masculine social mores. By "felt self," we are referring to the intimatizing of lived experiences as embodied sensual encounters, noting that these are transgendered human traits belonging to the lexicon of masculinities as well. Such rejoinders include experiences of felt loss, felt joy, and felt potentials of our bodies interacting with the material (biotic and abiotic, as well as biosocial) world that enable us to connect and grow. The "felt self" is an intersubjective self-of-always-becoming in always-ongoing social, psychological, spiritual, physical, emotional, and intellectual levels. As social beings, we recognize that feeling anger and sadness is unavoidable (and very natural), particularly in response to societal injustices, and/or destruction of Earth. That said, they are not commonplace in malestream socializations of masculinities.[3] Traditionally, and when liberated, the "felt self" is deeply bonded in feminized solidarity with Earth-others, setting masculine socializations on a course toward nature and away from the logics of domination that pervade human culture—particularly evident throughout Global Northern socio-cultural contexts (Plumwood 1993). Constraints and conditionings such as these that are placed upon the "felt self" are informed by our respective subjectivities, constituencies, and relations, which determine the lens through which we encounter and experience life, and also how we treat it in return. Consequently, this chapter is offered as a celebration of a particular (masculine) patina of the "felt self" that encounters the world with broader, deeper, and wider care for Earth, others, and self.

With this in mind, we begin by introducing (and locating) ourselves. Todd: a straight, white, cis-male, radical environmentalist who is married, a father of two, and has deep roots nourished by an intimate dwelling in the barrier coast of South Carolina. Paul: a Maltese, Italian, Lebanese Australian, born and raised of post–World War II refugees, who has assimilated and gentrified into white, Global Northern, straight culture with queer politics and deep roots nourished by an intimate dwelling in the ancient Australian landscape. Given the intersections of our positionalities, we focus here on cis-male, Global Northern, white, educated, and therefore privileged masculinities, placing particular attention on their impacts upon our world. In this sense, we offer an intimate (and gendered) analysis that we consider to be at the very heart of the planetary problems we face, which are also characteristic of our respective histories. We do so in order to seek a crucial leverage point for change by reconfiguring masculine gender norms. We contest harmful forms of masculinization that have silenced and kept the intimatized and caring "felt self" at bay for too long in too many men, noting that our global social and ecological problems find the lion's share of their origins in this (our) particular constituencies. In doing so, we expose the inner and outer transgressions, amendments, and transformations of two key types of modern masculinities while offering a third way forward that can actively engage in the mitigation of current and future catastrophic losses of planetary life. We argue in favor of affective and performed intimate, vulnerable internal and external communications in masculinities.

LINKING MEN AND MASCULINITIES TO SOCIAL AND ECOLOGICAL CRISES

Most readers are likely familiar with the work of the preeminent international body responsible for analyzing the most recent climate science, the Intergovernmental Panel on Climate Change (IPCC). Scientists working through the auspices of the IPCC have gathered an overwhelming amount of evidence to conclude that Earth is indeed warming, global snow/ice reserves are melting, sea levels are rising, rainfall is more erratic, intense storm surges are increasing, devastating fires are more frequent, marine and fresh-water hydrological systems are collapsing, terrestrial ecosystems are subject to unprecedented cyclic shifts, and biodiversity is declining. These biospheric changes are now being felt in our bodies and are impacting our psyches, triggering moments of intense anger, grief, and mourning in many global citizens. When examined alongside climate trends, threats to vulnerable ecosystems have become so great that we have entered a sixth mass extinction (Barnosky et al. 2011; Ceballos et al. 2017; Crutzen 2002; Steffen et al. 2011; Wake and Vredenburg 2008). A key cause of these planetary shifts is the excessive emissions of carbon dioxide into the atmosphere as a direct consequence of industrialization (IPCC 2014, 13–16). In other words, pressures that are of human making are placing great strain on Earth's living systems, severely impairing ecological fecundity, and with that, our affective (and therefore our inner) flourishings as a species.

This planetary devastation is tightly coupled to a new epoch broadly termed the "Anthropocene." To highlight that the devastation has been human-induced, the era is alternatively being referred to as the "Sociocene," "Technocene," "Homogenocene," "Econo-cene," and "Capitalocene" (Angus 2016, 230). Another term, which speaks directly to the analyses we offer in this chapter, is "(m)Anthropocene"; as implied by the (m) prefix, the term emphasizes the pivotal role of a small and influential group of men in creating and promulgating the human-centeredness that has driven climate change (Di Chiro 2017; Hultman and Pulé 2018; Raworth 2014). We find this term especially evocative since it calls our attention to those most responsible for the climate shifts we are facing and feeling and paves a way for the mourning we hold for each new species lost to extinction and the many faces of societal fracturing to which we are bearing witness. For example, when we introduce a gendered analysis of the onset of the Anthropocene, we note that eighty billionaires control more wealth than three-and-a-half billion people's combined wealth. Three sobering realities confront us as we grapple with such willful and blatant disparity.[4] First, 90 percent of the richest people in the world are men. Second, 85 percent of them are over the age of fifty-five. Third, almost 70 percent of them are white (Dolan 2017). Welcome, indeed, to the (m)Anthropocene. These wealth disparities are profoundly gendered and geopolitical, as are the impacts on those who suffer the most from them (Anshelm and Hultman 2017). For us, they are the tell-tail signs of a hegemony of select masculinities that assure that men of Global Northern, white, wealthy, and educated constituencies hold positions of primacy above all others. We consequently echo Di Chiro's (2017) and Raworth's (2014) contentions that our times are reflections of a (m)Anthropocene much more so than an Anthropocene.

The sources of these inequities are not biological. Rather, they are constructions. Consequently, we focus our critiques not only on select groups of men, but, more importantly, on the aspects of masculinities that have justified and promulgated global hegemonies that dwell as destructive and self-serving potentialities in us all, and the systems that created them. In light of these (m)Anthropogenic concerns, we look to the gendered roots of the substantial threats to human and other-than-human life (Quintero and Wiens 2013; Henehan 2019; WWF 2018). The burgeoning consequences of a global climate emergency and its impacts on human and other-than-human life have yet to be fully fathomed or to enter popular consciousness with the degree of alarm that such trends deserve. We feel frustration at this lack of urgency and are often overwhelmed by the depth of mourning such personal and professional loss engenders in the both of us. However, this inaction is not unexpected, as Hultman and Pule (2018) argue that such inertia is a direct product of masculine hegemonization—or the hierarchicalizing of masculine constructs that impact the unequal distributions of wealth, power, and privilege (Connell 1990). Here business-as-usual persists even in academia: malestream logics of domination continue to reify and prioritize dualized thinking despite alarming social and ecological trajectories.[5] This suggests that academia is as guilty as governments and businesses for failing to take a lead role in slowing or offering alternative visions to (m)Anthropogenic climate collapse and its resultant species die-offs and social fracturings

(LeVasseur 2014, 2015). Granted, innovations have been created to address our social and ecological conundrums in all three sectors, but they have thus far proven to be ineffectual. Recent attempts to offer regulatory responses to decades-long climate trends are largely devoid of caring and myopically reformist. Efforts to manage our way through crises have failed to steer us boldly away from the precipice upon which we teeter. Even when not blatantly extractive, these reforms languish in spaces that have historically been created and policed by hetero-cis-gender (white) male power in the academy, as much as in the government and businesses. Attendant to these spaces are logical modes of communication that have long dominated and avoided intersubjective immersions in the felt, erotic intimacies of our bodies. We maintain that this is a conundrum of ecocidal and sociopathic proportions that finds its origins in the ways that select men, and masculinities, as a privileged elite, are socialized, mechanized, and systematized toward planetary primacy.

Born of policies created by white men of power, environmental racism holds currency here as well, even in the academy. For example, the discipline of "white Geology makes legible a set of extractions, from particular subject positions, from black and brown bodies, and from the ecologies of place" (Yusoff 2018, 4). In short, the field facilitates the 500-year-long colonial project of violent dispossession of nonwhite bodies and the bioecological places and minerals of the "New World." As Yusoff explains: "The origins of the Anthropocene continue to [erase] and dissimulate violent histories of encounter, dispossession, and death in the geographical imagination" (2018, 101). Here, black, brown, and indigenous bodies, along with the Earth, are devalued through the justification of exploitation for profit. This manifests today in toxic saturation strategies, pipelines running through landscapes sacred to indigenous peoples, and a view of Earth as only having material value correspondent to the minerals that can be mined from it. The parallels with notions of toxic masculinities are overt.

The view of fungible bodies and Earth grafts onto the view of black and brown bodies as chattel that society is now confronting. The tragic murder of George Floyd in 2020 by four Minneapolis police officers made resonant the message that Black (Brown) Lives Matter. Writing in the wake of this modern-day lynching, we note that it was not only an act of racism (fueled by white supremacy). It was also an overt display of masculine violence that added to the life-destroying legacy of white males acting as institutional agent(s), holding primacy over the body of another. Such tragedies are no different than those rooted in gender inequalities and ecocide. However, the eruption of the voices of those who have long been targeted by the institutionalization of oppression on the streets of the United States and beyond has signaled a shift in the wake of the #MeToo and global warming movements. From this resistance, we are hopeful that the "felt self" is indeed rising, as made palpable in Floyd's heart-wrenching phrase, "I can't breathe" that sparked an international reaction against the injustices of white supremacy and holds currency for so many who have been oppressed—women, gender-queers, and Earth alike. Communicating oppression on a visceral level thrusts the tragedies into all of our faces, touching our humanity in the place where differences meet.[6]

With the above in mind, we introduce two key premises to frame our critique of the detrimental social and ecological impacts of masculine hege-monization on felt, embodied intimacies:

1. Engage with and then move beyond anger.

As a visceral emotion, anger is a great conduit for change. However, it is not a place to dwell. Because anger is often associated with the hypermasculinist logic of domination that has led to shifting biogeochemical patterns, extinc-tions, and violence against intersectionally "othered" bodies, we advocate spring boarding beyond the emotion. This does not mean denying anger but rather acknowledging it and then looking beyond its charged terrain, especially when it is leveled at those who are the prime beneficiaries of the (m)Anthropocene. In spite of the linkage between hypermasculine discourse and anger, we also recognize ecocidal masculinities as social constructions; they are not innate nor intractable. This insight is key, as it takes us beyond blaming and shaming men, while not letting them (us) off the hook. It is to the sources of these problems, which we consider to be masculinities as socializations that dwell in us all, and especially in cis-males, that we turn our primary attention and action. To be grounded in a healthy response, our recommendation of intimatizing and mourning planetary (and personal) loss must do the same. While a necessary and understandable initial reflex response to the tragedies of our times, gestures of pointed anger and blame are, ultimately, not effective in leveling structural critiques at masculinist systems in ways that ensure change. To deal with anger and grief triggered by the recognition of looming collapse and male violence, we advocate for pro-portional accountability, responsibility, and amendment of the structural con-straints placed upon Earth, others, and self (Hultman and Pulé 2018, 235–41).

2. Engage with and move beyond grief.

Grief is a great medium for healing and recovering the fullest functioning self. As such, it is vital to life. Still, in feeling the tragic urgency of our times, there is little room for bargaining with our Earth realities nor collapsing into hopelessness and depression.[7] Since mourning is a necessary part of grief, to move forward we must come to accept planetary and personal loss and the felt pulses of bodily pain that accompany them.[8] This is intentionally contradictory to the mores of masculine hegemonization. To transform the social constructions of masculinities, men in particular must locate their (our) respective complicities at the heart of both our global and our personal problems. Solutions and transformation originate from the (masculine) "felt self." In this way, (we) men will be primed to discover pathways leading to roles beyond dominator that are more fully human. They (we) garner the agency to contribute as equals to collective efforts for systemic change.

This redressing of masculinities can equate to an existential retraining or an ecologization of masculinities that celebrates felt and honored relationalities, effectively pulling men and the social machinations of masculinities toward deeper planetary citizenship. Here, vulnerability in our communicative interactions with the rest of life aids in building pathways of emotional and ecospiritual literacy that awaken a fuller humanity. Cultivating such intimate vulnerability in men supports urgently needed policy actions that create antiracist, antispeciesist, antisexist, antihomophobic, and gender equitable communities of greater global care.

The premises presented here invite active engagements with the "felt self," which, in the context of masculinities' socializations, remain novel. From this innovation, we are compelled to honor "our pain for the world . . . [as] a way of valuing our awareness, first, that we have noticed, and second, that we [all] care. Intellectual awareness by itself is not enough. We need to digest the bad news. That is what rouses us to respond" (Macy and Johnstone 2012, 71). In this way, we confront the "monstrosities of masculinities" (Akomolafe 2020) that ail us all, but hypermasculinized men in particular. Doing so allows us to feel and mourn loss (of the planet and our place in it) rather than dismiss it. It is from dwelling deeply within our losses (and feeling the anger and grief they provoke) that change can indeed happen.

MONSTROUS MASCULINITIES: FRAGILE EGOS AND THE SUPPOSED SAFETY OF VULNERABILITY AVERSION

We recognize that there are many pathways to communicating beyond the monstrosities of malestream masculinities. Through them, we find multiplicities of intersubjectivities to reawaken the human as animal. These pathways are Earthen and house many voices, including those of the supposed voiceless: the myriad other-than-human others with whom we share this Earth. Listening to these voices can allow us to access our attentive care, leading us toward increasingly vital remedies to the (m)Anthropocene. Two notable conundrums also emerge along these pathways. First, despite many masculinist constructs to the contrary, we cannot avoid engagements with our world; our animal selves steep us in and of Earth whether we like it or not. We always dwell in a variety of Earthly relations. Many of us resist, deny, or ignore this. Second, subverting the masculinist constructs of the (m) Anthropocene is too big a task for any one person or positionality to assume. As a result, we take a stepwise approach, contending with the logics of domination emblematic of the constrained socializations shaping many men's lives, which are largely detrimentally impacting the planet. This is especially so for men in power in the Global North, whether under- or over-educated, whose wealth and domination compels them to remain wedded to myopic modalities of caring that resist Earthen intimacies.

The monstrosities of masculine hegemonies articulate political, economic, and cultural power that is differentially layered among all peoples, regardless of gender. Some (especially bolted to wealthy, white, masculinist, and Global Northern constituencies) are unapologetic about their disproportionate accumulation of wealth, power, and privileges and the ways that they benefit from systems that enable them to indulge in the abundances of life. Others are (at-times violently) pushed far from the accoutrements of global socio-economic and political primacy. The willful greed and pursuit of power-over by the privileged few who ride high on the labor of others is what Hultman and Pulé (2018) refer to as industrial/breadwinner masculinities, one of the two dominant strains of masculinity that have largely triggered the (m)Anthropocene. These masculinities are the product of patriarchal or male domination[9] and have been bolstered by the rousing rhetoric of capitalists, libertarians, incels, nationalists, and white supremacists.[10] Such are the logics of domination that have reified the idealized masculine self as a strong, conquering, dominating, emotionally absent, controlling breadwinner, and industrial inventor.

Attempts to move beyond industrial/breadwinner masculinities have been with us for some time. The most pervasive of these, what Hultman and Pule (2018) call ecomodern masculinities, has been instrumental in leading us through the limitations of neoliberalism. This type of emergent masculinity was signaled through a critical analysis of the highly energy dependent/ wealthy/powerful persona of Arnold Schwarzenegger as California State "Governator" by Hultman (2013, 97). Hultman and Pulé (2018) note that ecomodern masculinities emerged in the wake of rising social and ecological concerns but notably stopped short of compromising the select advantages of the capitalist system. In this sense, ecomodern masculinities represent a paper tiger, engaging with the same systems of extraction, dispossession, and violence against the planet and certain bodies that are reflective of industrial modernization. However, ecomodern engagements with our world attempt to "nice" (a.k.a. greenwash) our responses to planetary problems (e.g., the Paris Accord).[11] With the failings of neoliberalism, ecomodernism has proven to be little more than an effort to soften the blow of the (m)Anthropocene. Notably, "ecological modernist priorities place industrial capitalism ahead of social and environmental imperatives; they are insufficient responses to growing evidence of the unsustainability of industrialization, designed to placate evidence-based concerns and extend business-as-usual for as long as possible" (Hultman and Pulé 2018, 46). In doing so, this second set of masculinities has socially and environmentally failed us as well, since it does not require us to cultivate deep care, vulnerability, or intimacy nor to relinquish unearned positions of power over others.

For the remainder of this chapter, we advocate a third way forward in alignment with Hultman and Pulé's (2018) efforts to ecologize masculinities. This third option, ecological masculinities, offers more intimate engagements, immersing us in tactile, emotive, and relational exchanges with Earth, others, and self. Ecological masculinities draw from gender studies (especially profeminist views associated with critical studies on men and masculinities [CSMM]), deep ecology, ecological feminism, and feminist care theory (Hultman and Pulé 2020). As a recent contribution to gender and environment discourse, ecological masculinities is positioned as a pluralized starting point that builds on existing conversations about men, masculinities, and Earth. It aims to help us dwell in intimacy, feel connection to community (human and more-than-human), and support men (and other-gendered and sexed bodies) to honorably mourn the ending of what has been the largest flourishing of planetary biodiversity to date.

Ecological masculinities offer a new theoretical framework that advocates for pluralized praxes. This emergent discourse notes the need to transform the hegemonization of the Global Northern sociopolitical landscape into ecologization. Central to such a transformation is the broadening of embodied scopes of care in masculine socializations. While encouraging the application of these transformations across systemic fronts (policy, education, economics/business, family dynamics, relations with Earth, systems of incarceration, health care, etc.), ecological masculinities highlight the simultaneous need for felt personal transformations that foment intimate encounters with Earth, others, and self. The focus on facilitating global care through the local (or "glocal commons") posits an alternative path that moves us beyond the alarming consequences of the (m)Anthropocene. The theoretical framework is built on the central premise that masculinities contain infinite capacities to care, which can be expressed at the same time toward Earth, others, and self. It thereby functions as a constructive response to our times that allows us to realize and act on the masculine capacity for care. As Connell (1995, 220–24) explains, the transition from hegemonization to ecologization is a type of "exit politics," liberating men from the logic of domination that structures industrial/breadwinner and ecomodern masculinities. Intimatizing the encounters between men, masculinities, and Earth holds great potential to awaken care for Earth-others and self—simultaneously.

MOURNING LOSS AS AN ECOLOGIZED ALTERNATIVE FOR MEN AND MASCULINITIES IN A TIME OF COLLAPSE

As has been explained, industrial/breadwinner and ecomodern masculinities fail to yield planetary health because their respective enmeshments with extractivism render them psycho-spiritually empty—both in their compositions and societal and ecological impacts. Despite their compulsions for innovation, both pursue power at the expense of the relational self that dwells in and of Earth. Their intimacies are that of *Thanatos*—a mercilessness, indiscriminate hatred toward the felt realm that Freud termed a "death drive."[12] As implied, it has potentially catastrophic corporeal consequences, which have manifested in the COVID-19 pandemic. Along with the lethal consequences the pandemic has had for hundreds of thousands of people, it has also put a pause on the logics of domination that underpin industrial/breadwinner and ecomodern masculinities, giving us the time to fully feel the complexities of the self and other. The subsequent impact on the global economy and patterns of movement has awakened a broadscale celebration of *Eros* that brought us home—literally and metaphorically (indeed, necessarily)—to dwell more fully in our senses. However, this has not come without considerable resistance, as seen in the scramble to reignite the economy by kickstarting business-as-usual with financial bailouts and mixed messaging about public health so that we could carry on with the killing of Earth, others, and ourselves.[13] Such are the *Thanatophoric* intimacies of the industrial/breadwinner and ecomodernist logic that hold particular currency for men. As a consequence, entering into the "felt self" as a result of the pandemic exposed the emptiness and conditioning that had cauterized the inner musings of our Earthen/animal selves. The normality of domination, exclusion, competition, and status were muted for long enough to notice what so many of us had seemingly forgotten: that our feelings and relationships are indeed precious. However, we also learned that masculinist responses to the public health crisis, especially those proffered by conservative and right-wing extremist leaders (e.g., in the United States and Brazil), were inimical to life. Championing money over health. Such responses verified the moral bankruptcy of industrial/breadwinner models of manhood, the inefficacy of reformist responses, and the lack of care that these masculinities yield (Madani 2020). For us, as men committed to justice for all, the pandemic called us both to stand in solidarity with millions of others, to honor the "felt self" and celebrate the strangeness of a slowed world. In the process, we began to grapple with the question: What might masculine ecologization look like in a world rocked by a pandemic? The tangible homeboundness imposed on us by COVID-19 cauterized the usual forums of malestream power broking. We were all domiciled whether we liked it or not, foisted into the ecological reality that we truly are connected and no amount of social/physical distancing could bring the spread of contagion to a halt. The pandemic provided us with an inescapable sense that behind the façade of masculine hegemonization, we are left with a visceral sense that life is about caring for ourselves, each other, our communities, and Earth.

We also saw the COVID-19 pandemic as a preview of how we will have to live in a climate-changed future: slowing down, building community resilience, getting to know our neighbors, helping each other, supporting local food production, increasing civic engagement by writing to elected officials about closing schools and demanding mask-wearing, playing with our children more, educating them at home, sinking into place, and marveling at the sounds of birds and insects in the airplane-less skies. On the many walks we both took, we remembered that we always and already dwell in communities of intricate relationship. We made efforts to feel, know, and come home through our feet and senses, reaching beyond damaging partisan politics and resisting the addiction to hide behind screens. Doing so, we were able to find personal versions of ecologization that paralleled those occurring across the globe, as dolphins replaced Venetian gondolas, the Himalayas emerged from a smog-free distance, goats and bears roamed streets, and spring birdsongs filled the suburbs. Like a seedling growing between the cracks of concrete, these fugitive spaces of erotic love confronted the edifices of domination.[14] By showing us that this is possible, the pandemic exposed the softer, tenderer, more relational priorities in our lives that matter most. It could thereby be described as a virally induced queering of the "apocalyptic narrative of the Anthropocene [and its] ontological dimension . . . [that] brings forth a temporarily wounded yet ultimately redeemed Man who can conquer time and space by rising above the geological mess he has created" (Zylinska 2018, 15).[15] As we got in touch with our "felt self," we both viscerally experienced that being stopped reduced our socialized malestream urges to make, insert, assert, forge, hold, control, contain, manage, strive, produce, and dominate. We were able to focus instead on our respective callings and to be loved (toward Earth, others, and self) all the more. Doing so, however, also brought to surface the anger, grief, and mourning we feel as Earth dwellers. By allowing us to acknowledge the anger and grief associated with loss for many, COVID-19 also presented a trial run of the changes we believe are required to better live through and beyond the (m)Anthropocene. Beyond the pandemic, we need to stop consuming so that we can redefine community, wealth, health, and the purpose of a human life. Industrial/breadwinner and ecomodern masculinities do not facilitate this process or aid in an authentic transition toward justice, equity, resilience, and regenerative culture. Ecological masculinities does.

The great lesson of an ecologized masculine awareness is the prioritization of relationality that lies at the very foundations of life. Such awareness provides a redoubling of the capacity for care that exists in all humans—and for traditional notions of masculinities in particular. A movement toward ecological masculinities purposefully reiterates masculine aspects of caring, while recognizing that care pervades the feminine aspects within us all as well. The capacity to dwell in and embody intimate care is alive in us all. Key to our argument, and crucial for dealing with the anger, grief, and mourning that comes with cultivating intimate relations with a planet in bioecological turmoil is the intentional filtering into the nuanced and gendered microscales of emotional socialization. From the macro-level of human socializations to the psychoanalytical and existential microscales, this process builds on an understanding that all gender norms must cultivate an ecological conscience that celebrates all life as sympoietic. Gender norms must also cultivate the tenderness that informs healthy familial relations,[16] which are taken here to be the foundation of innate goodness of the fully human self. These are some of the intimatized core tenets that the theoretical framework for ecological masculinities and its practical applications offer.

There are practical applications to ecological masculinities as well, which include the familial rites of passage that transition us into adulthood. For men who have been conditioned by dominant discourses, new, ecological adult responsibilities may threaten traditional notions of manhood. If interpreted as a feminization of the masculine self, they can conjure misogynies and queerphobias. Yet, when embraced, masculine ecologization promotes (ritualized) care, giving back to community and family rather than using others to sustain an isolated, autonomous (masculine) self. It provides a communitarian alternative to patriarchy, where the concept of care reaches beyond the nuclear family, difference is celebrated and change embraced. This type of care allows for grieving the losses of climate change and human conflict that have resulted from industrial/breadwinner and ecomodern lifestyles. It is not a romanticized notion of ecotopic fantasy, but a cultural and evolutionary understanding of the broad level of familial care that must be extended to all of our Earthly kin who are suffering loss. It embraces the tensions of strife, exclusion, upset, and alterity often experienced within community, seeking resolutions beyond naive and romanticized unions between Earth, others, and self.

Transitioning into ecological masculinities means confronting the sobering reality of our communities and our Earthly relationalities as they are being willfully destroyed. It requires facing the costs of destruction for ourselves as well. The anger and grief triggered by accounting for these costs initiates the mourning process we refer to throughout this chapter. To allow such mourning to take its course, care must be available for both the marginalized and for those in power. In this way, we intimatize the masculine self and still the pendular swing between the dominator and the dominated. To be clear, such care does maintain accountability as it actively dismantles unequal intersectional power dynamics. It does so when the masculine forms alliances with the marginalized and uses privilege to yield power from behind. Masculinities that are traditionally privileged by action, entrepreneurship, vision, and focus thus uncover spaces where caring praxes can emerge, allowing for an awakening of generative Earth restorations. Meanwhile, traditionally masculine identities can be placed in service of ecologization as we recognize the masculine self in all of us. In this manner, ecological masculinities facilitates healing from the cauterization of the (m)Anthropocene, allowing us to take a stand against the wanton decay, death, and extinction that are products of manufactured patriarchal systems.

The ontological shift of the masculine self toward ecologization can be guided through spirituality as well—be it through the Earth-reverence and societal care of organized religion or through nature-based practices.[17] Doing so affirms life and champions love (McIntosh and Carmichael 2015), simultaneously nurturing the sentient self both "out-there" and "in-here." As a pathway to ecological masculinities, spirituality also opens the possibility of becoming vulnerable to the beauty, joy, fragility, and depth of life. In this space, the masculine ideal reaches beyond the judging, distant, disembodied, abstract, male sky god and brings focus back to the bedrock of life here, on this vibrant Earth. This need not mean that ecological masculinities should or should not shun organized religion or spiritual vulnerabilities as a prerequisite for ecologization. It does mean, however, that communicating intimacy should remain open to religio-spiritual forms of guidance throughout the (m)Anthropocene. Whether this communication is through church, meditation, yoga, Death Cafes, social media chat rooms, ritualized grief sessions, pagan rites, or what Johnson (2018) terms "radical joy," it opens an opportunity to reconcile our "felt selves" with the Earth tragedy of our times. These practices are particularly useful because they engender humility, foster connection across evolutionary and ecological boundaries, and speak to a holistic understanding of life (Taylor et al. 2020).

When applied systemically as well as personally in the ways we have argued above, our views are in fact post-gendered. They can have applications to femininities and masculinities alike (prioritizing a genderqueering beyond the feminine and masculine binary), since the potentialities are not uniquely male. Rather, they can apply to all genders. As a result, we call on men to reach beyond the allure of masculine hegemony and strive for

ecologization by joining in the pluralities of a post-(m)Anthropocene community, capable of honoring felt anger and grief at climate injustice while maintaining solidarity with and advocating for climate-just policies in support of
Earthen/family/community relationality. This includes not only leading with
care but also following from behind as allies supporting the leadership of the
marginalized. Such shifts in masculine social constructions reach beyond the
isolated self, helping us to develop fresh notions of inclusive, connected, and
caring manhood. Through ecological masculinities, the value of manhood is
located in the service and strength gained from connecting the intimate and
vulnerable self with others. In this sense, ecological masculinities provides
men in particular with a pathway back to their full humanity in and of Earth,
community, family, and self, offering them (us) a great (re)intimatizing in
defiance of the logics of domination.

IN SUMMARY AND EARTHLY SOLIDARITY

Throughout this chapter, we have advocated for intimacy in masculine social
constructions. By normalizing mourning and rendering the loving embrace
of life as a very human quality, it is possible to form a new "ethos" of masculine ecologization rooted in bioecological places where we are always
in intersubjective and inter-somatic relation with those around us. Such an
ethos builds agentic character while having the capacity to transform religio-
spiritual ways of being. Core to ecological masculinities is witnessing and
experiencing the felt aspects of life, which makes us vulnerable to relational
communion. We have argued that what matters most for men and masculinities (in the context of pressing Earth needs) is the provisioning of masculine
ecologization such that care touches loss and exposes the anger and grief of
the felt self. Through those feelings, it awakens momentum for change that
supports our co-existence with a fecund Earth.

While we extend the invitation to explore ecological masculinities to men
in particular, we also encourage women and genderqueer people to revise
the masculine in their identities. Ecological masculinities is posited here as
celebratory attunements to Earthly otherness. Doing so allows us to shift the
destructive complexities of traditional industrial/breadwinner and ecomodern
masculinities into an intimate celebration of "the many" who co-exist on
Earth. For men, in particular, this means seeking care in the self in order to
care for others, foment community, and sustain Earth.

This enmeshment with otherness is already in and around us. That is, we
are steeped in this ecological reality and have been for as long as our species
has existed. In this sense, the intimatizing of the felt self through ecological
masculinities is ancient; it is something Earth has been demonstrating through

the eons-long flourishing of ecological unfolding. Our task now, especially as men, is to reanimate what humanity has long known. Caring for others through our words, actions, and spiritual practices represents an essential form of liberation in a time of catastrophic loss. Herein lies the intimate ecologizing of the masculine self that we consider to be urgently needed, both now and into the tragic, climate-changed future to come.

NOTES

1. A holobiont is a host organism along with the assemblage of diverse species (for humans this would be microbes and bacteria) that reside in or near it, making a unique ecosystem. Sympoietic derives from "sym," meaning together or with, and poiesis denotes creative becoming, so joined together they signify creative becoming between life forms and processes. Both terms imply that there is no singularity and no isolated existence. Humans are made of other life forms, and everything we are is co-created with the rest of life in never-ending moments of intimate becoming.

2. We use this term as singular, not plural, even though "masculinities" is pluralized to indicate the inescapable plurality of masculinities within the ecologization process proposed.

3. The term "malestream" is attributed to Mary O'Brien's (1981, 62) writings on women's reproductive rights. Loosely, it is used synonymously with "patriarchy." However, "malestream" refers specifically to those socially sanctioned norms that are supportive of patriarchal domination and pave the way for modern Western men and masculine identities to conform to patriarchal thoughts, words and actions such that men and traditional renditions of masculinity flourish best within the social structures created. These norms are typically accompanied by an internalized sense of superiority in some men over other men, women and Nature.

4. Note that the wealthiest five hundred million people on Earth (approximately seven percent of the total human population) produce fifty percent of all the carbon dioxide emitted into the atmosphere, compared with the poorest three billion people, who emit a mere six percent (Assadourian 2010). Further, in 2014 the top one percent of the planet's richest individuals controlled forty-eight percent of global wealth compared to the poorest eighty percent, who controlled a mere five-and-a-half percent (Hardoon 2017).

5. For a fuller disposition on "logics of domination" as they relate to dualized thinking, see Plumwood 1993, 1–5; Warren 1990, 133.

6. In the case of the George Floyd killing, it can be argued that Kübler-Ross's (1969) five stages of the grief cycle have been triggered on international scales.

7. This is not to discredit valid feelings of depression, with which we both grapple as authors, especially as more studies emerge of how bad things are economically, socially, and ecologically. We also recognize and value various therapies that support pathways to living with, and even healing, depression. We encourage readers who are

feeling depression, especially related to eco-grief, to find experts or communities of care that can provide support for such valid, intimate feelings.

8. For example, Todd feels this every time he commutes home to a barrier island on the Atlantic Ocean. He recognizes that he, or, at best, his kids, will be the last human generation ever driving this road while looking at the marsh ecosystem, as it will all likely be underwater in the coming decades.

9. "Patriarchal domination" refers to the structural oppression of marginalized groups of human beings by economic, political and social systems that have been created and maintained to advantage men ahead of all others. "Male domination" is a consequential and personalized subset of patriarchal domination that emboldens men to engage in mechanisms of power and control in their immediate lives to gain and maintain advantages over more-than-humans. In both cases, male violence plays a key role in creating and sustaining these mechanisms of oppression from structural to personal levels. Research on masculine hegemonization has exposed these intersecting terrains of men, masculinities, and Earth (Connell 1995; Kimmel 2013). Hultman and Pulé (2018) introduced the term industrial/breadwinner masculinities as an alternative to "hyper-masculinity" and "toxic masculinity," which amplify traditional expressions of masculinities through physical strength, aggression, sexual prowess, military might, domination, being a "winner" and not being a "girl" (Kivel 1999; hooks 2004; Katz 2006).

10. Incels is a contraction of "involuntary celibates" that can be considered a subculture within the Men's Rights Movement that decries some men's struggles to gain sexual access to women on demand. Members are characterized by articulations of victimization, self-pity, entitlement, overt misogyny, misanthropy, and, in some cases, make direct reference to racist tomes. The most alarming aspect of this subculture is an endorsement of violence (esp. toward women), rationalized as "pay back" for rejection (either real or imagined), which has resulted in some mass murders since 2014 as the subculture has gained traction.

11. It is notable that the Trump administration's classic industrial/breadwinner motivated withdrawal from the Paris Accord has effectively rendered that international agreement redundant. It remains to be seen what mitigating actions to the alarming social and ecological consequences of climate change the incoming Biden administration will adopt.

12. We are inspired in this analysis by the work of Alastair McIntosh (1996), who applied Freud's concepts of *Eros* and *Thanatos* to cigarette advertisements, reflective of his understandings and interpretations of ancient Greek and psychoanalytical philosophies.

13. In nations of the Global North (such as the United States), COVID-19 quickly became a partisan issue, as conservatives and nationalists demanded a return to familiar levels of economic production and consumption, with large corporations (e.g. airlines) holding out their hands for the bulk of government stimuli. This demonstrated just how powerfully systems are built around fossil-fuel driven logics of domination (both those that are unapologetically industrialized as well as those that reach for regulatory reform), as they drew on habits of thinking and practice that aimed to skip over the great opportunity that a virally induced pause offered. The pressure to resist reassessing, and, in doing so, implement transformative change, was considerable.

That those willing to wear masks, slow down, and critique the hegemony of modernization afforded by COVID-19 were at times ridiculed and confronted with hostility indicates just how far removed those wedded to industrial/breadwinner and ecomodern forms of masculinities are from a vulnerability to the presence of life along with its fecundity and fragility.

14. Freud's *eros* stood against *thanatos*.

15. We use "queer/queering" here as a verb, in the sense of moving beyond binary categories that form the basis of domination logics. It conveys gaps and new horizons in received patriarchal, heteronormative ways of being and of conceiving all bodies. To queer in this sense means to embrace a place of discordance, to delight in the possibility of new assemblages (political, economic, bodily), and to challenge socialized ways of being by the erasure of stultifying and policed boundaries that always lead to hierarchies and violence. We celebrate queering, and the work of ecological masculinities helps queer spaces fill with care and with new ways of being in solidarity with all bodily others, regardless of class, gender, sex, age, nationality, and other assumed binary identities.

16. Family is used here to refer to a place of nurturing, growth, support, socialization, learning, and shame, and, in this sense, is not gender specific or based on heteronormative and nuclear family ideologies (see Jordan et al. 2012).

17. We recognize that indigenous peoples have their own ecological-relational dwelling practices and nonindigenous peoples should not colonize or appropriate these lifeways. Such colonization is symptomatic of the emptiness at the core of Global Northern malestreams, and appropriation without consent is a form of industrial/breadwinner taking and ecomodern privilege.

BIBLIOGRAPHY

Akomolafe, Bayo. 2020. "The Monsters in Perpetual Exile." *The Mythic Masculine.* Podcast audio. June 9, 2020. https://open.spotify.com/episode/1m5Lzc32nbjonf TL1ILOUF.

Angus, Ian. 2016. *Facing the Anthropocene: Fossil Capitalism and the Crisis of the Earth System.* New York: Monthly Review Press.

Assadourian, Erik. 2010. "The Rise and Fall of Consumer Cultures." In *State of the World (2010): Transforming Cultures: From Consumerism to Sustainability*, edited by Worldwatch Institute. Washington: Norton, 3–20.

Barnosky, Anthony, Nicholas Matzke, Susumu Tomiya, Guinevere O. U. Wogan, Brian Swartz, Tiago B. Quental, Charles Marshall, Jenny L. McGuire, Emily L. Lindsey, Kaitlin C. Maguire, Ben Mersey, and Elizabeth A. Ferrer. 2011. "Has the Earth's Sixth Mass Extinction Already Arrived?" *Nature* 471, no. 7336 (March 2): 51–57. http://doi.org/10.1038/nature09678.

Ceballos, Gerardo, Paul R. Ehrlich, and Rodolfo Dirzo. 2017. "Biological Annihilation via the Ongoing Sixth Mass Extinction Signaled by Vertebrate Population Losses and Declines." *PNAS* 114, no. 30 (July 25): E6089-E6096. http://doi.org/10.1073/pnas.1704949114.

Connell, Robert. 1990. "A Whole New World: Remaking Masculinity in the Context of the Environmental Movement." *Gender and Society* 4 (4): 452–78.

Connell, Raewyn W. 1995. *Masculinities*. Berkeley: University of California Press.

Crutzen, Paul. 2002. "Geology of Mankind." *Nature* 415, no. 6867 (January 3): 23. https://doi.org/10.1038/415023a.

Di Chiro, Giovanna. 2017. "Welcome to the White (m)Anthropocene? A Feminist-Environmentalist Critique." In *Routledge Handbook of Gender and Environment*, edited by Sherilyn MacGregor, 487–507. Oxon: Routledge.

Dolan, Kerry. 2017. "Forbes 2017 Billionaires List: Meet the Richest People on the Planet." *Forbes* (Online), March 20, 2017. https://www.forbes.com/sites/kerrya dolan/2017/03/20/forbes-2017-billionaires-list-meet-the-richest-people-on-the-pl anet/#2f63045e62ff.

Global Health 5050. 2020. "Covid-19 Sex-disaggregated Data Tracker: Tracking Differences in COVID-19 Illness and Death Among Women and Men." Global Health 5050: Towards Gender Equality in Global Health. Last modified August 7, 2020. https://globalhealth5050.org/covid19/sex-disaggregated-data-tracker/.

Hardoon, Deborah. 2017. "An Economy for the 99%: It's Time to Build a Human Economy That Benefits Everyone, Not Just the Privileged Few." Oxfam briefing paper, January 16, 2017. http://policy-practice.oxfam.org.uk/publications/an-eco nomy-for-the-99-its-time-to-build-a-human-economy-that-benefits-everyone-620 170.

Henehan, Michael J., Andy Ridgwell, Ellen Thomas, Shuang Zhang, Laia Alegret, Daniela N. Schmidt, James W. B. Rae, James D. Witts, Neil H. Landman, Sarah E. Greene, Brian T. Huber, James R. Super, Noah J. Planavsky, and Pincelli M. Hull. 2019. "Rapid Ocean Acidification and Protracted Earth System Recovery Followed the End-Cretaceous Chicxulub Impact." *PNAS* 116, no. 45 (November 5): 22500–4. http://doi.org/10.1073/pnas.1905989116.

hooks, bell. 2004. *We Real Cool: Black Men and Masculinity*. New York: Routledge.

Hultman, Martin. 2013. "The Making of an Environmental Hero: A History of Ecomodern Masculinity, Fuel Cells and Arnold Schwarzenegger." *Environmental Humanities* 2 (1): 79–99.

Hultman, Martin, and Jonas Anshelm. 2017. "Masculinities of global climate change." In *Climate Change and Gender in Rich Countries: Work, Public Policy and Action,* edited by M. Cohen. 19–34. New York: Routledge.

Hultman, Martin, and Paul M. Pulé. 2018. *Ecological Masculinities: Theoretical Foundations and Practical Guidance*. Oxon: Routledge.

———. 2020. "Ecological Masculinities: A Response to the Manthropocene Question." In *Routledge International Handbook of Masculinities Studies*, edited by Lucas Gottzén, Ulf Mellström, and Tamara Shefer, 477–87. Oxon: Routledge.

IPCC (Intergovernmental Panel on Climate Change). 2014. *Climate Change 2014: Synthesis Report*. https://www.ipcc.ch/report/ar5/syr/.

Johnson, Trebbe. 2018. *Radical Joy for Hard Times*. Berkeley: North Atlantic Books.

Jordan III, William, Nathaniel Barrett, Kip Curtis, Liam Heneghan, Randall Honold, Anna Peterson, Leslie Paul Thiele, Todd LeVasseur, and Gretel Van Wieren. 2012. "Foundations of Conduct: A Theory of Values and Its

Implications for Environmentalism." *Environmental Ethics* 34, no. 3 (September): 291–312.

Katz, Jackson. 2006. *The Macho Paradox: Why Some Men Hurt Women and How All Men Can Help.* Naperville: Sourcebooks.

Kimmel, Michael. 2013. *Angry White Men: American Masculinity at the End of an Era.* New York: Nation Books.

Kivel, Paul. 1999. *Boys Will Be Men: Raising Our Sons for Courage, Caring and Community.* Gabriola Island: New Society.

Kübler-Ross, Elisabeth. 1969. *On Death and Dying.* New York: Scribner.

LeVasseur, Todd. 2014. "Environmental Philosophy in a Post-Ice Cap North Polar World." *Environmental Ethics* 36, no. 3 (Fall): 303–18. http://doi.org/10.5840/en viroethics201436331.

———2015. "'The Earth Is *sui generis*:' Destabilizing the Climate of Our Field." *Journal of the American Academy of Religion* 83, no. 2 (June): 300–19. http://doi .org/10.1093/jaarel/lfv023.

Macy, Joanna, and Chris Johnstone. 2012. *Active Hope: How to Face the Mess We're in Without Going Crazy.* Novato: New World Library.

Madani, Doha. 2020. "Dan Patrick on Coronavirus: 'More Important Things Than Living.'" NBC News, April 21, 2020. https://www.nbcnews.com/news/us-new s/texas-lt-gov-dan-patrick-reopening-economy-more-important-things-n1188911.

McIntosh, Alistair, and Matt Carmichael. 2015. *Spiritual Activism: Leadership as Service,* Cambridge: Green Books.

O'Brien, Mary. 1981. *The Politics of Reproduction.* London: Routledge & Kegan Paul.

Phoenix, Joaquin. 2020. "Joaquin Phoenix Wins Best Actor." Oscars. Streamed on March 11, 2020. YouTube video, 0:05:41. https://www.youtube.com/watch?v=qii WdTz_MNc.

Plumwood, Val. 1993. *Feminism and the Mastery of Nature.* London: Routledge.

Quintero, Ignacio, and John J. Wiens. 2013. "Rates of Projected Climate Change Dramatically Exceed Past Rates of Climatic Niche Evolution among Vertebrate Species." *Ecology Letters* 16, no. 8 (June 26): 1095–1103. https://doi.org/10.1111 /ele.12144.

Raworth, Kate. 2014. "Must the Anthropocene be a Manthropocene?" *The Guardian*, October 20, 2014. https://www.theguardian.com/commentisfree/2014/oct/20/a nthropocene-working-group-science-gender-bias.

Steffen, Will, Åsa Persson, Lisa Deutsch, Jan Zalasiewicz, Mark Williams, Katherine Richardson, Carole Crumley, Paul Crutzen, Carl Folke, Line Gordon, Mario Molina, Veerabhadran Ramanathan, Johan Rockstrom, Marten Scheffer, Hans Joachim Schellnhuber, and Uno Svedin. 2011. "The Anthropocene: From Global Change to Planetary Stewardship." *AMBIO: A Journal of the Human Environment* 40, no. 7 (November): 739–61. http://doi.org/10.1007/s13280-011-0185-x.

Taylor, Bron, Jen Wright, and Todd LeVasseur. 2020. "Dark Green Humility: Religious, Psychological, and Affective Attributes of Pro-Sustainable Behaviors." *Journal of Environmental Studies and Sciences* 10 (1): 41–56. https://doi.org/10.1 007/s13412-019-00578-5.

Wake, David B., and Vance Vredenburg. 2008. "Are We in the Midst of the Sixth Mass Extinction? A View from the World of Amphibians." *PNAS* 105, supplement 1 (August 12,): 11466–73. https://doi.org/10.1073/pnas.0801921105.

Warren, Karen. 1990. "The Power and the Promise of Ecological Feminism." *Environmental Ethics* 12, no. 2 (Summer): 125–46. https://doi.org/10.5840/enviro ethics199012221.

WWF (World Wildlife Fund). 2018. "Half of Plant and Animal Species at Risk from Climate Change in World's Most Important Natural Places." News release, March 14, 2018. https://www.worldwildlife.org/press-releases/half-of-plant-and-animal-species-at-risk-from-climate-change-in-world-s-most-important-natural-places.

Yusoff, Kathryn. 2018. *A Billion Black Anthropocenes or None.* Minneapolis: University of Minnesota Press.

Zylinska, Joanna. 2016. *The End of Man: A Feminist Counterapocalypse.* Minneapolis: University of Minnesota Press.

Chapter 26

The Climate Gaze and Koalas in Extremis

Lyn McGaurr and Libby Lester

Tourism today is increasingly indistinguishable from that which is not tourism. Online technology has annihilated the getaway by allowing "normal" life to colonize our holidays and tourism to infiltrate the everyday. Imagined and virtual experiences of desirable landscapes and wildlife are ever-present, quietly hybridizing in public diplomacy, place branding, and environmental politics (Lester 2007; McGaurr 2015; McGaurr and Lester 2017). This was strikingly evident in July 2020 when Qantas airline's last jumbo jet took its final journey to an "aircraft 'boneyard'" in California (Dye 2020) and along the way used its flightpath over the Pacific Ocean to draw the shape of its logo, the flying kangaroo (Dye 2020; Xiao 2020). Whether corporeal travel is cheap and easy or we are in a pandemic lock-down, the banality of tourism in the twenty-first century produces a world in which nonhuman animals selected for aestheticization by destination promotion are our intimate companions. But because these mediated attractions are also part of the natural world, they have other lives, and deaths. Koalas, unlike kangaroos, are not swift, but their faces have something of the friendly old man about them, and their limbs are designed to embrace the tree trunks they climb, giving the upper ones the impression of being arms. These features, together with their fluffy fur, make them appear cuddly and endear them to humans. In the massive Australian conflagrations of spring and summer 2019–2020, a long legacy of tourism marketing set the stage for injured koalas to become "the international face of the fires" (Childs 2020). This interested us, because studies in the field of environmental communications have argued that visual images of charismatic fauna and landscapes threatened by climate change tend to be presented as a problem for wildlife and places rather than people (Doyle 2007, 142), while pictures of fire-fighting are read as neither salient

nor productive of individual efficacy (O'Neill et al. 2013). In the research
that produced the latter results, participants were shown pictures and asked to
categorize, sort and talk about them. We take a different path, with a different
view. In this chapter, we use media about Australia's 2019–2020 bushfires to
help us build our theory of the climate gaze. In so doing, we are indebted to
John Urry (1990, 2002; Urry and Larsen 2011), who for more than 20 years
considered how another gaze—the tourist gaze—ordered a particular form of
engagement with various cultural objects. We start our chapter by presenting
a case study of the fires and then develop our theory iteratively, using the case
to illustrate what we believe to be some of its defining elements.

CASE STUDY

At the height of an Australian bushfire season like no other, domestic and
international tourists flocked to the continent's southern and south-eastern
coasts. These places are not just the habitat of summer holidaymakers; they
are home to some of the most recognizable and popular Australians on the
planet: koalas (Commonwealth of Australia 2011; Hundloe and Hamilton
1997; Son and Pearce 2005). In November 2019, dramatic vision of a woman
rescuing a koala near Port Macquarie in New South Wales was posted to
social media and soon circulated internationally. The fact that she had taken
off her shirt to wrap the animal in and thus been filmed running after the koala
through smoldering bush in her bra contributed to her reputation as selfless.
Interviewed about her actions for television, she recalled, "The poor koala,
he was crying and screaming, because he was being burnt. He was burning
underneath, on his little back legs . . . I've never heard a koala before. I didn't
realise they could cry out. It was just so heart-rendering [*sic*]" (in Ciccarelli
2019). The koala, christened "Ellenborough Lewis," was taken to the Port
Macquarie Koala Hospital, which attracts 100,000 tourists a year (NSW
Koala Country 2019), where its recovery could be monitored by thousands
of social media followers. Farther south, koalas, kangaroos, and less popu-
larly recognizable wildlife died in large numbers in forests surrounding the
seaside settlement of Mallacoota in Victoria. On the morning of New Year's
Eve, 3,000 tourists and 1,000 residents became stranded in the holiday town.
Smoke, flames, and falling trees cut roads, a dark-orange sky rained ash,
and they fled to the water for safety (Thiessen 2019). Although much of the
town was ultimately spared, nearby blazes raged on, and it took a week for
Australian Defence Force (ADF) planes, helicopters, and ships to evacuate
all those wishing to leave. So extensive were the country's fires that summer
that even as the first thousand seaborne evacuees were being ferried to naval
vessels for the 17-hour voyage out of Mallacoota (Hope 2020; McGuire and

Butt 2020), reports of their relief competed with news of a massive fire-breaking containment lines on South Australia's Kangaroo Island, famous for its own natural attractions, including 50,000 koalas. In subsequent days and weeks, scenes of the Mallacoota evacuation, compared in one report to the movie *Dunkirk* (Hurley 2020), shared the global stage with photographs of a local hunter shirtless in a blackened forest with a rescued koala in his arms (Zappavigna 2020), as well as vision of dead kangaroos and injured koalas on Kangaroo Island (Tarabay and Simons 2020). Later, Mallacoota tourists told their own stories. In an article illustrated by a koala with bandaged paws, a Sydney woman wrote of furious nature, climate change, and koalas shrieking as they were burnt alive (O'Malley 2020a; see also O'Malley 2020b); a German couple pictured against a red-black daytime sky told a journalist that once back in Dusseldorf, their children had attempted to "consolidate the good" by inventing games in which koalas were rescued by firefighters instead of being left to die (Hope 2020); and a Canadian family pictured in a Chinook helicopter described an aftermath of nightmares and panic (Hope 2020). For a long time before and after, news and social media awash with images of injured koalas and their rescuers drew international attention to the wellbeing of individuals, the nation, and the planet. Barack Obama, already known for cuddling koalas (*NBC* 2014) and chiding Australia for failing to act decisively on climate change to ensure there would always be a Great Barrier Reef for his children and grandchildren to visit (Lester 2019), tweeted that Australia's fires were the latest consequence of climate change (Obama 2020). This elicited an angry rebuke from the Mayor of Kangaroo Island, who called the former U.S. president "pathetic" (Pengilly 2020). Undeterred, people in the United States and many other countries knitted, sewed, and dispatched koala mittens, in the hope of helping victims recover (Albeck-Ripka 2020; Paul 2020; Levison-King 2020). Some did, some didn't. Among the most celebrated individuals, "Frankie" from Mallacoota (WWF 2020; Phillip Island Nature Park 2020) and "Anwan" from Port Macquarie (Wellauer and Rubbo 2020) survived, while "Ellenborough Lewis" from Port Macquarie (Chambers 2019) and "Billy" from Adelaide in South Australia (ABC 2020) were less fortunate. By Australia Day, January 26, such a deluge of mittens, pouches, and other items for wildlife had arrived from overseas that the Animal Rescue Cooperative Craft Guild asked people to stop sending them. A *BBC* report on the phenomenon cited the contribution to climate change of international airline emissions among reasons to send money instead of such goods (Levinson-King 2020). But even this did not stem interest in the koalas' fates: when survivors started being returned to the wild in March, releases were reported in the United Kingdom, the United States, and Europe, including an article by tourism magazine *Travel + Leisure* (Rizzo 2020)—a good news story amid rising coronavirus restrictions and alarm.

The fires, which had started in earnest in October, were finally brought under control in February. By then, more than 10 million hectares (38,610 square miles) had burned (CSIRO 2020), perhaps 1 billion animals had died (University of Sydney 2020) and somewhere between 650 million and 1.2 billion tonnes of carbon dioxide had been released, equating to the annual emissions of the world's commercial airlines before they were grounded by the coronavirus pandemic (Climate Council 2020). In New South Wales, where koalas are listed as vulnerable, it was estimated that 8,000 had died. On Kangaroo Island, where overpopulation was a concern before the fires, the sheer number of deaths created news, with estimates as high as 25,000. In Victoria, where the species is not considered to be threatened, the news was less of overall deaths and more about how Mallacoota koalas were rescued by the public, triaged by the State Government, evacuated by the ADF, treated and rehabilitated in zoos, animal hospitals, and wildlife parks and, if they survived, released in places where suitable habitat remained intact or seemed to be regenerating. There were also articles about koalas starving in destroyed forests, and up to forty deaths due to commercial logging of a fenced plantation in the State's south-west, a story made all the more newsworthy for the *BBC* and *Time* by its temporal proximity to koala deaths from the fires (*BBC* 2020; Godin 2020).

FROM THE TOURIST GAZE TO THE CLIMATE GAZE

Revisiting these stories of Australia's bushfire summer of 2019–2020 after six months, we are struck by how much tourism is enmeshed in their discourses. For more than 50 years, Australia has projected idealized images of koalas as must-see attractions (Markwell 2020), and its success is evident in studies that demonstrate their economic and cultural significance (Commonwealth of Australia 2011; Huang and Gross 2010; Hundloe and Hamilton 1997; Son and Pearce 2008). The koala is now so closely identified with Australia and Australianness that a 2011 Senate inquiry into whether it should be listed as threatened called its report "Saving an Australian Icon" despite finding the species was vulnerable in only three of the five jurisdictions where it occurs naturally. This is the tourist gaze at work: the self-conscious selection and projection by professionals of images authorized by different discourses ordering people's engagement with cultural objects (1990, 2002; Urry and Larsen 2011). Urry argues that even as people bring their own meanings to their reception of photographs and videos, the visual images projected by destination promotion are capable of influencing not just prospective tourists' choices but the way visitors to the destination remember and reproduce the physical objects they encounter in their corporeal, imaginative, or virtual travels. Jenkins's description of a "circle of representation" partly explains the process:

> Images of the destination are projected collectively by the mass media. These images are perceived by individuals and may inspire travel to the destination. At the destination the tourist will likely visit the main attractions or tourist icons seen in the projected images and record his or her experience using a camera. These personal photographs are displayed back home to friends and relatives partly as proof of the visit. They may be thought of as another form of image projection, which begins the cycle again by influencing the perceived images held by other individuals. Tourism advertisers and marketers aiming to propagate attractive images may also be involved in image projection. (Jenkins 2008, 308)

The beach is another Australian "icon" that features prominently in tourism brochures and travelers' perceptions (Conrad 2014; Huang and Gross 2010; Hundloe and Hamilton 1997; Jenkins 2003; Son and Pearce 2008). This is hardly surprising when we recall that Urry believed an examination of departures could help scholars interrogate the "normal." Urry conceptualized tourism as an escape from a "normal" life primarily characterized by home and work (Urry 2002, 12). Written and visual discourses of "escapes" and "getaways" are a mainstay of English-language travel journalism and Australian tourism marketing. Holiday "escapes" that promise to put spatial, temporal, and psychological distance between holidaymakers and everyday life tap into Western cultural understandings of the "normal" as serviceable but tiring and insufficient for a life well lived. To embark on a holiday "escape," therefore, is to flee work and home with the dream of leaving care behind. Speed may be of the essence but only until the holiday destination is in sight, at which moment all sense of haste is meant to dissolve. But Australia's 2019–2020 bushfires turned these notions on their head. Instead of tourism icons bestowing a sense of wellbeing, the beach was remade as terrifying and koalas encountered as suffering casualties. Suddenly, escape meant returning home as fast as possible. Tourists no longer sought freedom from "normal" life but yearned to reclaim it.

Of course, the possibility of escaping "normal" life in the twenty-first century simply by taking a physical holiday is illusory: technology connects tourists with work even when they are away; access to online devices gives almost everyone the opportunity to mediate their experiences for family, friends, or strangers around the world in real time; and climate change means the environmental consequences of our "normal" lives can materialize in the most distant destinations. This knowledge is incipient in last-chance tourism that encourages us to see threatened places and species "before it's too late" (McGaurr 2015; McGaurr and Lester 2018). Physical consequence is layered upon this nascent awareness when Jenkins's circle of representation is disrupted by photographs of koalas with terrible burns, holiday skies filled with smoke, and beaches populated by defence force personnel and military craft. Such images recalibrate our understanding of "escape" and in so doing help make the temporalities of climate change comprehensible at multiple scales. Through an emergent climate gaze, scenery and wildlife rendered desirable by tourism can be encountered as symbols of interconnected vulnerability. Even in an era of coronavirus, when travel is being promoted as a defining feature of a pre- and post-COVID-19 "normal," tourism scholars referencing Australia's bushfire summer are looking for ways that the tourism industry and tourists can evolve after the pandemic to perpetuate environmental gains delivered by reduced travel during lock-down (Crossley 2020; Prideaux et al. 2020; Sun in Gray 2020). Crossley (2020) goes so far as to consider the possibility that environmental grief does not only encompass grief at environmental losses but also grief at the necessary loss of the prosperity-producing "normal" that will be required to make environmental reparation. For Crossley:

> Action on carbon emissions has come, just not in response to pressure from the climate movement. The tourism industry finds itself at the centre of this historic confluence. Mounting climate-related concerns about the ethics of flying to holiday destinations have been answered by COVID-19's abrupt cessation of almost all non-essential air travel. (Crossley 2020, 5)

Crossley asks whether fascination with the supposed rewilding of Venice during the pandemic might be an expression of ecological grief and environmental hope working together to pave the way for projects of hopeful tourism in the post-COVID-19 world, particularly as the pandemic occurred so soon after 2019's climate strikes and Australia's 2019–2020 bushfires. Whereas Murphy sees "ecological ambivalence" arising from media caught in a "cycle of passive recognition and weakly ecological, consumer-based action" (Murphy 2017, 145), and Mkono (2020) finds evidence of eco-hypocrisy in the gap between ecotourists' attitudes and behavior, for Crossley these are challenges for the design of tourism futures but ones that can be addressed by "harnessing and channelling environmental hope in a way that truly does heal the natural world and, in the process, heals our ecological grief" (Crossley 2020, 8).

Aestheticization and Spectacle

Aestheticizing landscapes and animals to render their loss more shocking is a common practice of environmental groups (Lester 2007; Doyle 2007; Lester and Cottle 2009; McGaurr 2015; McGaurr and Lester 2017, 2018). Particular landscapes and wildlife are promoted and reported as evidence of what is being threatened. Many of these places, animals, and plants will already have been aestheticized by tourism, but some may be aestheticized directly by climate and other environmental lobbying or activism and then appropriated by tourism. Our earlier studies have found extensive evidence of this in protracted conflicts over British Columbia's Great Bear Rainforest and Tasmania's wilderness, as well as in the deployment of the Great Barrier Reef in climate change discourse. In each case, visual symbols circulate between tourism and environmentalism, fuelling each other's campaigns (Lester 2007; McGaurr 2015; McGaurr and Lester 2017). At the same time, spectacles of damaged nature and extreme weather events are made salient through publicized contestation (Lester 2007; McGaurr 2015). These processes are structured by the climate gaze to order public reception and reproduction of extreme weather events and their consequences. Typical images of the bushfires in stories of extensive and ferocious fires in Australia told in the 2019–2020 spring and summer included vision of emergency workers dwarfed by flames, fire trucks screeching through ember attacks, and time-lapse photography of pulsating red horizons. In the aftermath, scenes of comparative stillness were published to remind audiences of the cost but also how rapidly the fires had advanced: carcasses of kangaroos and wallabies that could not outrun the flames; silent shells of destroyed homes; blackened stock; and devastated survivors grieving among the ruins. But amid this swirling imagery, the globally mediated lives of Australia's koalas and beaches rendered the crisis far more newsworthy than it might otherwise have been, via, for example, dramatic footage of a koala being burned and tourists being evacuated from beaches. Thus, the aesthetic of beaches and koalas, like their symbolic narrative as noted earlier, was grossly destabilized by spectacles of suffering, attack and military-style maneuvers.

Visual "Truth" and Surveillance

In theorizing the tourist gaze, Urry pays tribute to Foucault's interest in "visual domination in the operation of power" (Urry 1992, p. 175) and the interiorization of the all-seeing eye of the panopticon. Jonas Larsen, the co-author of Urry's last edition of the *Tourist Gaze*, has observed that the "making of seductive images and destinations [can be seen] as institutional mediation by 'expert gazes' within which spectacle and surveillance intersect" (Larsen 2014, p. 306). Surveillance in terms of the climate gaze often generates controversy about what climate change does and doesn't look like. In his book *Weathered: Cultures of Climate*, Mike Hulme (2016) addresses such questions of visual truth when he relates the difficulty of visualizing climate change to the constructed nature of climate itself. For Hulme:

> If "seeing is believing," then giving visual form to the idea of climate (and its changes) becomes a pre-condition of belief in climate (and its changes). But there is no simple instrument, nor a complex one, that extends the human senses such that climate can be witnessed. (Hulme 2016, 94)

Debates about visual truth do not invalidate the climate gaze. Rather, contestation among actors who share a desire for action on global warming is one of its defining features. The climate gaze is authorized by an uneasy discourse coalition of actors, storylines and practices from science, journalism, the environmental movement and, crucially, tourism. Discourse coalitions are key features of Maarten Hajer's (1993) "argumentative approach" to explaining political change in terms of struggles for discursive hegemony. At the heart of those struggles are narratives that frame problems in ways that can satisfy actors from multiple discourse domains—that is, domains that impose a degree of structural constraint on the discourses of the actors in those domains. The discourse coalition that organizes the climate gaze engages in, is subjected to and is ever aware of surveillance from within as well as without. Media coverage of Australia's bushfire summer provided many opportunities for surveillance by discourse-coalition experts concerned about the accuracy of visual climate-change discourses. Once koalas became "the international face of the fires" (Childs 2010), contestation about whether they were now in greater danger of extinction were enmeshed with discussions of climate change and its role in the increased prevalence and intensity of fires (Castagnino 2020a, b, c; Childs 2020; Fortin 2019; Markwell 2020; Ritchie 2020). One example indicative of this is a series of three interviews about the koala's environmental status published by U.S. environmental news site *Mongabay*. In the first interview, the Port Macquarie Koala Hospital's Cheyne Flanagan responds to the question "How can people get involved with koala conservation?" by encouraging them to lobby governments to legislate a reduction in carbon emissions (Castagnino 2020a). In the second, with Rebecca Montague-Drake from the Koala Recovery Partnership, the interviewee nominates addressing climate change "to stop the drivers of impacts such as drought and bushfire" as the second-most important action required to reverse koala decline in New South Wales, after land clearing (Castagnino 2020b). However, in answer to the question "What can we learn from these past months?" she passionately engages with people's experiences of the fires as "climate refugees" (Montague-Drake in Castagnino 2020b). In the third interview, entitled "Koalas vs Climate Change," John Zichy-Woinarski of the International Union for the Conservation of Nature (IUCN) strongly advocates for a reduction in greenhouse gas emissions to benefit wildlife generally but gives much greater prominence to other threats to koalas, as demonstrated in the following extracts. In the question and answer we present first, which is actually the last in the published interview, Zichy-Woinarski constructs climate change as an urgent global problem for biodiversity:

[Mongabay:] What can we learn from this devastating bushfire crisis?

[John Zichy-Woinarski:] Yes, there are many lessons, and they are apposite globally: 1., [*sic*] climate change will have devastating consequences for biodiversity, so if we are serious about species conservation then we need to strive harder to constrain it. (In Castagnino 2020c)

Prior to this, however, he had repeatedly foregrounded land clearing, disease, and habitat fragmentation rather than climate change as the most pressing threats to koalas, despite implicit encouragement by the interviewer to make a stronger climate-change link:

Mongabay: What are some measures that the Australian government can implement to get this species back on track considering that climate change will possibly increase the intensity of bushfires in the future?

John Zichy-Woinarski: Probably the single factor that could make the most improvement to koala conservation is tighter control on land clearing. (In Castagnino 2020c)

And here:

[Mongabay:] The risk of inbreeding increases as climate change isolates koala populations. How important are breeding programs to maintain the continued existence of viable koala populations in the wild for the species' long-term survival?

[John Zichy-Woinarski:] Koala populations are isolated by many factors, notably habitat loss and fragmentation. Climate change is probably not so important for koala continuity and maintenance of genetic diversity: climate change is mostly reducing the peripheral (lower rainfall edge of range) populations. There is a long history of koala translocations to try to rebuild local populations and manage genetic diversity but such translocations are somewhat constrained by risks of the spread of disease. (In Castagnino 2020c)

Only on one occasion does Zichy-Woinarski allow himself to be led, somewhat reluctantly, to make his comments about climate change specific to koalas:

[Mongabay:] Increased carbon dioxide concentrations in the atmosphere leads to a decrease in nutrients stored in trees, and therefore a degradation in the quality of eucalyptus leaves. How important is it to consider factors like this in recovery plans for the species?

[John Zichy-Woinarski:] That's an emerging threat, but not readily resolved by management actions. I'm afraid that the only known solution is to strive harder to constrain greenhouse gas emissions and climate change and to help reduce the intensity and effects of other threats. (In Castagnino 2020c)

Scientific discourse features in all the interviews but is most consistent in the guarded answers given by Zichy-Woinarski. That is, the discourse of the other two interviewees tends to environmental activism more than Zichy-Woinarski's. All three interviews feature photographs of bushfires, with the image used in the second interview including a firefighter in the frame. However, differences between the other images selected for each article demonstrate the operation of surveillance in the climate gaze. Zichy-Woinarski is speaking on behalf of a global body comprising both government and non-government members. The remaining photographs that accompany his interview are of blackened forest, regenerating forest, an apparently healthy koala eating eucalyptus leaves and a wombat. Here, the imagery, considered in the context of the written text is somewhat hopeful, pointing to short-term recovery and the possibility of long-term survival if land is better managed and carbon emissions are reduced. The introduction of a photograph of a wombat to a story about koalas responds to Zichy-Woinarski's reservations about the effectiveness of using koalas as "flagships" and "umbrellas" to attract attention to, and preserve, habitat that will benefit other, less charismatic species, and his view that "the public wave of support for koalas is also driven largely by animal welfare concerns rather than species conservation per se" (Zichy-Woinarski in Castagnino 2020b). However, it also respects Zichy-Woinarski's choice to keep his comments about climate-change impacts on fauna mostly generic rather than endorsing the interviewee's apparent desire to make them specific to koalas. In the second interview, three images of apparently healthy koalas in trees and one of a healthy forest are contrasted with a photograph of cleared trees and another of burnt cars—the only image of direct impact on humans in the series. By contrast, images in the interview with the clinical director of a koala hospital that is also a tourist attraction tap into a popular discourse of suffering prominent in coverage of the bushfires. Images accompanying Flanagan's interview feature a photograph of "a rescued koala" in the arms of a man. The man is patting the koala, which suggests he is reassuring it, but his head is out of frame, focusing our attention on the koala's head resting on his shoulder and the koala's paw appearing to embrace him. Interpreted anthropomorphically, the koala's expression is concerned or sad, while the position of its paw and the prominence of its splayed claws make it appear to be clinging to the man for comfort. The third photo in the article is a close-up of a koala's paw. The significance of koala paws and distress in the media about Australia's bushfire summer will be discussed at greater length in the final section of our chapter. For now, we note that the difference in koala imagery in the above three interviews highlights the suppleness of the climate gaze when contestation occurs. For *Mongabay*'s audiences, the universal celebrity of koalas deployed in the series of interviews functions to enmesh its fate with climate-change concern even when friendly surveillance is at work.

The panopticon of social media also enables members of the public who have internalized the climate gaze to enact surveillance in support of discourse coalition members who link increasing extreme weather events and climate change. In December 2019, when the environmental movement was expressing outrage via social and news media that Prime Minister Scott Morrison—a former managing director of Tourism Australia—was holidaying in Hawaii instead of being on the ground with people affected by the fires, his concern about public opinion was almost certainly responsible for his eventual grudging concession reported by *NBC*:

> There is no argument . . . about the links between broader issues of global climate change and weather events around the world . . . But I'm sure people equally would acknowledge that the direct connection to any single fire event— it's not a credible suggestion to make that link. (Morrison in Associated Press 2019)

Tourism discourse and symbols were also overtly deployed, as when the tagline of an unsuccessful Tourism Australia marketing campaign launched under Morrison's leadership, "Where The Bloody Hell Are You," became a hashtag that frequently appeared in tweets with varying combinations of #ScottyfromMarketing (another reference to the prime minister's Tourism Australia days) and climate-change words in the body of tweets or their hashtags. #ClimateEmergency and other climate hashtags were also combined with koala hashtags and images of koalas throughout the disaster.

The Reverse Gaze, Intimacy, Grief and Hope

There is another feature of the tourist gaze that is called into the service of the climate gaze. This is the reverse tourist gaze (Gillespie 2006), which refers to the discomfort tourists experience when the facial expressions of those they photograph challenge their preconceptions of themselves as benign and welcome guests. While we fully acknowledge the validity and value of critiquing images of koalas during the 2019–2020 Australian fires as anthropomorphic and infantalizing (for critiques of animals in tourism, see Markwell 2015), the concept of the reverse climate gaze offers an opportunity for an alternative reading of our case study. Whereas conservation science tends to subordinate the welfare of individuals to the fortunes of the species (for example, Zichy-Woinarski in Castagnino 2020c), and tourism discourse foregrounds the economic value of charismatic wildlife (Commonwealth of Australia 2011; Conrad 2014; Tisdell 2014), the reverse gaze accommodates intimacy between humans and nonhumans. In photographs of Australia's bushfire spring and summer, injured koala after injured koala stares back at the viewer from social media and news websites. Koalas are slow-moving. As explained by the *New York Times* in a story about Australia's fires published in January 2020, when trying to escape bushfires, they do not usually move away but attempt to climb into the forest canopy. If the fire passes before spreading to the canopy, they may be safe, but very intense and fast-moving fires can crown and jump from tree top to tree top:

> Even if the fire itself does not reach the tree canopy, the animals may overheat and fall to the ground, where they can be burned to death. They can also suffer smoke inhalation, or burn their paws or claws when trying to climb down trees. (Albeck-Ripka 2019)

This is why so many koalas that were rescued had bandaged paws and mittens. Indicative of this is the image of "Billy" posted by the *ABC* on the announcement of his death (ABC 2020). All four of his paws are covered in white bandages and bright blue cloth. Although seated, he is leaning on his front paws and appears to be staring intently at the viewer. Far more so than visual images of an idealized koala being projected to forge bonds between Australia and its consumers, but indebted to the tourist gaze nevertheless, this photograph has the capacity to establish a sense of relationship between human and nonhuman animals experiencing climate-change impacts and a sense of responsibility for the koala's plight. Viewed in combination with photographs of terrified tourists, landscapes that look like war zones and Mallacoota's holiday beach recast as a refugee camp and landing base for evacuation, these images contribute to a climate-gaze discourse that constructs koalas and humans as climate refugees together and fellow travelers in distress.

CONCLUSION

Our case study demonstrates the potential for the climate gaze to help navigate "a discursive terrain of environmental messages" that are "confusing, often contradictory, and obscured by mixed regimes of truth" (Murphy 2017, 145). It can do this because it accommodates and accounts for aestheticization, contestation by the professionals from multiple discourse domains whose discourses authorize it, and the generation of a progressive reflexivity. Most importantly, perhaps, in the context of this edited collection, it makes space for a sense of intimacy between individual human and nonhuman animals cultivated by tourism to be harnessed in the interests of environmental communication despite tension between discourses of animal welfare and species conservation, as well as legitimate critiques of anthropomorphism in the visual discourses of tourism.

ACKNOWLEDGMENT

This research was funded in part by the Australian Research Council DP150103454.

BIBLIOGRAPHY

ABC. 2020. "RIP Billy the Koala." Facebook, January 30, 2020. https://www.fac ebook.com/abcinsydney/photos/rip-billy-the-koala-%EF%B8%8Fsad-news-billy -unfortunately-didnt-make-it-to-the-end-of-hi/10158243125179015/.

Albeck-Ripka, Livia. 2020. "Koala Mittens and Baby Bottles: Saving Australia's Animals After Fires." *New York Times*, January 7, 2020 (updated January 8, 2020). https://www.nytimes.com/2020/01/07/world/australia/animals-wildlife-fires.html.

Albeck-Ripka, Livia. 2019. "Saving the Fire Victims Who Cannot Flee: Australia's Koalas." *New York Times*, November 14, 2019. https://www.nytimes.com/2019/11 /14/world/australia/australia-koalas-fire.html?searchResultPosition=3.

Associated Press. 2019. "As Wildfires Rage, Australia's PM Apologises for Family Vacation and Defends Climate Policies." *NBC*, December 22, 2019. https://ww w.nbcnews.com/news/world/wildfires-rage-australian-pm-apologizes-family-vac ation-defends-climate-policies-n1106241.

BBC News. 2020. "Koalas Found Dead on Australian Logging Plantation." *BBC News*, February 2, 2020. https://www.bbc.com/news/world-australia-51346637.

Castagnino, Romina. 2020a. "How are koalas doing in the aftermath of the Australian fires? Q&A with Cheyne Flanagan." *Mongabay*, March 17, 2020. https://news .mongabay.com/2020/03/how-are-koalas-doing-in-the-aftermath-of-the-australian- fires-qa-with-cheyne-flanagan/.

———— 2020b. "How to help koalas recover after Australia's fires? Q&A with Rebecca Montague-Drake." *Mongabay*, March 19, 2020. https://news.mongabay .com/2020/03/how-to-help-koalas-recover-after-australias-fires-qa-with-rebecca-montague-drake/.

———— 2020c. "Koalas Vs Climate Change: Q&Q with John Zichy-Woinarski." *Mongabay*, March 24, 2020. https://news.mongabay.com/2020/03/koalas-vs-c limate-change-qa-with-john-zichy-woinarski/.

Chambers, Alice. 2019. "Koala Rescued in Dramatic Viral Video Dies of Injuries." *ABC* (US), November 26, 2019. https://abcnews.go.com/International/koala-re scued-dramatic-viral-video-dies-injuries/story?id=67314846.

Childs, Jan Wesner. 2020. "Koalas, Under Stress From Wildfires and Climate Change, Could Become Extinct in One Part of Australia." *Weather Channel*, July 3, 2020. https://weather.com/science/nature/news/2020-07-03-koalas-extinct-new-south-wales-fires-climate-change.

Chow, Denise. 2019. "Australia is on Fire, Literally—and So Are Its Climate Politics." *NBC*, December 19, 2019. https://www.nbcnews.com/science/environm ent/australia-fire-literally-so-are-its-climate-politics-n1104351.

Ciccarelli, Rafaella. 2020. "This Mallacoota Local is Putting His Life on the Line to Save Koalas." *Today*, January, 2020. https://9now.nine.com.au/today/victoria-fires-mallacoota-local-puts-life-on-line-to-save-koalas/f20708ae-b97f-4815-a2b9-7099e0859816.

———— 2019. "He was crying, because he was being burnt." *Today*, November 2019. https://9now.nine.com.au/today/nsw-fires-koala-lewis-reunited-with-aussie-who -took-shirt-off-her-back-to-save-him/32de4eb0-85e4-4357-871f-b746d37097d1.

Climate Council. 2020. *Summer of Crisis*. Climate Council of Australia Ltd. https:/ /www.climatecouncil.org.au/wp-content/uploads/2020/03/Crisis-Summer-Report -200311.pdf

Commonwealth of Australia. 2011. *The Koala: Saving Our National Icon*. Canberra: The Senate Environment and Communications Reference Committee, Parliament of Australia, September, 2011, Chapter 1, 9–12. https://www.aph.gov.au/Parliam entary_Business/Committees/Senate/Environment_and_Communications/Compl eted_inquiries/2010-13/koalas/report/index.

Conrad, Emily. 2014. *The Economic Value of the Koala*. Australian Koala Foundation, August 6, 2014. https://www.savethekoala.com/sites/savethekoala.co m/files/uploads/Conrad%202014%20The%20Economic%20Value%20of%20the %20Koala%5B2%5D.pdf.

Crossley, Émilie. 2020. "Ecological Grief Generates Desire for Environmental Healing in Tourism After COVID-19." *Tourism Geographies*, online first (May): 1–8. https://doi.org/10.1080/14616688.2020.1759133.

CSIRO. 2020. "The 2019–2020 Bushfires: A CSIRO Explainer." Commonwealth Scientific and Industrial Research Organisation, February 18, 2020. https://ww w.csiro.au/en/Research/Environment/Extreme-Events/Bushfire/preparing-for-cl imate-change/2019-20-bushfires-explainer.

Doyle, Julie. 2007. "Picturing the Clima(c)tic: Greenpeace and the Representational Politics of Climate Change Communication." *Science as Culture*, 16 (2): 129–150.

Dye, Josh. 2020. "Qantas Boeing 747 farewell: Tears as last jumbo jet departs Australia for final time." July 22, 2020. https://www.traveller.com.au/qantas-boei ng-747-farewell-tears-a-last-jumbo-jet-departs-australia-for-final-time-h1pisg.

Ferreras, Jesse. 2018. "This Polar Bear Is Starving, But It's Not 'What Climate Change Looks Like': National Geographic." *Global News*, August 1, 2018. https:// globalnews.ca/news/4361868/polar-bear-climate-change-national-geographic/

Filipovic, Jill. 2019. "Lewis the Koala's Death is a Sad End to a Terrible Tale." CNN, November 27, 2019. https://edition.cnn.com/2019/11/26/opinions/lewis-the-koala-fire-death-climate-filipovic/index.html.

Fortin, Jacey. 2019. "Koalas Aren't Extinct, but Their Future Is in Danger, Experts Say." *New York Times*, November 25, 2019. https://www.nytimes.com/2019/11 /25/world/australia/koala-fires-functionally-extinct.html?searchResultPosition=5.

Gillespie, Alex. 2006. "Tourist Photography and the Reverse Gaze." *ETHOS*, 34 (3): 343–366.

Godin, Mélissa. 2020. "'Australia Should Be Ashamed' After More Than 40 Koalas Killed on Logging Site." *Time*, February 4, 2020. https://time.com/5777362/austr alia-koalas-killed-logging-site/.

Gray, Lachlan Moffat. 2020. "Coronavirus Causes 150 Million Job Losses, Largest Greenhouse Gas Emissions Drop in History." *Australian*, July 10, 2020. https ://www.theaustralian.com.au/business/economics/coronavirus-causes-150-million -job-losses-largest-greenhouse-gas-emissions-drop-in-history/news-story/f9a35f 56fb71db5475801c995b73acc.

Hajer, Maarten A. 1993. "Discourse Coalitions and the Institutionalisation of Practice: The Case of Acid Rain in Great Britain." In: *The Argumentative Turn in Policy Analysis and Planning* edited by Frank Fischer and John Forester, 43–67. London: Duke University Press.

Hope, Zach. 2020. "When Trauma Comes Home: Tourists of Mallacoota Relive Their Summer." *Age*, February 22, 2020. https://www.theage.com.au/national/victoria/w hen-trauma-comes-home-tourists-of-mallacoota-relive-their-summer-20200216-p 5418f.html.

Huang, Songshan and Michael J. Gross. 2010. "Australia's Destination Image Among Mainland Chinese Travelers: An Exploratory Study." *Journal of Travel and Tourism Marketing*, 27: 63–81. DOI: 10.1080/10548400903534923.

Hulme, Mike. 2017. *Weathered: Cultures of Climate*. London: SAGE.

Hundloe, Tor, and Hamilton, Clive. 1997. "Koalas and Tourism: An Economic Evaluation." Australia Institute, Discussion Paper no. 13 (July). https://www.tai .org.au/sites/default/files/DP13_8.pdf

Hurley, David. 2020. "Inside the Delicate Operation to Save Mallacoota Locals." *Herald Sun*, January 4, 2020. https://www.heraldsun.com.au/news/victoria/in side-the-delicate-operation-to-save-stranded-mallacoota-locals/news-story/b05e5d 516cf9dedbe4d18ce7f7eb98b4.

Larsen, Jonas. 2014. "The Tourist Gaze 1.0, 2.0 and 3.0." In *The Wiley Blackwell Companion to Tourism*, edited by A Lew, C Hall and A Williams, 304–313. Chichester: Wiley Blackwell.

Lester, Libby. 2019. *Global Trade and Mediatised Environmental Protest: The View from Here*. Cham, Switzerland: Palgrave Macmillan.

———— 2007. *Giving Ground: Media and Environmental Conflict in Tasmania*. Hobart: Quintus.

Levinson-King, Robin. 2020. "Why Australia Probably Doesn't Need More Koala Mittens." *BBC*, January 26, 2020. https://www.bbc.com/news/world-us-canada-51197129.

Markwell, Kevin. 2020. "Koalas Are the Face of Australian Tourism. What Now After the Fires?" *Conversation*, January 7, 2020. https://theconversation.com/koalas-are-the-face-of-australian-tourism-what-now-after-the-fires-129347.

———— (editor) 2015. *Animals and Tourism: Understanding Diverse Relationships*. Bristol: Channel View Publications.

McGaurr, Lyn. 2015. *Environmental Communication and Travel Journalism: Consumerism, Conflict and Concern*. Abingdon: Routledge.

McGaurr, Lyn and Libby Lester. 2018. "See It Before It's Too Late: Last Chance Travel Lists and Climate Change." In *Climate Change and the Media Volume 2*, edited by Benedetta Brevini and Justin Lewis, 123–140. New York: Peter Lang.

———— 2017. "Environmental Groups Treading the Discursive Tightrope of Social Licence: Australian and Canadian Cases Compared." *International Journal of Communication* 11: 3476–3496.

McGuire, Amelia, and Butt, Craig. 2020. "Cut Off: How the Crisis at Mallacoota Unfolded." Age, January 19, 2020. https://www.nytimes.com/2020/02/04/world/australia/kangaroo-island-fire.html?searchResultPosition=6.

Murphy, P, 2017, "Conclusion," *The Media Commons: Globalization and Environmental Discourses* Chicago: University of Illinois Press.

NSW Koala Country. 2019. "Cheyne Flanagan: Koala Hospital Director." https://koala.nsw.gov.au/portfolio/cheyne-flanagan/.

Obama, Barack (@BarackObama). 2020. 8am, January 10, 2020. https://twitter.com/BarackObama/status/1215377738858663937.

O'Malley, Mary. 2020. "'Nature Has Spoken and She Is Furious': On the Beach in Mallacoota." *Age*, January 6, 2020. https://www.smh.com.au/national/koalas-shrieked-as-they-burnt-on-the-beach-in-mallacoota-20200106-p53p4a.html.

———— Mary. 2020. "'Koalas Shrieked as They Burnt': On the Beach in Mallacoota." *Stuff*, January 6, 2020. https://www.stuff.co.nz/world/australia/118614106/koalas-shrieked-as-they-burnt-on-the-beach-in-mallacoota.

O'Neill, S., M. Boykoff, S. Niemeyer and S. Day. 2013. "On the Use of Imagery for Climate Change Engagement." *Global Environmental Change*, 23: 413–421.

Paul, Kari. 2020. "Kangaroo Pouches, Koala Mittens: Knitters Unite to Aid Animals in Australia." Guardian, January 8, 2020. https://www.theguardian.com/australia-news/2020/jan/07/australia-wildfires-animals-shelters-knitting.

Pengilly, Michael (@MichaelPengilly). 2020. 12.56pm, January 10, 2020. https://twitter.com/PengillyMichael/status/1215452299880845317.

Phillip Island Nature Parks. 2020. *Koala Rehabilitation Report*. May 2020. https://www.penguins.org.au/assets/Conservation/Environment/PDF/Koala-Rehabilitation-Report-2020.pdf.

Prideaux, Bruce, Michelle Thompson and Anja Pabel. 2020. "Lessons from COVID-19 Can Prepare Global Tourism for the Economic Transformation Needed to Combat Climate Change." *Tourism Geographies*, online first (May): 1–12. https://doi.org/10.1080/14616688.2020.1762117.

Ritchie, Emily. 2020. "Bushfires: Koala Deaths a Catastrophe but Extinction a Long Way Off Say Wildlife Experts." Australian, January 13, 2020. https://www.theaustralian.com.au/nation/bushfires-koala-deaths-a-catastrophe-but-extinction-a-long-way-off-say-wildlife-experts/news-story/a11d46db422dfe25f26ec50be802a9ce.

Rizzo, Cailey. 2020. "Koalas Rescued from Australia's Bushfires Are Finally Getting Released Back into the Wild." *Travel + Leisure*, circa March 2020 (updated July 18, 2020). https://www.travelandleisure.com/animals/koalas-released-into-wild-australia-bushfires.

Son, Aram, and Pearce, Philip. 2005. "Multifaceted Image Assessment: International Views of Australia as a Tourist Destination." *Journal of Travel and Tourism Marketing*, 18 (4): 21–35. DOI: https://doi.org/10.1300/J073v18n04_02.

Tarabay, Jamie, and Simons, Christina. 2020. "There's No Place Like Kangaroo Island. Can It Survive Australia's Fires?" *New York Times*, February 4, 2020. https://www.nytimes.com/2020/02/04/world/australia/kangaroo-island-fire.html?searchResultPosition=6.

Tisdell, Clement A. 2014. *Human Values and Biodiversity Conservation: The Survival of Wild Species*. Cheltenham: Edward Elgar Publishing.

University of Sydney. 2020. "More than One Billion Animals Killed in Australian Bushfires." University of Sydney, January 8, 2020. https://www.sydney.edu.au/news-opinion/news/2020/01/08/australian-bushfires-more-than-one-billion-animals-impacted.html.

Urry, John. 2002. *The Tourist Gaze*. Second edition. London: Sage Publications.

——— 1990. *The Tourist Gaze*. London: Sage Publications.

Urry, John. 1992. "The Tourist Gaze 'Revisited,'" *American Behavioral Scientist*, 36 (2): 172–186.

Urry, John, and Jonas Larsen. 2011. *The Tourist Gaze 3.0*. London: Sage Publications.

Wellauer, Kirstie, and Rubbo, Luisa. 2020. "Port Macquarie Koala Hospital Releases Its Most Famous Bushfire Victim Anwen." *ABC* (Aus), April 3, 2020. https://www.abc.net.au/news/2020-04-03/bushfire-koala-victim-anwen-returned-home/12119994.

Wharton, Jane. 2019. "Lewis the Koala Dies a Week After Being Rescued from Bush Fires." Metro, November 27, 2019. https://metro.co.uk/2019/11/27/lewis-koala-dies-week-rescued-bush-fires-11225346/.

WWF. 2020. "Update on Frankie the Koala." WWF, April 23. https://www.wwf.org.au/news/blogs/update-on-koala-from-mallacoota-australia-bushfires#gs.b2ebpt.

Zappavigna, Adrianna. 2020. "Local Hunter Turned Koala Hero Becomes Viral Sensation." *news.com.au*, January 4, 2020. https://www.news.com.au/technology/environment/local-hunter-turned-koala-hero-becomes-viral-sensation/news-story/b923f9c75b0a30e83cc7c880d6653ef8.

Chapter 27

From Fatbergs to Microplastics

New Intimacies of an Extruded World

Paul Alberts

PERSPECTIVES: PRECISE AND FUZZY

We live in a time when the deep complicity between knowing and see-ing—one of the oldest of epistemic patterns that humans employ—has been shaken yet again, this time by news from everywhere. Many perspectives have arrived at once. How is this so? Not because the globe is "smaller"— something which we have experienced now for several centuries, beginning perhaps with the invention of the telescope, and further as railways, roads and then air routes segmented space, domesticating our transits, commodifying landscapes. Rather because anywhere on the globe today we might nominate as "this place" can now be disclosed and documented in immaculate and rigorous empirical detail as an outcome, in fact, of complex physical inter-connections and processes, most of them vast in scale compared with the experience of a single human life. Saying something like, as humans have always wanted to do, "I know this place in this present moment," can now be counted, given a knowledgeable listener, as a certain naiveté. Our dominant paradigms of proper knowledge, the natural sciences, have now generated the most amazingly detailed considerations of how life is disposed in its biotic and physical settings, from the microscopic to the macro-scales of global systems. In circuits of elements (for example, water, carbon dioxide, nitro-gen, and phosphorous) or ecological waves of successive species, decades or centuries long, or through the detailed processes of erosion, sedimentation and dispersal of soils, somewhere, in fact anywhere, is explicable as part and parcel of processes immensely longer in duration, distant in origination, and yet more determining than the cycles of seasons we might remember or the rapid blinks of day and night that flicker through our human life spans. Earth

sciences, ecology, and climatology have in the space of a few decades, and
with the impetus now of almost daily reportage and explanations of dramatic
ecological and climatic shifts, opened our eyes to long perspectives that make
each place and its present, a temporary collation of fragile moments of planetary becoming.

Of course, we (who can afford to be part of this knowing "we") still
desire to feel the intimacy of knowing a place in nonquantifiable fashion,
perhaps of belonging in some traditional or comforting way, or longing to
belong—and standing before somewhere reflecting how we ourselves are
also included, and included in some way which is immeasurable, and must
be intrinsically immeasurable. This contrary perspective—the affect or feeling for place, for the things or objects we experience there, and of being
simultaneously *emplaced* cannot/must not be calculated or reduced to numbers, as it intimates a sense of the expansive opening of human experience to
the world, a receptivity that a long lineage of philosophers, perhaps at least
from Rousseau to Heidegger plumbed, and a vast body of art also sought to
represent or articulate as plenitude surpassing any of our narrowed measured
truths. When drawn beyond our definitions of home or the belonging that can
be expressed in culture, signs, and our shared languages, we moderns can
quite readily conjure up an affirmative sublime when in the right places—the
places that take us close to a pleasurable beyond. Even just "the walk," the
view, my shading tree, or the landscape as the light changes—all the alternate moments that city-dwellers across the globe cherish. The pleasure of
these intimacies is also the joy in being open to the immeasurable and being
able to repeat that without necessary closure. Such has been the success of
that coiled counterexperience lying deep within the last two centuries of
modernity's industrial machinery, that we see so many successful variations
of it across global culture, perhaps so many intimate embraces that refuse to
acknowledge just what might be passing, and the "passage" that has already
been coming and that we are now coming to know.

EXTRUSIONS

While many would like to find themselves still at home within these strands
of romantic orientation, thus accompanied by the consolation of feeling
emplaced within a world, while informed with the statistics of a world in
turmoil, the early Anthropocene is a time of increasingly discordant experience of places, and of the objects and things within them. Both the knowledge
bases that explain, count, and calculate, and then the fading traditions of
finding genuine intimacy in the nonhuman natural world have not been able
to "translate" the shock of globalizing disruption into a unified normative

stance. The very real possibility of the destruction of our "life support systems" has not induced a type of radical reorientation of the values of modern
industrial expansion. What are these? We can posit three that are crucial: the
absolute value of continued economic growth for national economies, calculated annually; the right to partition and control nonhuman nature, validated
simply by accumulating fungible wealth in any manner whatsoever; the sup-
position that all individuals can and should aspire to increased material goods
into the future, without limit (see Monbiot 2017). As many have pointed
out—unlimited or ill-limited material expansion on a finite planet is impossible: absolutizing economic growth, radical fungibility, and unlimited material
aspiration are precisely contra-limits. Those guiding values are all but ruinous
without rejection or intense revision. Now, the affective experiences that individuals enjoy away from the system of those values cannot be, of themselves,
ethically effective *at scale*, and the empirically detailed reports of the damaged state of the planet cannot imaginatively create the principles that would
have as a central concern, a restrained and limited exploitation of the natural
world. In fact, because we can see the strength of such values in our social
worlds, and the difficulties of binding perspectives of knowledge with affects
of care and connection, we have to think in a *preliminary* way about what the
Anthropocene means. We should be compelled to think the Anthropocene not
as a crisis to be overcome, if that implies taking us back, out of the wrong
branch of decisions and reorientation in the premodern modes of life, nor as
overcoming the sort of human creature that is so successful in dominating
and manipulating its ecotopes, as if we could leap apart from the dangers that
lie *within* the human condition—its "inhumanity aggravated to the point of
monstrousness" as Janicaud decries the technological dream of posthuman
transcendence (Janicaud 2006, 26). The Anthropocene is the name of the
global passage through which humanity is *already* travelling, irreversibly,
necessarily compelling all other living things to come with us, apart but par-
titioned with us. It is a movement, unstable, plural, and engulfing. As Bruno
Latour points out, we cannot in fact attain a simple singular understanding of
the present "profound alteration in our relation to the world" (2017, 9–11),
because the "alteration" has been happening already, without us registering
its accumulating force. We are late for our own emergencies. How can we
not have seen this? Already too numerous and too diverse are the alterations,
the extinctions, the metamorphoses appearing everywhere that don't fit our
modern mythologies, our self-important understandings of ourselves as rational creatures capable of *sufficient* knowledge. The industrial human imprint
all over the earth's skin—the scar tissue which might still be observable millions of years from now, yet paradoxically laid down in the space of decades,
is far more varied and *reactive* than our dreams of progress could imagine
with any precision. We were to rise about nature, be emancipated from cruel

necessity, and the oppressed were to be emancipated from domination, but
we have been altering the very conditions underlying our modern "mansion
of freedom" in becoming a geological agent on the planet (Chakrabarty 2008,
207). In still thinking of solving a crisis, of being in control, but in a better way we tell ourselves, we are likely missing the complex reactions now
woven with our continued industrial productive actions. This forms the locus
of concern for this chapter.

In particular, amid the contemporary concern to rethink objects and materiality, there will need to be critical thought of the *scales of objects*—the
emergence of different *aggregated* objects which appear in our landscapes
as disturbances but which are as important to reading the momentum of the
early Anthropocene as the readings of atmospheric carbon dioxide from
Mauna Loa Observatory or measuring the loss of Arctic sea ice. We are
entering a global space in which new aggregations are being counted and
assessed and present to us the evidence of both immense dispersals of minute objects, traces of expelled materials, both organic and inorganic, and
larger accumulations that were not imaginable a short time ago. The early
Anthropocene is also a long-term mass human industrial process which has
leeched its materials—gases, liquids, solids, microbes, radiation, hormones,
antibiotics, pharmaceuticals—into the world, either onto that which we
imagine as a retreating "outside" natural world, or of course within the infra-
structures of human-social domains. What we are registering now are types
of "precipitation," increasing in variety, complexity, and amounts. The best
summary figure for this might be the technical dynamic of extrusion. In using
this figure, which recalls production—output, a shaping of something, this
chapter aims to extend the thinking of the human as both deeply embedded
in a finite natural world that cannot be transcended, and yet also, as a creature
ingesting and expelling on immense new scales, it is now subject itself to an
auto-experiment over which it so far has limited control and understanding.

An extrusion happens by forcing inputted materials through a "die," a form
translating through its internal channel that is to be externalized. The process
requires energy, a containment structure, and the setting out of inputs and
outputs. While this is a simple metaphor at the level of an individual body, or
even of village life, industrial societies have configured their material support
for social life as a complex of social-technical "chambers," utilizing immense
amounts of energy, specialized technical knowledges, and procedures to
through-put materials to produce required and desired goods. The logic in
its pure form is simple transformation but paradoxically the scale of such
processes is now commingling intake with what is expelled as by-product,
waste, or obsolete product. In a positive sense, industry produces and makes
readily available what is required for human existence, but the co-products
have been dumped and dispersed so widely that we simply cannot know fully

(as yet—indeed if ever) what trails of contamination are returning to recondition and alter human life.

It is not just that I can now know my body contains fragments of plastic refuse, like millions of other humans, and likely my urine and stools expel microscopic particles regularly, perhaps along with other trace chemicals clinging to their structures (Revel et al. 2018). Rather what continues to emerge from the boundaries of our ecological investigations are novel issues, difficult to weigh, such as the interactions of wild animals with excreted human antibiotics, or the question of to what extent chemicals flowing into the rivers and oceans might be altering fish reproduction rates, thus altering the distribution of other species, and eventually biotic conditions far more widely. What we have considered as "biodegradable" might not in fact remain inert for all biota in contact with those materials, and the pathways of further interactions in food chains, possibly including human food chains remains unknown (González-Pleiter et al. 2019). Thinking our situation as not only embedded but furthering the technological passages through which elements (in the wider sense of inanimate *and* living elements) of the world are being forced leads to the question of our confrontation in the early Anthropocene with the dispersed accretions that now reactively "experiment" with the human form, its morphology and biological structures. If we are undoubtedly dispersing across the globe innumerable by-products from our capacities to produce on immense scales, which in turn re-enter our processes of gathering and extrusion, then we too are implicated in the processes as co-products. Human populations, and indeed the human body then is perhaps nothing more than an immense auto-experiment (without goal) through extensive environmental background accumulations—a far more prosaic, subtle, yet perhaps powerful manipulation of "the human" than the projects of genetic manipulation or fabricating artificial intelligence. Industrial humanity is accelerating on unknown scales of effectivity the re-environing of itself. Of course, that we are at some essential level conditioned bodies that can *recondition* them through our actions is not an activity of recent novelty; there's no doubt that prehistoric groups were capable of extinguishing mega-fauna from a shared ecological niche, thus both enjoying a diet of protein for a period of time, but then also pacifying, in fact part-domesticating the landscape for human activity. Human history is also a complex natural history of reconditioning human existence. Like all life forms, we are adaptive and malleable in particular ways. However, the early Anthropocene is a period of reconstructing our landscapes at scales of micro and nano-objects. The processes underway are repeated and dispersed across the globe, so that mega-collations of human artifacts are emerging, and in their own way impinge on human life, individual and collective. The plastic gyres in the oceans are today probably just the most visible sign of immensely varied human detritus dispersing throughout the biosphere; what we can't see clearly are many "clouds" of micro-particles interacting in the web of life in ways we are yet to discover.

At another level, within the social systems removing by-products from our population centers, we have learned of the accretions of waste that can over-burden existing systems, so that large objects form to block or even break channels of waste removal. A "fatberg" is the name given to a large compacted object clogging a part of a city's sewer system—"an iceberg of fat" (Denton 2019). They might in one sense be the prime comic environmental discovery of the early twenty-first century: the massive signs (as large as 800 feet in length and over a hundred metric tons) of unhealthy consumer tastes in many countries—with Britain and the United States perhaps leading examples (Engelhaupt 2017). But what they signify is far more disturbing. Fats mostly contribute to their basic substance, thus providing a sticky base for innumerable other objects to conglomerate together—including all the domestic detritus that usually should not be disposed of in sewer waste systems: plastic combs, false teeth, cloth wipes, diapers, bandages, and so on. So, in a more serious light, their risks to sewer systems signifies the emergence of "sclerotic infrastructure"—the problems of transporting and expelling wastes on immense scales in growing cities across the world (Marvin and Medd 2010). While individuals and their tastes for fatty foods might be a central element of the phenomenon, the problems are also tied to wider social processes: burgeoning availability of low-cost dietary fats, and the burdens now at the levels of various systems—scaled-up food production and its wastes, the consequences of making available cheap fast calorie-rich foods for huge populations, and the continuing decline in public infrastructure in some urban centers. The fatty excess not only does produce obstructing accretions and objects but also collects long enough to feed excess scavengers and species adapted to human urban populations—rats, mice, birds, and the various insects, parasites, and bacteria that they can carry as hosts. In other words, the appearance of fatbergs is also indicative of human metropolitan life reaching new levels of intensive dietary energy flows. Cities ingest and extrude metabolically, transferring energy potentials beyond human populations. The remains of a greasy dinner crosses metabolic interfaces; an array of other life forms live and multiply on secondary gradients (Marvin and Medd 2010, 96). Close, just below the surfaces of cities, scavengers and parasites live off our fabulous excesses. If the densities of cities continue to increase, then the interfaces of metabolic flows with other creatures will only become more active, more intense. The industrialized diets rich in fats and sugars will leak into creaking systems of disposal, relegating some populations with less developed infrastructure to deal with emergent problems of parasitic species and perhaps declining sanitation: fatbergs not only clog but threaten to crack pipes and cause overflows. Apart from the concern for human, and to some extent companion animal obesity, we have barely the beginnings of an understanding of what secondary species and interspecies relations the new assemblages of objects, blockages, and waste channels are going to produce as technologically advanced cities continue to grow into the twenty-first century.

We should note the forms these problems take outside of advanced cities. Mike Davis's focus on the sprawling mega-cities of developing nations recounts how the problem of sewerage is less blockage, but unsewered diffusion, leading to the return of diseases such as typhoid, cholera, and hepatitis (Davis 2006, 142–147). In part, urban extrusions invite back these bacteria and viruses because they continue to cannibalize wilderness, abandoned industrial land or marginal farmlands, creating frontier conditions that do not manage food and sanitation properly. The precarious character of human existence tied to disease and poverty—which the optimists of modern human progress imagined would be overcome across the twentieth century, given we knew the importance of sanitation and careful urban planning—continues to malign vast numbers of people. Urban sprawl diffuses its waste only onto fringes which in turn must supply daily food and energy demands. The intensities of the frontier processes atop each other produce risks, not only of old diseases already adapted to human population dynamics but new ones as well—the appearance of successful pathogens such as SARS and SARS-CoV-2 (Settele 2020).

MONSTROUS INTIMACY

The populations of the industrialized world are thus moving through the early Anthropocene into new proximities with unintended products and by-products extruded and distributed in ways that reach into our lives, even into us. We might hope that we are increasingly committed to learn to live in different, somehow healthier, less damaging, controlled ways, because in re-forming the conditions for life right out to the limits of the biosphere we should either accept the responsibility for our technologies and products or become lost in drifts of refuse and accumulating interactions of indeterminate consequences. But it is far from clear how well we can actually shape a normative direction for such responsibility. The demand for a thorough-going responsibility would be to take some dangerous steps with the meaning of Latour's slogan that we must "love our monsters" as an initial commitment (Latour 2011, chap. 3). Love in what sense: all our technologies, their systems, and the extruded landscapes that increasingly extend across the planet. But how can we love the things that fragment and react against our intentions? Latour's stance is to be deliberately polemical and bracingly direct. If we cannot be "unentangled" from the nonhuman world—less so with each passing day—then we must accept fully the creativity and destructive potency of modern technologies and embrace a "compositionist" attitude, which is to accept "our becoming ever-more attached to, and intimate with, a panoply of nonhuman natures," thus to recompose and not emancipate ourselves (Latour 2011, chap. 3).

The risk here many would say immediately is to acquiesce to technology's monstrous damage of the world. Surely the Anthropocene demands stringent judgment, rejection of established ways; the time of the early Anthropocene must ruthlessly pivot against existing technological processes. But the critical path of thinking here is rather to disarm the negative which Latour sees as haunting environmental stances, far more than can be productive. We disavow, we despair, we imagine a "letting be" of nature and species, without *doing the work* of composing the conditions for that to be possible. It is not an answer now to retreat from the machinery of modernism but rather to retake its mechanisms, accept that pristine nature is gone, and see ourselves as responsible for composing as best as we can, accepting that many unintended consequences will happen, but they must then be consistently pursued and ameliorated. Taken as a positive program, this is to insist on our immanence in the world of our making and a demand for constant care. Do not abandon your monsters, as Victor Frankenstein mistakenly did with his creation, otherwise they will be troubled and destructive, returning the suffering visited upon them. The claim would then be that only in the full and open acceptance of the potentials and dangers of technological power, the extent of our ecological penetration, accepting all of what we are spreading across the world, can we then start to approach the level of redefining what we have become, as creators and co-created, and the need then to re-create. Latour's arguments are in fact demands for very deep and careful attention to technological entanglements. The demands are very difficult—something that Latour's style of rhetorical presentation does not affirm enough. We are deliberately unsettled, pushed away from many common assumptions. But certainly, he brings home the issue that if we dwell in denial or despair, we might remain in the phases of pseudo-activity—repeating the mantras of "what must be done," but mechanically doing the ineffectual and temporary, thus in fact disavowing the full truth of our trajectory (see also Žižek 2009, 178). We would then be disavowing our saturation of environments with human-caused extrusions, continuing to hope that we are excerpted above the worst and can continue to alienate the natural world in our projects, creating human-social interiors which operate supposedly through utterly nonnatural principles. To affirm rather that we begin with social-natural entanglements, to *start* from their hybridity must be to accept the landscapes of the planet have changed and are changing irrevocably under our dominion, and that the traditions of science and technology, their uses in modernity *have* to embrace responsibility for what have been mere "externalities" in our thinking.

Undoubtedly challenging to contemporary environmental philosophy facing the shock of the Anthropocene, these claims can be seen as turning us to confront our paradoxical ability to know only contours of our problems but deny the really difficult challenge to the deep frameworks of modernity—that Nature should be a distinct realm of calculation or personal rapture but not thought as always already entangled with human artifice. We are living through a staggering revelation that even the gathering threats of global catastrophes can be psychologically disarmed, or many hope to be able to turn to science to "find solutions" in the way we see it working in the technological revolutions of modernity, without radically altered practical commitments, without revolutions in our most common evaluations and turning the machinery of extrusions to different *remediating* purposes—to neither idealize nor errantly despoil a natural world which we should feel as our constant attachment, our constant responsibility.

We have to recognize in existing irresponsibility toward expanding technological powers a lineage that is not just only recent ecological insight. The wars of the twentieth century and the hyperbolic increase in destructive weapons raised deep questions about whether the powers of scientific understanding could be ethically or politically delimited. Hannah Arendt, who, while not much of a direct environmentalist, provided a particular *reflexive* character to this modern predicament; that is, a sense of the bind we find ourselves in, while apparently leaping forward in our powers. Her prescient ideas on scientific perspective in fact serve as valuable precursors to Latour's monstrous challenge today, and in some ways have been perhaps neglected (apart from several astute commentators—Whiteside 1994; Macauley 1996; Smith 2011) for their contributions to unraveling the particular binds of modernity on subjects' potential commitments or refusals to engage in ecological politics. Modernity's world-making projects, for her, were already disintegrating under through the captivating paradigms of scientific advances and the phenomenal growth of consumer society (Arendt 1975, 262). But there was a particular figure Arendt dwelt upon in several late essays on the powers of modern science that are most useful to consider here.

UNWORLDING

Hannah Arendt used the ancient figure of the Archimedean point, in its philosophical guise, to try to capture the momentous increase in human power in the postwar era. Cited in *The Human Condition* (1958), and then influential in two later papers (1963, 1969), Arendt twice deployed an aphorism by Kafka in which he interpreted the sense of the Archimedean point in a particular paradoxical way: "He found the Archimedean point, but he used it against himself; it seems that he was permitted to find it only under this condition" (Arendt 1958, 248). Archimedes's imaginary point had been the idea of the "firm ground" from which the whole world might be levered or moved; for philosophers, it was the image of the perspectival point or ground from which the whole of nature could begin to be known through elaborating sufficient reason. In earlier forms, the Point signified the sense of sure ground amid fluidity or single base principle from which a metaphysics could be initiated (see Tokarzewska 2014). But, the most well-known example is the surety of the cogito for Descartes (*Meditations* 1641), of experiencing the ground of the knowing self through the ungrounding procedure of doubt—the inward turn toward the pure spontaneity of the "I think" providing one of the steps toward modern subjectivist paradigms (Descartes 2008, 16). Kafka seems to have grasped the philosophical move and amplified through the literary cypher that which thinkers following Descartes realized had been opened up—pursuing the Archimedean point *within* implied including the very per-formance of seeking it. "Levering" the world must also affect that creature that imagines and seeks such capabilities. Any "outside and distant" appar-ently transcendent point of surety determined rather as being "inside" also must turn whatever transcendent power against the internalizing operation. Kafka captures this in the ironic twist—permissibility on condition of "use against the self"—suggesting that whatever is gained through such a truth, the rules, perhaps metaphysical, demand the gain operate on the self-same know-ing subject. At the imagined extreme, we might say—if you seek to lever the universe, then be prepared for some terrible reciprocity, for such power when harnessed grasps the levering body as well. Distance and mastery through knowledge rebound intimately—a repeated key in Kafka's musings on human power.

For Arendt, the leaps of physical sciences in the twentieth century—split-ting the atom, realizing fission and fusion energy in weapons and power plants, theorizing the distant universe, and overcoming the earth's grav-ity in spacecraft—indicated "we have found a way to act on the earth and within terrestrial nature *as though we dispose of it from outside*, from the Archimedean point" (Arendt 1958, 262, stress added). We are able to "carry" the Archimedean point through scientific representation to scenes of great disclosure. The sciences were enabling such technological power, thought Arendt, such that the very stability of earth as our home was under threat from the forces unleashed (Arendt 1958, 268). Of course, that chiefly meant the threat of nuclear annihilation, but Arendt also foresees the prosthetic mutation of human life with nonhuman technological things—an instability that she seems unwilling to evaluate. She approves of Heisenberg's image of "looking down" and seeing the cars in which we travel "as inescapabl[y] a part of ourselves as a snail's shell to its occupant" as an apt condensed metaphor of technology as a "large-scale biological process" ranged against ourselves (Arendt 1969, 413). The science-fiction image of hybrid human-machine beings is confirmed as a matter of finding and adopting a suitable "levering" perspective. Similarly, bringing into play both the sense of physical perspectives from above the globe and the perspectives of knowing *as though* we are universal creatures, Arendt wondered whether the coincidence of population explosions with the development of nuclear weapons could both be therefore interpreted as part of a "large-scale biological process" which might "prevent life on earth from being thrown out of balance"; possibly revealing she thought of homeostatic balance or a normativity for life on the planet submitted to human domination (Arendt 1969, 413). Human life had thus crossed a threshold of advancing knowledge, beyond which we could see ourselves as elements in terrestrial behavioral patterns, opening up the questions for us of immense scales of control or threat, similar but hyperbolically increased, when compared to the authoritarianism and mass politics which Arendt diagnosed following World War II.

From the time when we could see the globe and the totality of earthly life, beginning with Sputnik I in 1957, adopting such extra-terrestrial perspectives through the power of the sciences also undermined humanistic traditions—"a diminishment of man's self-respect" (Arendt 1969, 412). Threatening both the continuity of those traditions, and unleashing destructive powers, Arendt foresees the dissipation or destruction of our modern "world making" projects, and the values of continuity and longevity in social landscapes undermined. Her diagnoses then already saw the success of scientific endeavor and instrumental reason leading to the logic of bureaucratic oversight of populations by government, and correlated declines of what she considered was genuine political participation in deciding the direction of modern polities. We were entering a time of power overtaking its human origination. She pointedly pleaded for "a new realization of the factually existing limitations of human beings . . . we may let loose what we shall never be able to stop" (Arendt 1969, 417). In these speculative arguments, Arendt foreshadows, from admittedly different directions located by the concerns of the 1960s, problems Latour later sketches in *We have Never Been Modern* (1991)— problems framed by our present time almost-deifying scientific activity and results, our inability to articulate properly their translation into an ethos, and corresponding inadequate critical attention to the ways in which many small things, the minor problematic patterns diffused in ordinary life connect outward to larger social and political structures. Latour cites Arendt's diagnosis of totalitarianism in this way favorably, since it avoided easy demonization of large actors, and turned attention to creeping networks of acceptance (Latour

1991, 125). Both recognized our long journey out of premodern metaphysics of nature was incomplete, in fact a sort of partitioning of the natural has been instituted, and then constituting social realms in distinction, with limitations placed on how they can be related (Latour 1991, 34). We struggle to find the means to overcome those limitations. Billions have been inexorably positioned in vast systems of production and consumption, so that we can now extrude and jettison on enormous scales, and what happens "out there" is disgusting, we can be disgusted in ourselves but struggle to create through our advanced technological systems the dynamics at scale required to properly alter our aggregating trajectory.

ALLOTMENT IN THE EXTRUDED WORLD

What has gone wrong with modernity is often obvious every day—in the smallest and nearest of the things we have at hand. We have now so much that is new, every day, but in a trivial repetitive way, that disposing of it— returning it to the world is nothing. But now the expelled excess is blown back in our faces by the winds off the sea for us to breathe in. Are we not deferring the great global projects of remaking the human niche, which includes the many creatures now dependent on our existence, out of self-disgust? We can walk through the deep woods now and see tiny fragments of plastic silted into the soil; we walk on wondering "What vile things are we doing?" But disgust in itself is not the answer. The refuse we are in fact returning to the world is itself refused from being properly recognized as a significant part of our existing human project; it should not be just set aside, excluded as pollution, "defilement," but as truly ours to include as meaningful core element of the new landscape of the Anthropocene. The excesses of toxic waste dumps, and rivers of sludge, these pathological features should be moved from their status as excrescences of modern success to that of a central feature of the world-making now underway. This disturbing, paradoxical, and monstrous initial acceptance would be the precursor to then reconstruct the engines of extrusion: all environmental externalities will appear on balance sheets; all production is at the same time implicated in maintenance of our life support systems; all monstrousness can be cared for, brought back into the thought of the social, provided with representation in the universe of rights. Returning to the world so many billion tiny fragments of industrialized life must start to appear in our accounting for our activities. Then the question can be what other activities address the problems of our landscape; what remodeling should be written into the fundamental accounts, and further still, the fundamental ethos of how we live. Remediation will have to become the valuable project, the work that recreates the bounds of commons, not merely the bill that someone must pay.

The allotment which the modern industrial acceleration imagined it had, and was justified in having, that is, bordering a free natural world apart, which was to be considered available, standing ready for supposedly unlimited exploitation has to be redrawn. The human allotment—what we could well be thinking following Arendt—has to be considered as approaching limits and could be therefore imagined as the return to world-building efforts which will include many ecosystems and species currently under threat of extinction; the "letting be" which we would like to be possible would rather have to be a construction of borders, of great care, of great understanding and even large-scale technological interventions. Letting things be and respecting the diversity of life on the planet will take, not some hopeful withdrawal in the sense of "live less like moderns" but efforts of construction, of cleaning, of repair, of accepting human effects and ongoing forces of disruption nonetheless, but not an overcoming, which would amount to a rejection of what we are and have been doing. As Janicaud argued in a discussion of humanism under technological strain, a constant caution against our capacity toward inhumanity, or destruction twinned with technology, should be affirmed as intrinsic to any contemporary revised humanism (Janicaud 2006, 58). He meant by this, that we should not be seeking to lift the human condition onto a new level of existence as if that would annul the violence and damage we now constantly decline into. What could count still as a progressive responsibility toward our condition would be a *vigilance* toward our "inner partitioning"—our ability to deny the full range of our creations, the things we are happy to hold intimately as part of our lives, and also all that has been made distant, or placed under the sign of refuse—of refusal to accept the facts of the planet reshaped. Thus, standing before the new landscapes of the Anthropocene, we should aim to lift our sights above disconsolation or disgust with the enormous machineries of dispersal that are changing the planet as they change us and accept that we will have to become active throughout all of our dispersed creation. The project starts not in looking *out* at a damaged and alienated nature and thinking we must somehow "stop" but rather do more in different ways. We need to find ways to take account of what we cannot abide the planet to become and include part by part the different mechanisms within the powerful machinery we dwell with which can begin to reconstruct and remake from the world as it is. This is a sobering form of self-acceptance, but from those lines of self-definition, an ethos or a better dwelling-with might start to be drawn.

BIBLIOGRAPHY

Arendt, Hannah. (1958)1998. *The Human Condition*. 2nd edition. Chicago: University of Chicago Press.

Arendt, Hannah. (1963)2006. "The Conquest of Space and the Stature of Man." In *Between Past and Future, Eight Exercises in Political Thought*, 260–274. New York: Penguin Books.

Arendt, Hannah. (1969)2018. "The Archimedean Point." In *Thinking without a Banister, Essays in Understanding, 1963–1975*, edited by Jerome Kohn, 406–418. New York: Schocken Books.

Arendt, Hannah. (1975)2003. "Home to Roost." In Responsibility and Judgement, edited by Jerome Kohn, 257–275. New York: Schocken Books.

Chakrabarty, Dipesh. 2008. "The climate of history: Four theses." *Critical Inquiry* 35: 197–222.

Davis, Mike. 2006. *Planet of Slums*. London: Verso.

Denton, Jack. 2018. "Icebergs of fat, oil, and grease are growing in the sewers beneath our feet. Here's why." *Pacific Standard*, January 18, 2018. https://psmag.com/en vironment/teenage-mutant-ninja-fatbergs.

Engelhaupt, Erika. 2017. "Huge Blobs of Fat and Trash Are Filling the World's Sewers," August 16, 2017, *National Geographic* online, https://www.national geographic.com/news/2017/08/fatbergs-fat-cities-sewers-wet-wipes-science/.

González-Pleiter, Miguel, Miguel Tamayo-Belda, Gerardo Pulido-Reyes, Georgiana Amariei, Francisco Leganés, Roberto Rosal, and Francisca Fernández-Piñas. 2019. "Secondary nanoplastics released from a biodegradable microplastic severely impact freshwater environments," *Environmental Science: Nano*, 6, 1382–1392.

Janicaud, Dominique. 2005. *On the Human Condition*. Translated by Eileen Brennan. London: Routledge.

Kafka, Franz. 2012. *A Hunger Artist and other Stories*. Translated by Joyce Crick. Oxford: Oxford University Press.

Latour, Bruno. 1991. *We have Never Been Modern.* Translated by Catherine Porter. Cambridge, Mass.: Harvard University Press.

Latour, Bruno. 2011. "Love your Monsters" in Shellenberger, Michael and Norhaus, Ted, eds. 2011. *Love Your monsters: Postenvironmentalism and the Anthropocene.* California: Breakthrough Institute. Kindle.

Latour, Bruno. 2017. *Facing Gaia: Eight lectures on the new Climatic Regime.* Translated by Catherine Porter. Cambridge: Polity Press.

Marvin, Simon and Will Medd. 2010. "Clogged Cities: Sclerotic Infrastructure," in *Disrupted Cities; When Infrastructure Fails*. London: Routledge.

Monbiot, George. 2017. *Out of the Wreckage: A New Politics for an Age of Crisis*, London: Verso.

Revel, Messika, Amélie Châtel, and Catherine Mouneyrac. 2018. "Micro(nano) plastics: A threat to human health?," *Current Opinion in Environmental Science & Health*, 1: 17–23.

Settele, Josef, Sandra Díaz, Eduardo Brondizio, and Peter Daszak. "COVID-19 Stimulus Measures Must Save Lives, Protect Livelihoods, and Safeguard nature to Reduce the Risk of Future Pandemics," 27 April, 2020. Intergovernmental Science-Policy Platform on Biodiversity and Ecosystem Services, https://ipbes.net /covid19stimulus.

Smith, Mick. 2011. *Against Ecological Sovereignty: Ethics, Biopolitics and Saving the Natural World.* Minneapolis: University of Minnesota Press.

Tokarzewska, Monika. 2014. "Archimedean Points in a Network of Cosmological Metaphors: Fontenelle, Locke, Fichte, and Kant," *SubStance*, Volume 43, Number 3: 27–45.

Žižek, Slavoj, 2009. "Ecology." In *Examined Life: Excursions with Contemporary Thinkers*, edited by Astra Taylor, 155–183. New York: The New Press.

Whiteside, Kerry. 1994. "Hannah Arendt and Ecological Politics," *Environmental Ethics*, 16/4: 339–58.

Chapter 28

Doğa İçin Çal (Play for Nature)

Çağrı Yılmaz

Doğa İçin Çal is a music project initiated by agaclar.net and advocated by Playing for Change that was put into effect in the face of the current ecological crisis (Doğa İçin Çal 2009a).[1] Founded on the belief that "union is strength" and using music as a common language, it strives to remind us that our responsibilities to incite an ecological change can bring us together. As publicized on its official YouTube channel, its goal is "to create awareness for nature. We do this with music, the job we know best!" (Doğa İçin Çal 2009b).

The project's vibrant YouTube channel has had hundreds of thousands of subscribers and millions of views since its inception in 2009. Its success seems rooted in the principle that difference lies in diversity. Inspired to unite for nature, local Turkish musicians of a wide range of ethnicities—including Turkish, Kurdish, Armenian, and Laz—come together with musicians from other countries, such as the United States, Iran, China, Georgia, Somali, Canada, the Republic of Korea, the Turkish Republic of Northern Cyprus, and Greece. Performers with impaired hearing, walking disabilities, and Down syndrome have also shown up to contribute, widening the project's circle of unity and solidarity. The musicians, some of whom are also renowned actors, actresses, writers, and television presenters/announcers, perform traditional Anatolian folk songs that incorporate local and global styles. For instance, songs are played on local and universal instruments and range in musical genre from Anatolian folk music to Turkish and Western classical music, pop, rap, country, rock n' roll, jazz, soul, R&B, and opera. But, why these songs? What do they tell us?

Anatolian folk songs intimately engage with nature and abound in images that remind us of who we are and what nature means to us, sedulously demanding for a reconsideration of our relations with it. The emotions

387

conveyed by the songs—including misery, sadness, lament, happiness, bliss, and celebration—are transmitted through distinctly nonhuman subjects, creating a resonance that indicates our inextricable interconnection to nature. The geographical specificity of the songs details the flora and fauna of specific regions and indicates how natural phenomena, events, and disasters affect life, constantly reminding us of how humans and their practices implicate nature.[2]

For instance, in a video clip, Doğa İçin Çal performs "Divane Aşık Gibi" (Like a Mad Lover; Doğa İçin Çal-1 2011), written and composed by Hasan Tunç, which narrates the story of two lovers who fail to reunite. Both characters express their grief through nonhuman subjects:

(*Woman*)
I, the bird of high mountains,
will perch on a cypress.
Beg my pa of our marriage,
Should he naysay,
Then will I elope with you.
(*Man*)
You, the rain,
Me, a cloud,
Down in Maçka,[3]
Shall we meet.

"İki Keklik" (Two Partridges; Doğa İçin Çal-10 2018b), is based on an elegy of a mother who wails for her martyred son. She expresses her misery through partridges:

Two partridges, singing on a rock,
Don't, oh partridge,
For I've already had a lot on my plate!
. . .
Two partridges, drinking water from a creek,
Oh, grief-stricken partridge causes pain,
To those free as a bird!

In "Allı Turnam" (My Rufescent Crane; Doğa İçin Çal 2018a),[4] a folk poet who longs for his homeland sends his best to his loved ones via cranes:

O, rufescent crane!
Should you come by our land,
Give [my] sweet, kaymak, and honey.[5]

O, my Rose! My arm,
My hand, all broken, ah cranes!
. . .
O, rufescent crane!
What fly high in the sky?
I, with a broken wing,
Stuck in here.

In "Çarşamba'yı Sel Aldı" (Çarşamba Flooded; Doğa İçin Çal-11 2019),[6] another folk song about unfulfilled love, sorrow is expressed through an analogy between a natural disaster and the pain of love:

Çarşamba flooded,
The one I loved,
Taken away by a stranger.
. . .
I, predestined by God,
For a fortune ill-starred.
Oh mountains, lofty mountains!

But in "Dere Geliyor Dere" (There Flows the Creek; Doğa İçin Çal-10 2018b), the image of water works as a mediator:

There flows the creek,
Washing its sand away.
Take me, too, oh creek,
To where my beloved is!

In "Çemberimde Gül Oya" (A Rose Embroidery on My Hoop Frame; Doğa İçin Çal-3 2011), natural entities are employed to verbalize the pain of love, which infiltrates into daily life practices and evokes a premodern sense in which humans and their handicraft are compatible with nature before machines:

A rose embroidery on my hoop frame,
Oh, to my heart's content,
Have I failed to laugh!
. . .
Once a pink rose,
I, now, all grown pale.
We, once, cheek to cheek,
I, now, with a longing for your face.

"Çayeli'nden Öteye" (Beyond Çayeli; Doğa İçin Çal-3 2011) manifests these intricate relations between nature and humans:

Along Kanlıdere,
Sweep green tea plants.
Girls with waist clothes,
Pick tea sprouts.

And interrelatedness, interconnection, and interaction between the two are elaborately described in "Hayde!," written and composed by Melek Akman (Let's go!; Doğa İçin Çal-8 2017):

Let's go,
To the mountain, cherry laurels!
How dare I say let's go,
To somebody else's lover!
Up did I climb a pine,
To lop off the half.
What kind of love it is,
Alas, shame on it!
Say, is an alder,
lopped down from the top?
Does one get shy,
About her/his beloved?

Doğa İçin Çal raises its voice on behalf of nature, saying "You've *played* enough with nature! Now, *play* for nature!" (Doğa İçin Çal 2009b).[7] It reappropriates songs of the past for today and the future with an aim to hold nature dear to our hearts through music. The songs performed are a glocal call for us all to reunite against the ecological crisis. We therefore need to listen to nature, for, as rightfully put by agaclar.net, "If you don't care about nature, nor does it about you at all" (Agaclar.net 2004).

NOTES

1. The Turkish *ağaç* means *tree* in English.
2. Most of the Turkish folk songs which are mentioned in this writing are anonymous. Those created by known writers and/or composers are stated. I translated the lyrics myself.
3. A county of Trabzon province known for its splendid nature and located in the eastern Black Sea region of Turkey.

4. The video was collaboratively produced in cooperation with the office of World Wide Fund for Nature (WWF) in Turkey to draw attention to the Anatolian crane population threatened with extinction. See http://www.wwf.org.tr/calismalarimiz/yab an_hayati/tur_koruma_calmalar/turnalar_hep_ucsun/.

5. The words *sweet, kaymak* (a creamy dairy product consumed at breakfast, often with honey and jam, and with desserts), and *honey* imply that the speaker of the poem sends all the best to his beloved ones.

6. A county of Samsun province located in central Black Sea region of Turkey.

7. This is the motto of Doğa İçin Çal. The literal translation from Turkish is: "You've stolen enough from nature! Now, play for nature!" However, the translation is complicated by the double meaning of the Turkish verb *çalmak*: (i) to steal something (as in the first sentence), and (ii) to play an instrument (as in the second). While there is an obvious play on the word *çalmak* in the phrase, I chose to translate the first as *play* instead of *steal* to facilitate readability and comprehension in English.

BIBLIOGRAPHY

Agaclar.net. 2004. "Amaçlarımız." Dec. 14, 2011. http://www.agaclar.net/?id =amaclarimiz.

Doğa İçin Çal. 2009b. "Açıklama." YouTube. Dec. 9, 2009. https://www.youtube. com/user/dogaicincal/about.

Doğa İçin Çal. 2018a. "Allı Turnam." YouTube. Jan. 13, 2018. https://www.youtube. com/watch?v=DJwYQsop2mU&list=PL3E85345102C14249&index=10&t=0s.

Doğa İçin Çal-11. 2019. "Çarşamba'yı Sel Aldı." YouTube. Dec. 7, 2019. https:// www.youtube.com/watch?v=4C010aOLw4I&list=PL3E85345102C14249&index =2&t=0s.

Doğa İçin Çal-3. 2011. "Çemberimde Gül Oya, Çayeli'nden Öteye." YouTube. Dec. 17, 2011. https://www.youtube.com/watch?v=MbPOFfdvOZk&list=PL3E85 345102C14249&index=7&t=0s.

Doğa İçin Çal-1. 2011. "Divane Aşık Gibi." YouTube. Dec. 14, 2011. https://www .youtube.com/watch?v=r3OwxXw0v9c&list=PL3E85345102C14249&index=11 &t=0s.

Doğa İçin Çal-8. 2017. "Hayde!" YouTube. May 6, 2017. https://www.youtube.com/ watch?v=Hu97Hk8MT8U&list=PL3E85345102C14249&index=5&t=0s.

Doğa İçin Çal-10. 2018b. "İki Keklik, Dere Geliyor Dere." YouTube. Dec. 8, 2018. https://www.youtube.com/watch?v=u2kBNb79bN8&list=PL3E85345102C14249 &index=3&t=0s.

Doğa İçin Çal. 2009a. "Önsöz." Doğa İçin Çal. http://www.dogaicincal.com/index .asp?sayfa=biz.

Chapter 29

Subversive Art

Communicating the Climate Crisis on a Planetary Scale

Catherine Sarah Young

"How can we convince people to care about climate change?" is a question scientists have asked for decades. Climate change is a slow burn, a threat that seems out there with asteroids, which makes it difficult to comprehend or empathize with here and now.

As an artist, I have often wrestled with this question while travelling the world on art residencies and fellowships. Each city was besieged with a different kind of climate impact, be it stronger typhoons, intense drought, rising sea levels, or others.

In 2013, as artist-in-residence at the Singapore-ETH Future Cities Laboratory, I observed scientists doing cutting-edge research on critical issues involving sustainability and simultaneously, I worked with high school and university students. Of the questions I asked the students about climate change, it was one on clothing that got them excited: What will you wear in a climate change apocalypse? The question led me back to the lab, where I co-designed garments based on the scientists' research and got these brilliant researchers to model them around Singapore in the series, *Climate Change Couture* (figure 29.1). At the time, which coincided with Supertyphoon Haiyan in the southern Philippines, something about those images seemed to signal a growing awareness of climate change. The public began asking things like: "What is the difference between climate and weather?" Or, "what *is* the Anthropocene?" In those days, I was often criticized for "fear-mongering," which I thought was a privileged, if not ignorant, comment—many countries, especially those in the Global South, have been sounding the alarm for decades.

Figure 29.1 *Climate Change Couture. Credit*: Catherine Sarah Young.

I expanded this body of work around the world as I saw the need for art projects that could not only inspire people to empathize with climate change but also help them find a safe, inclusive space to share their understandable confusion and concerns. The resulting body of work became *The Apocalypse Project*, which explores climate change and our environmental futures. In the process, I realized that interactive pieces worked best; when people did something to the work, they seemed to engage with it longer and were able to share their vulnerability and curiosity about the piece with the strangers around them. They also seemed to have more fun. I think the most effective, impactful art works are experiential, not didactic.

As the piece I believe to be the most successful in the artistic body of work, *The Ephemeral Marvels Perfume Store* (2014) (figure 29.2) transcends culture and language through its use of the most intimate of senses to arrest people's reality: scent. In this collection of perfumes of the things we could lose and are losing because of climate change, people are invited to smell and contemplate their relationship with various scents. The atypical medium, coupled with the memories and opinions evoked by these smells, creates an inclusive space and an experience that people can hopefully take with them beyond the exhibition.

Figure 29.2 *The Ephemeral Marvels Perfume Store. Credit*: Catherine Sarah Young.

Not all art projects are so inviting. Indeed, *The Apocalypse Project*'s most contentious piece *The Sewer Soaperie* (2016) (figure 29.3) left people with more questions than answers. The piece was inspired by the experience of being trapped in a cab on a street in Manila that had flooded when fatbergs clogged the sewers. Being submerged in a flood caused by fatbergs sparked my curiosity to examine the journey of palm oil from rainforests into cheap cooking oil that sometimes ends up in sewers because of improper waste practices. Using a process of saponification with sodium hydroxide, I turned the oil in the fatbergs into soap. In some exhibitions, visitors were invited to wash their hands with the soap. Part of the work thereby becomes that dare: Will they or won't they? Reactions have ranged from excitement to disgust, and indeed this work has been viewed through both art and design lenses. From the speculative, "what-if" scenario that framed the project when it was created in 2016, some have now come to see it as a potential design solution to the worsening sewer situation in many large cities.

The works within *The Apocalypse Project* usually take forms that subvert the familiar. Indeed, they may be seen as substitutions for items we are used

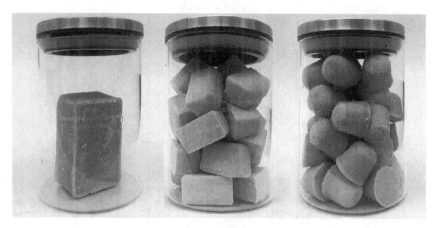

Figure 29.3   *The Sewer Soaperie. Credit*: Catherine Sarah Young.

to, such as clothing, perfumes, and soap, commodities that in their own way have contributed to the extractivist relationship we have with nature. The effect of using such items as art is twofold. First, viewers tend to do a double take because they resemble things we use every day, but they are radically different from what we purchase for ourselves. Second, because of the participatory nature of these works, they achieve another level of engagement with the viewer, who becomes part of the work and the issues that these pieces interrogate.

As I continue to build upon this project, I have also observed that people (myself included) have what I think of as Polar Bear Fatigue. Images of the destruction of homes and decimation of habitats, which have led to starving polar bears, are so common in this age of easy, dopamine-fueled "doomscrolling" on the Internet that they no longer have the impact that one might hope they would. Now, in 2020, as I see the normalization of mask-wearing herald a new normal, be it because of the extreme bushfire season in Australia or the coronavirus pandemic, the next important question thus becomes: "How can we convince people to act on climate change?" This becomes the impetus for even more participatory art, such as the *Wild Science* body of work, where I ask people in *Letters for Science* (2018–present) to write letters to science denialists, asking them to change their views. By choosing to exhibit work outside of the art world, I hope to reach more people.

As an artist, designer, academic, and writer, I believe that art and scholarship are part of a long-term solution. One art piece won't change the world; it is the consistent deployment of these pieces in society and the discussion and debates that ensue that make a tiny ripple in the larger societal context.

Index

ableism, 232, 241, 245. *See also* cognitive ableism
Abram, David, 35–36, 41–42, 46, 48–50, 164
activism, xi, 18; internatural, 254–58, 260, 262, 267–71
acute threats, 59
aestheticization, 353, 358–59, 365
affect, 5, 55–57, 64, 76, 155–56, 168, 206–7, 372–73
affective assemblages, 76
agency: aquatic, 39, 225; horticultural, 219; human, 75, 163, 200; plant, 185, 201–2; relational, 5, 73; shared, 73
aggression, experienced by elephants, 130, 138
agriculture, 36–37, 130; degradation of traditional, 288
áhsen nikontate'kén:'a. See Three Sisters
AIDS Memorial Quilt, 18
alternative symbolics, 257–59, 267, 269
animacy, 179–80, 322; plant, 174, 182, 204, 206, 209, 322
animalitas, 306
animalization, 232. *See also* dehumanization
animal liberation, 231–36, 240–43, 246–49

animism, 179; animist worldviews, 164, 179, 190
Anthropocene, 2–3, 39, 46, 56–58, 64–65, 163, 197, 247–48, 275, 372–79; how to live in the, 29, 36, 60, 111, 123–24, 233, 293–94. *See also* (m)Anthropocene
anthropocentrism, 36, 43, 56, 132, 175, 218–21, 277, 285, 300, 312–13, 315–16; cognitively ableist, 233–35, 241–48
anthropodenial, 107
anthropomorphism, 40, 73, 107, 179–80, 183, 226–28, 255–61, 301–2, 362–65; strategic, 7, 256–58, 260, 268
anthropotechnics, 163
anthrozoology, 255
antiracism, 59–60, 339
The Apocalypse Project, 394–95
aquaculture, 85–97; commercial, 88, 90, 96
arachnophilia, 74
Aristotle, 177
art therapy, 69–72
Atrato River, 287–90; Guardians of the, 289; legal personhood of, 288
Audubon, John James, 20–21

autonomy: indigenous, 197, 199, 204, 289; practical, 233, 235, 241–47

Bakhtin, Mikhail, 132
banding, 114–17
Barthes, Roland, 18, 26
Benjamin, Walter, 303, 315–16
Benthos, 105–9
bioaccumulation, 96
bio-philial sense, 133
bird feeding, 117–19
birthing, 175–79, 181–87, 260–62
Black Lives Matter, 60, 337
Buck v. Bell, 246
Buddhism, 132–38
Burwell v. Hobby Lobby, 234
bushfires, 69–71, 72, 354, 356–62, 396
Butler, Judith, 16, 18, 66n9, 205

cannabis, 165–67
capitalism, 8, 37, 135, 156, 175, 340–41; land use, 127, 139, 142–43
Capitalocene, 5, 335; racial, 60–61
captive class, 256, 258
care, 3, 35–36, 38, 117–24, 333, 339–46, 377–78
caretakers, 218–21
chena, 130, 135–37, 140
childhood, 174–76, 182–83
chimpanzees, 83, 236–38, 245–46; Tommy and Kiko, 236–38, 241, 244–46
Chinook salmon, 134, 261. *See also* endangered species
chronic stressors, 58–59
Chthulucene, 2, 157, 163, 168
Circe, 186–88
Citizens United v. FEC, 234, 279
Clean Water Act (CWA), 276–77
climate change, 2, 53–59, 62–64, 69, 86, 88, 96–98, 134, 143, 197, 228, 253, 259–62, 269–70, 285, 293, 322, 326, 335–36, 343–47, 355, 357–64, 393–94; denialists, 396
coexistence, 13–15, 19, 29–31, 129

cognitive ableism, 231, 233, 241–47
cohabitation, 127, 129–32, 138–42
colonialism, 62, 92–93, 109, 130, 133, 208, 235, 282, 328, 337; as a major driver of HEC, 130; praxes of domination, 106
Colorado River, 275, 283, 290–93
communal storytelling, 59
communication: ecocultural, 321; environmental, 2–3, 6, 54, 123–24, 257, 321, 353, 365; environmental animal, 255; internatural, 35, 255–58, 321–22; kinesthetic, 76; multispecies, 132
compassion, 35–36, 81–82, 122–23, 175
compassionate contamination, 37–39, 44–45, 49–50
connectedness, 4–5, 82, 121, 161–62; psychedelic, 161–62
conservation, 36–37, 41, 43–44, 48–49, 85–88, 90–97, 127–29, 228, 255, 260, 268, 360–64; compassionate, 37, 44
Controlled Substances Act, 159
coronavirus. *See* COVID–19
COVID–19: impacts of, 1, 82, 96, 111, 124, 127, 234, 257, 342–43, 348n13, 356, 358; as a preview of a climate-changed future, 343
critical animal studies, 231–32
critical disability studies, 231–32
critical legal studies, 231–32
cultural animal studies, 75
Cultural Keystone Species, 209
CWA. *See* Clean Water Act (CWA)
cyanotype, 70–71

de-anthropomorphized imagery, 301–2
de-centering, 205, 209, 233
decriminalization, 157, 166–67
Decriminalize Nature movement, 166–67
dehumanization, 232. *See also* animalization
Deleuze, Gilles, 35, 156, 302–3

denial, 70, 255, 268–69, 378
dependency, 128, 133, 164–65, 248
Derrida, Jacques, 13, 17, 306
Descartes, René, 307, 380
development, 95, 119, 127–31, 134–37, 140, 142, 285, 311, 316
dialectics, 41, 43, 168; exploitation-idealism, 43; mastery-harmony, 41; othering-connection, 43
dialogism, 131–32
dialogues, 48, 127–29, 131–32, 134–38, 141–43, 304–5, 323; dialogic, 132, 141; monologic, 132; multispecies, 127–28, 131–32, 134, 142–43
digital revolution, 136
disability: activists, 242–43; social model of, 232; studies, 232
disruption, 14, 19, 128, 132, 136, 257–58, 307, 316, 372, 383
Doğa İçin Çal, 387–90
domesticity, 177–78, 186
domination, 105–6, 200, 231, 235, 305–6, 311, 334, 340, 342–43, 346, 348n13, 359, 374, 381; male, 336, 340, 348n9; patriarchal, 340, 347n3, 348n9

Earth Jurisprudence, 248
ecocentricity, 175–76, 183, 235, 248
eco-criticism, 300
ecocultural perspective, 321
ecofeminism, xii, 123
eco-hypocrisy, 358
ecological ambivalence, 358
ecologization, 339–46
ecomodernism, 340
Econo-cene, 335
economies, 2, 85, 133, 140, 342, 373; capitalist, 37; divorced from local ecological knowledge, 131
ecosystem destruction, 2, 29, 227, 333, 383
ecotourism, 129, 142
Ectopistes migratorius. See passenger pigeon

elephants, 127–43; Asian subspecies found in Sri Lanka, 133; crop raiding, 133–34; feeding of, 132–34; Happy, 238; Minnie, 237–38, 241, 246; Rambo, 138; sociality, 134, 139
embodied connections, 176, 315
empathetic identification, 268
emplacement, 372
empowerment, 53, 58, 64; community-based, 136
endangered species, 25–26, 45, 105, 261–62
entanglement, 2–7, 39, 77, 90, 158, 168, 203, 218, 254, 262, 378; of biological bodies with fabricated technologies, 218; in *Leviathan*, 305, 317
environmental law, 231, 275–76, 280–83
Environmental Protection Act of 1970, 283
Environmental Protection Agency (EPA), 276
Ereignis, 300, 311–12, 317n8
ethic of care, xii, 111, 124
exit politics, 341
extinction, 2, 6, 14, 19–22, 25–29, 53, 56, 105, 128, 183, 190, 233, 240, 335–36, 345, 360; anthropogenic, 29

familiarity, 14, 42, 188, 268; urgent, 188
fatberg, 376, 395
fatigue, 57, 263, 396
felt self, 334–35, 338–39, 342–43, 345–46
femininization, 344
fences, 133, 140, 142
film movements, 316, 327
First Nations Technical Institute (FNTI), 198, 203–10
fission-fusion, 141
Floyd, George, 94, 337, 347n6
fluidity, 311, 314, 380

FNTI. *See* First Nations Technical Institute (FNTI)

Foucault, Michel, 157, 199, 359

Freud, Sigmund, 13, 15–17, 26, 30, 164, 342, 348n12, 349n14

fungi, 156–57, 176, 187. *See also* mushroom; psilocybin

Geo-Doc, 325–29

Ge-stell, 300, 309–12

global emissions, 53

globalization, 130, 372

Global North, 135, 334, 340–41, 348n13; socio-cultural contexts, 334

Goodall, Jane, 236–37

Green Revolution, 136

greenwash, 340

grief, x, 7, 14–19, 21, 23–27, 29–31, 39, 42, 46, 62–65, 69–70, 72, 253–60, 262–64, 267–70, 338–39, 343–46, 358, 363–64, 388; climate, 64–65, 69–70, 72; ecological, 19, 27, 30–31, 358; as a medium for healing, 338; as public protest, 62, 253, 268; white, 54, 62–63

Handsome Lake Code, the, 203

haptic, 300–305, 312, 315–16; art, 302–3

Haraway, Donna, 1, 4, 19, 73, 121, 157, 163, 306

Haudenosaunee cosmology, 202, 206, 208

HEC. *See* human-elephant conflict (HEC)

Heidegger, Martin, 300, 309–12, 317nn4–8

hierarchical anthropocentrism, 56

Hinduism, 132–34

holobiont, 333, 347n1

Holocene, 333

Homogenocene, 335

hubris syndrome, 41, 47

human-elephant conflict (HEC), 127–42

human exceptionalism, 5, 43–44, 180, 198, 201, 205, 210, 255, 306

humanimal, 267

human-nature binary, 97

hybridity, 86, 92, 98, 378

hyper-individualism, 201, 207

hyperobject, 5–6, 164, 168

hyper-surveillance, 199, 207

iconophobia, 304

identities, 36, 44, 46, 91, 180, 208, 246, 312, 346, 347n3; hybrid, 135; intimate, 46, 131; permeable, 132

ideological rhetorical criticism, 232

Indian Control of Indian Education policy paper, 197

Indigenizing higher education, 197–98

indigenous: ecological-relational dwelling practices, 349n17; Institutes, 198, 204, 208; legal consultation, 288, 292; oral traditions, 322; Peoples of Turtle Island, 197; recognition of medicinal value, 156; seizure of lands from, 106; use of psilocybin, 156–57, 159–60, 164–67

individualism, 4–5, 199, 203

industrialization, 175, 335, 341, 377, 382; diet, of, 376; excessive emissions due to, 335

inequities, 54, 336; social constructions of, 336

injustice, 18, 58, 60–61, 64, 116, 198, 334, 338, 346; gender-based, 116

Inslee, Jay, 265–66

integration, 60, 71–72

interconnectedness, 4–5, 36, 76, 256, 268, 276

interdependence, 201, 321; orcas and humans, 260

Intergovernmental Panel on Climate Change (IPCC), 53, 335

intersubjectivities, 339

intimacy, 3–8, 30, 39, 54, 59, 62, 74–77, 82, 84–86, 96, 107, 254–55,

268, 270, 276, 282, 290, 300, 305, 316, 333, 341, 345–46, 363–65, 372; continuity, through, 92–94; ecological, 111, 120–23; existential, 247; fragility of, 76; monstrous, 377–79; more-than-human, 74, 76–77; performance, and, 258–60; performative writing, through, 182
invasive species, 37, 41, 137, 219
IPCC. *See* Intergovernmental Panel on Climate Change (IPCC)
isolationism, 156

Jardin d'Incertitude, 217–20, 221n1, 221n3
Jünger, Ernst, 308–9

Kafka, Franz, 379–80
Kangaroo Island, Australia, 355–56
ka'nikonhri : io, 200
Kariwiyo. See Handsome Lake Code
kasasten'sera, 200–201, 208, 210
killer whale. *See* orca whale
kinship, 134, 157, 163, 166, 178, 183, 190, 217; renewal of, 163; tree, 183, 190, 192n11
koalas, 353–64; Billy, 355, 364; Ellenborough Lewis, 354–55
Kubler-Ross Grief Cycle, 70, 347n6

Latour, Bruno, 76, 128, 138, 168–69, 306, 373, 377–79, 381–82
Law of Mother Earth, 281–82
Leopold, Aldo, 15, 19, 23, 30, 41
Leviathan, 299–17; aesthetic framework of, 300; bodily entanglement, 317; multi-perspectivism, 312; shift away from human perspective, 301
Ley de Derechos de la Madre Tierra. See Law of Mother Earth
liquid modernity, 199–200
logophobia, 304
logos, 199, 304, 306, 316–17
Luckiamute River watershed, 37
Lummi Nation, 134, 266

magic, 164; motherhood, 181–83, 187
Mailhot, Terese Marie, 54, 64–65; *Heart Berries*, 64–65
malestream, 334, 336, 339, 343, 347n3
(m)Anthropocene, 333–36, 338, 340–41, 345–46
Maori, 286–87, 290
marginal cases, argument from, 241–43, 245, 247
marginalization, 197, 271; elephants, 128; indigenous people, 198
masculinities, 333–47, 348n9; ecocidal, 338; ecological, 333, 341–42, 344–47; ecomodern, 340–42, 344, 346; industrial/breadwinner, 348n9; monstrosities of, 339–40
masculinization, 335
mass extinction, 2, 6, 14, 25, 233, 240, 335
material connections, 174, 177–78, 181
medicine, 147–51, 155–57, 166–68, 201, 205, 209
melancholia, 16
mental health, 55–59, 69, 82, 159, 161, 164
Merleau-Ponty, Maurice, 303
merroir, 91, 93. *See also* terroir
#MeToo, 337
Millennium Drought, 283–85; ecological consequences of, 284
mindfulness, 55, 57, 81–84, 157
minimization, 269
modernism, 128, 130–31, 138, 309, 378
monocultures, 131, 136
Monument to the Passenger Pigeon, 20–25, 28, 31
moral community, 233–35, 241, 247–48. *See also* personhood
more-than-human, xii, 14, 19, 29–31, 35, 40, 46, 73–74, 77, 174–81, 190–91, 191n1, 199, 203, 208–10, 228, 231, 235–36, 254–57, 259–60, 262, 268, 341; mourning the, 27; power, 199–204; rhetoric, 235, 254
Morton, Timothy, 5, 14, 168

motherhood, 174, 176–83, 190–91;
green, 178–79; mourning, 182; as a
shared identity, 190–91
mourning, 13–19, 21, 23–31, 38–40,
49, 182, 188–90, 254, 259, 333, 336,
338–39, 342–46; ecological, x, 26–
27, 29–30; planetary loss, 338–39;
successful, 13, 15–16; vigilant, ix,
14–15, 18–19, 21, 23, 25, 29, 31
mushroom, 155–56, 159–60, 163–65,
168, 190. *See also* fungi; psilocybin
mycelium, 155–56; "rhizomatic"
structure of, 156

naiad, 105–7, 109
naming practices, 40
nature as partner, 322–23
National Oceanic and Atmospheric
Administration (NOAA), 266
Native American. *See* indigenous
Navigable Water Protection Rule, 276
neoliberalism, 90, 201, 203, 207–8, 210,
340–41; conservation, 95; economic
policies, 130–31; gamesmanship,
156; Indigenous higher education,
and, 198–99; masculinity within,
340–41
NhRP. *See* Nonhuman Rights Project
(NhRP)
NOAA. *See* National Oceanic and
Atmospheric Administration
(NOAA)
Nonhuman Rights Project (NhRP), 231,
233, 235–49; central argumentative
objectives, 237

Obama, Barack, 276, 355
objectification, 264
ocean: acidification, 88, 96, 98;
anthropomorphism of, 226–28;
personhood of, 225
ocularcentrism, 316
Oliver, Mary, 82
oppression, xii, 61, 65, 176–79, 198,
232, 235–36, 243, 246, 248, 337–38,

348n9, 374; institutionalization of,
337–38
optical art, 302–3
oral traditions, 322; of the Athapaskan
and Tlingit, 322
Orange, Tommy, 54, 62–63; *There
There*, 62–63
orca whale, 134, 253, 257–68, 270–71;
agency of, 260, 267; birthing process
of, 260; familial bonds, 261; grieving
practices of, 253; pollution of,
261–65; Tilikum, 257–58. *See also*
Tahlequah
Oregon State University's College of
Forestry, 51n2
Other, 15–17, 46–47, 50, 60, 82–83,
142, 164, 166, 168, 175, 191n1, 217,
258, 264, 338–42; Animal, 82–83
overconsumption, 178
oyster, 85–98; aquaculture, 85–97;
racial/ethnic representation of
workers, 94; restoration, 88–90, 93–
95, 97; symbolism of, 86, 90–94, 97

Pada Yatra pilgrimage, 133
pandemic, x, 18, 176, 342–43, 358. *See
also* COVID–19
Paris Climate Accord, 340, 348n11
Paris Climate Summit, 326
participation, 14, 70, 279, 381
Participatory Mode, 327–29
passenger pigeon, 19–26, 28, 31;
Martha, 20
path dependence, 276–78
pathologies of pain, solution-oriented,
65
performative writing, 174, 181–82
persistence, 15, 20–25
personhood, 129, 175, 177, 179–80,
190–91, 200, 225, 231, 233; legal,
233–37, 239–42, 244–48, 277–82,
286–90, 292–93; plant, 198, 204–9.
See also moral community
Pittsburgh Community Bill of Rights,
282

place: identity, 41–42, 87; meaning, 86–88, 90, 96–88; pathology, 41
plantations, 129–31, 135–36, 139–41
plant prostheses, 218–19
plastics use, 96–97
Polar Bear Fatigue, 396
policy competition, 278–80, 291
policy cycle, 279–82, 292–93
policy incrementalism, 282
Pollan, Michael, 156, 158–59, 164, 166
pollution, 2, 94, 96–97, 262; noise, 261, 263–65; regulation, 277
poverty, 56, 128, 377
practical autonomy, 233, 235, 241, 244–47
practice-orientation, 128
premarket societies, 131
privilege, 63, 65, 178; human, 233, 322; language of, 59; male, 334, 336–37, 340, 345; white, 54
psilocybin, 155–68; authoritarianism, links to, 161; colonial history of, 160; long-term behavioral change due to, 161; Mazatec use of, 159; medicinal properties of, 156; politicized stigma of, 160. *See also* fungi; mushroom
psychedelic-assisted psychotherapy, 159, 164
psychedelic prohibition, 159–60, 167
public policy, 2, 270, 275, 278–79, 326–27; anthropocentric, 285

quasi-objects, 168
queering, 343, 349n15

radical empiricism, 159
relational knowledge, 111, 115, 123
relational ontology, 4, 201
relations: intimate, xi–xii, 3, 35–39, 42–43, 46, 72, 76, 85, 94–95, 133, 255, 333, 344; reciprocal, 134–35, 209–10
Remembrance Day for Lost Species, 15, 25–29

Renaissance, 303; perspective, 303
repetition, 15, 25–29, 31
resilience, 6–7, 53–65, 66n5, 128, 155, 344; climate, 54, 56–59, 66n2; emotional, 57, 59
resistance, xii, 17–18, 26, 62, 65, 138, 199, 207, 210, 337, 342; organized, 62
rewilding, 37, 50, 358
rhetorical studies, 231–32; climate rhetoric, 56
rituals, 18, 27, 254, 269; significance of, 27

Saraceno, Tómas, 73–77
scales of objects, 374–76
scent, 141, 394; as speech, 3
scholarship, xi–xii, 53, 65, 182, 232, 242; siloed nature of, xii, 128
SeaWorld, 239
self-determination, 199, 204
self-efficacy, 58
self-responsibility, 58
sentience, 174, 235, 242
Sierra Club v. Morton, 281, 292
silence, as a resource, 322
Singer, Peter, 236–37, 242, 244
social media, 325, 354–55, 363–64
social support, 59, 111–12
Sociocene, 335
socioeconomic status, 55, 58–59
solastalgia, 36, 38, 41–42, 44–46, 57, 69–72, 192n12
soliphilia, 49
spatial features, 139–40
speciesism, 231–33, 239, 241–42, 245, 247
species loneliness, 82
spider, 73–77
spirituality, 306, 345
stakeholders, 232, 287, 292, 321–23
stewardship, 106, 228, 259
Sumbiotude, 38–39, 43
surveillance, 359–63
sustained observation, 114–15

Symbiocene, 38–39, 46, 49–50
symbol, 86, 257; tourism, 358–59, 363

Tahlequah, 253–71; internatural
    activism, 254, 257–58, 260, 267–71;
    Tour of Grief, 253, 258–60, 267, 270
tank cascade system, 130
Te Awa Tupua Act. *See* Whanganui
    River Claims Settlement Act
Technocene, 335
technology, 217–18, 300, 305, 308–13,
    316–17, 325, 353, 357, 378–79;
    agency, 305, 308, 311; as a barrier to
    learning, 55
terroir, 91. *See also* merroir
Thanksgiving Address, 202, 204–5
Three Sisters, the, 201–10; curriculum
    around, 204, 207–8; obligations to,
    207, 210
tides, 28–29
time: cyclical, 139; linear, 139
topos, 199
tourism, 85–88, 90, 92–93, 128, 140,
    261, 353, 356–60, 363–65; discourse,
    356–57, 360, 363–65; as an escape,
    357–58; industry, 87–88, 93, 358
tourist gaze, 354, 356, 359; reverse,
    363–64
transcorporeality, 179–81
trauma, 55–58, 69, 120–22, 243, 269;
    suffered by elephants, 129–30
Trump, Donald, 276, 348n11
Truth and Reconciliation Commission
    of Canada, 197

UNFCCC. *See* United Nations
    Framework Convention on Climate
    Change (UNFCCC)
United Nations Declaration of
    the Rights of Indigenous Peoples,
    197

United Nations Framework Convention
    on Climate Change (UNFCCC), 326
unworlding, 379–82

VEWH. *See* Victorian Environmental
    Water Holder (VEWH)
Victoria, Australia, 283–85
Victorian Environmental Water Holder
    (VEWH), 284
Victorian Water Act of 1989, 283
violence, 6, 30, 58, 62–63, 127, 130,
    236, 269, 338, 340; masculine, 6,
    337
visual truth, 359–63
vital materialism, 179–80
voyeurism, environmental, 267
vulnerability, 27, 65–66, 156, 247, 253,
    339, 341, 358, 394

watershed, 35–50; council, 36–37, 42,
    45–46, 48–49; theology, 36
weird naturalism, 157
Western culture, 3, 6, 175, 182, 190,
    203, 306, 308
The Whale Trail, 265–66
whale-watching, 261, 263–65
Whanganui River, 286–87; disputes
    over ownership of, 286; legal
    guardian of, 286; legal personhood
    of, 225, 286
Whanganui River Claims Settlement
    Act, 286
white environmentalism, 54, 64, 334
white Geology, 337
white supremacy, 337–40
Wild Law. *See* Earth Jurisprudence
Wise, Steven, 231, 233–48
Women With A Vision (WWAV), 54,
    61

zoo'd animals, 256–57

About the Editors, Contributing Authors, and Artists

Alexa M. Dare

Alexa Dare is associate professor of Communication at the University of Portland where she also directs the Social Justice minor. She works and teaches at the intersection(s) of cultural studies and environmental communication and is guided by an overarching interest in materiality and embodiment, especially in the context of protest and activism. Much of her recent research examines questions related to interspecies solidarity and human-nonhuman relations.

C. Vail Fletcher

Vail Fletcher is associate professor in the Department of Communication at the University of Portland and codirector of the Gender and Women's Studies program. Vail currently teaches courses related to Ecofeminism, Critical Nonhuman Animal Communication, and Conflict and the Environment. Her research broadly focuses on the intersections of nature culture, land and animal rights, and environmental communication. She lives on a farm that practices interspecies collaboration on a large river island in Oregon (on unceded Chinook land).

Carol J. Adams

Carol J. Adams is a feminist-vegan advocate, activist, and independent scholar and the author of numerous books including her path-breaking *The Sexual Politics of Meat: A Feminist-Vegetarian Critical Theory*. She is the coeditor of several important anthologies, including most recently *Ecofeminism: Feminist Intersections with Other Animals and the Earth* (with Lori Gruen). *The Carol J. Adams Reader: Writings and Conversations 1995–2015* appeared in the fall of 2016. She has a master's of Divinity from Yale University. In the 1970s, she and her spouse, the Rev. Bruce Buchanan started a Hotline for Battered Women in upstate New York. She is the author of *Woman-Battering* (1995) in Fortress Press's Creative Pastoral Care and Counseling Series. With Marie Fortune, she edited *Violence Against Women and Children: A Christian Theological Sourcebook* (1995). She is the author of the training manual, *Pastoral Care for Domestic Violence: Case Studies for Clergy—for Christian Audiences— Training Manual* (2007) published by the FaithTrust Institute. She wrote one of the earliest articles theorizing why batterers harm animals, "Woman-Battering and Harm to Animals" (in *The Carol J. Adams Reader*). Carol is also the author of books on living as a vegan, including *Never Too Late to Go Vegan: The Over-50 Guide to Adopting and Thriving on a Vegan Diet* (with Patti Breitman and Virginia Messina), *Living Among Meat Eaters: The Vegetarian's Survival Guide*, *How to Eat Like a Vegetarian Even if You Never Want to Be One.* Her most recent book is *Even Vegans Die: A Practical Guide to Caregiving, Acceptance, and Protecting Your Legacy of Compassion*, with coauthors Patti Breitman and Virginia Messina.

Paul Alberts

Paul Alberts teaches philosophy at Western Sydney University and a member of its Philosophy Research Initiative. He has published in both philosophy and literary studies and recently contributed to a special edition of the Oxford Literary Review (2016) on the theme of overpopulation. Previous publications on the Anthropocene and Foucault's conceptions of nature have also been oriented to the work of rethinking environmental theory through appropriate lenses available in the critical traditions of continental philosophy. Extending this work in a monograph, the author aims to contribute to the project of theorizing the early Anthropocene, this emerging period which threatens to derange the principles and forces of modernity's global expansion.

Katharina Alsen

Katharina Alsen holds a master's degree in art history and visual culture from the University of Oxford and a state certificate (MA equiv.) in literature, theology, and philosophy from the University of Hamburg. After graduating, she was a fellow of the international research training group "InterArt" at Freie Universität Berlin and a one-year visiting scholar at the Doctoral School of Cultural Studies, University of Copenhagen. She was awarded a PhD scholarship from the German Research Association (DFG) to pursue her dissertation on the topic of staged intimacy in the performing arts. Following this, she received a Global Humanities Junior Fellowship from the network "Principles of Cultural Dynamics" at Freie Universität Berlin. Currently, she is working as a research associate at the University of Music and Theatre in Hamburg (HfMT). Her publications include: *Bruch—Schnitt—Riss. Deutungspotenziale von Trennungsmetaphorik in den Wissenschaften und Künsten* (ed.), Berlin: LIT 2014, and *Nordic Painting. The Rise of Modernity*, New York: Random House 2016.

Anne K. Armstrong

Anne K. Armstrong is a PhD candidate in the Department of Natural Resources at Cornell University and a member of the Civic Ecology Lab. She has a professional background in environmental education, and she is the lead author on *Communicating Climate Change: A Guide for Educators* (Cornell University Press, 2018). Her research areas include climate change communication, environmental education, social-ecological symbols, and the links among place meanings, social practices, and identity in environmental stewardship.

Joshua Trey Barnett

Joshua Trey Barnett is an assistant professor in the Department of Communication Arts and Sciences at Penn State University, where he holds a joint appointment in the Huck Institutes of the Life Sciences. He has published widely in rhetorical studies and in the interdisciplinary environmental humanities. His scholarship on ecological rhetoric can be found in the journals *Environmental Communication, Communication and Critical/ Cultural Studies, Quarterly Journal of Speech, Communication, Culture & Critique, Ethics & the Environment, Culture, Theory & Critique, Departures in Critical Qualitative Research*, and *ISLE: Interdisciplinary Studies in Literature and Environment*, among others. He is currently completing a book about ecological mourning

Christianna Bennett

Christianna Bennett is a landscape designer and architectural instructor in Troy, New York, where she teaches in Design Studios, Final Project/ Thesis Studio and Seminar, and the History and Theory of Landscapes and Urbanism. She is interested in the landscape imaginary, landscape-related research and design, the ideation of public space, especially in rural areas, and in living materials, material energy, massive living-and-inert hybrid systems, and the histories, philosophies, and ethics implicated in practices of design. Her personal and theoretical research focuses on examining and interpreting water as design material and philosophical framework.

Peggy J. Bowers

Peggy J. Bowers is a scholar whose work focuses on communication ethics as well as on cultural critical media studies, media ethics, and free expression.

Her research examines relationships among ethics, visuality, culture, and the environment. Her work has been published in such venues as *Journal of Mass Media Ethics, Free Speech Yearbook, Communication Monographs, American Communication Journal*, and the *International Journal of Media and Cultural Politics,* as well as in scholarly book chapters. She has received awards for her scholarship and has professional journalism experience. Bowers received her doctorate in communication from Stanford University, and an MA in communication and a BA in journalism from Wichita State University.

Suzanne Katsi'tsiarihshion Brant

Suzanne is Mohawk from the Tyendinaga Mohawk Territory situated on the Bay of Quinte. As President of First Nations Technical Institute (FNTI), Suzanne is focused on ensuring that indigenous knowledge is woven through all aspects of the institute and committed to the idea that "responsive education" remains the hallmark of her vision for FNTI. She has a MA in environmental studies from York University. Areas of interest include but are not limited to traditional uses of medicinal plants and their positive influence on health, and the role culture plays in the preservation of the natural environment. Suzanne is a member of the Haudenosaunee Environmental Task Force and formerly served on the Board of Governors for St. Lawrence College.

Chelsea Call

Chelsea Call is an interdisciplinary artist and art psychotherapist currently residing in the high desert of Santa Fe, New Mexico (unceded, occupied Tewa land). Her intersectional work focuses on facilitating healing through integrative investigations. She holds an MA in counseling and art therapy from Southwestern College, along with a BFA from Colorado State University. Grounded in an eco-psychological framework, Call has worked with various groups and individuals through nonprofit sectors to facilitate creative processes exploring dialogues between identify and environment. Concerned with the future of the Anthropocene, her work aims to invite viewers toward a place of stewardship with the natural world. She currently teaches counseling psychology at Sofia University.

laura c carlson

laura c carlson is an artist researcher dedicated to queer ecologies, multispecies ethnography, and environmental justice. carlson assembles speculative stories through resurrecting myths and imagining speculative futures, focusing on often-erased imperiled species including freshwater mussels, snails, and lichen. carlson received their MFA in Interdisciplinary Art from the University of Pennsylvania (2017) and their BFA in Art History and Studio Art from Creighton University (2013). An upcoming Mountain Lake Biological Station ArtLab resident, carlson has attended residencies and participated in group and solo exhibitions across the United States and Australia and has lectured and held workshops nationally and internationally. carlson has received multiple awards, most recently the Puffin Foundation Environmental Award.

Patrícia Castello Branco

Patrícia Castello Branco (PhD) is a senior researcher at Nova Institute of philosophy (IFILNOVA), New University of Lisbon, Portugal. She works mainly on the relations between technology and haptic visuality and its links to Posthumanism. Her book, *Image Body, Technology* (Lisboa: Fundação Calouste Gulbenkian, 2013) investigates on technology and the renewed sensory awareness in cinema, video, and contemporary art. Her most recent articles include: "An Eco-Posthuman Reading of Avatar" (2017); "Herzog's Sublime and *Ecstatic Truth*: From Burke's Physiological Aesthesis to the Dionysian Unveiling" (2020); and "The Awakening of the Body: 'Film as Sensation' in the First French Avant-Garde" (2020). She is the editor and founder of *Cinema: Journal of Philosophy and the Moving Image*. She has edited, among others, the following issues: "Embodiment and the Body" (2011) and "Posthumanism. Human and Non-Human: Links, Continuum, Interplay" (2015).

Amal Dissanayaka

Amal Dissanayaka has over seven years of experience working on socio-economic issues of rural agrarian communities in Sri Lanka. He obtained a bachelor's degree in sociology from University of Ruhuna, a master's degree in sociology from University of Colombo, professional qualifications from Chartered Institute of Personnel Management (CIPM) Sri Lanka, and certificate in anthropology from the University of Queensland Australia. Currently, he works as a research officer at Hector Kobbekaduwa Agrarian Research and Training Institute (HARTI) in Colombo, Sri Lanka, and represents the HARTI as an active member in "National Committee on Managing Wildlife Crop Damages in Rural Agrarian Areas" under the Ministry of Agriculture. He is actively working in the field of Human Wildlife Conflict (HWC) in Sri Lanka, which has become a prominent socioeconomic issue in the country.

Marybeth Holleman

Marybeth Holleman is the author of several nonfiction books including *The Heart of the Sound* and *Among Wolves* and is a coeditor of the poetry and essay anthology *Crosscurrents North*. Pushcart-prize nominee and finalist for the Siskiyou Prize, Holleman has had essays, poems, and articles in dozens of journals, magazines, and anthologies, among them *Orion, Christian Science Monitor, Literary Mama, ISLE/OUP, Sierra, North American Review, AQR,* and *The Future of Nature,* and on National Public Radio. Holleman holds a BA in environmental studies from UNC-Chapel Hill and an MFA in creative writing from UAA, where Holleman taught literature, women's studies, and creative writing. Raised in the Appalachian Mountains of North Carolina, Holleman transplanted to Alaska's Chugach Mountains after falling head-over-heels for Prince William Sound just two years before the EVOS oil spill. Holleman has held artist residencies at Ninfa, Mesa Refuge, Denali National Park, Hedgebrook, Weymouth Center, and Tracy Arm Ford's Terror Wilderness.

Jessica Holmes

Jessica Holmes is a PhD candidate in English at the University of Washington in Seattle, where she teaches in the Interdisciplinary Writing Program. Her research areas include environmental humanities, contemporary poetry, and vegan studies. She is a 2019 Mellon Fellow for New Public Projects in the Humanities. She received a Master of Fine Arts in poetry from the University of Washington and a Bachelor of Fine Arts in English from Lewis & Clark College. Her creative and critical work has been published in *TRANSverse Journal, West Trade Review,* and *Auto/Biography Studies,* and is forthcoming in the *Routledge Handbook of Vegan Studies* and *Critical Animal Theory: Critical Theory, Social Constructions, and Total Liberation.*

Kathy Isaacson

Kathy Isaacson, PhD, is a faculty member in the Communication & Journalism Department at the University of New Mexico. Her teaching, consulting, and research interests include environmental communication, conflict management, and interpersonal communication. Isaacson is the author four books and numerous articles and videos, including the following with coauthor Stephen Littlejohn: *Communication, Conflict, and the Management of Difference; Facework: Bridging Theory and Practice; Engaging Communication in Conflict: Systemic Practice;* and *Mediation: Empowerment in Conflict Resolution.* She received her PhD in communication and social change from Tilburg University in the Netherlands.

Deepani Jayantha

Deepani Jayantha is a veterinarian and a conservationist. She studied elephant behavior and human-elephant interactions for more than a decade and has been working on community conservation projects excelling citizen science. She is a member of IUCN SSC Asian Elephant Specialist Group and currently works as the Country Representative of Elemotion Foundation. She closely works with several government and nongovernment organizations.

Michaela Keeble

Michaela Keeble is a white Australian writer living in Aotearoa New Zealand. She works independently and in a collective of poets engaged with resisting neocolonization, including in climate writing. This is an urgent issue that nonindigenous writers and researchers must take responsibility for, as they increasingly look to indigenous knowledges for solutions to the crises we are living through. Michaela's poetry and fiction are published widely in Australia and Aotearoa, including in *Plumwood Mountain, Pantograph Punch, Westerly, Not Very Quiet, Cicerone Journal, The Spinoff Ātea, Capital, Turbine|Kapohau,* and *Community Lore.* Michaela has a background in community development and social justice publishing. She currently works for a research organization, communicating the challenges of climate adaptation across Aotearoa.

Marianne Krasny

Marianne E. Krasny is professor of natural resources and director of the Civic Ecology Lab at Cornell University. Her recent books include *Civic Ecology* (with K Tidball), *Urban Environmental Education Review* (with A. Russ), *Communicating Climate Change: A Guide for Educators* (with A. Armstrong and J. Schuldt), and *Grassroots to Global.* She conducts environmental education online courses for international audiences and is an International Fellow of the Royal Swedish Academy of Agriculture and Forestry.

Libby Lester

Libby Lester is director of the Institute for Social Change and professor of media at the University of Tasmania. Her research focuses on how issues are raised, understood, and responded to in public debate, and she is recognized internationally for her work on environmental communications. She works across industries, government, and NGOs to understand and promote the role of communication and media in good decision making about shared social and environmental futures. Recent Australian Research Council–funded research has focused on trade, resources, and global communications, drawing on case studies on forestry, aquaculture, tourism, and mining to examine the flows of information, resources, and people between Australia and its Asian trading partners. She has authored, coauthored, and coedited seven books. These include *Leadership and the Construction of Environmental Concerns* (2018, Palgrave Macmillan), *Environmental Pollution and the Media: Political Discourses of Risk and Responsibility in*

Australia, China and Japan (Routledge 2017), and *Media and Environment: Conflict, Politics and the News* (Polity 2010; Arabic ed 2013). She has been awarded four Australian Research Council discovery grants. Her research appears in leading international journals, including *Media, Culture & Society, International Communication Gazette, Journalism, Forestry, International Journal of Communication, Environmental Policy and Governance,* and *International Journal of Press/Politics.*

Todd LeVasseur

Todd is visiting assistant professor of religious studies and also environmental and sustainability studies at the College of Charleston in Charleston, South Carolina. He also directs The College's Sustainability Literacy Institute. His research resides within the environmental humanities, broadly, with a specific attention to religion-nature interactions within the context of sustainability sciences. He is author of *Religious Agrarianism and the Return of Place: From Values to Practice in Sustainable Agriculture* (2017, SUNY Press).

Lyn McGaurr

Lyn McGaurr is a university associate in the School of Creative Arts and Media at the University of Tasmania, where she received her PhD in 2013. Her research focuses on environmental communication, particularly in relation to the way tourism destinations and their brands can be politicized during conflicts over resource extraction. Among her many interests is the deployment in environmental campaigns and place branding of visitor concern for animals, such as the Tasmanian devil and British Columbia's spirit bear. She is the author of the monograph *Environmental Communication and Travel Journalism: Consumerism, Conflict and Concern* (2015, Routledge) and coauthor of the book *Leadership and the Construction of Environmental Concern* (2018, Palgrave Macmillan). Her research has appeared in journals such as *Journalism Studies*; *Journalism Practice*; the *International Journal of Communication*; *Ethical Space*; the *International Journal of Press/Politics*; *Environmental Communication*; and *Environment and Planning E: Nature and Space*.

S. Marek Muller

S. Marek Muller is assistant professor of rhetorical studies at Florida Atlantic University. Her work is at the intersection of rhetorical criticism, ecofeminism, and critical animal studies. Her book *Impersonating Animals* describes the complexity of animal rights rhetoric within the contemporary U.S. American legal system and advocates for a "critical vegan rhetoric" as a guiding rhetorical tactic in the pursuit of animal rights and broader social justice.

Anna Ijiri Oehlkers

Anna Ijiri Oehlkers is a digital media specialist currently working with The Metropolitan Museum of Art. Her research involves media archeology, particularly proto-social media forms of communication, and contemporary issues in digital museum practices. She graduated with a degree in media studies from Vassar College.

Peter W. Oehlkers

Peter Oehlkers is associate professor in the media and communication department at Salem State University, where he teaches social media, global communication, and social marketing. He has written about the role of agricultural periodicals in bird protection and the work of author and naturalist, Thornton W. Burgess. He studies the rhetoric of Baltimore orioles. He is on the editorial staff of *Bird Observer*.

Elizabeth Oriel

Elizabeth Oriel is a PhD researcher based at University of London, studying human–elephant relations and conflict in Sri Lanka. She is also a conservation biologist and founded the arts-research-science collaborative, StoriedSeas.org. She facilitates community projects in the United States and United Kingdom around relations to natural systems and creativity.

Emily Plec

Emily Plec (PhD, University of Utah) is professor of communication studies at Western Oregon University, where she teaches courses in rhetoric, media, intercultural, and environmental communication. Editor of *Perspectives on Human Communication: Internatural Communication* (Routledge, 2013), Plec advocates for a communication discipline that considers meaningful interaction to be a more-than-human enterprise. Her scholarship on humans focuses on communication and social justice, with emphases on: the rhetoric of racism in sports, the discourse of women leaders, the labor rights of farmworkers, prison communication and death penalty discourse, and environmental communication pedagogy and practice. She has served on two watershed councils, one in Michigan and one in Oregon, and is a past recipient of the Luckiamute Watershed Council's Educator of the Year Award.

Josh Potter

Josh Potter is a PhD candidate in communication and media at Rensselaer Polytechnic Institute, where he previously served as the manager of communications at EMPAC/The Curtis R. Priem Experimental Media and

414 *About the Editors, Contributing Authors, and Artists*

Performing Arts Center. Drawing on his prior career in arts journalism, his research interests include human-scale mediation, sensory theory, embodied cognition, rhetorics of wellness, and mind-body practice within hybrid, immersive spaces.

Paul M. Pulé

Paul is an Australian Gender and Environment scholar and activist specializing in men, masculinities, and their impacts on others and self. His research and community education efforts are dedicated to creating a healthier planet for all. He is research fellow at Chalmers University of Technology in Göteborg, Sweden, working with his collaborator Martin Hultman on conceptual and practical approaches to Men, *Masculinities and Earth: Exploring Ecological Masculinities*.

Jenny Rock

Jenny Rock has a multidisciplinary background in science and the arts and humanities, including a BA in human ecology and a PhD in zoology. She is an interdisciplinary academic researcher in both spaces, with much of her current research now focusing on transdisciplinary approaches where scientific and artistic practices meld. She holds positions at research institutions including the University Centre of the Westfjords (Iceland) where she teaches climate change communication and supervises research projects within the multidisciplinary master's program in Coastal and Marine Management and Coastal Communities and Regional Development. She is adjunct faculty and research associate at College of the Atlantic (Maine, USA), lecturing multidisciplinary courses integrating practices in science and the arts. For ten years, she was senior lecturer in science communication at the University of Otago (New Zealand) where she continues to hold research and postgraduate supervision contracts.

Madrone Kalil Schutten

Madrone Kalil Schutten (PhD, University of Utah, 2007) is associate professor of communication studies teaching at Northern Arizona University in Flagstaff, Arizona. Her research passions focus on new social movements, the relationship between mass media and social movements, and the alternative symbolics between humans and more-than-humans. The bulk of her academic career has been spent studying Inter*natural* Communication with recent publications in *Frontiers in Communication*. Her work can also be seen in *Rhetoric Society Quarterly* and in *Environmental Communication: A Journal of Nature and Culture*. She recently published a chapter exploring the care and fatigue of activists in *Activism and Rhetoric: Theories and*

Contexts for Political Engagement (2nd Ed). Madrone's scholarship, activism, and teaching are woven into all of her work with community and various social justice movements.

Ellen Sima

Ellen Sima holds a master's in science communication, and the experimental component of this chapter comprised a portion of her thesis research under J. Rock's supervision. She also participated in community social art and environmental conservation projects with J. Rock, as part of The Sandpit Collective. She currently works as exhibit developer at Questacon: The National Science and Technology Centre (Canberra, Australia).

Richard C. Stedman

Richard Stedman is professor in the Department of Natural Resources and associate director of the Center for Conservation Social Sciences at Cornell University. His research and teaching focus on social-ecological systems, particularly the role of human subjectivity in interpreting and acting in ways that affect transitions. Much of this work has used a sense of place/place attachment lens. Current projects in this area focus on environmental stewardship, energy transitions, water quality challenges, invasive species, and changes to fishery systems.

Carie Steele

Carie Steele is assistant professor of politics and international affairs at Northern Arizona University. She earned her PhD at University of Illinois, Urbana-Champaign, in 2011. Her research interests are in international and comparative political economy, development, and international cooperation on collective and public goods related to health and the environment.

Mark Terry

Mark Terry is a documentary filmmaker and digital media scholar currently teaching in the faculty of environmental studies at York University in Toronto and Wilfrid Laurier University in Waterloo, Ontario, Canada. After publishing his book *The Geo-Doc: Geomedia, Documentary Film, and Social Change*, he took up a postdoctoral fellowship at York with the faculty of environmental studies and the Dahdaleh Institute for Global Health Research. Dr. Terry is also a fellow of the Royal Society of Canada; a member of the College of Fellows of the Royal Canadian Geographical Society; and an International Fellow member of The Explorers Club. During his time in isolation, he composed a book of poetic musings on life during the coronavirus, *Pandemic Poetry*.

Mariko Oyama Thomas

Mariko Oyama Thomas, PhD, is a writer, instructor, and independent scholar currently living in the mountains of Taos, New Mexico, with her partner and baby daughter. She has an MS in communication and research from Portland State University (2013) and a PhD from University of New Mexico in environmental and intercultural communication (2019), as well as a background in creative writing and performance. Her research interests are largely focused on plant-human relationships, environmental justice and racism, and more-than-human communication, with a methodological focus on oral history's ability to access these subjects.

Keith Williams

Keith is the director of research and social innovation at First Nations Technical Institute, a post-secondary institution based on Tyendinaga Mohawk Territory in southern Ontario. Keith has family roots in Tyendinaga and is also a PhD candidate (Educational Studies) at St. Francis Xavier University.

Çağrı Yılmaz

Çağrı Yılmaz is a member of Ordu University's Faculty of Fine Arts, Department of Radio, Television, and Cinema. He holds a BA in English language and literature from Hacettepe University, Ankara. He received his MA and PhD in cinema and television from Anadolu University, Eskişehir. He offered an eco-critique of the contemporary Turkish films for his PhD dissertation. He can be contacted at CagriYilmazAcademia@gmail.com.

Catherine Sarah Young

Catherine Sarah Young is an award-winning artist, designer, scholar, and writer who uses her background in molecular biology, fine art, and interaction design to create experimental artworks on the environment. Her bodies of work include *The Apocalypse Project* which explores climate change and our environmental futures and *Wild Science* which interrogates the role of science in society. She has lectured widely around the world and has received grants and fellowships to do her work most recently around China, Southeast Asia, Uganda, Austria, and the Amazon. She is currently a Scientia PhD scholar at the University of New South Wales, Sydney and an Obama Leader for Asia-Pacific.